Making Magic

RECENT TITLES IN
AMERICAN ACADEMY OF RELIGION
REFLECTION AND THEORY IN THE STUDY OF RELIGION SERIES

SERIES EDITOR
James Wetzel, Colgate University

A Publication Series of
The American Academy of Religion and
Oxford University Press

Healing Deconstruction
Postmodern Thought in Buddhism and Christianity
Edited by David Loy

Roots of Relational Ethics
Responsibility in Origin and Maturity in H. Richard Niebuhr
Melvin Keiser

Hegel's Speculative Good Friday
The Death of God in Philosophical Perspective
Deland S. Anderson

Newman and Gadamer
Toward a Hermeneutics of Religious Knowledge
Thomas K. Carr

God, Philosophy, and Academic Culture
A Discussion between Scholars in the AAR and APA
Edited by William J. Wainwright

Living Words
Studies in Dialogues about Religion
Terence J. Martin

Like and Unlike God
Religious Imaginations in Modern and Contemporary Fiction
John Neary

Beyond the Necessary God
Trinitarian Faith and Philosophy in the Thought of Eberhard Jüngel
Paul DeHart

Lessing's Philosophy of Religion and the German Enlightenment
Toshimasa Yasukata

American Pragmatism
A Religious Genealogy
M. Gail Hamner

Opting for the Margins
Postmodernity and Liberation in Christian Theology   .
Edited by Joerg Rieger

Making Magic
Religion, Magic, and Science in the Modern World
Randall Styers

AMERICAN ACADEMY OF RELIGION

Making Magic

Religion, Magic, and Science
in the Modern World

RANDALL STYERS

UNIVERSITY PRESS
2004

OXFORD
UNIVERSITY PRESS

Oxford   New York
Auckland   Bangkok   Buenos Aires   Cape Town   Chennai
Dar es Salaam   Delhi   Hong Kong   Istanbul   Karachi   Kolkata
Kuala Lumpur   Madrid   Melbourne   Mexico City   Mumbai   Nairobi
São Paulo   Shanghai   Taipei   Tokyo   Toronto

Copyright © 2004 by The American Academy of Religion

Published by Oxford University Press, Inc.
198 Madison Avenue, New York, New York 10016
www.oup.com

Oxford is a registered trademark of Oxford University Press

Library of Congress Cataloging-in-Publication Data

Styers, Randall.
Making magic: religion, magic, and science in the modern world / Randall Styers.
p.   cm.—(Reflection and theory in the study of religion)
Includes bibliographical references (p.) and index.
ISBN 0-19-515107-0; ISBN 0-19-516941-7 (pbk.)
1. Magic.   2. Magic—Religious aspects.   3. Magic—Social aspects.   I. Title.   II. Series.
BF1611.S855 2003
133.4'3'0903—dc21   2003049859

9 8 7 6 5 4 3 2 1

Printed in the United States of America
on acid-free paper

Acknowledgments

My work on this project was originally funded by a dissertation grant from the National Endowment for the Humanities. I am extremely grateful for this support, and I am saddened that such grants are no longer provided for other American doctoral students. In addition, Union Theological Seminary in New York City funded a sabbatical leave that allowed me to continue my work on the project, and I am pleased to acknowledge Union's generosity and nurture.

My work here is also profoundly indebted to a large circle of extraordinary teachers, colleagues, and friends. Let me simply mention their names, in the assurance that each of them knows the depth of my affection and gratitude: James Applewhite, John Blevins, Winona Butler, Marilyn Chapin-Massey, Robert Cover, Sutton Edlich, Alberto Garcia, Robert Goodwin, Andrew Hamid, Gail Hamner, Lynn Harmet, Beverly Harrison, Stanley Hauerwas, Peter Hawkins, Elizabeth Hawley, Betty Hobbs, Kelly Jarrett, Daniel Keifer, Rosemary Keller, Wesley Kort, Roanne Kuenzler, Deborah Malmud, Dean Marks, Dale Martin, Katherine Oberlies O'Leary, Donald Lopez, Harry Partin, Grant Rockett, Kathy Rudy, M. J. Sharp, Kenneth Surin, Nancy Thompson, John Trump, Thomas Tweed, Ruel Tyson, Mark Wakefield, and Vincent Wimbush.

In addition, let me offer a few further words of gratitude. Elizabeth Clark provided generous wisdom and inspiration throughout this project. Mary McClintock Fulkerson worked diligently to make this book possible. Ann Burlein, Euan Cameron, Elizabeth Castelli, Bruce Lawrence, Tomoko Masuzawa, and Brian Schmidt offered remarkably attentive readings and insightful critique. My parents,

Donald and Carolyn Styers, have given constant love and encouragement through the many steps in this path.

Finally, for me as for many others, William Poteat served as an intellectual and personal mentor, and I will always be indebted to him for modeling a productive and generous scholarly form of life. My efforts here are dedicated to his memory and to the memory of Michael Brown, Chee Davis, Mark Miller, and Michael C. P. Ryan. Numberless, indeed, are the world's wonders.

Contents

Making Magic

Introduction

Do not trust those who analyze magic. They are usually magicians in search of revenge.

— Bruno Latour

This is a book about the making of magic. Its principal objective is to explore a body of literature devoted to the production of magic as an object of academic study. My focus is a range of texts produced by Western scholars since the late nineteenth century dealing with magic from a wide array of disciplinary perspectives. Magic has been a central theme in the theoretical literature of the modern social sciences and religious studies since the very emergence of these disciplines. Western scholars have engaged in extended debates on the definition and nature of magical thinking, and innumerable academic texts claim to tell us the truth about magic. The pages that follow will be occupied with that truth.

Yet as Bruno Latour warns, we should be wary of those who purport to analyze magic, since they are usually themselves magicians.[1] My objective here is to demonstrate various ways in which scholarly texts on magic have exerted potent forms of surreptitious—and often mystifying—power. The core of my argument is that these theories of magic are, in essential respects, magical. Modern scholars have been in the business of making magic.

And Latour's cautionary word extends even further: theoretical magicians of the sort encountered in these pages are rather inherently duplicitous, even prone to vengeance. Latour warns against too glib a reliance on any truth about magic, and he directs us to attend closely to the subtleties of the magician's craft, particularly the self-interests at its core. As these theories of magic unfold, we will see scholars assume a posture of detachment, transparency, and cool reason. But we will also find many interests in play—some petty, others malign. Perhaps the most significant subtext that will emerge from these theories is the scholarly effort to conjure—or conjure away—what it means to be modern. Debates over magic provide an extraordinarily rich ground for exploring the nature of modernity, its values, and its limits.

Magic and Modernity

Between the sixteenth and eighteenth centuries, Europe experienced massive economic and political transformations. This era saw the fracturing of religious unity, the consolidation of the nation-state, and the emergence of new capitalist economic structures. During the same period, European powers launched an extended program of discovery and conquest of the non-European world that produced not only new riches but also a startling array of information from missionaries and explorers. Through this era, a distinctive form of "modernity" took hold within European culture. Scholars debate how this notion should be most productively understood—whether it should be seen primarily in chronological or economic or ideological terms, the role of secularization and rationalization in this cultural formation, the specific social and material forces in Western history that contributed to its rise.

Among the aspects of the "modern" most relevant for our purposes here, Gustavo Benavides underscores its essentially comparative, oppositional nature. As he explains, "A condition of modernity presupposes an act of self-conscious distancing from a past or a situation regarded as naive." The very notion of the modern depends on a mode of self-referential opposition to the nonmodern, a mode of difference and differentiation that leads, in turn, to the sense that the future is open—things can be otherwise. Western modernity developed distinctive forms of technical and institutional power that fueled its processes of modernization, but at its heart was this fundamental mode of reflexive differentiation.[2]

In the early modern context of cultural contact and transformation, a new notion of "religion" gained currency among European intellectuals. Prior to the sixteenth century this term had referred largely to the dutiful performance of ritual obligations. But in various sixteenth-century accounts of non-European social practices, the word began to designate a cross-cultural, and potentially universal, phenomenon related to systems of ritual practice. By the eighteenth century, the cross-cultural aspect of religion was firmly established, but usage of the term had shifted dramatically away from attention to ritual toward an internal state of mind. Religion had become principally a matter of ideas and beliefs. Amplifying important themes of the Protestant and Catholic Reformations, the knowledge-making classes of the Enlightenment disparaged all visible manifestations of religious life and practice—communities, institutions, rituals, various other types of behavior—as dubious encrustations. Religion had come to designate an expansive genus encompassing disparate cultural species, but at the same time true religion was localized within the private intellect as a matter of properly warranted cognition.

One of the paradigmatic formulations of this new notion of religion was David Hume's *Natural History of Religion* (1757). Hume mocked deist and rationalist apologetics for religion, but as Robert Baird has shown, Hume shared with his opponents two crucial presuppositions. First, the core of religion was properly to reside in a set of coherent propositions, and further, religious faith was reducible in its essence to a cognitive assent to the truth of these propositions.[4] For Hume and those who followed him, even as religion was universalized as a phenomenon present in all (or almost all) human cultures, its proper scope was dramatically delimited.

In the centuries that followed, this idealized notion of religion had wide-ranging effects, reverberating through Western culture and beyond. It assumed particular potency in liberal political theory and came to predominate the social and legal institutions of the modern West. And the concept was so thoroughly naturalized among Europe's intellectual classes that it functioned as one of the primary tools with which the West sought to understand human culture. As European scholars evaluated various social groups—both their own and those of their neighbors and conquests—this privatized and intellectualized notion of religion played an essential role in their analysis. It served as the standard against which alternative cultural configurations and modes of behavior were measured.

Only in recent decades have Western scholars come to acknowledge the very particular cultural provenance of this concept of religion—that it is far more provincial than it purports to be. Following on the work of Wilfred Cantwell Smith in his pivotal text, *The Meaning and End of Religion* (1962), scholars have come to explore central aspects of the linguistic and cultural development of this Western notion of religion.[5] Social theorists now accept as a commonplace the claim that this concept is a distinctive product of the modern (or early modern) West, thoroughly shaped by the presuppositions of reformed Christian theology. Yet despite this recognition and recent efforts by a number of important scholars to excavate the genealogy of religion, much work remains in tracing the specific ways in which this notion has taken shape and in which it has functioned. This text is a contribution to those efforts.

Despite its prevalence in modern Western thought, this intellectualized notion of religion has proved extraordinarily amorphous. European and American social scientists, philosophers, and scholars of religious studies—those very scholars most eager to invoke religion as a discrete cross-cultural phenomenon—have had enormous difficulty in seeking to formulate a coherent definition of religion. They have engaged in long and entangled struggles to pin down the concept, to demarcate religion in relation to other cultural systems of knowledge and meaning. Social scientific studies of religion regularly begin with discussions of the problem, and the effort to find a stable definition of religion persists in contemporary theoretical and philosophical texts.[6] This issue has been particularly acute for the field of religious studies: its institutional legitimacy as a distinct academic discipline demands a clearly defined object of study, yet quite often the nature of that object remains elusive.

It is at this point that magic enters the scholarly discourse with a distinctive allure. Since the emergence of religious studies and the social sciences as academic disciplines in the late nineteenth century, theorists have regularly invoked "magic" as a fundamental category of cultural analysis. In innumerable texts by the leading theorists of these disciplines—including such founding figures of modern anthropology, sociology, psychology, and religious studies as Tylor, Mauss, Durkheim, Freud, Malinowski, and Weber—understanding magic has seemed key to understanding human society.

One of the primary functions of magic in this scholarly literature has been to serve as a foil for religion. Some theorists have seen magic as standing outside the category of religion, others as marking religion's outermost boundary. But in either case, there has been widespread scholarly consensus that magic is "the bastard sister of religion."[7] Magic has been configured as the illegitimate (and effeminized) sibling, and through contrast with this form of deviance, scholars have sought to give religion clearer definition. Magic has played a central role in scholarly efforts to define the nature of religion and to demarcate its proper bounds.

But magic has proved a remarkably pliable analytical tool in these academic texts, serving multifarious functions. Magic not only has offered a foil for religion but also has been positioned in the scholarly tradition as occupying some sort of middle ground between religion and that other great Western social formation, "science." Science has proved no less difficult to define than religion. As Latour pointedly states, " 'Science'—in quotation marks—does not exist. It is the name that has been pasted onto certain sections of certain networks, associations that are so sparse and fragile that they would have escaped attention altogether if everything had not been attributed to them."[8] Yet given the centrality of these scientific networks to modern social organization, such an assessment has been untenable for many scholars, and they have again turned to magic as an invaluable foil promising to bring the boundaries of science into sharper relief. And with magic positioned as a middle ground between religion and science, it has functioned in the scholarly literature to mediate—even police—relations between the two. Throughout the history of modern Western social science and religious studies, numerous scholars have struggled to reify magic as a discrete entity and to map the precise relations among magic, religion, and science.

Yet the efforts to formulate distinctions among these categories have proved notoriously unstable, the subject of repeated critique and deconstruction. Edward Burnett Tylor was one of the principal architects of this analytical structure, yet as Wouter Hanegraaff has recently shown, Tylor himself demonstrated great ambivalence in demarcating the precise boundaries among the categories. In 1900, R. R. Marett challenged the efforts of British intellectualists such as Tylor and Frazer to differentiate religion and magic. More than a half century later, in *The Savage Mind* (1962), Claude Lévi-Strauss rejected the notion that magic could be reified as a category analytically distinct from either religion or science. After considering various efforts at contrasting magic and practical action, Lévi-Strauss concluded that attempts to see magical practices as fundamentally subjective—in contrast to practical and objective scientific behavior—are fallacious, since magic is based on the fundamental belief that humanity can intervene in the order of the natural world to modify or add to its system of determinism. Recognizing this aspect of magic, Lévi-Strauss asserted, helps us better understand the proper relation between magic and religion. Religion consists in "a *humanization of natural laws* and magic in a *naturalization of human actions*—the treatment of certain human actions *as if* they were an integral part of physical determinism." But, he continued, we should not see these two as alternatives or evolutionary stages:

> The anthropomorphism of nature (of which religion consists) and the physiomorphism of man (by which we have defined magic) constitute two components which are always given, and vary only in proportion. As we noted earlier, each implies the other. There is no religion without magic any more than there is magic without at least a trace of religion. The notion of a supernature exists only for a humanity which attributes supernatural powers to itself and in return ascribes the powers of its superhumanity to nature.[9]

Marett and Lévi-Strauss are only two of the many prominent voices who have challenged the effort to reify magic and to fix clear boundaries among magic, religion, and science. Yet even as Marett and Lévi-Strauss critique the attempts of other theorists to circumscribe magic, they themselves are drawn to put forward new definitions of the phenomenon. Other commentators go even farther to argue that, given the inherently problematic nature of the concept, magic should be completely discarded as a category within scholarly analysis. In 1956 Erland Ehnmark asserted that the effort to differentiate magic and religion "is unpractical in its logical rigidity, exactly because it is built on opposites *excluding* each other": each term only has meaning through the exclusion of its contrary. The following year Olof Pettersson argued that the debate over the relation between magic and religion is "an artificial problem created by defining religion on the ideal pattern of Christianity." The proper response, in Pettersson's view, would be to give magic "a decent burial." And in 1982, as he considered the notion of magic, Edmund Leach concluded that "after a lifetime's career as a professional anthropologist, I have almost reached the conclusion that the word has no meaning whatsoever."[10]

But despite the force of such arguments, scholars continue to invoke magic as a meaningful analytical category, and efforts to delineate the boundaries among magic, religion, and science persist. Introductory texts in religious studies and the social sciences regularly recount debates over the definition of magic and its relation to religion and science, and new theories of magic proliferate. In one bold example, Daniel Lawrence O'Keefe's *Stolen Lightning* (1982) rejects the argument that magic is a mere "construct" and sets out to formulate "a general theory of magic . . . a complete explanatory account of the whole thing, past and present, all the provinces, rather than a single hypothesis." Scholars continue to put forward definitions of magic, particularly in connection with the broader effort to define religion as an object of study. Despite its indeterminacy and elusiveness, magic retains a tantalizing power. Many theorists seem to share the hope voiced by Stanley Tambiah that one day when magic is adequately embedded in "a more ample theory of human life," its "now puzzling duality" will disappear.[11]

This book was sparked by the persistence of theories of magic as a topos in European and American social theory. More than a century of thwarted attempts to reify and define magic—to contain and circumscribe this phenomenon—by many of the West's most prominent cultural theorists would seem to provide a rather clear indication that this enterprise might be suspect. But despite that troubled legacy, scholars continue in this endeavor. This very persistence signals that more than mere intellectual curiosity may be at stake in these debates. My purpose in the following chapters is to explore why a category as amorphous and indeterminate as magic has maintained such currency in the theoretical literature of anthropology, sociology, and religious studies. Given the problematic nature of magic as an analytical concept and the apparently insurmountable difficulties in efforts to define it, why has the category maintained such intellectual vitality?

My fundamental contention is that theoretical debates over magic have persisted in large measure because of their resonance with broader contemporary social concerns. Whatever the many areas of disagreement among scholars in their competing definitions of magic, one common feature throughout these debates has been the broad consensus that magic is an archetypically nonmodern phenomenon. Magic has offered scholars and social theorists a foil for modern notions of religion and science and, more broadly, a foil for modernity itself. As Benavides underscores, the very notion of modernity is based on an oppositional mode of self-referentiality. Debates over the nature of magic have provided scholars with a particularly apt occasion to articulate the nature of modernity through the process of differentiating the nonmodern. The plasticity of magic, its pliable and permeable nature, has made the concept readily adaptable as a polemical and ideological tool, especially when coupled with the long-standing stigma attached to the notion. The following chapters will explore various modern cultural disputes refracting through the debates over magic.

Magic and the Boundaries of Religion

At the most obvious level, theories of magic have provided a prominent site for scholarly elaboration of the modern concept of religion and the proper role of religion in the modern social order. Through the process of reifying magic in contrast to more acceptable forms of internalized religious piety, theorists have found an extremely well-suited mechanism to aid in formulating norms for religious belief and behavior. Scholarly debates over the relation between magic and religion have been lengthy and complex, and through these competing theories, magic has served a wide range of functions that will be considered in detail in subsequent chapters.

For example, many important theorists have invoked magic as a weapon in their efforts to prescribe appropriate religious belief and practice. For centuries Protestants regularly denigrated Catholic sacramental and devotional practices as magical, and this polemic has echoed through modern social scientific theory. The specter of magic has regularly been deployed in order to promote an idealized notion of religion as private, intellectual, and spiritualized—a norm based on decidedly Protestant views of appropriate religious piety. Yet as numerous recent scholars have stressed, the interiorizing of religion was a prominent theme of the Catholic Reformation as well, and it is not uncommon to find recent writers seeking to explain that Catholic sacramental practices fall properly within the bounds of religion rather than magic.[12]

For other theorists, however, the debates over magic have not so much served as an opportunity to promote reformed, spiritualized norms for religion as they have provided cover for a thinly veiled attack on all religion as superstitious and magically benighted. A vivid—and thoroughly unveiled—example of this use of magic appears in H. L. Mencken's *Treatise on the Gods* (1930). Mencken here attributes all forms of religion to "the same sense of helplessness before the cosmic mysteries, and the same pathetic attempt to resolve it by appealing to higher powers." In his discussion of religion's nature and origins, Mencken notes the scholarly "frenzy to differentiate between religion and magic":

[margin note: Magic vs. Religion (Mencken)]

The magician, it is explained, is one who professes to control the powers he deals with; the priest attempts only to propitiate them. The magician pretends to be able to work evil as well as good; the priest works only good. The magician deals with all sorts of shapes, some supernatural and others not; the priest deals only with gods and their attendant angels. The magician claims a control over material substances; the priest confines himself to spiritual matters.

Scorning these distinctions, Mencken launches a broadside against "the indubitable magical quality" of "the rev. clergy of Holy Church," a magic demonstrated most visibly in the rite of the Eucharist:

[margin note: Transubstantiation]

The simple carbohydrate of the bread, a purely material substance, is changed into a complicated congeries of other material substances, and so with the alcohol of the wine. . . . Here we have all the characteristics of a magical act, as experts set them forth: the suspension of natural laws, the transmutation of a material substance, the use of a puissant verbal formula, and the presence of an adept. . . . But the point needs no labouring, for it doesn't make much difference what a thing is called, so long as its intrinsic character is clearly apprehended. Magic or religion: it is all one.[13] *[margin note: For Catholics]*

Mencken's mockery of the doctrine of transubstantiation follows a long tradition of Protestant attacks on Catholic magic, but he also demonstrates how readily a polemic that most often serves to promote nonmagical norms for religion can transmute into a polemic that sees all forms of religion as equally besotted with magic.

Evans-Pritchard addresses this issue in his *Theories of Primitive Religion* (1965). In considering the scholarly use of magic to impugn religion, Evans-Pritchard focuses on the personal beliefs of important protagonists. He explains, for example, that Tylor had been raised Quaker; Frazer, Presbyterian; Marett in the Church of England; Malinowski, Catholic; Durkheim, Lévy-Bruhl, and Freud, Jewish. Yet despite these religious backgrounds, "with one or two exceptions . . . the persons whose writings have been most influential have been at the time they wrote agnostic or atheists."[14] Thus, Evans-Pritchard asserts, the polemics against magic by these various theorists were shaped by their condescension toward all forms of religion.

Evans-Pritchard need not have been so concerned with this sort of psychologizing. One of my objectives here will be to demonstrate that, regardless of scholars' personal motives, the dominant theories of magic have functioned to delimit religion in a manner that renders it increasingly extraneous to modern culture. Whether framed as a polemic against all beliefs in the supernatural or merely as a polemic advocating certain narrow religious norms, scholarly arguments against magic have commonly prescribed an increasingly limited

[margin note: Dominant theories of Religion]

role for religion, leaving it relevant—if at all—only as a tenuous source of private comfort or subjective validation. The dominant theories of magic have regularly served to untether religion from life in the material world, to configure religion as an ungrounded abstraction decidedly irrelevant to pragmatic affairs. These theories have reinforced a harsh antinomy between the natural world and the increasingly vaporous realm of religion. In this frame, religion becomes extraneous to the world of human experience. John Milbank has written at length on the efforts of modern social theory to "police the sublime."[15] No more overt example of this policing can be found than these theories of magic.

This domestication of religion has proved an essential component of liberal social thought. Timothy Fitzgerald has recently underscored the crucial role played by the liberal containment of religion in producing a sense of the secular, a nonreligious world under the "rational" control of politics, science, capitalism, and "individuals maximizing natural self-interest." This "separate 'non-religious' conceptual space, a fundamental area of presumed factual objectivity," can take shape only through delimiting the realm of the religious. The modern notion of religion has thus proved a central tool in "establishing the naturalness and ideological transparency of capitalist and individualist values." As Fitzgerald states it, "The category religion is at the heart of modern western capitalist ideology. . . . it mystifies by playing a crucial role in the construction of the secular, which to us constitutes the self-evidently true realm of scientific facticity, rationality, and naturalness."[16] Modern modes of secularization depend on the construction of a discrete and autonomous religious sphere, a sphere that both constrains religion and clarifies, through contrast, the meaning of the secular. Throughout the traditions of social thought explored in this book, magic is invoked to demarcate and police the boundaries of the religious realm, a move that serves to reinforce the stability of modern social organization.

At the same time, magic serves even more subtle ideological functions. Throughout the theoretical literature, we learn that magic is preoccupied with social power, entangled in a web of improper and disruptive desires, murky relations with materiality, arrogant self-seeking. In contrast, these texts configure a model of religion insulated from contamination by any sense of power—it is abstract, rarefied, otherworldly. As Fitzgerald states, modern "'religion' constructs a notion of human relations divorced from power. One of the characteristics of books produced in the religion sector is that they present an idealized world of so-called faith communities—of worship, customs, beliefs, doctrines, and rites entirely divorced from the realities of power in different societies." In a similar vein, Russell McCutcheon has powerfully attacked the efforts of religious studies scholars to configure religion "as sui generis, autonomous, strictly personal, essential, unique, prior to, and ultimately distinct from, all other facets of human life and interaction." McCutcheon underscores that this construction of religion "deemphasizes difference, history, and soci-opolitical context in favor of abstract essences and homogeneity," a gesture with the insidious corollary that "certain aspects of human life are free from the taint of sociopolitical interactions." Defining religion in this rarefied man-ner serves to mystify the material realities within which religious systems—and the production of knowledge about religion—function.[17]

As we will see, the scholarly deployment of magic is a central component of this construction of religion. Magic is configured in these theories as ob-sessed with self-serving and vain power, but the very contrast with magic serves to deflect issues of power away from religion. This use of magic masks the values and material interests at work in the production of a delimited religious realm, and at the same time it also serves to occlude the power actually exer-cised by—and within—Western religious institutions. The dominant theories of magic offer a harmless, rationalized model of religion serviceable for liberal modernity.

Magic and the Modern Subject

These debates on the relation of magic to religion and the role of religion in liberal society have been only one aspect of far broader modern cultural agendas. Throughout the theories of magic, scholars have engaged in wide-ranging exploration of various aspects of modernity. So, for example, in dis-putes over the relation between magic and science, theorists have struggled to define the precise nature of modern forms of rationality and how that ration-ality might differ from other modes of thought. And the debates over magic have ranged far beyond issues of piety and rationality into broader considera-tions of the nature of modern subjectivity itself.

Charles Taylor has highlighted the role played by the suppression of mag-ical thinking in the emergence of modern Western forms of subjectivity and individual identity (which developed, he says, from a post-Reformation sense of "inwardness"). As Taylor explains, in the earlier magical worldview the boundaries between the self and the natural world were seen as essentially permeable. But with the arrival of "a new moral/spiritual stance to the world . . . a new piety," those boundaries were reinforced, bringing in their wake "a new notion of freedom and inwardness." This new, disenchanted sense of freedom stands in sharp contrast to the confinement of the past: "The decline of the world-view underlying magic was the obverse of the rise of the new sense of freedom and self-possession. From the viewpoint of this new sense of self, the world of magic seems to entail a thraldom, an imprisoning of the self in uncanny external forces, even a ravishing or loss of self. It threatens a possession which is the very opposite of self-possession."[18]

Taylor is surely correct in his claim that modern notions of subjective autonomy and freedom have been constructed through contrast with past forms of magical thought (much as the modern sense of social progress has tracked this liberatory narrative). Yet as Lyndal Roper has asserted, the triumphal tone of Taylor's account of the consolidation and stability of this modern sense of autonomous identity is rather thoroughly unwarranted. Michel Foucault and the generation of his followers have amply demonstrated that the consolidation of the modern subject is far less secure than Taylor implies and, further, that the maintenance of modern subjectivity turns on complex new forms of repression and constraint. Building on Foucault's insight, Roper rejects Taylor's simplistic account of the effects of historical and social conditions on individual subjectivity. Not only have magic and the "irrational" been far more integrally involved in the emergence of the modern bourgeois subject than Taylor recognizes, but also the disciplinary processes that produce this subject often contradict the very values they espouse.[19] As I will discuss in later chapters, while "freedom" from magic is certainly invoked as a constitutive element of modern modes of subjectivity, this freedom is purchased only at the price of potent new forms of social control and regimentation.

The dominant scholarly theories of magic have had as a central theme the prescription of idealized norms for modern subjectivity. The modern subject configured in these theories demonstrates properly delimited forms of religious piety, properly rationalized modes of thought, and properly disenchanted relations with the material world. This subject conforms to distinctive norms of individual agency and autonomy (seeing itself as fundamentally independent from other individuals and the natural world), while tempering that autonomy with a suitably submissive attitude toward the social order. This subject demonstrates a requisite respect for the abstract regularity of the material world, while repressing any awareness of the mystifications of the commodity form. Subjects who fail to conform to these norms are denigrated as trapped in decidedly nonmodern and subversive forms of magical thought.

These theories of magic are permeated with overt forms of moralism, a mode of social discipline comparable to what Stuart Clark has called "acculturation by text." Max Weber's term for the modern disenchantment of the world was *Entzauberung*—"removing the magic"—and the dominant theories of magic have as their objective an insistence that the modern subject conform to an emphatic disenchantment.[20] As I will argue, a crucial factor contributing to the persistence of magic as a major theme of scholarly concern is the resonance of the topic with broader efforts to prescribe and regulate modern forms of subjectivity and modern relations to the material world. Magic has assumed the role of modernity's foil, and debates over magic have provided an important site for the articulation of modernity's norms.

Yet as is already clear, this moralizing narrative is no mere passive lesson. Even as the scholarly debates over magic have foregrounded fundamental questions of social order, material and political interests have taken visible shape

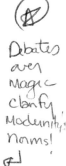

within these disputes. Magic has functioned as a powerful marker of cultural difference, one with ready application in the political and economic sphere.

Magic and Social Control

In social scientific literature of the late nineteenth and early twentieth centuries, magic was seen as a definitive characteristic of the "primitive" mentality. Magical thinking was viewed as a prime index of the nonmodern and non-Western, and theorists commonly attributed magic to marginal peoples, locations, and eras. Even scholars who acknowledged that magic was more widespread and pervasive than this narrow attribution regularly restricted their consideration of magic to its preliterate and non-Western manifestations (offering disclaimers to the effect that magic is particularly "well exemplified in rude communities").[21]

In recent decades, the discourse on "primitive" cultures and mentalities has become intellectually untenable. Yet contemporary theories of magic still often invoke these earlier traditions analyzing primitive and nonmodern mental and social processes, either through the very structure of their analysis or through other types of scholarly sleight of hand. Even as theories of social evolution have become more muted, texts still regularly consign the primary discussion of magic to chapters dealing with "primitive," "folk," "traditional," or "indigenous" religion. The principal evidence of magic is still today drawn largely from anthropological studies of non-Western cultures, and earlier evolutionary theory continues to resound through recent theoretical formulations of magic. While it might appear unseemly to speak of "primitives," it remains perfectly acceptable to speak of "magic in the life of traditional peoples";[22] there is little ambiguity as to who constitutes a "traditional" person and who does not.

This link of magic with the "primitive" underscores one of the most important functions of scholarly discourse on magic. These theories served through much of the past century as an important ideological tool in the aid of European and American imperialism and colonialism. Theories of magic confirmed that the mental processes of nonmodern, non-Western peoples are benighted and superstitious, and this conclusion served in turn to affirm, in Edward Said's phrase, "that certain territories and people *require* and beseech domination."[23] A propensity to magic demonstrates an incapacity for responsible self-government: people prone to magic call out for enlightened control.

Euro-American imperialism has commonly been overlaid with a religious mission, and this missionizing theme has been prominent in theoretical texts concerning magic. In Western theories of religious development throughout the nineteenth and twentieth centuries, Christianity was regularly positioned as the ultimate development of rational, enlightened religion, and the logic of this evolutionary view thoroughly informed the response to magic. For example, the influential philosopher Frank Byron Jevons concludes a lengthy 1908 examination of the nature of magic with suggestions as to how "the sensible missionary" might war against magic by exposing it as "wicked" and "silly"; Jevons offers his study as a tool in the effort to convert the heathen to Christianity.[24] Opposition to magic—both through missionizing and through colonizing—was seen as an appropriate Christian duty.

Yet imperialism also had far more secular bases, and these economic and political interests also feature prominently in the theoretical literature on magic. Near the conclusion of his 1948 study of magic, the sociologist Hutton Webster encourages "white settlers" (including missionaries, traders, and European administrators) to use ridicule and contempt in the effort to eradicate forms of magic disruptive to colonial interests and to institute more manageable forms of piety. Throughout the various permutations of this scholarly preoccupation with magic, the theories have formed an important component of what Said calls the broad Western "imagination of empire."[25] As numerous cultural theorists have underscored, the modern Western social sciences emerged in the context of Euro-American colonial exploration and conquest, and these disciplines provided invaluable resources to colonialist efforts to define and control non-Western peoples and territories. Orientalist tropes and rhetoric have permeated the literature of the social sciences, particularly theoretical formulations of magic.

Yet magic could not be so stably consigned to the colonial frontier. In *Primitive Culture* (1871), Tylor wrote of magic as a cultural "survival." The very notion of survival underscores central tensions that have haunted Western theories of magic. By definition, survivals persist; they refuse to be contained in the chronological or geographic distance. In fact, Tylor's own charting of where magic is to be found provides an instructive example both of the obvious difficulties in seeking to consign magic to distant times and locales and of the pressing domestic concerns that animate his theory.

In *Primitive Culture* Tylor asserts that magic is primarily a problem of the colonial periphery, but it is clear that he also sees magic as an issue for contemporary domestic policy. Tylor attributes the pernicious and delusional belief in magic "in its main principle to the lowest known stages of civilization, and the lower races." But he immediately affirms that magic persists even in "modern cultured nations." Magical practices can thus be traced from "the lower culture which they are of, to the higher culture which they are in." The very prevalence of these magical survivals so confounds Tylor's evolutionary principles that his cartography is threatened with inundation: "For the stream of civilization winds and turns upon itself, and what seems the bright onward current of one age may in the next spin round in a whirling eddy, or spread into a dull and pestilential swamp."[26]

Tylor finds examples of magic not only among "savages high and low like the Australians and Polynesians, and barbarians like the nations of Guinea," but also within the population and folklore of Europe. Indeed, Tylor finds a surviving European equivalent for almost every form of symbolic magic. Divining with animal entrails and bones is common, he tells us, among Malays and Polynesians, Peruvians and central Africans, North American Indians and ancient Romans, but these practices survive in Brandenburg, Ireland, and England itself. Palmistry, which "flourished in ancient Greece and Italy as it still does in India," "has its modern votaries not merely among Gypsy fortune-tellers, but in what is called 'good society.'" Magical thought is shared by "the negro fetish-man" and "the modern clairvoyant," and comparable magical practices appear among "the Red Indian medicine-man, the Tatar necromancer, the Highland ghost-seer, and the Boston medium." As Tylor strings together examples of the symbolic magic and superstition of "the lower races" of the Zulu and the Obi-man of West Africa, he acknowledges that these examples are "fully rivalled in superstitions which still hold their ground in Europe" among such types as the "German cottager" and the "Hessian lad," sailors and the "Cornishman." This exotic and animated landscape encroaches near at hand: an astrologer, we are told, has opened shop within a mile of Tylor's own door.[27]

Tylor is dismayed by the persistence of magic within the heart of Europe, and his concern with this social threat has been echoed throughout the scholarly tradition. While the primary discussions of magic focus on its non-Western manifestations, theorists also regularly assert that particular groups within the West demonstrate strong proclivities to magic. It is little surprise that these are groups posing the specter of social disruption: women, children, people of color, members of lower social classes, other deviants. There has been a widespread, explicit consensus among scholars that magic incites antisocial appetites and subversive passions among the dispossessed and thus places good order at risk.

The scholarly discourses on magic have regularly conformed to the interests of the dominant classes of Europe and America seeking to regulate and control both their colonial possessions and their domestic populations, especially the troublesome groups on the margins of society. In the context of colonialism, non-Western cultural systems were regularly configured by scholars so as to provide a contrasting foil that could bring Western modernity into clearer relief. Particularly in anthropological and ethnographic literature, this juxtaposition of cultures could produce a heightened sense of cultural difference, rendering non-Western societies an "oppositional Other."[28] Through the scholarly production of "primitive" or "traditional" culture, nontraditional culture itself takes form. But the alleged magical proclivities of this primitive Other could be used not only to contrast the enlightened West with its primitive possessions but also to naturalize distinctions between the enlightened and elite social classes in Europe and their less privileged compatriots within the metropole.

These scholarly theories of magic provide a powerful example of the ways in which notions of cultural difference can be constructed and deployed in the effort to exercise social control. As Foucault underscores, one of the principal strategies of modern Western disciplinary technologies has been to reify the identities of marginal groups. Many forms of deviation have been configured as deviance and consigned to specialized modern institutions (prisons, hospitals, mental institutions). The modern era has also given rise to a range of new scholarly disciplines working to classify and normalize modern subjects. While magic proved more amorphous and less pressing a concern than the forms of deviance that Foucault studied, it has taken its place nevertheless among the markers of cultural difference.

One of the most effective tactics in this reification of deviant identities has been the deployment of various codes of stigma and marginalization intersecting in a mutually reinforcing overlay, gaining strength through association. Through these intersecting rhetorics, the cultural weight of discourses on gender, sexuality, race, and various other forms of marginality is powerfully amplified.[29] As we will see, the dominant scholarly theories of magic echo and reinforce the rhetoric of various modes of deviance, most notably the rhetoric of sexual nonconformity. The effort to consolidate Western social norms has been an abiding subtext of these theories. Through a complex interweave with other stigmatized identities and behavior, magic has been configured as one further marker in the chain of Otherness against which the ideals of modern social order have been articulated.

Magic and the Critique of Modernity

Throughout the dominant modern theories of magic, the category has served as a foil for use in the self-fashioning of modernity. Yet magic has proved far too elusive and indeterminate to remain a stable and contained rhetorical tool. Modernity itself has always been fractured, contested, and ultimately illusory. As Bruno Latour emphatically declares, "we have never been modern" at all.[30]

Latour argues that one of the foundational gestures of Western modernity has been the effort to formulate and police a heightened antinomy between nonhuman nature and human culture. Modernity has been constituted on this ideology of purification, on an insistence that we disentangle the nonhuman from the human. To be modern, we are told, is to recognize the essential differentiation between these "two entirely distinct ontological zones." Yet as Latour demonstrates, the modern bifurcation of nature and culture has always

lines of demarcation are

been thoroughly ambiguous and contradictory. Despite the ostentatious efforts to police their separation, to configure the nonhuman and the human as if they were separable, the perverse success of Western modernity has actually depended on the ingenious and profligate intermingling of nature and culture. Under the ideological cloak of their ontological differentiation, nature and culture have interwoven to produce astounding networks and "mixtures between entirely new types of beings, hybrids of nature and culture." Latour concludes in fact that the dualistic rhetoric of a separation between nature and culture has actually played an indispensable role in their intermingling: "The more we forbid ourselves to conceive of hybrids, the more possible their interbreeding becomes—such is the paradox of the moderns. . . . the modern Constitution allows the expanded proliferation of the hybrids whose existence, whose very possibility, it denies."[31] And through these paradoxical and duplicitous processes, the incessant efforts to consolidate some sort of stable modern identity inevitably falter. The pure, modern subject is an elusive figment, always incoherent and impossible.

Modern theories of magic provide a particularly apt confirmation of Latour's claim. These theories configure magic as blindly artificial, inserting human desire and machination futilely into the workings of natural causality (in contrast, of course, with universalized and naturalized forms of religion and science built on the modern differentiation of culture and nature). Repeatedly modern scholars will assert that practitioners of magic fail to recognize the essential differences between the human and the nonhuman, the psychic and the material, desire and reality. Yet even as scholars have struggled to articulate these distinctions and to formulate norms for the proper relations of modern subjects to the natural world, strange voices intrude. These moralizing theories of magic are always ambiguous and riven; as we will see, they regularly veer into overt self-contradiction, tautology, or incoherence.

Just as the effort to disentangle nature and culture has proved incoherent, so also magic can never be stably distinguished from its contraries. Though scholars persist in the attempt to define and contain magic, to hold this reification steady, magic is prone to dematerialize under the watchful scholarly gaze only to reappear with ghostly power at the very heart of the modern. So, for example, in one of the more ironic twists of the story that follows, the ardent self-proclaimed rationalist James George Frazer was dismayed at the ways his work fed the booming turn-of-the-century spiritualist subculture. The scholarly effort to reify and contain magic has regularly had the inadvertent effect of making more magic.[32]

Frazer's difficulty was no isolated episode. Alex Owen and Pamela Thurschwell have both recently explored striking parallels between the interests of late Victorian occultists and spiritualists and those of their more secular scholarly contemporaries in such fields as psychology and emerging information technologies. Owen and Thurschwell demonstrate that far from representing some premodern survival, Victorian occultism was a demonstrable product of modernity, turning on the heightened modern preoccupation with the nature and boundaries of the individual consciousness and rehearsing important tensions lurking within the modern sense of subjectivity. As Owen asserts, Victorian occult practices reflected "a modern sensibility that remained immured in and fascinated by the performance of the irrational even as it sought to measure, understand, and to some extent control or manipulate it."[33]

Modern occultism is thus as modern as it is occult, and it demonstrates the deep level at which the "secular" and the "sacred," the "rational" and the "irrational," refuse separation. While many prominent scholars have worked to stigmatize and condemn magical thinking, their efforts have met with little success. Like the scholarly establishment, other inhabitants of the modern world have remained fascinated by magic. Occultism, astrology, various forms of supernaturalism—all have had an effervescent life in the modern popular imagination. Nineteenth-century commercial culture launched the marketing of new forms of "magical" entertainments, and with varying degrees of solemnity and kitsch, magic and occultism have proved a staple of modern cultural life, especially in film, television, and popular literature. Simon During's recent work has vividly demonstrated the constitutive role of a broad form of "secular magic" (commercial magical entertainment and literature making no claim to involve supernatural powers) within modern popular culture. As During explains, this type of magic illuminates the deep power of "puzzlement, fictiveness, and contingency" within modernity, the degree to which modern culture is "oriented toward illusions understood as illusions." So, for example, the vernacular of magic is often invoked to describe the appeal of celebrity, to supplement or substitute for concepts of the sublime and the beautiful, and "to express perceptions of modern society's astonishing, unpredictable, or uncontrollable qualities."[34]

And beyond this broad secular magic, a variety of more supernaturally inclined magical subcultures have thrived in Europe and America throughout the modern period. These subcultures are a prominent feature of the alternative religious and spiritual landscape that has emerged since the 1960s, and new information technologies (particularly the Internet) have fueled their growth. Like Victorian occultism, these groups are deeply informed by central ideologies and values of modernity, and again like their Victorian predecessors, they often directly address alienations and tensions within the contemporary world.

Many people seize on magic specifically because of what they see as its political valence. Magic and witchcraft have been most notably invoked by feminists and gender activists as tools in their efforts to subvert dominant systems of social power. As Starhawk explains: "*Magic* is another word that makes people uneasy, so I use it deliberately, because the words we are comfortable with, the words that sound acceptable, rational, scientific, and intellectually correct, are comfortable precisely because they are the language of estrangement."[35] Generations of social theory dismissed belief in the supernatural with the broad brush of Marx's assertion that religion is the "opium of the people." Yet in recent years various cultural theorists have expressed a renewed interest in the operations of magic and religion on the margins of society.[36] Michael Taussig, a prominent example of this new critical perspective, has built on the thought of Walter Benjamin to explore the ways in which various magical practices can function as forms of social critique. In *Shamanism, Colonialism, and the Wild Man* (1987), Taussig distinguishes the magical rites of the indigenous Indian and peasant inhabitants of the Putumayo region of southwestern Colombia from the religion of state Catholicism imposed on the Indians by Western colonialism. He demonstrates the important subversive functions served by the Indians' magical practices. Not only do these practices provide the peasants a vehicle through which to articulate the antagonisms they experience at the hands of capitalism and alien Western social structures, but these forms of magic can also serve as lines of empowerment for marginal groups in response to oppressive social structures. As Taussig frames it, his work is focused on "the possibilities and even necessities for reconceptualizing the power of imageric and magical thinking in modernity."[37]

Starhawk and Taussig offer valuable examples of the deployment of magic as a tool in the critique of modernity. Their efforts have been joined by activists and social critics from a range of perspectives. Theologians have worked to rethink disembodied norms for religious practice and to break down artificial barriers between the natural and supernatural in order to make religious life more tactile, concrete, and engaged. Other cultural and political theorists have recognized the power of magic as a mechanism for challenging the estrangements and alienations of European and American cultural structures. With magic configured as the epitome of the non-Western and the nonmodern, it has proved a potent medium with which to contest the hegemonic social structures and norms of modernity.

Since the 1950s, postcolonial theory has emerged as one of the most prominent academic resources for interrogating the ways in which Euro-American modernity has defined itself in opposition to cultural Others. The first generations of postcolonial theorists often painted starkly Manichean portraits of Western appropriation of this Other, seeing Orientalist scholarship as uniformly objectifying and derogatory and Western scholars as sharing a narrow and monolithic set of objectives. But in recent years these images have become increasingly nuanced, with theorists recognizing the important variety and complexity of Western depictions of the non-Western Others.

John MacKenzie, for example, has shown that in many contexts the Orient could be invoked rhetorically by Western writers for the purpose of critiquing and challenging Western self-identity, for the formulation of "a counter-western discourse." As he explains, while Western scholars regularly deployed the tropes of Orientalism to bolster imperial hegemony, many scholars could also join with colonized writers to contest colonialism through counterhegemonic practices. As MacKenzie concludes:

> A fascination with Orientalism was as likely to be oppositional as consensual in relation to established power structures, a promoter of a ferment in ideas as in artistic innovation. . . . It is difficult to discover in any of the arts at whatever period sets of clearly delineated binary oppositions, sharp distinctions between the moral Self and the depraved Other. Rather has the whole experience been one of instabilities and fusions, attraction and repulsion, an awareness of characteristics to be peremptorily rejected as well as devoutly embraced.[38]

MacKenzie might well underestimate the degree to which this mode of self-critique depends on a reifying Orientalist appropriation of the non-Western Other. Yet he makes an important contribution to the growing body of literature demonstrating the variable, contingent, and ambivalent nature of colonialist representational practices. The discourses of colonialism—like all discourses—are marked by fluidity and heterogeneity; as Reina Lewis has argued, that very fluidity proved an essential component of their power.[39] And the discourses of colonialism—like all discourses of difference—have remained a site of shifting and contested struggles for power. These discourses could be readily deployed in the effort to confirm Western self-identity, but they could also be used to expose the frailty of that identity. They could legitimate colonial hegemony, but they could also puncture the pretensions of the colonizer.

The broad colonialist representations of the non-Western Other proved an important arena for Western self-critique, and so also the theories of magic have provided an important occasion for questioning and contesting Western cultural norms. This mode of critique has turned on a cultural logic that frames magic as alien, subversive, and nonmodern, but within that frame scholarly debates over magic have provided valuable resources for challenging reified and idealized notions of modern identity and for interrogating the insidious binary logics and dualisms on which modernity has been founded.

Magicians in Search of Revenge

My basic argument in this text is that debates concerning magic have maintained a great appeal for social theorists in large measure because they provide such a rich site for articulating and contesting the nature and boundaries of modernity. In the context of these debates, scholars have found a ready opportunity to articulate norms for modern modes of identity and subjectivity and for the relation of those subjects to the social and material worlds. But magic has also offered particularly useful resources for contesting those norms—for challenging modernity's hegemonic narratives of autonomy, rationality, and progress. Modernity might conceal its wizardry behind a naturalizing veil, but magic tantalizes with a peek behind the curtain.

This book seeks to excavate the genealogy of modern Western theories of magic and to explore their operations, with particular focus on the most influential theories in religious studies and the social sciences. Chapter 1 examines the social and intellectual context in which academic theories of magic emerged in the latter half of the nineteenth century. Beginning with a discussion of witchcraft and magic in early modernity, the chapter explores a number of the cultural factors crucial in shaping Western understandings of magic and modernity.

The remaining chapters explore major themes in the scholarly literature on magic since the late nineteenth century. Chapter 2 examines the construction of magic in relation to liberal religious piety, chapter 3 in relation to modern scientific rationality, and chapter 4 in relation to modern social order and capitalist economic relations. These chapters seek to address a basic set of questions: How has magic functioned in modern thought to demarcate the limits of religion? How have constructions of magic served to give definition to science and scientific rationality? Finally, with magic positioned as a buffer between religion and science, what social and political norms have been promoted through these theories?

Before proceeding, let me make three disclaimers. First, magic features as a prominent theme in an enormous range of Western scholarly literature, and I make no pretense of being comprehensive in my discussion here. I have limited my focus largely to major trends within religious studies and the social sciences. Even within that context, I have explored literature derived primarily from nineteenth-century theories of "primitive" culture and the resultant genre of "anthropology of religion." Magic was also a major concern among nineteenth-century Orientalist historians of religion whose philological study of the civilizations of the ancient Near East exerted profound influence on the discipline of religious studies. Comparable constructions of magic emerged in both traditions of study (with the anthropological configuration of "religion/magic/science" effectively mirrored by the triad "Israel/Egypt/Greece").[40] And, again, given the innumerable texts exploring magic even in my relatively constrained arena, I have focused largely on texts written in English or particularly influential in English-speaking countries. These limitations serve only in the interest of space. It is important to recognize that modern discourse on magic is as polymorphous and boundless as the phenomenon it purports to describe.

Second, my focus here is squarely on Western theorizing about magic. Recent years have seen invaluable scholarly contributions to the study of magic by non-Western theorists from a variety of disciplines, but that material is beyond the scope of this book. My goal is more narrow, an exercise in what a number of recent scholars have called the "anthropologizing of the West." For both practical and theoretical reasons, I have limited my focus to Western scholarly literature. My hope is that this focus allows the fissures and tensions within this literature to emerge with heightened clarity. The tradition of Western theories of magic readily demonstrates the contradictions and ambivalences on which it has been built, and these tendencies toward self-deconstruction make the prominence and persistence of this scholarly preoccupation even more remarkable. I leave to other scholars, with different forms of expertise and training, the task of bringing other tools to bear on this literature.

Third, while my objective in this text is to trace what I see as centrally important aspects of these scholarly debates on magic, I have no interest in making a reductive claim that this reading should eclipse other ways of approaching this literature. I am convinced that much of the appeal of debates concerning magic lies in their resonance with broader—and often unstated—concerns, but this study has also persuaded me of the thoroughly mobile and polyvalent nature of this cultural site. Many widely divergent issues are at stake in these debates over magic, and I am addressing only those that I find most compelling.

I began with a warning from Bruno Latour that scholars of magic should be approached with caution: they are often magicians in search of revenge. Many aspects of this scholarly vengefulness have already emerged. Social power is at stake in theory-making, but the workings of this power are often unacknowledged—and overdetermined. Even as social scientists and scholars of religion frame their accounts of magic as dispassioned theory, these accounts often surreptitiously replicate the very processes they purport to contain. The scholarly formulation of distinctions between rational analysis and magical spell can serve to mask the subterranean conjuration always at work in the cultural text and, in this masking, give license to the production of novel hybrids of profound, enchanting power. With a cloak of naturalized rationalism, scholars can deflect our attention from the power effected in their theory-making.

Power is an important aspect of scholarly vengefulness, but so also is desire. One of the most persistent themes in modern efforts to reify and comprehend magic is the scholarly rejection of the desires on which magic is based. These theories have as a central objective the disciplining of wayward desire. But in this process, scholars often disclaim the very pleasures that animate their own craft. Theories of magic have proved a source of great puzzlement and satisfaction to generations of theorists. The half-illusion of the magic show can give enormous delight, as can the mock seriousness of the psychic hot line or the astrology column. Yet the far more sober business of cultural analysis can also provide comparable forms of pleasure. How might we understand this allure?

Emily Apter offers some clues in her discussion of that venerable magical trope, the fetish. As scholars from a broad range of disciplines have taught us, the fetish is a focus of inordinate and immodest attention, regularly invested with magical import. Yet as Apter points out, scholars themselves have fetishized the concept, seeing it as a key to religion, psychology, art. In seeking to account for this ironic preoccupation, Apter looks to the power of the fetish to destabilize our normal modes of thought and representation—and to do so in an eminently pleasing manner:

> Desublimating the aura of falsity and bad faith in consumer consciousness; unmasking the banal sexisms of everyday life; undercutting aesthetic idealism with the seductive spectacle of kitsch, camp, or punk; exposing the postmodern infatuation with transgression, "gender trouble," and erotic fixation; smoking out the Eurocentric voyeurism of "other-collecting"—fetishism as a discourse weds its own negative history as a synonym for sorcery and witchcraft (*fetiçaria*) to an outlaw strategy of dereification. . . . a consistent displacing of reference occurs, paradoxically, as a result of so much *fixing*. Fetishism, in spite of itself, unfixes representations even as it enables them to become monolithic "signs" of culture.

Apter argues that this "unfixing," this dereification, has been the persistent function of the fetish. Refusing to stay in its allotted place as the property of the Other, the fetish has worked its way through bourgeois curiosity cabinets and the European literary imagination as a potent talisman through which Europe has "made itself strange to itself."[41] The fetishized process of estrangement and transgression has proved extraordinarily pleasurable through a double movement that reinscribes and subverts norms.

Magic has functioned in modernity with the very estranging and destabilizing vitality that Apter sees in the fetish. Magic has demonstrated a novel capacity to reinscribe and simultaneously to subvert modernity's self-representations. And further, modern theories of magic have exercised the paradoxical and expansive magical power of words, a power with its own distinctive satisfactions and one to which we will return. These theories have prescribed a reified modern identity, even as they have displayed the fictiveness of that reification. They have rigorously declared the fixity of scholarly representation, even as they have evanesced and dissipated. They have mocked the efficacy of "mere words," even as they have conjured powerful spells. As we will see, these theories have boasted of a pious will to truth, even as they have served a distinctly modern will to power "precisely because of their capacity to disguise themselves as transparencies."[42]

I

The Emergence of Magic in the Modern World

It is natural, that superstition should prevail every where in barbarous ages, and put men on the most earnest enquiry concerning
those invisible powers, who dispose of their happiness or misery.
—David Hume

Magic has a long and complex history. And crucial to any recounting of that history is an awareness of the broader context within
which magic takes shape. The effort to mark off a region of the conceptual and social terrain as magical involves, at the most basic
level, an act of demarcation, a juxtaposition of magic with other social practices and modes of knowledge. As the social context shifts,
so also magic is transformed, assuming new forms and exerting
new powers.

The nature and role of magic in Western society have changed
profoundly over recent centuries as the social order itself has
changed, the most significant of these developments involving
transformations in economic and political structures and concomitant shifts in the demarcation and social position of religion and
science. By the latter decades of the nineteenth century, a range of
major Western thinkers struggled to define and explain the nature
of the modern cultural formations that had taken shape around
them. But this focus on the modern also gave rise to an intense cultural preoccupation with the nonmodern. As discussed in the introduction, the very notion of modernity involves a sense of self-
referential differentiation from, and opposition to, the nonmodern.
One of the central strategies in efforts to define modernity has

been the attempt to reify nonmodern, superstitious thought and social practices in a manner that configures them as modernity's foil. In scholarly literature this foil has commonly assumed the form of magic. The position of magic within the intellectual and cultural terrain of the modern West has thus been a product not only of the distinctive confluence of social and material factors that gave shape to modernity but also of modernity's need to consolidate its own identity.

My primary objective in this book is to chart the role of magic in influential modern discursive structures since the late nineteenth century, to explore the significance that magic has held in modern thought. In order to approach this task, it is important to begin with an account of the social and intellectual context within which definitions of magic emerged in the latter decades of the nineteenth century. Three major epistemic changes profoundly affected the shape of magic in the modern world. First, through the course of the Reformation and the Enlightenment, religion came increasingly to be seen as properly a matter of the private intellect, a view deeply informed by generations of religious reform—and particularly by Protestant polemics against Catholic ritual and devotional practices. Coupled with this development was the astounding proliferation of capitalism and modern science, social practices sharing related forms of mechanistic and rationalized manipulation of the material world. Finally, the late nineteenth century saw the consolidation of European control over much of Asia and Africa, and colonial conquest and exploitation gave rise to new forms of scholarly analysis of "primitive" culture. These three developments exerted profound influence on almost every aspect of European and American culture. But for our purposes here, they particularly altered cultural perspectives on the natural world and the proper role of religion and science within modern society. As various thinkers struggled to come to terms with the norms for life in this seemingly disenchanted new world, to articulate appropriately modern forms of piety, efficiency, and rational control, magic emerged as a remarkably useful analytical tool. A host of social theorists, philosophers, and scholars of religion turned to magic as a central theme in their efforts to delineate the nature of the modern.

As Gustavo Benavides has asserted, the differentiation between magic and religion must be approached historically—"in the context of state formations and the centralization of political power."[1] The purpose of this chapter is to explore the social and intellectual context within which magic took shape as a category of modern cultural analysis. In order better to understand this context, it is productive to excavate important elements of Europe's past. The chapter begins with an examination of central aspects of the history—and historiography—of early modern witchcraft and magic, including the role of the European Reformations on the witchcraft persecutions and on evolving discourses concerning magic and superstition. Through this period we find significant cultural contestation over the proper understanding of the "natural" world and the relation between the natural and supernatural realms. Many of the strands of argument raised in opposition to the witch-hunts are echoed in later scholarly theories of magic, particularly those arguments that move to configure the belief in witchcraft not as heresy but as pathology.

The chapter then explores the rise of new mechanical views of nature and related notions of natural religion feeding the Enlightenment war against superstition. I will conclude by examining the colonial and racial context that gave rise to new Western theories of cultural and religious evolution. Particularly with the tremendous spread of European colonial power in the latter nineteenth century, Western social thought—including theories of religion and magic—was profoundly shaped by the interests of colonialism.

Through the historical period traced in this chapter, a major epistemic transformation occurs in the understanding of magic. At the dawn of the early modern period, magic was understood by European intellectuals within the context of the dominant synthesis of Aristotelian and Thomistic thought, and negative manifestations of magic were seen as constituting grievous sin. By the nineteenth century, Europe's intellectuals would no longer frame magic primarily as sin, but instead as an aberrational mode of thought antithetical to the dominant cultural logic—a symptom of psychological impairment and marker of racial or cultural inferiority.

Early Modern Witchcraft and Magic

I begin this account of the development of magic as a modern social and analytical category with a consideration of early modern perspectives on witchcraft and magic. Lyndal Roper underscores that "it is in the arena of the magical, the irrational, in witchtrials that—paradoxically enough—the individual subject of the early modern period unfolds."[2] As Roper and other scholars have demonstrated, these particular contested arenas illuminate central aspects of the emergence of the early modern subject. With the transformation of dominant social views on these issues, modernity itself becomes more clearly demarcated.

During the early modern period, concern with magic took two distinct forms in European culture. First, from around 1450 to at least 1750, secular and religious authorities in various parts of Europe and its colonies engaged in a prolonged effort to identify and punish suspected practitioners of witchcraft. Over these three centuries, tens of thousands of people were accused of and executed for witchcraft. Robin Briggs has recently estimated that the period saw around one hundred thousand witchcraft trials, with between forty and fifty thousand executions. As Briggs underscores, these numbers must be understood in the harsh context of early modern judicial procedures and social violence, but even within that context, the witch-hunts constitute a widespread and sustained cultural preoccupation.[3]

This era also saw a second significant manifestation of magic, as a large number of prominent early modern intellectuals engaged in extended investigation of various forms of natural magic. By the late Renaissance, traditions of "high magic" flourished among a stratum of Europe's learned elite pursuing various forms of Neoplatonic magic, alchemy, astrology, and hermetic divination (quite distinct from the practices of the illiterate peasantry and strongly influenced by various Arab and Byzantine practices and Greek sources). In 1460, texts attributed to Hermes Trismegistus arrived at the court of Cosimo de' Medici, and Marsilio Ficino's translation of these and other newly recovered Platonic texts prompted widespread interest in hermetic and Neoplatonic traditions. These traditions became linked with cabalistic studies through the influence of Pico della Mirandola, and a rich tradition of natural magic developed, remaining influential among Europe's intellectual and scientific elites throughout the sixteenth and seventeenth centuries.[4] As we will see in the third chapter, the role of these traditions of natural magic in the emergence of modern science has been a subject of lengthy controversy.

Early modern concern with witchcraft and magic provides a useful entry into the study of modern constructions of magic for three major reasons. First, far from being a primitive or medieval throwback or survival, belief in witchcraft and natural magic flowered in the very era in which Europe began its move toward modernity—the Renaissance, the Reformation, and the age of early modern philosophy, science, and capitalism. The witchcraft persecutions were a prominent feature of the social landscape as early modern thinkers explored the nature of rationality and superstition. The brutality of the witch-hunts also provides a vivid demonstration of early modern concerns with the identification and containment of deviance and of the social conflicts and antagonisms that can underlie a preoccupation with magic. Moreover, demonology and iconography from the witchcraft persecutions have lingered in the modern cultural imagination, and various tropes from the traditions of natural magic thrive in contemporary popular culture.[5]

Second, intellectual disputes over the witchcraft persecutions and natural magic proved a central site for the negotiation of new boundaries concerning the place of religion and the supernatural within the emerging modern world. As I will discuss later, many prominent early modern philosophers responded directly to issues raised by the witchcraft persecutions, a fact often occluded by the ways these philosophers are studied in disregard of their historical contexts. Arguments against the witchcraft persecutions by various philosophers, social thinkers, and theologians were a significant factor in the development of modern discourses concerning nature and religion. These arguments reflect the shift in Western culture toward modern forms of rationality, a rationality often constructed in explicit contrast to the superstition of magic beliefs. Yet even as various skeptical voices challenged the violent persecution of alleged witches, they also pointed toward new forms of social control. These critics themselves began to formulate new medical and psychological theories of who might be prone to irrationality and superstition, a theme greatly amplified in nineteenth- and twentieth-century theories of magic. Debates over the witch-craft persecutions provided a prime opportunity for articulating new notions of magical thinking as irrational, benighted, and pathological.

Finally, early modern concern with witchcraft and natural magic provides a useful entryway to this discussion of modern views of magic because the very historiography of the early modern period itself provides a vivid demon-stration of the themes of this study. Various twentieth-century attempts to ac-count for the cultural logic of the early modern period run headlong into a thicket of terminological confusion. Historians struggle to distinguish various forms of social practice and belief, often turning to categories and concepts far removed from those used by their objects of study. As G. R. Quaife rather succinctly expresses the situation, "Magic is a label applied to phenomena which have certain characteristics in common. There is little agreement on the phenomena or the characteristics." This difficulty is evident even in one of the most substantive and influential scholarly works on the witchcraft persecu-tions, Keith Thomas's *Religion and the Decline of Magic* (1971). While Thomas's work provides invaluable historical insight, numerous scholars have properly pointed out that Thomas himself sometimes lapses into an uncritical use of the notion of "magic," paying insufficient attention to the ways in which our modern understanding of the term is itself a product of the very social conflicts he is excavating.[6]

Thomas is far from alone in such problems. Efforts to uncover the social history of the witchcraft persecutions often turn on the formulation of a whole range of problematic distinctions, distinctions first between religion and magic and then among various types of "magical" behavior and belief. The scholarly attempt to untangle medieval and early modern social practices is regularly confounded. Historians find themselves plagued by the ambiguity of the his-torical record, particularly trial records and demonological literature that hope-lessly contort testimony and evidence. And historians often appear at a loss in their efforts to translate modern notions of religion and magic onto social contexts that refuse to conform to these concepts. The range of practices des-ignated as "magic," "witchcraft," "superstition," and the like has varied greatly through European history. The elasticity and imprecision of these terms makes early modern social history profoundly difficult.

One point on which there is a wide degree of scholarly consensus is that the persecution of witchcraft flared only when notions of simple sorcery and popular magic were overlaid with a demonological theory in which these prac-tices were seen as involving socially threatening, diabolical, and heretical pacts with Satan. There are long traditions of Christian condemnation of magic, but through the early medieval period it appears that secular and religious authorities were relatively unconcerned with practices of simple sorcery or folk magic. Citing particularly the position of Augustine on these issues, theologians and church officials taught that witchcraft was illusion or fantasy, a form of pagan superstition. The influential *Canon Episcopi* (dating perhaps from the tenth century) codified the doctrine that folklore concerning the exploits of witches was based only on illusion or phantasm inspired by the devil.[7]

While medieval secular and ecclesiastical authorities viewed a broad array of folk practices as manifestations of residual paganism, these practices were regularly ignored. When they came into conflict with church teaching, the common penalty was merely a stiff penance. Various forms of folk healing appear to have been widespread, particularly in a culture in which effective alternatives were practically nonexistent and in which the predominant philosophical and medical systems taught that analogies and sympathetic correspondences existed among various parts of the created order. While alleged *maleficium* might prompt private vendetta, public authorities rarely intervened. Over time *maleficium* came to be associated with heresy, but well into the twelfth century the usual prescription for such behavior was excommunication rather than execution.[8]

Scholars regularly note that many aspects of popular folk magic were commonly incorporated into Christian religious practices, and various layers of European society engaged in behavior that would later be considered superstitious. Popular Christianity included active devotion to miracle-working shrines and holy relics, and the medieval church promoted its power as a conduit of divine blessing. Keith Thomas points out that while medieval theologians maintained a distinction between proper religion and "superstition," the notion of superstition was used in an extremely elastic manner to designate ceremonies or practices of which the church disapproved and which fell outside its control. As he states: "The difference between churchmen and magicians lay less in the effects they claimed to achieve than in their social position, and in the authority on which their respective claims rested."[9]

Through the nineteenth and early twentieth centuries, a tone of Enlightenment positivism shaped much of the analysis of the witch persecutions. Scholars portrayed alleged witches as the unfortunate victims of mass superstition and false confessions elicited by torture. Such superstition was defeated only by the march of modern scientific reason as Western culture moved toward a progressive secularization. By contrast, an influential counteranalysis with roots in nineteenth-century Romanticism asserted that witch beliefs had their origin in pre-Christian folk religion. This line of argument is most prominently associated with the Egyptologist Margaret Murray, who claimed that the victims of the witchcraft persecutions were actually members of a widespread fertility cult constituting the predominant popular religion in Europe until the seventeenth century.[10]

Murray's work gained great popular appeal, and aspects of her argument, particularly concerning witchcraft practices as a form of resistance against Christian hegemony, repressive social structures, patriarchy, and exploiting landlords, were pursued by a number of subsequent historians. Scholars read various forms of social critique within the alleged practices of witchcraft subcultures. For example, Mircea Eliade claimed that European witch cults engaged in prohibited sexual practices in the effort to return to an archaic cultural past—"the dreamlike time of the fabulous beginnings."[11] Others suggested that witchcraft practices constituted inchoate forms of feminism or the early modern inklings of gay and lesbian identities. And in a striking example of the interaction between historical text-making and the texts' social field, Murray's claims concerning the existence of organized early modern witchcraft have been often invoked by various twentieth-century neopagans to establish a venerable lineage for their practices. The "history" developed by Murray and her successors helped stimulate a proliferation of witches' covens in Europe and the United States.[12]

Despite such enthusiasm, the claims by Murray and her followers that organized forms of witchcraft existed in opposition to Christianity have been roundly debunked by numerous critics. Yet these critics themselves then face the difficult task of sifting through the layers of evidence and testimony concerning witchcraft accusations and confessions to determine the outlines of early modern social practices.[13] Debates persist among historians concerning the magical and religious practices of the European population in the medieval and early modern periods. Scholars work to distinguish various layers of popular healing practices, *maleficia*, superstition and simple sorcery, white magic, divination, blessings, exorcism, and high (or natural) magic through various strata of European society.

Historians also struggle to account for the dramatic shift from the relatively benign medieval views of sorcery as illusion or fantasy to the virulent beliefs that swept through Europe concerning the reality of witches and their demonic powers. Toward the end of the medieval period, religious and political authorities became increasingly concerned with nonconformity and heresy, particularly in response to groups that appeared to challenge religious orthodoxy and hierarchy (often in the name of religious reform). As Norman Cohn and Jeffery Russell both point out, the stereotypical array of charges raised against medieval heretics (night meetings, desecration of the sacraments, sexual orgies, sodomy, infanticide, cannibalism) echo the charges traditionally made against Jews and other nonconformists and the charges soon to be made against witches. A series of thirteenth-century papal condemnations of heresy and commissions of inquisition gave, in the words of Jeffery Richards, "official imprimatur ... to the idea of a linkage between heresy, witchcraft, sodomy, promiscuity, and obscenity, rendering them more or less indistinguishable from each other."[14]

Through the late thirteenth and early fourteenth centuries, various forms of peasant sorcery and folk magic came to be seen as diabolical apostasy involving explicit or implicit pacts with the devil, and all heresy came to be linked to devil worship. In response to dualist theological heresies such as Catharism, scholastic theologians developed elaborate theories of the devil and the devil's kingdom, in which sorcerers were considered to be heretical servants of Satan. Before the 1420s, there were a growing number of cases involving various forms of *maleficia*, sorcery, and ritual magic (sometimes involving claims of heresy), and by the late 1420s, the stereotype of the witch engaged in a diabolical pact with the devil, flying through the night sky to participate in orgiastic, cannibalistic, and satanic assemblies, and practicing various forms of *maleficia* had taken hold.[15] With the various elements of the witch stereotype in place, the fear of witches could spread widely through the European population and lead in many areas to violent persecutions.

There were significant regional variations in the intensity and duration of witchcraft persecutions in Europe and its colonies, with the persecutions largely beginning in southern and western Europe and spreading over time to central, eastern, and northern areas. Different regions formulated differing conceptions of the nature of witchcraft and utilized differing prosecutorial mechanisms, and these variations greatly affected the intensity of the persecutions. Areas of Europe such as the Holy Roman Empire, Switzerland, and parts of France in which the full-scale image of diabolical witchcraft thrived saw extended and virulent witch panics.[16]

Many historians have sought the causes for this upsurge in concern with witchcraft in the massive social upheavals of the early modern era, particularly the religious conflict and warfare arising from the Reformation and various other types of social disruption. Jean Delumeau has argued that the era of the witchcraft persecutions coincides with the final Christianization of Europe through the period of the Reformation and Counter-Reformation. He claims, in fact, that the reformers "called Satanism what was really residual paganism."[17] More recent studies have pointed toward other important social and political changes fueling the witchcraft persecutions, including the growing efficiency and centralization of the nation-state and bureaucratic elites (which, in turn, sought to extend their control into the countryside and to extirpate elements of older folk culture); important developments in legal procedure (including the widespread acceptance of torture); demographic shifts, disease, inflation, and food scarcity; changes in family and kinship patterns; and the development and spread of new capitalist economic structures (which increased economic insecurity and dislocation).[18]

In one of the more engaging amplifications of this theme of social
political change, Jane Schneider has stressed the ways in which reformist aspects of Christianity (particularly efforts to extirpate animistic folklore and
other popular religious practices) aligned with the interests of emerging capitalism. Building on the arguments of Max Weber and Keith Thomas, Schneider
asserts that the witchcraft persecutions signaled a frontal assault on older, animistic social relations in favor of a universalizing (and rationally disenchant-
ing) Christian orthodoxy more closely conforming with the interests of the
developing economic system. The social hostility directed against witches, she
argues, served ultimately to facilitate the accumulation of private capital, the
enclosure movement, and the legislative authorization of new modes and relations of production.[19]

Support for this perspective can be found in the charges sometimes raised
against witches with respect to commerce. Witches were often portrayed as
seeking to obtain economic gain through impious machination rather than
through appropriate forms of labor. A number of historians have underscored
the economic tensions underlying the witchcraft persecutions, particularly in
the context of the spread of capitalist economic systems through Europe. In a
period of economic transition, witches were often construed as impediments
to—or polluters of—proper economic relations. For example, the famous demonologist Nicolas Rémy accused witches of perverting commerce. Other opponents of witchcraft and magic reiterated versions of Rémy's theme. Keith
Thomas notes the growing Protestant emphasis in early modern England
on self-help and labor as the proper solution to life's problems, and Thomas
cites various authors who saw the shortcut promised by magic as impious
and vain:

> Man was to earn his bread by the sweat of his brow. This was why
> Francis Bacon objected to magical remedies which "propound those
> noble effects which God hath set forth unto man to be bought at the
> price of labour, to be attained by a few easy and slothful obser-
> vances." The Northamptonshire physician, John Cotta, employed al-
> most *ipissima verba*, a few years later: "God hath given nothing unto
> man but for his travail and pain; and according to his studious in-
> dustry, care, prudence, providence, assiduity and diligence, he dis-
> penseth unto him every good thing. He hath not ordained wonders
> and miracles to give supply unto our common needs, nor to answer
> the ordinary occasions or uses of our life."[20]

Subsequent writers would amplify the theme that witchcraft and magic pervert
appropriate economic relations as practitioners of magic seek personal gain
through improper forms of manipulation.

Broad sociohistorical explanations of the witchcraft persecutions fail to account for the enormous variation in the intensity of the persecutions both by geographic region and over time, but given the proper confluence of factors the persecution of witches could serve a variety of important social and psychological functions in a period of profound cultural and economic transition. New forms of social organization and control required new norms for subjectivity and individual agency, and the witch persecutions demonstrate a deep concern with the articulation and enforcement of behavioral norms. The early modern period saw heightened concern with gender roles, and issues of gender and sexual behavior were a central aspect of the witchcraft persecutions. One of the most significant features of the persecutions is their disproportionate impact on women. While there were important regional variations, during the period of the major persecutions women appear to have constituted approximately 75 to 80 percent of those executed for witchcraft.[21] The early modern witch-hunts are commonly viewed as one of the most extended demonstrations of misogyny and fear of women in the history of Western Christianity. As Christina Larner has underscored, the persecutions were a highly efficient mechanism for attacking a broad range of deviant and nonconformist behavior. Witch trials demonstrated a preoccupation with the regulation of bodies, gender norms, and sexual practices, and they also coincided with increased legal regulation dealing with other behaviors related to procreation, gender, and sexual behavior (including infanticide, abortion, prostitution, and sodomy). As Robin Briggs states it, the witch-hunts can be understood as "one aspect of a search for order in a period when many established patterns underwent severe disruption."[22]

During the era of the witchcraft persecutions, an array of theologians, philosophers, physicians, jurists, and other scholars produced a voluminous body of demonological literature detailing the nature of witchcraft and specifying the proper means for its investigation and punishment. These texts are often obsessed with the definition and containment of social deviance; the most famous inquisitors' manual, the *Malleus Maleficarum* (1486–87), is notorious for its misogyny and preoccupation with sexual functions. Stuart Clark has recently published a major study of early modern demonological literature in which he underscores the ways in which these texts resonated with fundamental intellectual assumptions and concerns of their era. As Clark demonstrates, this literature drew on the common understanding that demons existed as a part of the natural order and that while demonic agents could produce unusual or "preternatural" effects, their powers were always limited by the laws of nature (only God, the creator, had the power to contravene the laws governing the natural order). This demonological perspective reflected the dominant natural philosophy, and thus, Clark states, "witchcraft theory presupposed a thoroughgoing naturalism . . . an application of the general principles of physics to one particular category of natural actions." Even as demonological literature "superimposed image upon image of disorder" in the portrayal of witchcraft, these texts affirmed widespread beliefs about the nature of the material world and demonic causation.[23]

At the same time the popular magic and the *maleficia* of alleged witches were actively persecuted in Europe, the learned, natural magic practiced by the educated class was broadly tolerated. An array of natural philosophers (including a number of Aristotelians, Neoplatonists, hermeticists, and even important advocates of the new mechanical views of nature) were drawn to natural magic. Natural magicians downplayed the role of demonic agency in producing extraordinary effects and explored instead the ways in which nature itself could produce marvels (often with the aid of esoteric human knowledge). As Clark emphasizes, numerous prominent early modern thinkers shared the assumption that this type of magic "was not only consistent with natural philosophy but one of its most elevated and rewarding forms." Natural magic involved extended investigation into the workings of natural causation (with causation understood as including angelic, spiritual, and intellectual influences) and an empirical mode of observation and experiment. While natural and demonic magic were "ontologically and epistemologically equivalent" in their shared assumptions about the natural world, the moral and religious implications of the two types of magic were seen in very different light.[24]

Just as the causes of the witchcraft persecutions remain perplexing, scholars also have difficulty accounting for their eventual cessation. Historians traditionally argued that the spread of Enlightenment views of nature was decisive in ending the witch-hunts, but critics of this view point out that the major witch persecutions ended well before new mechanistic notions of nature were consolidated and disseminated through the culture.[25] Current scholarship points to a broad array of cultural factors to account for the decline in concern with witchcraft among the dominant social classes. These include stronger centralized governments (which could standardize criminal procedure and utilize more subtle means of social control) and greater social stability. Theological explanations of witchcraft gradually gave way to medicalizing, psychological accounts, as witches came to be viewed as deranged hysterics rather than demonic heretics. The witchcraft persecutions subsided as the period Foucault calls the "era of confinement" took hold, an era in which various forms of social marginality were institutionalized in new regimes of social control. The legal persecution of witchcraft ended in various parts of western Europe and North America through the later seventeenth and eighteenth centuries, though popular beliefs in witchcraft have persisted in the West, and scattered lynchings and illegal attacks on alleged witches have occurred throughout the past two centuries (including attacks in Germany and France into the 1970s and a stoning in Mexico in 1981).[26]

The Reformation of Western Religion

The religious turmoil of the sixteenth and seventeenth centuries appears to have been a significant factor in the intensification of witchcraft persecutions in many parts of Europe. The effort to extirpate folk magic and witchcraft was an important component of broader efforts to reform European Christianity, and Catholics and Protestants shared in the persecution of witchcraft as part of their competing efforts to desacralize nature and spiritualize religion. As Stuart Clark states it, reformers both Catholic and Protestant pushed for "the spiritualization of misfortune, the abolition of magic, and the discrediting and eradication of a wide range of popular cultural forms as 'superstitions.'" Like their Catholic counterparts, Luther and Calvin both condemned popular magic and witchcraft in conjunction with their efforts to reform popular faith, and both agreed that witches should be burned as heretics. In 1597 the future James I of England published his *Daemonologie* and encouraged new legal measures against witches. Protestants further concurred with Catholics that women were particularly prone to witchcraft. For example, Luther argued that women were distinctly susceptible to magic and superstition because it was their nature to be timid and fearful. Sixteenth-century Protestants generally accepted the misogynistic arguments of the *Malleus Maleficarum* concerning witchcraft, and the text was popular in Protestant areas as well as Catholic.[27]

One of the principal legacies of the Reformation, and one with profound influence on modern scholarly views of magic and superstition, was the inter-Christian polemic concerning these themes. While Catholics regularly charged that the Protestant Reformation sprang from demonic apostasy, Protestants condemned Catholic liturgical and devotional practices as magical and superstitious. The Protestant charge had a long history in pre-Reformation Europe. The Twelve Conclusions of the Lollards (1395) asserted that exorcisms and hallowing by the church were "necromancy, rather than . . . holy theology." This Lollard theme was amplified by Jan Hus in his tract *De Sanguine Christi* (1405), where Hus broadened an attack on the clergy's abuse of relics of Christ (particularly his "true blood") to encompass miracles in general. Hus argued that all contemporary miracles were suspect as potential demonstrations of demonic magic and inducements to idolatry.[28]

This theme became a central polemic of the reformers. Theological disputes on such issues as divine grace and the means of its mediation were manifested in sharp attacks against Catholic sacramental practices. Lyndal Roper argues that prior to the Reformation, Catholic theology shared with popular magic a "belief in the profound interconnectedness of supernatural forces and the body." But the movement for reform, particularly in its Calvinist and Zwinglian forms, disrupted this link between materiality and the divine with a more radical dualism of flesh and spirit.[29]

For many reformers, the doctrine of transubstantiation came to stand as the pinnacle of Catholic magic. Martin Luther denounced the impiety of priests who reverenced the words of consecration "with I know not what superstitious and godless fancies." Calvin complained that Catholics saw the words of consecration in the Roman sacrament "as a kind of magical incantation," a superstitious murmur that contrasted sharply to the preached word of the gospel. For Calvin the performance of the Eucharist without assent to appropriate doctrine amounted to mimicry of the Lord's Supper as "a kind of magic trick"; he denounced "superstitious worship, when men prostrate themselves before a piece of bread, to adore Christ in it. . . . God himself has also been dishonored by the pollution and profanation of his gift, when his holy sacrament has been made an execrable idol." Zwingli declared the Catholic Eucharist "bread-worship." The Puritan William Perkins stated in 1591, "Surely, if a man will but take a view of all Popery, he shall easily see that a great part of it is mere magic," and Daniel Defoe claimed that "popery" was "one entire system of anti-Christian magic." As Keith Thomas states:

> Protestantism thus presented itself as a deliberate attempt to take the magical elements out of religion, to eliminate the idea that the rituals of the Church had about them a mechanical efficacy, and to abandon the effort to endow physical objects with supernatural qualities by special formulae of consecration and exorcism. . . . The Protestants were helping to make a distinction in kind between magic and religion, the one a coercive ritual, the other an intercessionary one. Magic was no longer to be seen as a false religion, which was how medieval theologians had regarded it; it was a different sort of activity altogether.[30]

The charge by early reformers that Catholicism was inherently magical would be rehearsed by Protestant polemicists well into the twentieth century. In fact, it has also been common in interdenominational battles for various Protestants to label other Protestant groups as prone to magic. And many prominent European philosophers would also repeat the claim that Catholicism—particularly the doctrine of transubstantiation—is magical.[31] This charge has had a long-standing rhetorical resonance.

As Protestants fought against witchcraft and demonic magic, they formulated theological and demonological theories emphasizing such themes as God's absolute sovereignty and providential justifications for human affliction. According to some historians, these strands of Protestant theology may have sometimes lessened Protestant witch-hunting. H. C. Erik Midelfort points out that by the end of the sixteenth century, Protestants and Catholics had come to formulate different perspectives on witchcraft. Protestants emphasized divine providence and moralized against witchcraft, while Catholics continued to stress the power of the diabolical (particularly the demonic nature of the Reformation itself). Protestant notions of predestination and election also placed constraints on human freedom that would conform with emerging mechanistic notions of nature. While in the mid–sixteenth century Calvin had affirmed that supernatural events occurred regularly, by the early seventeenth century many Protestant theologians asserted that divine providence operated by means of the laws of nature. Protestants largely came to argue that the age of miracles had concluded with the New Testament era and that nature now operated with order and regularity. For those Protestants who rejected contemporary miracles, any supernatural occurrence or magical claim was seen as either illusory or demonic.[32]

But Protestant theology also emphasized the threatening activity of Satan in the world, and Protestant believers who feared demonic activity were deprived of countermagical rituals that could be used against witchcraft. In the emerging Protestant view, some theologians even expressed concerns that petitionary prayer was a self-seeking offense against the majesty and omniscience of God. The acceptable options available to Protestants to counter diabolical *maleficia* were thus restricted to austere prayer and piety, but as a result the prosecution and execution of evildoers could appear even more attractive. Thus, certain elements of the Reformation may have exacerbated popular concerns with witchcraft. Areas of Lutheran Germany and areas strongly influenced by Calvinist reforms (such as Pays de Vaud and Scotland) were particularly hard hit by the persecutions.[33] The concern over witchcraft spread through both Catholic and Protestant regions, reaching its height between 1560 and 1660 during an era of intense religious conflict.

Opposition to the Persecutions

The demonological beliefs undergirding the witch trials elicited a broad range of critical responses during the centuries of the persecutions. Many demonologists and other thinkers were able to recognize natural scientific explanations for unusual phenomena without challenging the basic demonological premises of the era, and magic itself was understood as a component of natural causation (since demons and other agencies of magical causation were viewed as part of the created natural order). For example, in his *Disquisitiones Magicae* (published between 1599 and 1600), the famous demonologist Martin Del Rio defined *magia* as "an art or skill which, by use of natural not supernatural power, accomplishes extraordinary and unusual things, the manner in which these are done being such as to overwhelm people's emotions and their capacity to comprehend."[34]

Stuart Clark argues that rather than seeing the early modern debates surrounding the persecutions as a conflict between "occult" thinkers on one hand and "scientific" or "skeptical" thinkers on the other, we are better served by

understanding these debates as involving "differences of degree between varying conceptions of nature." Disputes over the extent and danger of witchcraft
often turned on competing understandings of the natural order and its capacities. As Clark states:

> Demonism was said to be part of the realm of the natural, for it
> lacked just those powers to overrule the laws of nature that consti-
> tuted truly miraculous agency. It must be stressed, therefore, that
> demonic intervention did not turn natural into supernatural causa-
> tion. . . . demonic effects were in principle part of natural processes,
> and in this sense demonology was from the outset a natural science:
> that is, a study of a natural order in which demonic actions and ef-
> fects were presupposed.

Thus, conflicts over demonic magic and witchcraft involved "an epistemological debate—a debate about the grounds for ordered knowledge of nature and
natural causation . . . what *counted* as a natural capacity." In this respect, Clark
concludes, the intellectual disputes over witchcraft should be seen as a significant contribution to the emergence of early modern scientific thought.[35] Indeed, one of the significant themes of modern social science that takes shape
in these debates is the growing tendency to pathologize social deviance: critics
of the persecutions come increasingly to describe alleged witches as melan-
cholic and delusional, in need of medical care rather than prosecution.

Arguments opposing various aspects of the belief in witchcraft date back
at least to the fifteenth century. As noted previously, prior to the late medieval
period Christian theologians had argued that witchcraft should be understood
as illusion and pagan superstition. Throughout the period of the persecutions,
a range of arguments developed questioning the belief in witches' powers and
the value of the persecutions. Even proponents of the persecutions who accepted the reality of witches' conspiracies with the devil rejected many of the
more fabulous claims concerning witches and their power. Other thinkers challenged central aspects of the persecutions.[36]

One early strand of argument questioning the witch-hunts asserted that
the persecutions distracted Christian believers from the appropriate response
to misfortune—recognizing it as God's punishment for sin. For example, in
1505 Samuel de Cassini argued that the witch persecutions distracted Christians from properly pious responses to suffering. Martin Plantsch's *Opusculum
de Sagis Maleficos* (1507) rejected the premises of astrology and demonology
and argued that believers should devoutly endure their troubles on the model
of Job. Others followed this line of argument, seeking to redirect public focus
away from notions of witchcraft toward more providential accounts of human
misfortune. Perhaps, as Johann Brenz wrote in the 1530s, God would permit
Satan to test believers and to punish their sins with misfortune, but the applicable power in such situations resided not with witches but with Satan acting

only in accordance with God's permission. Yet this emphasis did not necessarily lead its proponents to oppose the witch trials. For example, the Protestant minister George Gifford argued in the 1580s and 1590s that even though witches only exercised power permitted them by God and that God allowed misfortune only to test the faithful or to punish sin, witchcraft does exist, and witches ought to be executed according to Scripture because of their dealing with devils.[37]

A different mode of questioning the witchcraft persecutions came from critics who were troubled by the violence and social disorder caused by the trials. From the early decades of the sixteenth century, questions arose even among inquisitors concerning the validity of confessions and evidence obtained from accused and tortured witches (particularly the uneducated, the gullible, and the confused). One of the most prominent critiques of evidence obtained through torture was offered by Friedrich von Spee, a German Jesuit who served as confessor to numerous alleged witches at Würzburg in the late 1620s. In 1631 Spee anonymously published a tract that challenged the methods of the witchcraft trials, particularly the presumption of guilt and the use of threats and torture to obtain confessions. Spee urged judges to be skeptical particularly of charges against women, since women were "often crazy, insane, light, garrulous, inconstant, crafty, mendacious [and] perjured." But while Spee advocated reform in legal procedures, his objective was not to end the witch trials but to ensure that real witches could be more reliably detected.[38]

A more direct challenge to the worldview underlying the witchcraft trials came from thinkers who challenged the very notion of spiritual or demonic intervention in the material world. Pietro Pomponazzi, an extreme neo-Aristotelian naturalist, rejected the notion of God's direct intervention in the human world and, accordingly, the power—and very existence—of angels or demons (which could not be proved by natural reason). While Pomponazzi affirmed the influence of various celestial forces and occult properties in the flow of natural causation, he argued that all occurrences in the material world (including reported miracles and appearances of angels) had causes that could be determined through recourse to natural reason, observation, and experience. Pomponazzi's brand of determinist naturalism was, of course, highly troublesome to more orthodox Christians, and writers such as Marin Mersenne sought to defend the validity of Christian miracles in the face of this emerging naturalistic philosophy.[39]

The Protestant Reformation directly challenged traditional forms of religious and social authority, and particularly after the renewed circulation in the late sixteenth century of Sextus Empiricus's arguments for skepticism, new questions emerged among European intellectuals concerning the nature and epistemological foundations of human knowledge. Pyrrhonian skepticism became an important factor in theological and philosophical discussions. In keeping with these skeptical trends, important sixteenth-century humanists expressed grave reservations about the witchcraft persecutions. For example, Erasmus mocked popular beliefs in the occult and alchemy. Montaigne repeatedly wrote against the persecution of witches on the basis of his broader emphasis on the limits of human judgment and the need for toleration. In his essay "Of Cripples," Montaigne concluded that "it is putting a very high price on one's conjectures to have a man roasted alive because of them." (He goes on to declare that when confronted with a group of confessed witches, the appropriate response should be to prescribe them hellebore (a purgative) rather than hemlock.) Comparable skeptical arguments concerning the limitations of human knowledge were used by such thinkers as Mersenne and Gassendi to reject alchemy and various other forms of Aristotelian natural magic and occult science. And then following on these skeptical arguments, a number of the seventeenth-century *libertins érudits* attacked superstition as part of their broader campaign against religious fanaticism and dogmatism of every kind.[40]

Johann Weyer, physician to the duke of Cleves, was one of the earliest Protestant writers to mount a sustained challenge to the witchcraft trials. In his *De Praestigiis Daemonum* (1563), Weyer invoked his medical expertise to argue that while people may profess to be witches and to have entered into a demonic pact, these people are actually deceived and deranged by the devil (a delusion to which women, Weyer explained, are particularly prone because of their innate instability, superficiality, and stupidity). Weyer offered various physical and psychological hypotheses to account for the behavior of alleged witches, much of which he attributed to physical illness and melancholia. He concluded that the best protection from such delusions is not through the persecution of witches but through prayer. (Weyer explicitly attacked Catholic forms of countermagic.) While Weyer never denied the existence or power of the devil and demons (arguing that it was, in fact, demons who induced the delusions that made people confess to witchcraft), his text elicited harsh response, most famously from Jean Bodin, who accused him of atheism. A century passed before Nicholas de Malebranche could gain broader acceptance for psychological explanations of witch beliefs.[41]

One of the most important English critics of the persecutions was Reginald Scot, whose *Discoverie of Witchcraft* (1584) challenged the basis of witchcraft beliefs and prompted rebuttal from James VI of Scotland. Scot's *Discoverie* is in significant measure an attack on the magical and superstitious practices of Catholicism. In his critique of Catholic teachings on witchcraft, Scot concludes: "The pope maketh rich witches, saints; and burneth the poore witches." Scot argues that the Protestant faith demands skepticism toward witchcraft, since the belief in witchcraft attributed powers to witches that properly belong only to God. Except for cases that can be explained as instances of fraud, senility, or poisoning, all claims concerning witchcraft are "false and fabulous." To attribute divine power to a witch makes one "a blasphemer, an idolater, and full of grosse impietie"; it is "a whoring after strange gods." While Scot's primary objective appears to be theological, he has often been lauded as a fore-runner of modern empiricism because of his efforts to debunk claims concerning the power of witches and other superstitions and magical frauds. Scot argues that the devil works only by deluding the human mind and that God has ordained the regularity of the natural world and closed the age of miracles.[42]

The crux of Scot's challenge to demonology is his claim that demonic agents exist only in a noncorporeal state, a state that removes them from nature and denies them the ability to affect the workings of natural causation. In this view, natural magic can succeed as a work of nature only because its practitioners have special knowledge of secrets God has implanted in the material world. Scot concurs with Weyer's medicalizing argument that people confessing to witchcraft are deluded and superstitious, and he denies that these witches have the power to perform threatening acts or miracles. He argues, instead, that witchcraft is largely trickery and that both spiritual and demonic magic are illusory. Witchcraft is persuasive only to "children, fooles, melancholike persons and papists."[43]

Various forms of opposition to the persecutions spread through parts of European culture through the late sixteenth and early seventeenth centuries. In response, Catholic demonologists worked to combat what they saw as widespread incredulity concerning the dangers of witchcraft among the learned elites, particularly judges. William Monter recounts the episode of a Catholic priest in Luxembourg who was denounced as a "great magician" in 1616 after preaching against the witchcraft persecutions on the grounds that it was more sinful to punish the innocent than to free the guilty.[44] Over time various social and intellectual developments coalesced in Europe to give these arguments against the persecutions greater persuasive appeal.

During the latter half of the seventeenth century, a number of European intellectuals and religious authorities attacked various forms of superstition, including the belief in witchcraft. For example, Thomas Ady's *Candle in the Dark* (1656) attacked the biblical arguments supporting the witchcraft persecutions, arguing that contemporary notions of witchcraft were not mentioned in the Bible and were based only on Catholic superstition. The notion that the material world was governed by orderly and regular divine laws spread through the course of the seventeenth century. As John Webster stated in 1677, "It is . . . simply impossible for either the Devil or witches to change or alter the course that God hath set in nature."[45] Through the seventeenth century, European intellectuals came increasingly to view witchcraft as a phenomenon to be explained rationally, and they set out to fight such superstition with new notions of rational faith.

In *De Betoverde Weereld* (1691), Balthasar Bekker, a Dutch Reformed minister and Cartesian rationalist, reiterated Scot's basic claim from a century earlier that supernatural spirits could have no power over the material world and that the witchcraft persecutions were largely the result of a papist conspiracy to enrich the clergy. Arguing that conjecture concerning witchcraft should be limited by a pious focus on the power and goodness of God and on the laws of nature, scriptural revelation, and reason, Bekker challenged what he saw as the prejudice, superstition, and ignorance that led people to explain unusual occurrences by recourse to witchcraft. Bekker rejected on both theological and epistemological grounds the notion of a pact with the devil (arguing, for example, that the devil cannot have knowledge, since the devil does not have a body necessary for sense perception). After surveying various claims of witchcraft, Bekker concluded that the phenomena of magic and witchcraft are purely imaginary or delusional. Bekker's arguments were widely circulated, but they are particularly significant in the present context because, as G. J. Stronks has pointed out, Bekker's notion of superstition no longer turns on the issue of insufficient trust in God or God's created order, but rather on a rationalist notion of faulty judgment or prejudice stemming from inadequate knowledge.[46]

In the opening years of the eighteenth century Pierre Bayle joined the growing movement against belief in superstition and magic. One of the most important precursors of the French Enlightenment, Bayle rejected belief in the powers of witches from a position of rational antidogmatism akin to the earlier positions of Weyer and Montaigne. While never overtly challenging the biblical or theological bases of the belief in witchcraft and while concurring that sorcerers deserve punishment for their sins against God and their desire to cause harm, Bayle argued that contemporary witchcraft beliefs were commonly the product of fearful credulity and overly susceptible imaginations, a fervor that could produce psychosomatic symptoms and other physical effects. Bayle concluded that superstition was more dangerous than atheism because superstition gave the insidious illusion that one was obeying God.[47]

Numerous other theological challenges to the belief in witchcraft appeared through this era. Christian Thomasius's *De crimine magiae* (1701) offered another Protestant theological challenge to the witchcraft trials by rejecting the fundamental notion that witches formed pacts with the devil. Francis Hutchinson's *Historical Essay on Witchcraft* (1718) gave an English version of Bekker's attack on witch beliefs. Through the late seventeenth and early eighteenth centuries, a large number of Catholic clerics denounced various practices as superstitious and promoted a more spiritualized religious piety. One of the most famous of these texts, the *Civil History of the Kingdom of Naples* (1723) by the Italian priest Pietro Giannone, attacked devotional practices surrounding relics, images, and pilgrimages as superstitious and as driven by clerical greed. An even more radical challenge to Catholicism came from the French priest Jean Meslier, who around 1725 composed what William Monter identifies as "the first truly atheist-communist treatise in the history of western civilization," a text that was later discovered and published by Voltaire. Meslier argued that all religion was superstition born of ignorance and fear, "the art of occupying limited minds with that which is impossible for them to comprehend." Christianity was itself merely a tool for the oppression and subjugation of the poor.[48]

By the late seventeenth century, skepticism concerning the persecutions was finally widely translated into judicial procedures that increasingly demanded a heightened degree of proof for witchcraft accusations. By the end of the 1670s, major witchcraft trials had ended in much of western Europe. Stuart Clark argues that a decisive factor in displacing the worldview on which the persecutions were based was the emerging theological and moral perspective that demons were not a part of the natural world (and natural causation): "When devils were excluded . . . a whole range of phenomena then became available for natural magical, or, later, 'new scientific,' explanations to deal with." Brian Levack underscores the ways in which prominent opponents of the witchcraft trials came to ridicule the gullibility of the peasant classes in order to promote skepticism concerning witchcraft among the upper classes and learned elites. As Willem Frijhoff has pointed out, the very process of combating the belief in witchcraft gave rise to a new form of social differentiation between the popular cultural practices of the masses and the belief systems of the educated cultural elites. This new stratification of belief systems served to bolster other forms of social differentiation.[49] The belief in witchcraft had come to stand as a marker of cultural difference, a psychological pathology to be explained rationally rather than a demonic threat. Modern theories of magic would emerge within the context of newly medicalizing and psychologizing discourses on abnormality and deviance.

Mechanical Views of Nature

The seventeenth century saw dramatic changes in intellectual views of the natural world. One of the central shifts in European thought was the transition from an Aristotelian view of the natural world as governed by sympathies and correspondences toward the notion of nature as a regular, differentiated system. Through the course of the seventeenth century, scientists and natural philosophers offered a range of competing views as to the specific natural forces that were to be the proper subject of scientific inquiry and the precise nature of the emerging mechanical philosophy, and the results of these disputes were to have decisive significance for emerging modern views of magic.

England's Francis Bacon is renowned in the history of science for his pivotal role in advocating a rigorous mode of inductive observation and scientific knowledge. While Bacon rejected many of the excesses of natural magic, he was a proponent of a reformed, exoteric mode of natural magic focusing on the latent or internal features of natural bodies in order to produce practical results. Bacon argued in his *Novum Organum* (1620) for an empirical focus on the marvels of nature in order to uncover their complex underlying natural processes. He advised particular attention to—and suspicion of—any matter that depends for its explanation on religion, natural magic, or alchemy because such unusual occurrences had distinctive potential to shed light on the hidden operations of nature. In other texts Bacon argued that it is popular credulity that leads people to explain natural occurrences by invoking claims of witchcraft. In addition to his repeated attacks on alchemy and the excesses of esoteric natural magic, Bacon harshly objected to religious superstition, which he attributed to such factors as sensual pleasure, excessively demonstrative holiness, inordinate reverence for tradition, the ambition and greed of prelates, and "barbarous times, especially joined with calamities and disasters." He argued that it is preferable to be an unbeliever than to have an unworthy, superstitious notion of God. Superstition, Bacon concluded, compares to religion as an ape compares to a human being.[50]

The skeptical traditions elaborated by sixteenth-century thinkers such as Montaigne, Pierre Charron, and their successors had a significant influence on René Descartes. Descartes framed his philosophical method as a defense of Christianity against Pyrrhonian skepticism. In his formulation of the extreme radical skepticism setting the stage for the certainty of the *cogito*, Descartes poses an array of reasons to doubt human knowledge (the limitations of the senses, logical fallacies, illusions in dreams, etc.). One of the most famous of the arguments in Descartes's First Meditation (written between 1638 and 1640) is the hypothesis that "some malicious demon of the utmost power and cunning has employed all his energies in order to deceive me." This hypothetical demon seeks to ensnare Descartes's judgment. The relevance of this malicious demon for the present consideration of magic and demonology is, first, that Descartes gives at least hypothetical credence to the possibility that such a demonic force could actually interfere with human activity and judgment. Descartes's skeptical stance prevents him from dogmatically rejecting the possibility that demons can bewitch human judgment, even though he recognizes the severe epistemological problems posed by "human contrivances, apparitions, illusions, and in short all the marvelous effects attributed to magic."[51]

Further, when considering Descartes's malicious demon, it is important to recall that the witchcraft persecutions were at their worst in many regions of Europe in the early years of the seventeenth century. Richard Popkin provides a provocative suggestion as to one of the historical precedents for Descartes's deceiving demon. Popkin recounts the debates among French intellectuals concerning the 1634 trial in Loudun (just a few years prior to Descartes's First Meditation) of the priest Grandier, who was accused of spreading witchcraft within a convent. Grandier's trial turned on questions concerning the reliability of evidence, particularly the fear that demons might infect human judgment; the faculty of the Sorbonne eventually intervened to adjudicate whether testimony obtained from the devils that Grandier had allegedly commanded could be considered trustworthy. In this context, Descartes's hypothetical demon was not so completely hypothetical.[52]

As Descartes formulates his position of radical skepticism, he argues that the material world cannot provide sure evidence for the existence of God. Without prior proof that human senses are reliable, all external evidence is suspect. Thus Descartes seeks to establish the certainty of God's existence on the certitude of human thought itself, and he delineates a firm ontological differentiation between *res extensa* and *res cogitans* (with God functioning as the mediating link between the two). Descartes's formulation of this distinction gives him a pivotal role in the emergence of modern notions of the differentiation between nature and supernature.

Descartes is a central figure in the development of mechanistic views of nature. By the early seventeenth century, Aristotelian natural philosophy was under assault from a number of directions, including the astronomical theories of Copernicus, Kepler, and Galileo, the spread of newly recovered classical texts (both skeptical and scientific), and epistemological issues heightened by Reformation challenges to authority. While the idiom of natural magic remained prominent among numerous European intellectuals, through the seventeenth century a number of thinkers began to articulate new forms of mechanistic natural philosophy that removed occult and supernatural forces from the realm of causation. Margaret Osler has explored the influence of "intellectualist" Thomistic themes stressing God's rationality and omniscience in the creation of the world on Descartes's view of the mechanical operations of nature. Descartes argues that while God acted with absolute freedom in the creation of the world, God's perfect wisdom in the formulation of the laws of creation entails that God is now necessarily bound by those laws. On the basis of this necessity, Descartes can claim certainty with respect to the laws of physics, a certainty based on a priori, mathematical first principles.[53]

Osler contrasts Descartes's views in this respect to those of his contemporary Pierre Gassendi, who shared the fundamental presupposition of the mechanical nature of the created world but was more influenced by "voluntarist" nominalist views emphasizing the absolute freedom and omnipotence of God in relation to the creation. Gassendi favored an empiricist approach to science stressing the contingency and limits of scientific knowledge. In his effort to identify the limits of mechanical causality, Gassendi affirmed the Bible's testimony that angels and demons exist, but he rejected popular notions of magic as merely a product of fraud and nonsense. While sinful temptations and demonic possession do exist, God's providence limits the power of demons, and the proper concern of the believer should be to attend to one's spiritual and moral state. Gassendi concluded that human ignorance of the causes of various occult occurrences should not lead to the supposition that the ordinary principles of nature have been violated, but simply to the conclusion that those principles are insufficiently known. Throughout these discussions, Gassendi sought to oppose the determinism coming from thinkers such as Hobbes and to maintain a space for both human and divine freedom.[54]

In contrast, Descartes invoked the immutability of God as the basis for his belief in the possibility of absolute certainty of the laws of nature. In *Discourse on the Method* (1637), Descartes asserts, "I have noticed certain laws which God has so established in nature, and of which he has implanted such notions in our minds, that after adequate reflection we cannot doubt that they are exactly observed in everything which exists or occurs in the world." In *The World* (dating from the early 1630s), he includes among his fundamental suppositions the claims that God will perform no miracles and that spiritual forces will not disrupt the ordinary course of nature. And in his *Principia Philosophiae* (1644) Descartes affirms the immutability of God: "God preserves the world by the selfsame action and in accordance with the selfsame laws as when he created it." Thus the fundamental mathematical laws of nature can be known with certainty.[55]

While Descartes's stated objective was to defend the truth of Christianity from the onslaught of skepticism, his view of the world as decisively cut off from the realm of spirit and as operating mechanistically in accordance with immutable laws has direct, if inadvertent, implications. As Michael Buckley succinctly declares, "Descartes has left the world godless."[56] The world operates only according to its own mechanical principles, and inquiry into the world demonstrates only those laws. Knowledge of God is to be obtained solely through inquiry into the mind. Descartes's basic differentiation between the realms of nature and supernature provided the paradigm for ensuing differentiations of the proper realms of science and religion.

Subsequent natural philosophers and scientists amplified the view of nature as governed by invariable, mechanical laws. Spinoza argued that nature preserves a fixed and unchanging order that cannot be contravened; as he stated, "The universal laws of nature are decrees of God following from the necessity and perfection of the Divine nature."[57] Thomas Hobbes concurred that an appropriately material and mechanistic philosophy effectively precluded recourse to spiritual beings (such as demons) as causal agents in the material world.

Yet the rationalist Hobbes had an ambivalent relation to the witchcraft persecutions. In *Leviathan* (1651), Hobbes argued that scriptural passages concerning witchcraft and demons should be understood as metaphorical. Demons, devils, and ghosts are phantasms and "Idols of the braine"; there is no biblical testimony supporting the existence of immaterial or incorporeal spirits (such as specters or demons) or the possession of human bodies by corporeal spirits. In Hobbes's view, the proper task of the philosopher is to focus on material bodies and their deterministic, mechanical motion, disregarding all immaterial or spiritual issues. Yet Hobbes was also perplexed by the confessions obtained from alleged witches. He stated: "As for witches, I think not that their witchcraft is any reall power; but yet that they are justly punished, for the false beliefe they have, that they can do such mischiefe, joyned with their purpose to do it if they can." Hobbes argued that ridding society of "this superstitious fear of Spirits," prognostications, and false prophecies would make the populace "much more fitted than they are for civill Obedience."[58] Witches thus deserve punishment because of their malicious intent and the social disruption they can cause.

Hobbes asserted that the development of various religious notions, particularly the belief in spirits, was based on human ignorance of the laws of causation and human fear of unknown and invisible powers. In his index of human passions, Hobbes offered the following account of the origin of religion and the proper distinction between religion and superstition: "*Feare* of power invisible, feigned by the mind, or imagined from tales publiquely allowed, RELIGION; not allowed, SUPERSTITION. And when the power imagined, is truly such as we imagine, TRUE RELIGION."[59] While Hobbes acknowledged that religious authority has value in promoting peaceful social relations, he concurred with the ancient argument that all religion has its origins in human fearfulness. Religion is the socially accepted form of the fear of invisible powers, and the distinction between religion and superstition is to be found ultimately in public sanction.

A number of seventeenth-century thinkers saw the materialist tendencies of Descartes, Spinoza, and Hobbes as a great threat to Christianity. Prominent among this number were the philosophers Henry More and Joseph Glanvill, associated with the Cambridge Platonist movement. In response to the looming materialism, More and Glanvill argued that the evidence of witchcraft actually served to prove the existence and power of the spiritual realm. As Glanvill asserted, the existence of witchcraft constituted proof of the existence of God and the immortality of the soul. He argued that the existence of witches and apparitions constituted "a sensible proof of Spirits and another Life, an Argument of more direct force than any Speculations, or Abstract reasonings." While Glanvill acknowledged that there were excesses in the witchcraft persecutions, he and More set about recording empirical evidence of witchcraft in an effort to overturn materialist atheism and to authenticate genuine witch beliefs. In his investigations Glanvill deployed a skeptical experimental method against what he saw as the dogmatism of opponents of the witch persecutions, and in his effort to affirm Anglican orthodoxy he was able to formulate a version of mechanical philosophy accommodating demonic causation.[60]

Yet despite the designs of the Cambridge Platonists, both traditional Aristotelianism and various forms of Neoplatonic theory were quickly falling to the pervasive influence of more materialist forms of mechanical philosophy. As Keith Thomas states it, "The notion that the universe was subject to immutable natural laws killed the concept of miracles, weakened the belief in the physical efficacy of prayer, and diminished faith in the possibility of direct divine inspiration."[61] The leading English scientists of the seventeenth century, Robert Boyle and Isaac Newton, both sought to defend mechanical science from charges of atheism and materialism. The two challenged Cartesianism because of concern that it placed improper limits on divine freedom, and Boyle (who encouraged Glanvill's efforts) defended the notion of miracles as proof of an active divine providence. Newton believed the Cartesian system was dangerously prone to atheism, and he sought instead to formulate a mechanical worldview that could accommodate direct divine dominion over materiality. As Newton stated in his *Opticks* (1704), "It may also be allow'd that God is able . . . to vary the Laws of Nature, and make Worlds of several sorts in several Parts of the Universe. At least, I see nothing of Contradiction in all this."[62]

Newton has proved a notoriously complex figure in intellectual history. He was a student of the Cambridge Platonists, and his nearly thirty-year career of alchemical study and experimentation has remained a source of embarrassment for many historians of science. William Monter identifies Newton as "the last important alchemist in European history," and in John Maynard Keynes's famous assessment, Newton was "not the first of the age of reason," but rather "the last of the magicians." His theory of gravitation itself was attacked as occult by contemporaries. Yet Newton also came to deny that biblical references to spirits and devils should be interpreted literally. Newton's complex role in debates over the proper demarcation of the forces active within the natural order is emblematic of the profound intellectual and social changes taking place in the late seventeenth century. The early modern enthusiasm for various forms of natural magic and occult causation was fading.[63]

One of the more valiant efforts to combine mechanistic views of nature with Christian belief in a divine final cause appears in the work of Leibniz. A staunch anti-Spinozan, Leibniz sought to reconcile the possibility of miracles with notions of absolute divine harmony and perfection in creation. He argued that the subordinate laws of nature can be overturned by miracles "through consideration of some more powerful final cause," but that such miracles serve "not to satisfy the needs of nature but those of grace." Thus recourse to the notion of miracles is appropriate not with respect to the ordinary course of nature but only with respect to articles of faith. In Leibniz's view, the created order is governed by divine laws of perfect harmony, including the law of continuity that requires the orderly regularity of natural mechanisms. In his *Discourse on Metaphysics* (1686), Leibniz argues that the laws governing God's creation require that nothing extraordinary or miraculous happen to human beings or other substances, for otherwise the need of such extraordinary modifications would indicate flaws inherent in the system. As he states, "It would indeed be without rhyme or reason that God should perform miracles in the ordinary course; so that this do-nothing hypothesis would destroy equally our philosophy which searches for reasons, and the Divine wisdom which provides them."[64]

Seventeenth-century mechanical views of nature moved in the eighteenth century toward an increasingly secularized view of nature as a deterministic system governed by universal laws. In the seventeenth century, as G. Mac-Donald Ross states, "there was no clear line of demarcation between occultism, philosophy, religion, and science." Yet by the mid-eighteenth century, these demarcations had taken firm hold among European intellectuals. First, natural magic was abandoned, and all forms of demonic and occult causation were effectively expelled from the natural world. Moreover, the natural and supernatural realms were clearly differentiated, and the role of the supernatural was severely constrained. Paradigmatic of this Enlightenment view is Laplace, who refined central astronomical calculations in the Newtonian system and thus obviated the need that Newton had asserted for periodic divine intervention within the system. In an often recounted anecdote, Laplace is reported to have responded to Napoleon's query concerning the role of God in his scientific system: "I have no need of that hypothesis." By the end of the eighteenth century, through the work of physical scientists such as Laplace and Lagrange, physics was largely disentangled from theological questions concerning the existence of God, and nature was understood in thoroughly materialist terms.[65] As these differentiations gained broad popular acceptance, the stage was set for modern demarcations among religion, magic, and science.

The forms of mechanical philosophy developed under the influence of Descartes were modified first by Newtonian natural philosophy and then by subsequent physical models. Yet the materialist, mechanical view of nature has remained influential to the present day. As Brian Easlea states:

> In a fundamental sense the mechanical philosophy still provides the ontology against which advances in both the natural and human sciences are measured. . . . although modern physics is now inundated with all kinds of (precisely mathematically articulated) "sympathies" and "antipathies"—and although matter according to quantum theory is a rather "occult" substance to say the least—the mechanical philosophy has not been forced to concede any major defeat: sentience and consciousness are still not considered to be immanent properties of matter. . . . above all, the natural world is still held to lack creative powers and telos.

Despite the limitations of the mechanical view of nature and the challenges posed to it even by such prominent thinkers as Darwin, aspects of the mechanical perspective remain pervasive in contemporary scientific and popular thought. As Easlea concludes, "Modified the mechanical philosophy had to be—but its principal descendant, physicalism, remains—for better or worse—the dominant philosophy underlying the natural and, controversially, even the human sciences."[66]

Natural Religion and the Enlightenment War on Superstition

Throughout seventeenth-century debates over the nature of the material world, the relation of God to the created order remained a central concern. Yet as mechanical theories of nature became more exclusively materialist, God became more tangential to natural philosophy, and rationalized forms of natural religion became increasingly prominent among European thinkers. This notion of religion took shape as an overt response to the social strife of Europe's religious warfare, and it became an important site for the emerging struggle against intolerance, clericalism, and superstition. Yet as Timothy Fitzgerald has argued, the abstract and constricted notion of natural religion actually came to serve two related ideological functions: it declared the universality of a distinctively modern rationality, and it confirmed the existence of "secular nature" (thus securing emerging bourgeois values).[67]

While Bacon maintained that revealed theology was the proper province of faith, he argued that knowledge of God could also be derived in natural religion through the observation and contemplation of the natural world. Herbert of Cherbury argued in his *De Veritate* (1624) that humanity is endowed by God with certain "common notions" constituting innate truths. The central true dogmas of Christianity are derivable from these common notions (while religious practices are only of subsidiary importance). In his subsequent *De Religione Gentilium* (1663), Herbert asserted that various human religions arise through a process of degeneration from the pure revelation given by God to humanity, a degeneration caused not so much by human sinfulness as by the machinations of a greedy and self-seeking priesthood enslaving the masses.[68] Building on these themes, other seventeenth-century thinkers sought to resist the move toward materialism by promoting the notion of a natural religion that could be discerned through the use of reason alone.

Spinoza countered the beliefs in witchcraft and superstition with a rationalistic (perhaps mystical) monism, leaving no room for active agents of evil who could corrupt the divine laws of nature. Spinoza begins his *Theologico-Political Treatise* (1670) with an account of the origins of superstition in which he explains that human beings are prone to superstition both because of the fear and uncertainty that arise in the face of misfortune and because of greedy human desires for temporal advantage. Spinoza acknowledges that the passions breeding superstition are natural to all human beings, but he concludes that superstitions themselves are base "phantoms of imagination, dreams, and other childish absurdities" contrary to both nature and reason. Spinoza seeks to outline the ways in which properly rational religion has been disfigured into "a tissue of ridiculous mysteries" by misconceptions and superstition. In the pantheistic worldview Spinoza proposes, "Nature herself is the power of God

under another name." Those who impiously conceive of God's power as standing distinct from the power of nature and who see miracles when nature acts
in unexpected ways mistake both the nature of the divine and the nature of
revelation. To believe that God might intervene to overrule or correct the operation of the fixed and immutable laws of nature is to impugn the perfection
of creation itself.[69] Spinoza's rationalized religion maintained a place for the
divine only by aligning God seamlessly with the workings of nature, but many
critics quickly recognized that in this scheme talk of the divine readily dissipates as an extraneous—and insubstantial—addition to the description of nature.

John Locke sought a more dynamic balance between rational religion and
miraculous divine action. His *Essay concerning Human Understanding* (1690)
affirms the existence of spiritual substances (including individual mental operations) and the existence of God. As Locke considers the distinct provinces
of faith and reason, he argues that reason is to serve as arbiter of the authenticity of divine revelation and as the mechanism for interpreting revelation.
While the appropriate realm of faith consists of propositions beyond reason,
if human beings give too great a sway to faith and do not acknowledge the
proper role of reason in assessing religious truth, all sorts of superstitions,
extravagances, and absurdities can emerge (as witnessed by various religions
of the world). In Locke's view, neither God nor Satan intervenes to disrupt the
orderly natural flow of the contemporary world. As Brian Easlea states it,
Locke's is a reliable and predictable world in which "the new men of property
are . . . to be unimpeded in their objective of accumulating wealth—and of
using the labouring poor as a principal means."[70]

In the concluding sections of the *Essay*, Locke argues that miracles played
an important historical role in certifying Christian revelation to be divine.
While in the ordinary course, common natural events and experience assist
our rational judgments, in the case of miracles God used the very strangeness
of the occurrence to compel belief. God certifies divine revelation either by the
usual method of natural reason or by demonstrating its authenticity by outward
or visible signs, "by some Marks which Reason cannot be mistaken in."[71] Thus
even in the case of miracles, reason still serves as arbiter.

Locke expands the theme of miracles in *The Reasonableness of Christianity*
(1695), where he argues that the truth of the Christian revelation was made
manifest, and therefore reasonable, by Jesus' fulfillment of prophecies about
the Messiah and performance of miracles. Locke argues that while the works
of nature offer sufficient evidence of the deity, humanity fails to use reason
properly to discern God's truth. Instead, sensuality, lust, fear, and carelessness
deliver humanity into the hands of a greedy and self-interested priesthood who
warp rational notions of God and religious practice into foolish rites, vice, and
superstition. Jesus came to remedy this situation and restore true monotheism,
and the authenticity of his mission was attested by miracles "so ordered by the

divine providence and wisdom, that they never were, nor could be denied by any of the enemies or opposers of Christianity." God's revelation through Moses was "shut up in a little corner of the world," but the miracles of Jesus and his followers were addressed universally. The reformed religion that Jesus instituted offers "plain, spiritual, and suitable worship," in opposition to the "huddle of pompous, fantastical, cumbersome ceremonies" that had come to mark religion. Locke concludes: "To be worshipped in spirit and in truth, with application of mind and sincerity of heart, was what God henceforth only required. . . . The splendour and distinction of habit, and pomp of ceremonies, and all outside performances, might now be spared."[72] Despite its miraculous pedigree, Locke's rationalized Christianity is plain and spiritual; ritual, ceremony, "all outside performances" have become suspect.

As the theme of natural religion reached the hands of Enlightenment thinkers in the eighteenth-century, they pushed more assertively for freedom from revelation, ritual, authority, and other human institutions and customs. Many important eighteenth century intellectuals (notably Samuel Clarke) sought to maintain a place for revealed religion. But other influential Enlightenment thinkers argued that religion should be retained only to the extent that it was based on the dictates of reason, not revelation or mystical experience. Already in the seventeenth century, writers had begun to offer symbolic or metaphorical interpretations of such religious notions as the existence of hell. English deists of the early eighteenth century developed the naturalistic themes of Herbert of Cherbury to reject Locke's reliance on revelation or miracles. John Toland sought to contain Christianity strictly within the realm of reason, and Matthew Tindal argued that Christianity should be properly aligned with natural religion. In 1713 Anthony Collins argued that the superstitious are "incapable of believing in a perfectly just and good God. . . . And so they are more properly to be stil'd *Demonists* than *Theists*." These rationalist themes were reiterated through the course of the eighteenth century by a number of influential writers who sought to displace the specific claims of Christian revelation and tradition with a universalized, rational religion free from what they saw as the intolerance, fanaticism, priestcraft, and superstition of the past.[73]

Into this context, David Hume launched a broad, two-pronged attack, challenging, on the one hand, popular religion and orthodoxy and, on the other hand, the emerging Enlightenment deism and natural theology. In Hume's view, proper religion would consist only in the practice of morality and a meager "Assent of the Understanding to the Proposition that God exists." As Deleuze explains, Hume saw philosophy as reaching its completion "in a practical battle against superstition." All external manifestations of religion are simply the misapplication of principles of association and causality, and religion can thus be justified, as Deleuze frames it, only as the thin presumption of an "original agreement between the principles of human nature and nature itself," a presumption that resides "outside culture and outside true knowledge."[74]

The first prong of Hume's critique is directed against religious superstition and enthusiasm, two different (but similarly pernicious) corruptions of true religion. Hume links enthusiasm to the excessive piety of Protestant sects (characterized by emotional raptures and fanatic imagination), but he offers a different account of the origins of superstition, most vividly demonstrated by "the ROMISH church." Amplifying Hobbes's claims concerning the roots of religion, Hume asserts that superstition arises from "weakness, fear, melancholy, together with ignorance." In the face of invisible and unknown enemies, a wide array of absurd superstitious rites and practices develop to placate these mysterious powers. In his *Natural History of Religion* (1757), Hume expands this account of the origins of superstition to argue that polytheism has its origin in human anxiety and speculation concerning the unknown that leads to anthropomorphizing natural phenomena.[75]

Hume attributes superstition to mentally and emotionally feeble groups. He asserts that just as it is in the weakest and most timid periods of life that human beings are most addicted to superstition, so also it is the weaker and more timid sex that is most superstitious. Nothing is more destructive of superstition than "a manly, steady virtue, which either preserves us from disastrous, melancholy accidents, or teaches us to bear them." Similarly, as he argues that proper epistemology should lead us to deny the existence of miracles, Hume asserts that one of the prime reasons to discount testimony concerning miracles is because supernatural and miraculous events are to be observed primarily "among ignorant and barbarous nations."[76]

Hume explains that superstition promotes the concentration of power in the hands of impudent and cunning priests. Superstition enters into religion gradually, rendering the population "tame and submissive"; it is tolerated by the civil authorities as inoffensive until at last the priest becomes "the tyrant and disturber of human society, by his endless contentions, persecutions, and religious wars." An enemy of civil liberty, superstition renders the population "tame and abject, and fits them for slavery." Such lax beliefs cause a broad range of social ills: "factions, civil wars, persecutions, subversions of government, oppression, slavery."[77]

The second prong of Hume's attack is directed against efforts such as those mounted by Newton and Locke to base theism and natural theology on philosophical deductions of the existence and nature of God. Hume repeatedly maintains that it is appropriate to assent to the existence of a divine cause. Yet claiming to follow the rules of reasoning laid out in Newton's *Principia*, Hume also insists that the divine cause remains inexplicable and incomprehensible to human reason, and skepticism is the only pious response to claims concerning the nature of that divinity. As he states, "The whole is a riddle, an enigma, an inexplicable mystery. Doubt, uncertainty, suspense of judgment appear the only result of our most accurate scrutiny, concerning this subject. But such is the frailty of human reason." In Hume's *Dialogues concerning Nat-*

ural Religion (1779) the character Philo asserts that the only appropriate worship of God is a "plain, philosophical assent" to the proposition that God's existence is probable; any other worship is "absurd, superstitious, and even impious" in its attribution of human, or even demonic, characteristics to the deity. In this limited rational affirmation, speculation is contained within the appropriate bounds of human knowledge.[78]

Enlightenment France also saw a great interest in natural religion and deism. Chief among the French critics of superstition and fanaticism was Voltaire. In his *Philosophical Dictionary* (1764) Voltaire mounts a broad campaign against fanaticism and religious coercion. Voltaire argues that Christianity was contaminated in its very earliest stage by pagan and Jewish superstition, and he mocks an array of contemporary practices, including the veneration of relics, religious ecstasies, visions, even the belief in vampires. As he asserts, "All the fathers of the Church, without exception, believed in the power of magic. The Church always condemned magic, but she always believed in it." Further, Voltaire derides the confusion as to what constitutes superstition; as he states it, each sect and nationality condemns the practices of other sects as superstition, and even sects with the fewest rites are superstitious to the extent that they maintain absurd beliefs. "It is therefore evident that what is the foundation of the religion of one sect, is by another sect regarded as superstitious; the sole arbiter of this debate is raw force."[79]

Voltaire explains the origins of beliefs in ghosts and spirits by claiming that when human beings came to believe that they consisted of a nonmaterial component and that their identities persisted after death, they gave this nonmaterial spirit an aerial body resembling the physical one. He mocks the efforts to burn magicians, arguing that if they truly had magical power, they would use that power to escape the executions. Concerning the other alleged powers of witches and sorcerers, he states caustically that "it is unquestionable that certain words and ceremonies will effectually destroy a flock of sheep, if administered with a sufficient portion of arsenic." Throughout the *Philosophical Dictionary* Voltaire offers various accounts of the ways that natural events can be mistakenly ascribed to supernatural causes, a delusion, he asserts, to which Europe was particularly prone during prior periods in which "the majority of our provincial population was very little raised above the Caribs and negroes."[80]

Voltaire rejects the belief in miracles as an affront to the perfection and wisdom of God. He scornfully dismisses the claim that God would interfere with the laws of nature for the benefit of humanity: "Is it not the most absurd of all extravagances to imagine that the Infinite Supreme should, in favor of three or four hundred emmets on this little heap of earth, derange the operation of the vast machinery that moves the universe?" He argues that the biblical stories of the miracles of Jesus should be interpreted allegorically, and throughout the *Philosophical Dictionary* he attacks central components of traditional Christianity such as the belief in Jesus' divinity. In Voltaire's view, such superstitious beliefs are a crucial component of religious fanaticism, and the rampant sway of superstition throughout society must be purged by the light of reason. It is philosophy alone that has cured Europe of the delusion that witches and sorcerers exist and "has taught judges that they should not burn the insane." In opposition to these divisive and violent fanaticisms, Voltaire urges a universal rational religion based on general notions of justice and probity. As he concludes, "Nearly all that goes farther than the adoration of a supreme being, and the submission of the heart to his eternal orders, is superstition."[81]

Versions of Voltaire's deism were shared by other important figures of the French Enlightenment, including Fontenelle, Montesquieu, and Condillac. Various eighteenth-century French thinkers promoted new materialist doctrines rejecting the Cartesian distinction between mind and matter and promoting materialist or mechanistic notions of the soul and mental operations. Thus, for example, La Mettrie's *L'Homme machine* (1747) dismissed Descartes's notion of immaterial thinking substance in favor of a thoroughgoing mechanistic view of human intellection. As La Mettrie underscored, the notion of the deity in Enlightenment thought had become so vaporous as to constitute only a gratuitous "theoretic truth with very little practical value."[82]

It was Enlightenment France that first saw this materialist critique of revealed religion shift into overt atheism. In his study *At the Origins of Modern Atheism* (1987), Michael Buckley cites the career of Denis Diderot as emblematic of this transition. Diderot moved in a very short span from the advocacy of a Newtonian-inspired deism to a materialism that left no opening even for this ephemeral deity. Diderot joined other Enlightenment deists in dismissing all distinctively theological arguments for the existence of God as superstition and in focusing exclusively on abstract arguments from design. Yet the God at stake in these teleological arguments proved so elusive, transcendent, and hypothetical that this deity ceased to be a matter of consequence. Thus Diderot could declare in a 1749 letter to Voltaire: "It is . . . very important not to mistake hemlock for parsley; but to believe or not believe in God, is not important at all." For Diderot and other descendants of the Enlightenment, the question of God's existence receded in importance as the God at stake in these debates became an increasingly sublime and increasingly irrelevant conjecture. As Buckley states it, "Any discussion of the existence of a god whose reality cannot be proven and who does not interfere in the life of the universe is idle." Perhaps the most prominent French atheist of the eighteenth century was the Baron d'Holbach, who reiterates the claim that religion has its origins in human fear, uncertainty, and imagination. Gods are formulated, d'Holbach explains, when human beings come to the limits of their analytical and technical powers. In confronting those limits, human beings can respond either with superstition (based on ignorance and fantasy) or with sound philosophical inquiry (based on effective observation and rationality).[83]

With Kant, Continental philosophical thought took a decisive shift in relation to questions of religion. Reacting both to forms of German deism and to important themes of German pietism (individualism, emphasis on the practical aspects of religious faith, and opposition to dogma), Kant rejects all the forms of natural theology developed on the basis of mechanistic physics. Such theistic natural theology, he declares, inevitably fails to demonstrate the existence of God. And the metaphysical grounds for religion posed by speculative thinkers such as Descartes fare no better. In dismissing deistic transcendental theology, Kant asserts that "all attempts to employ reason in theology in any merely speculative manner are altogether fruitless and by their very nature null and void."[84]

Having demarcated the bounds of speculative reason, Kant turns to ground religion within the realm of practical reason. For our purposes here, the most notable aspect of Kant's reformulation of the ground of religious faith lies in the extraordinarily thin nature of the religious sensibility he advocates. He argues that his restrictions on speculative thought are aimed at preventing religion from falling into theurgy ("a fanatical belief that we can have a feeling of other supersensible beings and can reciprocally influence them") or idolatry ("a superstitious belief that we can please the Supreme Being by other means than by a moral sentiment"). Kant insists that proper service of God is restricted to the performance of moral duty, consisting "not in dogmas and rites, but in the heart's disposition to fulfill all human duties as divine commands." As he asserts, "The illusion of being able to accomplish anything in the way of justifying ourselves before God through religious acts of worship is religious *superstition.* . . . it is called superstitious because it selects merely natural (not moral) means which in themselves can have absolutely no effect upon what is not nature (i.e., on the morally good)."[85]

When a human being attempts to use actions possessing no inherent moral value as a means of gaining divine approval, that person "labors under the illusion that he possesses an art of bringing about a supernatural effect through wholly natural means." Such an attempt, Kant states, could be called sorcery, but to avoid the demonic implications of that term, he prefers the label fetishism. Kant denounces the supposition that the performance of actions that are not inherently moral can serve as a means or condition through which one can obtain satisfaction from God. Such actions are nothing more than an attempt to "conjure up divine assistance by magic," "a pseudo-service which is subversive to all endeavors toward true religion."[86]

Thus, Kant concludes, the true, moral service of God is "invisible . . . a service of the heart (in spirit and in truth)." "Every initiatory step in the realm of religion, which we do not take in a purely moral manner but rather have recourse to as *in itself* a means of making us well-pleasing to God and thus, through Him, of satisfying our wishes, is a *fetish-faith.*" Illusory faith can overstep the bounds of reason in the direction of the supernatural ("which is not,

according to the laws of reason, an object either of theoretical or practical use")
through improper faith in miracles, through faith in mysteries, or through an
illusory faith in external means of grace. Even the most chastened and pious
outward form of religious devotion (prayer, church attendance, baptism, communion) can degenerate into a formalistic and superstitious means of grace.
As Paul Tillich concluded, Kant "felt that it was not dignified for autonomous
men who control the world and possess the power of reason to be found in
the situation of prayer."[87] Kant carries the logic of reformed piety to its extreme.
Any human behavior other than purely moral action that seeks to foster a
relation with the divine or to affect the divine in any manner is a fetish-faith,
a form of magic; all that remains is the most austere and moralistic piety. True
religion has no distinguishing visible manifestations.

In Kant's scheme, the ground of religion was shifted definitively to the
human consciousness, and other thinkers followed him with new formulations
of the subjective nature of religious truth. Most relevant here is Schleiermacher, who echoed Kant's shift of the ground of religion into the individual
consciousness and who exerted enormous influence both on nineteenth-
century Christian theology and on broader nineteenth-century understandings
of religion and magic. With his argument that the fundamental source of all
religion is the human feeling of absolute dependence, Schleiermacher gave
theological legitimization to Kant's claim that the only adequate ground for
religion is to be found in human nature itself.

In *The Christian Faith* (1821–22), Schleiermacher argues that the proper
locus of the redemptive power of Christianity lies in the inner experience of
the believer. This redemptive experience constitutes the appropriate mean between forms of religion that Schleiermacher calls "magical" (in which natural
elements are seen as having some form of automatic power over Christ) and
"empirical" (which focuses entirely on mundane experiences of moral development). In the "magical" mode, participation in Christian blessedness is seen
as independent of "vital fellowship" with Christ; "something so absolutely inward as blessedness is supposed to have been brought about externally, without
any inner basis."[88] While Schleiermacher rejects Kant's thinly moralistic religious sense, he affirms Kant's suspicion of external religious behavior as magical.

Working to explain Christianity as a revelation that becomes natural when
it takes a manifest form, Schleiermacher argues that miracles, including even
the resurrection of Jesus, are neither necessary nor sufficient for the dawning
of true Christian faith; indeed, biblical episodes only appear to be miraculous
relative to limited human awareness of the laws governing physical nature. Not
only is it clear that Christ marks the end of all miracles, but also the biblical
miracles themselves are "altogether superfluous" to faith for the contemporary
Christian.[89] In discounting external religious behavior and rejecting the notion

of miracles, Schleiermacher seeks to formulate a version of Christianity that is thoroughly naturalized and thoroughly rationalized.

From the seventeenth century forward, rationalized forms of religion gained increasing influence in European thought. Reformed Christianity (in both its Protestant and Catholic forms) advocated newly spiritualized norms for proper piety in which external manifestations of religion became ancillary to true faith. By the eighteenth century, mechanistic views of nature had effectively expelled the supernatural from the flow of causation, and Enlightenment notions of rationality posed serious challenges to the particularity of religious rituals and revelations. Thus, for example, theological debates over an issue such as the existence of miracles turned on growing acceptance of the twin notions that nature was governed by regular, mechanical laws and that God stood outside that system of laws. New ideals for religion took shape, discounting all forms of external ritual and religious practice in favor of a private, intellectualized religious sensibility. While significant opposition to these trends persisted (particularly in Romanticism and various pietistic renewal movements), this ideal of rationalized religion came to hold increasing sway among the dominant classes and intellectual elites of Europe and America. With religion constrained into such abstraction, the material world could be configured as securely secular, and this in turn rendered it appropriately prone to commodification by the emerging bourgeois classes.

Colonialism and Comparative Theories of Culture

One of the principal assumptions linking Enlightenment deists and atheists was assurance in the value of science and scientific rationality. Many of the most prominent Enlightenment thinkers were themselves scientists, and they shared a belief that scientific rationality was the key to human progress. Among the intellectually and socially elite classes of Europe, Western science came to stand as a prime marker of Europe's cultural superiority, and this confidence in Europe's preeminence served as a valuable resource in the spread of European economic and industrial power throughout the eighteenth and nineteenth centuries. These beliefs were also central to new Enlightenment schemes of the progressive development of human history. Vico had seen history as progressing in accordance with natural laws through a series of cyclical stages. This comparative approach to cultural history was developed by subsequent Enlightenment thinkers such as Montesquieu and Turgot, who began to chart more linear evolutionary paths. Positivistic interpretations of human history became increasingly prevalent through the course of the eighteenth century. While there were prominent dissenting voices (most notably Rousseau), many major Enlightenment thinkers saw Europe's new scientific and social development as evidence of the dawning of a new era in human development.[90]

Nowhere is the progressivist strand of Enlightenment thought more overt than in the work of Condorcet. In his *Esquisse d'un tableau historique des progrès de l'esprit humain* (1794), Condorcet traces the evolution of humanity through various developmental stages; he argues that by charting the development of masses of human beings over time, we can come to understand the progress of the human intellect. Condorcet sets out a utopian vision in which the social divisions and tyranny occasioned by religious superstition fall with the spread of reason. Indeed, Condorcet declares, European colonialism is itself a central tool of social evolution. As European colonizers move into colonial territories, they will either civilize the savage inhabitants of these territories or drive the savages to disappear. These colonizers will diffuse the principles and example of European liberty, enlightenment, and reason throughout Africa and Asia. As social and educational equality are disseminated throughout humanity and as reason comes to banish the ridiculous prejudices of superstition, humanity will progress toward the perfect society created through reason itself. Science is the principal engine in this move toward perfection.[91]

Condorcet's emphasis on the role of colonialism in the spread of Western reason points us to the direct material context of the European confidence in progress. From the late fifteenth century, Europe had been engaged in the conquest of large expanses of the non-European world. Spanish and French victories in the Americas were followed by massive efforts to missionize the indigenous populations, efforts that often involved great violence against practices seen as heathen and idolatrous. European colonists brought their concerns with witchcraft with them to the New World. Historian William Monter cites a sixteenth-century Peruvian chronicler as stating that the devil came to the West Indies in a Castilian ship. Philip II sent inquisitors to the Americas in the 1570s, though in 1575 he declared that Indians (as opposed to Creoles or mestizos) were not "people of reason" sufficient to be subject to inquisitorial jurisdiction. The rhetoric of European witchcraft exerted a significant influence on early European views of indigenous American religious practices. For example, in 1585 the French explorer Jean de Léry invoked Jean Bodin's demonology to describe the ritual practices of Brazilian women.[92]

The initial stages of European colonial expansion were shaped by internal political struggles among Europe's emerging nation-states. During the early period, European powers had not yet developed the industrial and material superiority that would fuel later stages of colonial conquest, and they gained hegemony only in the Americas. But subsequent centuries saw the dramatic spread of European control. During the late eighteenth century and the first decades of the nineteenth, European colonial expansion largely involved indirect economic domination with only sporadic episodes of direct territorial conquest. In the latter decades of the nineteenth century, a major new phase of colonial conquest was launched as European powers competed for territories in the newly explored African inland and for the remaining uncolonized areas of Asia. By this point, Europe's industrialization gave it profound advantages in armaments and transportation. Edward Said underscores the sweep of European conquest through this period:

> In 1800 Western powers claimed 55 percent but actually held approximately 35 percent of the earth's surface . . . by 1878 the proportion was 67 percent, a rate of increase of 83,000 square miles per year. By 1914, the annual rate had risen to an astonishing 240,000 square miles, and Europe held a grand total of roughly 85 percent of the earth as colonies, protectorates, dependencies, dominions, and commonwealths.[93]

As we will see, the astounding spread of European colonial power through the nineteenth and early twentieth centuries thoroughly informed the context within which European and American scholars developed theories of magic.

Throughout the era of conquest, Europe produced a voluminous literature aimed at legitimating colonialism. Theories of social evolution prevalent in the eighteenth and early nineteenth centuries stressed the role of climate and geography in the development of human societies, a theme with roots in the work of Aristotle and particularly prominent since the sixteenth century. Theorists such as Montesquieu and Rousseau argued that the propitious climate of Europe was a primary determinant of Europe's cultural superiority.[94]

But from the closing decades of the seventeenth century onward, new racial theorizing developed to confirm that the "savage" was fundamentally distinct from the European. This new racial ideology promoted both conquest and slavery. The theme of racial difference grew in importance in Germany and England with new Romantic emphases on the links between geography and racial identity. Theorists such as Buffon and Blumenbach supported their theories of human monogenesis by attributing the differences among contemporary racial groups to the physical environment (including climate and dietary conditions), which produced "degenerations" passed on by heredity. Herder's account of divine providence and cultural predestination also turned on the geographic location of specific peoples in space and time.[95] This link between geography and human culture would persist as an important undercurrent in theories of magic even after the eclipse of such overt racial theorizing.

Enlightenment race theorists also came to stress the relation between anatomy and psychology, and they began a move from earlier notions of environmentalism toward the "neurological" concept of racial difference that was to predominate in the nineteenth century. In keeping with the emerging materialism of the eighteenth century, the predominant Enlightenment racial paradigm emphasized visible anatomical characteristics, a focus implying that behavior could be explained largely through recourse to physiology. In the nineteenth century, these reifications of identity and difference were further naturalized by burgeoning forms of empiricism. In the early decades of the century, the anatomist and founder of paleontology, Georges Cuvier, consolidated current racial thought and formulated his influential tripartite division of human racial groups. Through the first half of the nineteenth century, more elaborate racial doctrines began to appear, most notably from the historian Thomas Arnold and the anatomist Robert Knox. These new formulations focused heavily on the body's anatomical and physiological determinants. New theories of racial degeneration also appeared, further bolstering the demand for race-based political and economic policy both at home and on the colonial frontier.[96]

Later in the nineteenth century, the new academic fields of psychopathology, ethnology, and sociology emerged to offer further tools for the mapping of human development and difference. The study of primitive culture promised an opportunity to excavate earlier eras of human development through diachronic analysis. These emerging forms of racial and cultural theorizing were extraordinarily amorphous and pliable, but their very imprecision proved to be a prime source of heuristic efficacy as they were applied to wildly divergent contexts and bodies of "evidence." And these theories took on even greater cultural legitimacy through their intersection with other rhetorics stigmatizing cultural difference. One of the major tropes of these theories, to be rehearsed time and again in theories of magic, was the gendering and sexualizing of cultural difference. Europe was configured as the locus of appropriate forms of masculine autonomy and authority; other racial and cultural groups were portrayed as feminine and denatured. Rudi Bleys provides a striking example of the cultural relays between the rhetoric of race and gender as he quotes Cristoph Meiners's 1793 assessment of cultural difference: "In the end, black and ugly people are distinct from the white and beautiful ones due to a sad lack of virtues or to several dreadful anomalies. . . . They also combine a more than female cowardice and fear of visible danger and death with an unintelligible quietism."[97]

Many of the nineteenth-century theories of social and racial difference aimed at formalizing distinctions between European and non-European peoples, between the colonizer and the colonized. These theories were an important ideological tool for imperialism, particularly in the more extreme forms of the late nineteenth century. In 1894 John Westlake made the influential argument that cultural inferiority should preclude recognition of the legal sovereignty of "uncivilized natives" under international law. By the close of the nineteenth century, Europe faced new needs to control its expansive imperial possessions and to maintain popular domestic support for the colonial enterprise. In response to these needs, a massive literature arose across an array of academic disciplines serving to legitimate colonialism. The theme of racial and cultural difference regularly veered into an apologetic for colonialist social policy. Europe was configured in these theories as the seat of innovation, dynamism, and rationality. And throughout these texts, science was seen as a distinctively Western phenomenon.[98]

It is important to underscore that even from the earliest phases of this modern cultural and racial theorizing, dissenting voices could be heard. Rousseau and important Romantic theorists invoked "the noble savage" to challenge various aspects of contemporary European culture, a theme reflected in Schopenhauer's negative assessment of human progress. The nineteenth century also saw various cultural movements of *décadence* valorizing numerous aspects of cultural difference (even if those differences were carefully mediated). Primitivism could be deployed either to legitimate Europe's cultural hegemony or to contest it.[99] Yet whatever the valence attached to the notion of cultural difference, these arguments shared a fundamental structure. Europe could be understood only through cultural contrast; modern identity could be defined only through juxtaposition with cultural Others. In this context, I turn to examine the emergence of modern theorizing about religion and magic.

Self-definition against 'OTHER'

Theories of Religion and Religious Evolution

One of the significant aspects of the Enlightenment critique of revealed religion was a new interest among European scholars in the analysis of religion from a comparative perspective. In the period from the thirteenth to the fifteenth century, new information had arrived in Europe about various cultural practices in the non-European world. The voyages and conquests of the sixteenth and seventeenth centuries prompted more sustained European interest in the range of human cultural systems, and during this period the new notion of "religion" as a cross-cultural aspect of human society took hold. With the formation of the Society of Jesus, an active missionary movement began to spread into North America, India, and China, and missionaries soon provided even more information to Europe about non-Christian religious systems.[100]

In the seventeenth and early eighteenth centuries, numerous texts began to appear in Europe detailing the practices of various non-Christian religions. These books were often marked by an extreme anticlericalism (portraying the development of religious ritual as a degeneration from simple and pristine origins) and by the effort to identify a common source for all religions (most commonly in some form of natural religion). Charles de Brosses's influential *Du culte des dieux fétishes* (1760) proposed fetishism as the predominant form of religion of preliterate societies. The late eighteenth and early nineteenth centuries saw various new compendia of information concerning the mythology and religions of ancient and contemporary peoples.[101]

Nineteenth-century Romanticism emphasized the notion of religion as an inward, subjective experience, but Romantic idealism also gave new stress to the importance of history. On a popular level this focus on history was reflected in new interests in folklore. The works of Sir Walter Scott and the Grimms' *Deutsche Mythologie* (1832) offered compilations of folk beliefs and practices. Herder argued for the central role of religion in human history and sought to trace the historical laws governing religious development. Through the late eighteenth and early nineteenth centuries, European scholars began to translate and publish various Hindu religious classics, and the early nineteenth century also saw the growth of new archaeological and linguistic information about the ancient Near East and new interest in Indo-European languages and cultures.[102]

A number of philosophies of history were published through this era, setting forth the developmental principles of human life. Hegel's is the most prominent, and Hegel is particularly relevant here also because of the important role magic plays in his philosophy of religion. In his *Lectures on the Philosophy of Religion* (from lectures in 1827), Hegel offers an elaborate account of human religious development. He rejects the claims of English and French deists that religions degenerated from pure origins into corrupted ritualistic systems. Instead, he argues, religion is spirit realizing itself in consciousness, and this progressive realization unfolds over time, taking its ultimate form only with the development of Christianity.[103]

Hegel's primary discussion of magic appears in his phenomenological account of the three forms of "determinate, particular, and hence finite religions, the *ethnic religions* generally." In this typology, Hegel identifies nature religion (the first stage of determinate religion) as religion in which the spiritual is recognized only in the external, natural, and immediate form of particular and existing human beings. Magic is the first, and perhaps archetypal, form of this nature religion. In fact, Hegel repeatedly states that magic may actually be deemed "unworthy of the name 'religion.'" Magic demarcates the boundary of the emergence of the religious consciousness. The primitive magical stage can be understood, Hegel explains, only by the imaginative struggle to place oneself into a human position "devoid of consciousness of anything universal." In his memorable phrase, "To put oneself in the place of a dog requires the sensibilities of a dog."[104]

Magic is religion based solely on the consciousness of human power over the natural world. Human beings in the magical stage exist in "a state of immediate desire, force, and action, behaving in accord with their immediate will." Primitive human beings do not frame theoretical questions concerning cause and effect, and they fail to acknowledge essential limitations on subjective desire (such as the rights or duties that can lead to universal concerns). Living in "this undivided state, this benighted condition, a stupor in the theoretical domain and wildness of will," they are completely at the mercy of arbitrary desire. And these sad primitives are also prey to a constant fear of contingency and the uncontrolled forces of nature. Spirit is not recognized in its universality and is identified instead as "just the singular and contingent human self-consciousness."[105]

Members of the modern world exercise an indirect, mediated power over nature, recognizing the external world as subject to its own forms of autonomy and as governed by its own laws. This indirect control actually comes from the superior freedom that moderns manifest with respect to nature. In contrast, human beings who seek to practice direct, magical power over nature are thwarted by the lack of mediation in their relations to nature. Without "meditative thought," it is impossible to attain a consciousness of anything beyond the immediately surrounding natural objects. Yet this enslavement remains inexplicably alluring: the direct relationship to nature "continues to insinuate itself deeply into other, higher religions in a secondary way, for instance the practice of witchcraft in Christendom, and of invoking devils."[106]

Hegel rejects Kant's claim that prayer should be considered a type of magic in which human beings seek to bring about effects not through appropriate forms of mediation but directly from the spirit. Instead, Hegel argues, in prayer human beings are turning to God, who can grant or deny the petition in furtherance of the good. Prayer itself appears to be a form of mediation. Hegel contrasts this mode of prayer with black magic, in which human beings seek to control spirits or devils through the direct exercise of the capricious and subjective human will.[107]

The concrete examples that Hegel cites of magical practices emphasize that in his developmental scheme magic is primarily a non-European phenomenon. The higher religion of China is a relatively developed form of magical religion, he explains, but it remains mired in a magical subjective particularity. Various less developed systems of magic are to be found among "wholly crude and barbarous peoples" such as Eskimos, Africans, and Mongols. So, for example, the Negroes, who "have not yet attained to a universal rationality," demonstrate in their magic only a "wild sense." In his *Philosophy of History* (from lectures in 1822), Hegel reiterates the claim that African life lacks any notion of universality; in "Negro life . . . consciousness has not yet attained to the realization of any substantial objective existence." The Negro lacks any sense of reverence and morality, as well as consciousness of the "Higher Power" on which religion is based. The Negro is thus a sorcerer:

> In *Sorcery* we have not the idea of a God, of a moral faith; it exhibits man as the highest power, regarding him as alone occupying a position of command over the power of Nature. We have here therefore nothing to do with a spiritual adoration of God, nor with an empire of Right. . . . Although they are necessarily conscious of dependence

upon Nature . . . yet this does not conduct them to the consciousness of a Higher Power: it is they who command the elements, and
this they call "magic."

In their ceremonies, Negro magicians begin with "all sorts of gesticulations,
dances, uproar, and shouting, and in the midst of this confusion commence
their incantations." These magical rites are so depraved that they are often
accompanied by cannibalism. And while fetishism offers the illusion of a step
toward objectivity, this objectivity is false, since the fetish is merely the arbitrary
creation of its maker and leads to no true relation of dependence.[108]

The fundamental components of Hegel's account of magic will be rehearsed repeatedly throughout the nineteenth and twentieth centuries; magic
marks the boundary of religion (with magic's relation to that boundary an open
question); magic is largely a local, ethnic phenomenon; magic is based on
unconstrained and arbitrary desire and willfulness; magic lacks any notion of
transcendence and universality; magic is linked essentially to non-European
peoples, even though it maintains an inexplicable allure even in higher culture.
Subsequent scholars will also follow the basic structure of Hegel's discussion.
Like Hegel, they will invoke magic as a resource for giving content to idealized
notions of religion, a foil against which proper religion can be juxtaposed.

Hegel's view of religion had great initial appeal in Europe among various
reactionary religious and political movements, but other nineteenth-century
thinkers came to reinterpret Hegel's thought in ways that pointed toward a
radical critique of religion. Prominent among these thinkers was Feuerbach,
who argued that religion is a subjective creation of the human mind in which
humanity alienates its own nature. Feuerbach's most extensive comments re-
garding magic appear in his *Lectures on the Essence of Religion* (1851), where he
brings magic to bear as a weapon in his broader attack on religion. Feuerbach
explains that "uncivilized man," in his confusion and helplessness, seeks to
harness the forces of nature to human aims and desires either through the
"prayers and gifts or sacrifices" of religion or through magic ("which is only
an irreligious form of religion"). For Feuerbach, there is ultimately little distinction to be made between religion and magic. In magic, the believer projects
"the real or alleged power of magicians to control nature by mere words, by
sheer force of will—into beings outside of man." Even pious Christian prayer
often contains an element of magic, as the believer repeats magical formulas
in the hope of compelling divine assistance. Magic is only a more excessive
demonstration of the basic tendencies that Christians share with polytheists
and idolaters in their attempts to bend nature to the human will. Yet despite
these similarities, modern, educated Christians actually demonstrate an ironic
degree of progress over the idolaters: even as they persist in praying to be
protected from fire, "in practice . . . they put little reliance in the power of
prayer, but prefer to take out fire insurance." Feuerbach rejects Schleierma-

cher's claim that human beings have some special predisposition toward religion or religious sentiment. Instead, he asserts, "we should be more justified in assuming the existence of a specific organ of superstition," "a special organ for superstition, ignorance, and mental laziness." Superstition takes its strength from "the power of ignorance and stupidity, which is the greatest power on earth, the power of fear and the feeling of dependency, and finally the power of the imagination." If rationalists hope to find a basis for natural religion, Feuerbach concludes, let them also defend beliefs in the devil, ghosts, and witches, since the two sets of beliefs are identical in origin and nature.[109]

A critique of religion similar to Feuerbach's was offered by his French contemporary Auguste Comte, who exerted great influence on subsequent sociological theories of cultural and religious development. Comte built on Condorcet's triumphalist views of historical progress to formulate a more dogmatic and evolutionary positivism in which religion is reconfigured as the worship of humanity. He outlined his evolutionary social scheme in the six-volume *Cours de philosophie positive* (1830–42). Comte begins the *Cours* by asserting the "great fundamental law" that human culture passes successively through three phases: "the Theological, or fictitious; the Metaphysical, or abstract; and the Scientific, or positive." Comte argues that the theological stage begins with fetishism and moves through polytheism to monotheism. Priests and magicians appear in Comte's account as fetishism develops toward its highest stage, astrolatry, or star worship. They exemplify the ability of "superior men to make the utmost use of the civilizing virtue of this primitive philosophy" in order to attain leisure and dignity for the study of science and industry.[110] Comte's themes of the fundamental trajectory of culture and of the role of the ambitious magician in cultural development will appear repeatedly through the nineteenth and twentieth centuries.

By the later half of the nineteenth century, an evolutionary, historical approach to religion had gained prominence in Europe and America, and this methodology would persist well into the twentieth century. Advocates of the new "science of religion" such as Max Müller expressed great hope that this science would flourish and offer invaluable keys to the understanding of human life. In 1901 Morris Jastrow pointed to a broad new scholarly consensus on two related points shaping the late nineteenth-century study of religion: "that the religious development of mankind proceeds in accordance with definite laws, and that this development is on the whole an upward movement from crude ideas and primitive forms of worship to a philosophic conception of the universe, accompanied by a ceremonial correspondingly elaborated and refined."[111]

The historical and comparative study of religion became increasingly institutionalized in Europe and the United States in the closing decades of the nineteenth century through the coalescence of interest in a range of related fields (including comparative philology, ethnology, anthropology, and folklore).

As Joseph Kitagawa asserts, this new "scientific" study of religion was thoroughly shaped by the Enlightenment understanding of religion. At the heart of the new science was an Enlightenment notion of natural religion, a core seen as underlying all of the concrete, historical manifestations of religious phenomena.[112]

The theoretical focus on magic that emerged in the late nineteenth and early twentieth centuries among scholars of religious studies and the social sciences was also thoroughly informed by this rationalist, Enlightenment model of religion. A wide confluence of social and intellectual forces converged to inform these new theories of magic. From the cultural memory of the European witchcraft persecutions to the immediate material demands of empire, a complex array of associations and interests refract through these theories. In light of this broad social and intellectual context, let us now turn to examine modern theories of magic.

2

Magic and the Regulation of Piety

A religion without externals, must ever be fantastic and false.
　　　　　　　　　　　　　　　—John Williamson Nevin

Near the turn of the twentieth century, Alfred Haddon wrote a history of the newly institutionalized academic discipline of anthropology. As he considered the modern anthropological perspective on religion, Haddon quoted Parson Thwackum, a character from Henry Fielding's *Tom Jones*, as exemplifying a benighted, parochial approach to the subject: "When I mention religion I mean the Christian religion; and not only the Christian religion, but the Protestant religion; and not only the Protestant religion, but the Church of England." In contrast to the parson's perspective, Haddon claimed, the modern discipline of anthropology proceeds by the very opposite approach: not constraining the study of social phenomena to a single, narrow model of what constitutes religion but seeking instead to encompass all the religions of the world with no thought as to their truth or falsehood.

Haddon may have been a bit overly optimistic in his assessment of the cultural expansiveness of the European and American social sciences. Western anthropology, sociology, and religious studies have proved far more indebted to post-Reformation and post-Enlightenment models of religion than Haddon allowed. In fact, while it might not always have been the Anglicanism of Parson Thwackum that served as the norm, the analysis of religion through the history of these academic disciplines has been deeply informed by Christian—and often specifically Protestant—ideals.

The most vivid example of the power of these Christian norms in the pages that follow is to be found in the ease with which numerous scholars from a broad range of academic disciplines have located the specific pinnacle of human religious development, its most distilled expression. Repeatedly scholars will assert that this pinnacle is reached in the formulation of the Christian Lord's Prayer. It may be relatively unsurprising that scholars writing within the Western social sciences—even scholars claiming secular objectivity—would seize on the Lord's Prayer as the most rarefied and idealized form of religious expression. But more striking than the choice itself is the consistency with which these scholars reduce the prayer to the same thin message. In this social scientific frame, the Lord's Prayer is valorized because it is seen as teaching a distinctively appropriate religious response to the supernatural: pious and passive submission. "Thy will be done." In the view of a broad range of scholars, this statement—nothing more, and nothing less—is the goal to which all human religious development aspires.

As recounted in the prior chapter, increasingly rationalized models of religion took hold during the early modern era as new forms of social and economic organization emerged within European culture. These rationalized norms for religion served as one of the formative components of modern social organization. Liberal social contract theory, in versions from Hobbes and Locke through their nineteenth- and twentieth-century progeny, has displayed great ambivalence about the status of religion. On the one hand, religion is seen as serving socially adaptive ends—promoting forms of individual subjectivity well suited to the needs of the modern nation-state. On the other hand, religion also stands as a persistent threat to the state's autonomy and coercive power—offering competing visions of social order and competing demands for loyalty. Liberal social theorists have recognized religion as the most potent mediating institution in liberal modernity, intervening between the state and the liberal subject in a decidedly unstable fashion.

Because of religion's anomalous status and its political potency, liberal social thinkers have exerted a great deal of effort to bring religion under control. Since the eighteenth century, a range of important theorists have condemned religion as socially regressive, blocking the path of economic and scientific progress. Other scholars have set about the task of constraining religion into a tame and domesticated form more serviceable to modern economic and social interests. This domestication of religion, channeling it into a narrow, private realm, is an essential step in producing the secular sphere, a nonreligious realm given over to the rational control of science, economic markets, and secular political power.

Paul Tillich offers a pointed description of the specific ways in which rationalized religion comports with the interests of modern capitalism. Members of the enlightened and calculating modern bourgeoisie, Tillich explains, seek to exercise control over the material world, a control premised on the twin presuppositions that nature is regular and that nature displays consistent patterns that the mercantile class can rely on as a basis for sound business decisions. This calculating bourgeois mentality has held great sway in Western modernity. And it has been accompanied, Tillich asserts, by a religious sensibility that harmonizes with its fundamental assumptions:

Tillich

> Irrational elements which interfere with a calculable pattern of reality must . . . be excluded. This means that the irrational elements of religion must be eliminated. The bourgeois needs a reasonable religion which views God as lying behind the whole of life's processes. God has made the world and now it follows its own laws. [God] does not interfere any more. Every interference would mean a loss of calculability. No such interferences are acceptable and all special revelations have to be denied.[2]

Rationalization of religion for economic ends

(Is this changing now?)

Thus, Tillich concludes, a rationalized, disenchanted form of religion comports well with the interests of the bourgeoisie. God is banished from active involvement in the material world, and with divine or supernatural intervention no longer threatening to disrupt the regular, lawful operations of nature, scientific and economic calculations can be put forward with greater assurance. This rationalized religious sensibility has had a profound appeal among the Western bourgeoisie.

Religion unstable

But this notion of religion has never been particularly stable. Religion is far too unwieldy for easy containment, in theory or in practice. The extent of modern secularization has been exaggerated at every level, and even in the domain of social theory this rationalized model of religion is rather hopelessly abstract. For many generations, Western philosophers, social scientists, and scholars of religion have struggled to give content to this concept of religion and to prescribe its role in modern society. One of the pervasive strategies in these scholarly efforts to define the rationalized modern notion of religion has been to juxtapose it with a foil, nonrational forms of magic. Through a broad range of academic literature since the late nineteenth century, magic has been invoked as "the bastard sister of religion."[3]   *Magic as bastard sister*

In the premodern view—reflected most visibly in the early stages of the European witchcraft persecutions—magic was commonly portrayed as sin or idolatry. In the rationalizing scheme that took shape with modernity, magic came to be reconfigured as immature or improper religious practice. Magic was thus seen as constituting a new form of aberrational behavior, a disorder or delusion contravening appropriately rationalist, and post-Reformation, piety. In this view, magic signified a counterfeit, a deceptive and fraudulent imitation, "what is related to religion as false money is to genuine."[4] Since the late nineteenth century, innumerable scholars of religious studies and the social sci-

Pre-Modern
- Magic as sinful

Modern as
Magic as delusional/psychological disorder
- FALSE, counterfeit

ences have struggled to clarify the precise nature of this aberration and to articulate, in turn, the limits for appropriate religious behavior within modern liberal society.

The purpose of this chapter is to explore the various functions that magic has served in modern theoretical literature concerning religion. I will begin by examining the role of magic in efforts to account for the origins of religion. From the latter decades of the nineteenth century well into the twentieth century, the search for the origins of religion was a major scholarly preoccupation. Many important scholars offered competing theories of religious evolution, and magic regularly played a central role in these theories. The search for origins eventually subsided, but scholars continue to put forward theories of religious development, and magic remains an important component in these recent accounts. Some theorists have seen magic as designating a category distinct from (and external to) religion, while others have seen it as an internal subset of religion. But in either case, magic has functioned in these theories both as a means of demarcating the boundaries of religion and as a rhetorical and strategic tool for articulating a vision of religion's ultimate provenance.

Of course this search for origins was always an indirect attempt to uncover religion's essence. As Ruth Benedict frames it, "The study of 'origins' in religion has never been anything but a convenient way of designating efforts to isolate the core of religion." In this assessment, Benedict echoes Wilhelm Wundt's earlier assertion concerning the search for religion's origins: "The beginning is supposed to anticipate the end, as a revelation not yet distorted by human error."[5] Displacing controversies about the essence of religion onto debates about primitive history and cultural development served as a useful tactic for diverting (or diffusing) the heat of more pressing contemporary conflicts. Through the course of the twentieth century the search for origins fell into disrepute, but scholars moved to new strategies for seeking to identify the essential nature of religion (including various forms of functionalism and phenomenology). The second section of this chapter will explore the role of magic in these new approaches to religion. By serving as the marker of religion's limits, magic again proved useful in efforts to demarcate religion as a discrete object of study and to illuminate religion's essence. These accounts of the nature of religion are thoroughly shaped by post-Reformation and post-Enlightenment notions of religion as private, intellectual, and involving a distinctly constrained piety. Debates over magic proved an important arena for reiterating those norms. In addition, as the dominant theoretical formulations of magic stigmatize forms of practice that contravene rationalist, post-Enlightenment piety, they articulate central aspects of the modern notion of human identity and agency.

The final section of this chapter will explore another major theme that emerges from twentieth-century theoretical accounts of magic: the relation of religion to the material world—and the place of religion in the system of human economic relations. Throughout these theories, scholars regularly return to the theme of magic's fundamental materiality. Magic is seen as involving murky relations to the material world, in both its practices and its objectives. The chapter will conclude by examining the distinctive ways in which magic has been stigmatized in accounts of its practitioners seeking to subvert the regularity of the external world. In contrast, of course, religion is configured as seeking only internal (or transcendent, or supernatural, or supraempirical) objectives, objectives thoroughly in conformance with the regularized operation of materiality and with modern capitalist social relations. One of the abiding subtexts of the dominant theories of magic has been the effort to constrain the position of religion within the modern liberal social order and to police the role of religion in the modern economy.

The Origin of Religion

Magic first emerged as a topic of major analytical concern for nineteenth-century scholars of religion in theories of religious evolution. Religion was a central focus of early social scientific theories of cultural development. As the anthropologist Felix Keesing pointed out, religion and religious origins featured more prominently than any other aspect of culture in the literature of social evolution. Scholars sought to account for the origins of religion (and its formative role in human culture) by offering a wide variety of what Evans-Pritchard aptly described as "just-so stories," and magic proved an instrumental player in these early evolutionary tales.[6] Certain theorists argued that religion was a sui generis phenomenon and that magic was fundamentally distinct (possibly related to the evolutionary origins of science). Others argued that magic constituted an early stage in the evolution of religion, with more developed forms of religion growing from magical roots. A major theme of these debates was the question of what sort of boundary should be constructed around religion and what the ultimate etiology of religion might be.

As we will see, throughout these debates over the origin and development of religion, magic proved a remarkably pliable tool. For some scholars, placing magic at the origin of religion served to discolor religion's genesis, to malign contemporary religion by establishing its disreputable lineage. For others, identifying magic as the originary stage of religion could demonstrate the power and trajectory of social evolution; culture moved in a clear line of progress from humble beginnings to greater glory. For still others, an emphatic distinction between religion and magic was necessary to protect religion's purity; magic could stand as a vivid foil for religion or even as a protagonist in accounts of religion's degeneration from a stage of primordial monotheistic truth. And yet again, the debates over magic served as an opportunity to expound on the various social and existential functions of religion. Throughout these early theories, the discussion of magic provided an invaluable opportunity to debate the nature and role of religion in human development.

Fetishism and Other Early Theories

Through the course of the nineteenth century, a range of theories emerged concerning the origins of religion. Comte gave his imprimatur to Charles de Brosses's theory that fetishism constituted the initial stage of religion, and fetishism dominated most early nineteenth-century accounts of the religious practices of primitive and uncivilized peoples. In midcentury, Max Müller proposed that the roots of religion could be found in nature mythology, and his philologically based approach became widely influential.[7] Herbert Spencer, the primary figure of late nineteenth-century English evolutionary social thought, played a significant role in popularizing Darwin-inspired theories of social evolution and in expanding those theories to include the development of religion. Spencer advocated a naturalistic account of the origins of magic. In primitive oral societies, he explained, mistaken speculation concerning the effects of action on parts of an object or items associated with an object results in notions of magical power. Religion also originates in false speculation, as figures in dreams are interpreted as ghosts, and then ghosts of dead ancestors are elevated into deities. As religious beliefs develop, magic evolves to include notions of supernatural agency, and religion itself moves along a clear causal path from the initial stage of euhemerism into the more complex and differentiated forms displayed in modern society. Spencer rejected the widespread Enlightenment view that religious systems were merely invidious priestly inventions, claiming instead that they evolve from deep-seated natural causes and human experience.[8]

Magic played a key role in Hegel's account of religious development discussed in the prior chapter, and by the late 1860s it emerged as a central feature in accounts of social evolution. One of the first influential British texts to place focus on the role of magic in the development of religion was John Lubbock's *Origin of Civilization and the Primitive Condition of Man* (1870). Lubbock invokes newly amassed ethnographic data to correct the errors he sees in Comte's evolutionary theory. He outlines an elaborate scheme of six stages of religious evolution (atheism, nature worship or totemism, shamanism, idolatry or anthropomorphism, the deity as creator, and religion joined with morality). The proper boundaries of religion should be determined, he states, on the basis of "the conception formed of the nature of the Deity," "the estimate in which the Deity is held." Religion is not to be found at all among "the lowest savages" who have not yet arrived at a properly submissive attitude toward the divine. Using this standard, Lubbock determines that magic and fetishism should not properly be considered elements in the evolution of religion, since they stand outside its bounds. Unlike Comteans who argued that fetishism was the ear-

liest stage of religious evolution, Lubbock argues that fetishism is more properly understood as an "anti-religion," a developed form of witchcraft and magic
in which the practitioner attempts to coerce and control the deity. In Lubbock's
view, all forms of magic, including fetishism, have at their heart a desire to
control and dominate nature, which leads to the attempt to control and dominate the deity or lower spirits. Magic must not be confused with religion, since
it stands entirely opposed to "the true spirit" of religion. The one involves the
attempt to subject the divine to the human will, while the other involves human
submission to the divine. The priest stands in opposition to the wizard, because
the priest worships the deity, while the wizard attempts to coerce it.[9]

Lubbock's formulation of the difference between religion and magic echoes the differentiation that solidified during the cultural disputes discussed in
the prior chapter, particularly Protestant attacks on Catholicism. Lubbock links
magic and fetishism, and he challenges the Comtean view of fetishism as the
most primitive form of religion on the basis of his desire to establish a clear
differentiation between religion and magic. The debate over the relation between religion and magic would become far more contentious as new theories
of religion's origins emerged in the following decades, but Lubbock's fundamental understanding of the nature of magic would reverberate through subsequent formulations.

Animism (belief in souls & spiritual beings)

By far the most influential evolutionary account of religion from the latter
half of the nineteenth century was set out by Edward Burnett Tylor, widely
considered the founder of British anthropology.[10] In his *Primitive Culture* (1871),
Tylor argues that the earliest stage of religion is to be found in animism (belief
in the existence of souls and other spiritual beings) and that religious beliefs
develop through relatively clear stages of social evolution. Animism emerges,
he explains, as primitive people reflect on the difference between living and
dead bodies and as they work to account for the appearance of human figures
in dreams and visions. The notion of the soul takes shape as the primitive
philosopher struggles to find a rational and coherent interpretation of this
sensory data. While the animistic religions of "the lower races" show little
evidence of the moral element of religion, in more developed forms animism
comes to include an explicit belief in a future state that leads to true worship
and morality. And though its form changes, animism resides at the heart of
all religious systems, even those found in modern culture. Tylor rejects the
claims of missionaries and other scholars that there are tribes so low in culture
as to have no religious ideas: "For the most part the 'religious world' is so
occupied in hating and despising the beliefs of the heathen whose vast regions
of the globe are painted black on the missionary maps, that they have little
time or capacity left to understand them." Instead, he asserts, scholars would

be better served by a clear recognition of the commonality of human religious systems: "No religion of mankind lies in utter isolation from the rest, and the thoughts and principles of modern Christianity are attached to intellectual clues which run back through far præ-Christian ages to the very origin of human civilization, perhaps even of human existence."[11] Since there are no cultures without religion, religion constitutes an originary component of culture itself.

In this universalist light, Tylor posits a broad—and rampantly intellectualist—minimum definition of religion: "the belief in Spiritual Beings." As many commentators have emphasized, this definition of religion is Protestant to its core. Tylor directly affirms the Protestant insistence on religion as belief, and even further, his entire evolutionary scheme is shaped by a rigid Protestant differentiation between religious belief and magical act. In the words of Paul Bohannan, as Tylor put forward this thin, intellectualist understanding of religion, "the rest of the supernatural he left to magic."[12]

In *Primitive Religion* Tylor never demarcates an explicit boundary between religion and magic, but he underscores the importance of differentiating between the two. In a valuable recent study of Tylor's thought, Wouter Hanegraaff concludes that while Tylor displays a fundamental sympathy toward basic aspects of religion, "magic is clearly the enemy." Tylor discusses magic primarily in the context of cultural survivals. He explains that while many survivals could properly be described as "superstitions" (a word that, "in what is perhaps its original sense of a 'standing over' from old times, itself expressed the notion of survival"), he prefers the more neutral term "survival" to avoid the stigma attached to "superstition." Despite this professed desire to avoid stigma, Tylor asserts that belief in magic is "one of the most pernicious delusions that ever vexed mankind." This "Occult Science" "belongs in its main principle to the lowest known stages of civilization, and the lower races, who have not partaken largely of the education of the world, still maintain it in vigour." Yet magical beliefs persist, and they may be traced upward even into modern cultured nations, where many older practices are still performed and new rites continue to evolve. But despite the presence of this unfortunate cultural residue, Tylor asserts that the "modern educated world" rejects occult science as "a contemptible superstition" and "has practically committed itself to the opinion that magic belongs to the lower level of civilization."[13]

As discussed at greater length in the following chapter, Tylor attributes the ignorant belief in magical occult science primarily to a misapplication of the principle of association of ideas. Mental (or ideal) connections between objects or events are confused with causal connections. It is only the educated world that has slowly and painfully learned the folly of mistaken magical thinking that "would to this day carry considerable weight to the minds of four-fifths of the human race." But despite such indications of progress, magic maintains a great hold on human thought: "A once-established opinion, however delusive, can hold its own from age to age, for belief can propagate itself without reference to its reasonable origin, as plants are propagated from slips without fresh raising from the seed." Indeed, while the history of magic is largely a history of "dwindling and decay," the laws governing this history are so variable and imprecise that they can often appear to be "no law at all."[14]

Tylor points to the early modern witchcraft persecutions as demonstrating the bitter transformation from passive to active survival. The belief in witchcraft, itself "part and parcel of savage life," was revived in Europe from the primeval past. While "the guilt of thus bringing down Europe intellectually and morally to the level of negro Africa lies in the main upon the Roman Church," the Reformers also share blame for the persecutions. Only the Enlightenment succeeded in changing prevailing opinion, a transition that has not yet penetrated all of society. As he states:

> In our days, when we read of a witch being burnt at Camargo in
> 1860, we point to Mexico as a country miserably in the rear of civili-
> zation. And if in England it still happens that village boors have to
> be tried at quarter-sessions for ill-using some poor old woman, who
> they fancy has dried a cow or spoiled a turnip crop, we comment on
> the tenacity with which the rustic mind clings to exploded follies,
> and cry out for more schoolmasters.

Indeed, we cannot know with certainty that witchcraft beliefs will not reassert themselves in the contemporary world. The Victorian revival of spiritualism, particularly among intellectual and affluent circles, stands as a powerful object lesson concerning the power of superstitious beliefs to reemerge in modern culture: "The world is again swarming with intelligent and powerful disembodied spiritual beings, whose direct action on thought and matter is again confidently asserted. . . . Apparitions have regained the place and meaning which they held from the level of the lower races to that of mediæval Europe."[15]

Tylor concludes his discussion of magical survivals with a revealing defense of his decision to study such phenomena. Survivals are useful, he explains, in demonstrating the large role of ignorance, superstition, and conservatism in preserving important traces of the history of the human race. By studying antiquarian relics, particularly concerning such disreputable topics as superstition, the scholar can avoid the practical problems posed by a more direct intervention in "partizan diatribes on the questions of the day." Yet the results of this scholarly indirection are directly applicable to contemporary disputes, because the laws of culture that are thus uncovered apply universally to all human societies. As he states:

> It is no more reasonable to suppose the laws of mind differently
> constituted in Australia and in England, in the time of the cave-
> dwellers and in the time of the builders of sheet-iron houses, than

to suppose that the laws of chemical combination were of one sort in the time of the coal-measures, and are of another now. The thing that has been will be; and we are to study savages and old nations to learn the laws that under new circumstances are working for good or ill in our own development.[16]

Summary of Tylor

Tylor's theory of magic will feature prominently in subsequent chapters, but for now let me underline only a few of its most salient aspects. First, Tylor's liberal universalism dominates his account of animistic religion and magical survivals. Throughout his discussion of these themes, Tylor is intent on stressing the commonality of humanity, and despite the racial and class presuppositions underlying his views, his primary ire is steadily directed against theorists who would deny the fundamental unity of humanity. Second, the very nature of survivals poses a major threat to Tylor's notion of social development. As he acknowledges, the laws governing this development often appear to be no law at all. He regularly acknowledges important qualifications and limits to his claims of human progress, and in turn, his claims repeatedly founder and deconstruct. Third, as various commentators have noted, Tylor's distinction between animistic religion and magic is extremely unstable. Stanley Tambiah points out that in Tylor's account animistic religion and magic both involve manipulation of the spiritual realm to achieve practical ends. Wouter Hanegraaff underscores Tylor's ambivalence in explaining various practices standing at the boundary between animism and magic (including fetishism and other more "animistic" forms of magic).[17] The distinction Tylor would draw between religion and magic remains ambiguous in significant respects, an ambiguity compounded as he considers the interlocking persistence of animism and magical survivals from the most primitive to the highest cultures.

Finally, the tradition of scholarly debates over magic that followed *Primitive Culture* surely proved Tylor correct in his assertion that the study of such a phenomenon would allow theorists to speak to modern culture—and intervene in its diatribes—while maintaining the illusion of discrete distance. Tylor's discussion of magic inaugurated a lengthy and contentious debate among social scientists and scholars of religion concerning the primordial relation between magic and religion. But despite its pretensions of dispassionate, antiquarian objectivity, this debate was animated by contemporary concerns that were often quite palpable.

Tylor's theory of animism as the origin of religion was extremely influential, effectively eclipsing earlier theories of fetishism following from the work of de Brosses and Comte and theories of nature mythology prevalent among philologists and theologians influenced by Max Müller. His evolutionary sequence of human development is reflected in such prominent subsequent texts as Freud's *Totem and Taboo* (1913). But the theory of animism was itself soon contested. Other theorists expounded rival versions of the earliest stages of human social—and religious—development, some contending that animism was too primitive to constitute actual religion, others proposing alternative theories of the origins of religion. And in many of these competing theories, magic took on even greater significance.[18] A number of important scholars proposed either that magic was the initial stage of religion (prior to the recognition of a split between body and soul central to animism), that magic constituted a stage of social evolution prior to the emergence of religion, or that magic and religion both originated from an amorphous sense of the supernatural. Other theorists used magic as an ancillary factor bolstering their particular versions of religion's origins or illustrating their perspectives on the social functions of religion.

The Despair of Magic

Tylor's theory of animism was most prominently challenged by his fellow English intellectualist James George Frazer. Frazer's *Golden Bough*, elaborating his theories of sacred kingship, appeared in its first edition in 1890 and grew to twelve volumes by the third edition (1906–15), culminating in a widely circulated 1922 abridgment by Frazer. From the second edition of 1900 forward, Frazer gave particular emphasis to the distinction between magic and religion and amplified his typology of various forms of magic. It was in this edition that Frazer first divided the broad category of sympathetic magic into two subspecies: homoeopathic or imitative magic (based on the operation of the law of similarity that "like produces like, or that an effect resembles its cause"), and contagious magic (based on the law of contact providing that objects that have been in contact continue to act on one another over distance).[19]

Frazer shares Tylor's view of magic as "occult science," but he argues for a far more rigid evolutionary notion of human development than Tylor. Frazer sees humanity moving through a fixed sequence of stages: magic, religion, then science. He argues that magic operates on an intellectual foundation fundamentally different from that of religion, the former depending on a view of nature as regular and mechanistic, the latter seeing nature as subject to personal intervention by divine beings (and therefore more variable). In this respect, magic shares its fundamental conception with modern science, which also understands nature to be orderly and uniform: "Wherever sympathetic magic occurs in its pure unadulterated form it assumes that in nature one event follows another necessarily and invariably without the intervention of any spiritual or personal agency." In magic, as in science, humanity relies on its own strength to deal with difficulties and dangers by manipulating the established natural order.[20]

Frazer defines religion as "a propitiation or conciliation of powers superior to man which are believed to direct and control the course of nature and of human life." Religion thus entails the twin assumptions that the course of nature is elastic or variable in fundamental respects and that we can induce powerful beings to alter the flow of events for our benefit. In these basic presuppositions, religion is directly opposed to magic and science, which share a view of nature as "rigid and invariable," unmoved "by persuasion and entreaty . . . by threats and intimidation." There is a radical conflict between magic and religion in their core principles, a conflict demonstrated in the hostility between the priest and the magician. The magician demonstrates a "haughty self-sufficiency" and an "arrogant demeanour toward the higher powers" that appear to the prostrate priest to be "an impious and blasphemous usurpation of prerogatives that belong to God alone."[21]

As Wouter Hanegraaf underscores, Frazer advocates a far more emphatic differentiation between religion and magic than does Tylor, largely by consigning all forms of animism to the realm of religion and thus denying the existence of any form of "animistic magic." This means both that Frazer faces great difficulties in reconciling his theory with the range of ethnographic materials before him and that he has particular difficulty explaining the cultural transition from magic to religion, since his theory requires such antipathy between the two practices. Frazer acknowledges that magic and religion often appear intermingled, reinforcing one another as magical mimicry and imitation become joined to religious prayer and sacrifice. There are many situations where the two are practiced simultaneously, as practitioners combine prayers and incantations with little recognition of the theoretical inconsistency in the mixture. This intellectual confusion appears not only among the primitive but even among more advanced peoples, including contemporary peasants ("the ignorant classes of modern Europe," who, it would appear from Frazer's examples, are largely Catholic). In these cases, Frazer asserts, we may assume that the original magical practices have been suffused with subsequent religious elements. Indeed, magic often invokes spirits, but when it does so in a properly magical manner, "it constrains or coerces instead of conciliating or propitiating them as religion would do."[22]

Despite these forms of intermingling, Frazer maintains that it is important to understand magic as predating religion. He argues, first, that the thought process behind magic, the misapplication of the association of ideas, is more elementary than the relatively complex notions behind religion. Further, he asserts, the priority of magic to religion is confirmed inductively by ethnographic research on aboriginal peoples (among whom magic is universal, while religion remains unknown). As he states it, "Roughly speaking, all men in Australia are magicians, but not one is a priest." Finally, beliefs in magic demonstrate uniformity and permanence, while religious systems show a great deal of variety and change, and this too establishes that magic is evolutionarily prior to religion. Thus we can conclude that all "civilised races" have passed through a magical stage on their evolutionary path: "Just as on the material side of

Stone age to analogous to Magic age!

Stone age : analogous to Magic

human culture there has everywhere been an Age of Stone, so on the intellectual side there has everywhere been an Age of Magic."[23]

Frazer explains the shift from magic to religion by suggesting that as the more intelligent members of a society come to recognize the futility of their system of magic, they are forced to recognize human powerlessness and begin to seek a more adequate account of nature. They arrive at a notion of superhuman beings directing the course of nature on whom human beings are absolutely dependent. The "primitive philosopher" comes humbly to beseech the mercy of these beings and to prostrate before them (though Frazer makes clear that this religious sensibility never actually permeates the duller minds). In this manner, just as primitive democracy is replaced by a magical king, so also the magician is eventually succeeded by the priest, and the magical king exchanges the practice of magic for priestly prayer and sacrifice. After religion takes hold, magic is increasingly seen as a vain and impious encroachment on the domain of the gods. Sacrifice and prayer become "the resource of the pious and enlightened portion of the community, while magic is the refuge of the superstitious and ignorant."[24]

As discussed in the following chapter, Frazer proceeds to explain how science emerges as the limits of religion are sounded. Indeed, Frazer's construction of human social development has the effect of configuring religion as a largely unfortunate detour on the progressive path from magic to science. In his scheme, the benighted, magical primitive is ultimately on far surer ground with respect to the regularity of the laws of nature than the priest who vainly and demeaningly grovels for divine aid.

Magic more like science

Primitive High Gods

Other theorists more sympathetic to religion than Frazer rejected the claim that magic was older than religion and asserted, more in keeping with the biblical account, that primitive forms of theism were the original stage of religion. Adolphe Pictet's *Les origines Indo-Européennes* (1859) had argued for the existence of instinctive primitive forms of monotheism among Aryans and other cultural groups that later developed into more complex forms of polytheism, and Max Müller had concurred that humanity shared an originary inclination to monotheism.[25] This theme was picked up by a number of scholars who proposed new theories of primitive high gods.

In his 1898 Gifford Lectures, C. P. Tiele, the Dutch Egyptologist and leading figure in the development of Continental comparative religion, rejects the view that magic should be seen as an original component of religious worship, arguing instead that magical practices are "morbid phenomena" that devolve later. Tiele concurs with Robertson Smith that religion originates not in fear of the gods but in reverence for them. Thus even in its earliest stage, worship

Tiele

involves veneration of the deity and never arises from magical rites aimed at coercion. Magic is shaped by dread and abhorrence of the unknown, while religion responds to the unknown "with earnest longing . . . with awe." Though magic regularly intrudes into religious rites, and "the frequent and absolutely correct repetition of every word and sound" supplants the meaning of the words or actions, true prayer must exist before its magical corruption: "We may be quite certain that the Lord's Prayer was not originally intended to be used as a mere senseless incantation, as was practically done by mediæval Christendom." Worship degenerates into magic either through a slackening of the religious life that creates an opening for the intrusion of formalism or through the "imbecile superstitious awe" of the multitudes. Thus, Tiele asserts, while Max Müller had called mythology "a disease of language," it is more justifiable to call sorcery "a disease of religion." The early prayers of the primitive worshiper operate by entreaty and importunity, but they are fundamentally distinct from magic because of their earnest longing and reverence; as humanity evolves, its "prayers will become purer and worthier, until they attain their climax in the perfect submission implied in, 'Not my will, but Thine be done!' "[26]

Tiele was not alone in pressing the notion of primitive monotheism. One of the most prominent defenses of the notion of a primitive high god came from Tylor's student Andrew Lang in his critique of the theories of origin put forth by Tylor and Frazer. Lang argues that "the earliest traceable form of religion was relatively high, and that it was inevitably lowered in tone during the process of social evolution." Contesting particularly Frazer's claim that religion evolves only as people discover that their magic does not work, Lang asserts that anthropological evidence demonstrates even in the earliest forms of "savage religion" the belief in a powerful creator god. In earliest religion, these powerful beings are not propitiated by prayer or sacrifice, and they are not seen as existing to supply temporal desires, but belief in these beings does serve to satisfy "speculative and moral needs." Lang thus asserts that this early "non-utilitarian belief in a deity" overturns the theory that "gods were invented, in the despair of magic, as powers out of whom something useful could be got."[27]

For Lang, this preanimistic stage of religious development includes both primitive high gods and magic. Lang classifies magic into two main types, the first based on the principle that "the part influences the whole" or on imitation (a form of magic that is wholly materialistic and operates by the power of suggestion), and the second using spells to "constrain spirits or gods to do the will of the magician" (and which, because of this invocation of the gods, can become intermingled with religion). With respect to this second type of magic, Lang states that if the intention is to constrain the divine by spells, "then the intention is magical and rebellious. Though the official priest of a savage god may use magic in his appeal to that deity, he is not a wizard. It is the unofficial practitioner who is a witch, just as the unqualified medical practitioner is a quack."[28] This theme that magic is defined largely by the social status of its practitioner will recur in a number of subsequent theorists.

The theory of primitive monotheism attracted influential advocates, including the Swedish scholar Nathan Söderblom and the Austrian Catholic priest Wilhelm Schmidt, perhaps the most ardent champion of the theory of primitive high gods. Schmidt is extremely skeptical of the notion that magic had any positive role in the emergence of human society. He rejects the claim that primitive society is built on a notion of *mana* or some other undifferentiated supernatural substratum, as well as the evolutionists' argument that religion develops out of an earlier prereligious stage of cultural development. Schmidt asserts instead that monotheism is to be found in the oldest stratum of human cultural history. It is a serious misreading of this earliest stage to see primitive monotheism "on an equal footing as to strength and value with mythology and magic, or blended with them both in an undifferentiated something, to say nothing of all three being 'contained in one another.'" Monotheism is originary, while mythology and magic first appear only in weak and inchoate forms (reaching fuller development only in later cultural periods).[29]

Schmidt explains that magic derives from the effort to explain unusual experiences, from the encounter with new or extraordinary events eliciting excitement and emotional gesticulation. The struggle to understand unusual phenomena leads to the formation of new associations among various events, actions, and forms of behavior. But prior to any concern with abnormal causation is a more basic concern with the normal: "We must begin with power, not impotence; with the positive, not the negative; with effort and efficiency in the search for a cause, and not with 'primeval stupidity.'" Magical understandings of causation cannot have developed prior to the normal, and it is erroneous to surmise even that in the earliest era the two notions of causation were intermingled in an undifferentiated state. Instead, Schmidt declares, religion has its roots in the more rudimentary and pervasive effort "to classify and find reasons for normal, ordinary things and events." The desire to understand the ordinary coupled with a fundamental human tendency to personify leads to the recognition of a Supreme Being. The idea of the Supreme Being is "but the natural result of the personal conception of the universal cause, which is the prevailing one among mankind at this stage." Thus, "among all peoples of the lowest stratum, and among them especially, we find clearly and definitely the recognition and worship of a personal and moral Supreme Being."[30]

In Schmidt's view, primitive people reason their way to the notion of a Supreme Being (by way of a conception of personal, universal causation), and they respond to this Being not with attempts at coercion but with prayers, submission, and obedience. Even in this initial stage, magic is thoroughly distinct from religion, and despite the claims of various theorists, the two phenomena are never successfully interwoven. Magical actions exist in primitive societies only as "unconnected and occasional phenomena, growing chiefly on the edges and in the dusty corners of their existence, like any other weed." It is "unthinkable that these two forces, so different in quality and in size, should have sprung from the same root."[31]

In contrast to primitive monotheism, magic is thoroughly impersonal and turns on the potency of material objects and their secret latent powers to achieve its ends. Magic obtains converts even in preanimistic days "wherever men, for one reason or another, wished to cast off reverence for and obedience to the Supreme Being and thrust him [sic] into the background." Magic spreads, Schmidt explains, because it is "necessarily more agreeable to man's self-confidence than prayer to another personality than his own." Passive magic (the magic of omens and signs) develops in societies of matrilineal agriculturalists, societies dominated by "the more passive and timid character of women," while new, more active forms of magic develop as the tools and weapons of totemistic culture increase human self-confidence. Finally, in light of this understanding of magic, Schmidt repudiates the suggestion that there is any element of magic in the Christian sacraments. In such rites as the Eucharist and baptism, we find only "a simple and perfectly natural symbolism" owing its efficacy not to impersonal magic but to "the operation of the will of God's omnipotent personality." Moreover, the Christian sacraments require a refined moral attitude on the part of the recipient that inoculates them against any element of magical efficacy.[32]

The role of magic in Schmidt's theory requires little amplification. Schmidt is eager to vindicate the primacy of a natural and universal human monotheism. But if monotheism is the original form of religion, Schmidt needs an explanation for the massive degeneration from this stage of originary truth and harmony. Magic is well suited to his purposes. This contaminating form of materialism intervenes as a temptation to human pridefulness and arrogance. Like many other early theories of comparative religion, Schmidt's argument is structured to vindicate the truth, and superiority, of Christianity. In such theories, magic could serve as a useful tool to account for the degeneration of religion from a primordial, monotheistic purity into the murky forms of polytheism and fetishism.

Mana and the Magico-Religious

A very different challenge to the theories of religious development set forth by Tylor and Frazer came from scholars who argued that magic and religion were better understood not as successive stages in a path of cultural evolution but as comparable subsets of a broader category of supernaturalism, such as the "magico-religious" or the realm of mana (the amorphous supernatural force formulated by R. H. Codrington in his 1891 study of the Melanesians). By the closing decade of the nineteenth century, various theorists began to seek the origin of magic and religion in impersonal notions of spiritual power.[33]

One of the earliest theorists to move in this direction was the American anthropologist John H. King. In *The Supernatural: Its Origin, Nature, and Evolution* (1892), King argues that early humanity develops the notion of magic from its observation of impersonal physical powers in the natural world (a process older than the animistic theory of spirits derived from mental processes). King argues that "primary man, like the infant of to-day," is powerless in the face of natural forces and responds to this powerlessness by developing various "expositions of luck" that associate good or bad effects with various "supernal protecting powers." The very first human sentiment, in fact, and the one that today predominates in the least evolved peoples is a sense of "luck, fear of uncanny evil or the desire for canny good." Faced with incomprehensible, uncanny occurrences in the natural world, human beings attribute meaning to these occurrences and seek to deploy them to their advantage. As King explains, magic develops from these feelings of good and bad luck and the effort to standardize the protective influence of chance. As he states, "Every form of faith is the worship of luck."[34]

In a secondary stage of development, a simple religion of charms and spells emerges in which "each individual conceives he can produce whatever result he wills by the uncanny resources he has learnt how to utilize." Over time a third stage takes shape as specialists develop, leading to "the religion of the medicine man, or magic." Finally, under the influence of medicine men and on the basis of new mental stimuli, new notions of a different form of supernal power, notions of ghosts, spirits, and gods, emerge. Thus, King argues, "the impersonal forms of supernal faith have preceded the personal"—magic precedes animism. There are ultimately two distinct forms of supernatural force: "the impersonal derived from the attributes of things" and "the personal whose origin is seen in mental action—human or animal." While these two forms of power may be combined or blended in practice, in theory and in origin they are thoroughly distinct. Yet, King concludes, education and mental development lead all these forms of belief, magical and religious, to wither: "Is it not an unquestioned fact that as man advances the supernal, like the mirage it represents, glides away in the distant mist, and the time will come when the last gleam of the subjective supernal entities will permeate the soul of man like the unrecallable tones of a long-forgotten melody?"[35]

During the closing years of the nineteenth century, theories seeking the roots of magic and religion in an undifferentiated and impersonal spiritual force became increasingly prevalent. R. R. Marett developed the notion of impersonal spiritual powers in a direction very different from King. Like King, Marett challenged the definitions of religion and theories of religious development proposed by Tylor and Frazer, but Marett invoked the notion of diffuse supernatural power not to underscore the ultimate folly of religion but to configure religion as a fundamental component of human identity.

In various essays written around the turn of the twentieth century and compiled in *The Threshold of Religion* (1909), Marett rejects Tylor's claim that animism is the earliest stage of religion, arguing instead that a developmental stage of "pre-animism" or "animatism" is at least as old as animism. He asserts that the earliest stage of religion found among contemporary savages is both wider and vaguer than Tylor's "belief in spiritual beings." This early stage of human development is fundamentally mysterious and amorphous: "For me the first chapter of the history of religion remains in large part indecipherable." In fact, Marett is reluctant to adopt a rigid set of terms that would imply a false precision in his theory. Instead, he uses a variety of terms to characterize the sphere of the magico-religious ("mysterious," "mystic," "occult," "supernatural," "sacred"), in order to reflect the amorphous nature of his topic. Concerning the term "magic," Marett points out that the student of rudimentary religion is prone to define it sharply, "since it gives him his natural counterfoil." Rejecting this tendency, Marett opts instead to follow the popular use of the word, "which is liberal to the point of laxity."[36]

Marett describes the earliest stage of human religious development as characterized by "numberless dimly-lighted impressions of the awful that owned no master in the shape of some one systematizing thought." In preanimistic *mana*, various life forces are seen in nature without the addition of a notion of spirit or soul. This early stage of religion should be understood not through conjecture concerning the thought processes of some individual primitive philosopher (as in the theories of Tylor and Frazer) but through recourse to more fundamental human emotional states, to communal religious feelings and experiences. As summarized in Marett's most famous declaration, "Savage religion is something not so much thought out as danced out." In response to the intellectualist efforts by Tylor and Frazer to differentiate religion and magic as distinct modes of thought, Marett argues that magic and religion both arise from "a common plasm of crude beliefs about the awful and occult," a fundamental emotional sense of supernaturalism or awe (of which animism is logically and chronologically a mere subset). An array of emotions percolate within this awe of the supernatural: fear, but also "wonder, admiration, interest, respect, even love perhaps." Magic and religion are thus essentially joined in the notion of *mana*.[37]

Marett rejects Frazer's theory that distinct forms of religious prayer are generated from the failure of magical spells, arguing instead that magic should be understood as "part and parcel of the 'god-stuff' out of which religion fashions itself," and that magical and religious components are naturally intermingled in the transition from spell to prayer. Indeed, he asserts, any firm distinction between spell and prayer is as artificial and illusory as a distinction between magic and religion. Marett also rejects the theory of primitive high gods advocated by Lang and Schmidt. Such high gods "must have had a psychological prehistory of some kind which, if known, would connect them with vaguer and ever vaguer shapes—phantoms teeming in the penumbra of the primitive mind, and dancing about the darkling rim of the tribal fire-circle."[38]

As Marett explains, Frazer claimed that religious humility was born of the failure of pseudoscientific magic and thus "in effect that humility is the differentia of religion." Marett rejects this abstract differentiation but concurs that over time the human response to the magico-religious is moralized and shaped by social customs into a chastened, humble mode, and humility thus becomes a distinguishing mark of religion. So even as Marett stresses the fundamental continuity of the magico-religious realm, he states that he prefers to use magic primarily as a designation for condemned practices ("something anti-social and wholly bad . . . wonder-working of a completely noxious kind"). It is useful, he says, to maintain the "normative" distinction between magic and religion in order to distinguish between "the bad and good kinds of supernaturalism."[39]

Later in his 1931–32 Gifford Lectures, Marett returns to the issue of where the line should be drawn between religion and magic. While, he explains, the principal function of religious practices is to stimulate hope, craven forms of fear can inspire "religion's disreputable counterpart, namely black magic or sorcery." The normal development of social life leads to affirmative forms of religion, while fear can lead to magic, one of life's "morbid by-products." "The ignorant savage" is particularly prone to magic, both because primitive religion is so thoroughly communal that it provides few mechanisms for the resolution of individual misfortune and because the savage is "mentally tender": "The shrewdest blow on his thick pate will hardly make him wince; whereas he is delicately sensitive to the slightest hint of mystery." Yet even in this effort to differentiate religion and magic, Marett acknowledges that the distinction is an artificial framework imposed on practices that are not so clearly delineated by their practitioners. Magic and religion are both part of "one organic development."[40]

In the early years of the twentieth century other prominent theorists joined Marett in the argument for a preanimistic stage of religious development. Freud concurred with Marett that a preanimistic stage preceded the development of animistic spirits and that this stage is best understood by recourse to human emotion. The German anthropologist K. T. Preuss also asserted that a preanimist era occurred at the dawn of human development. As Preuss explained, in this earliest stage of Urdummheit (primeval stupidity), human beings act on the basis of instinct and imitation of other living things, and their efforts at self-preservation constitute the early forms of magic, which evolve over time into religion and art. In Preuss's view, magic and other forms of purposeful action blend indistinguishably in this earliest stage of development.[41]

A widely influential reformulation of the notion of *mana* appeared in Marcel Mauss's major contribution to the theorization of magic, *Esquisse d'une théorie générale de la magie* (1902–3), written in collaboration with Henri Hubert. Mauss and Hubert seek to build their general theory of magic on a broad and inclusive view of the subject. As they explain, representatives of the British anthropological school (including Tylor, Frazer, Jevons, and Lang) focused too narrowly on forms of sympathetic magic and thus misunderstood magic as primarily a form of pre-science. Mauss and Hubert argue instead that an underlying sense of magical power or potential (such as *mana*) is the ultimate cause of all magical effects: "We shall find—at the basis of magic—a representation which is singularly ambiguous and quite outside our adult European understanding." Indeed, if the fundamental concept of magical power is ambiguous and paradoxical, the same can be said for their description of this magical force:

> A concept, encompassing the idea of magical power, was once found
> everywhere. It involves the notion of automatic efficacy. At the same
> time as being a material substance which can be localized, it is also
> spiritual. It works at a distance and also through a direct connexion,
> if not by contact. It is mobile and fluid without having to stir itself.
> It is impersonal and at the same time clothed in personal forms. It
> is divisible yet whole.

Despite this vague and paradoxical account of magical power, Mauss and Hubert argue that the basic concept has been a universal category of collective thinking. *Mana* constitutes the rudimentary data of both magic and religion, with both phenomena deriving from a common source in "affective social states."[42]

Mauss and Hubert differentiate religion and magic on the basis of the relation of each practice to the social group (an argument going back to Plato's *Laws*). Religious rites are "solemn, public, obligatory, regular," in essence a collective phenomenon with society itself serving as the principal actor in the ceremonial drama. In contrast, magical rites are characterized by prohibition: "It is the fact of prohibition itself which gives the spell its magical character." Magic and religion are usually performed by different agents in different locations. While religious rites are performed in full public view, "magical rites are commonly performed in woods, far away from dwelling places, at night or in shadowy corners, in the secret recesses of a house or at any rate in some out-of-the-way place." The magician is set apart from society, usually even from colleagues; characterized by isolation and secrecy, both the magical act and its practitioner are surrounded by a sense of mystery. Magic is "mysterious, isolated, furtive, scattered and broken up." Thus, in a statement soon to be amplified by Durkheim, Mauss and Hubert assert that magic is "anti-religious," taking place outside of organized cults, "always considered unauthorized, abnormal and, at the very least, not highly estimable." In contrast, religion is "always predictable, prescribed and official," always cultic. If a magic cult does appear, it is a secondary development always modeled on the lines of religious cults and always in tension with the essential nature of magic.[43]

On this basis, Mauss and Hubert define as magical "any rite which does not play a part in organized cults—it is private, secret, mysterious and approaches the limit of a prohibited rite." Magical rites are practiced by individuals on the margins of the social group acting on the basis of individual interests (either their own or others'). In these rites, "all movements are the opposite of normal ones, particularly those performed at religious ceremonies. . . . materials are preferably unclean and the practices obscene. The whole thing is bizarre, involving artifice and unnatural features." Thus, magic is fundamentally antisocial, with its practitioners serving narrowly individualistic interests rather than the interests of the social group. As they conclude:

> Magic is a living mass, formless and inorganic. . . . Magical life is not compartmentalized like religion. It has not led to the growth of any autonomous institutions like sacrifice and priesthood. . . . Magic is everywhere in a diffuse state. In each case we are confronted with a whole, which, as we have pointed out, is more than the sum of its parts. In this way we have shown that magic as a whole has an objective reality—that it is *some* thing.[44]

Throughout this elaborate (and often convoluted) theory of magic, we see an insistence that magic must be identified as a distinct phenomenon, that it must be reified as a discrete entity. But the more that Mauss and Hubert attempt to describe this formless and diffuse phenomenon, the more amorphous it becomes. Their only firm conclusion seems to be that the vague notion of magical power stands disreputably on the social periphery, assuming many ambiguous forms, but always constituting a threat to the social order.

Marett's stress on a fundamental "magico-religious" plasm and on the theory of *mana* remained quite influential in subsequent generations. One of the most notable American reformulations of this notion came in 1924 from the anthropologist Robert Lowie. Rejecting the intellectualist view that religion emerges in response to abstract intellectual questions and needs, Lowie seeks instead for a definition of religion that follows Marett (and other theorists such as Nathan Söderblom and Alexander Goldenweiser) in stressing the dichotomy of human experience into the ordinary and the extraordinary. The "ordinary" is characterized by normal experience, rationality, and empirical cause-and-effect relations. But beyond the realm of the ordinary, "everywhere there is, in addition to such practical rationalism, a sense of something transcending the expected or natural, a sense of the Extraordinary, Mysterious, or Supernatural." This sense of the extraordinary is, in Lowie's view, the proper realm of religion.[45]

Lowie rejects Frazer's claim that an era of magic precedes religion, concluding that even "among very rude peoples" magic and religion always coexist.

Magic and religion must both be seen as fundamental and ancient components of the human worldview, sharing the same basic psychological character. There is no basis for a sharp differentiation between the two, since both partake in the larger whole of the extraordinary, "Supernaturalism" broadly defined. And just as Lowie rejects Frazer's basic distinction between magic and religion, he also opposes the sociological claim from Mauss and Durkheim that magic stands outside the organized social structures characterizing religion. Both magic and religion involve the acceptance of received social beliefs and observances, as well as the potential for improvisation with those traditions, so again no abstract differentiation is possible.[46]

Through all these notions of *mana* and the "magico-religious," various theorists argue that magic and religion partake of a common origin, that both participate in some overarching sense of the supernatural or extraordinary. In this manner, neither is given an evolutionary priority, and both are seen as fundamental aspects of human culture. Yet while the various theorists of this "magico-religious" realm share the assumption that magic and religion come from a common source, they differ in the conclusions this assumption moves them toward. Some stress the inherent commonality of the two phenomena, while others formulate various distinctions between them located in some subsequent aspect or process of social development. And persisting through all these competing theories of magic is an abiding concern with explaining the ultimate nature of religion itself.

Totemism and Clan Gods

Rather than relying merely on a generalized notion of the magico-religious as the source of religion, a large number of theorists in the late nineteenth and early twentieth centuries sought the origin of religion in the notion of totemism or clan gods. In these theories, religion is seen as evolving from a stage in which social groups worship various types of totemic creatures (animals, birds, plants) and understand the group as being descended from the totemic creature. Magic played a central role in the theories of totemism.

In his *Lectures on the Religion of the Semites* (1889), W. Robertson Smith developed the work of his teacher, J. F. M'Lennan, to identify totemism as the originary form of religion. In explaining his theory, Robertson Smith uses magic as a foil enabling him to demonstrate the distinctive nature of totemic religion. He rejects the ancient claim that religion is born of fear or terror, arguing instead that it arises from reverence for the benevolent totemic god. It is magic, Smith claims, that is born of fear. In times of great social distress, when human beings feel powerless, "magical superstitions based on mere terror, or rites designed to conciliate alien gods, invade the sphere of tribal or national religion." Magical superstition is built on the notion of mysterious hostile powers, unlike totemic religion based on the notion of a friendly and benevolent local deity. In this respect, magic is "the barrenest of all aberrations of the savage imagination," standing as an impediment to progress and industry. Even in antiquity private magical superstitions are regarded as offenses against the morals and norms of the social group. In times of stability, "the religion of the tribe or state has nothing in common with the private and foreign superstitions or magical rites that savage terror may dictate to the individual." Religion is thus in its essence "a relation of all the members of a community to a power that has the good of the community at heart, and protects its law and moral order."[47] I will return to this theme of the individualism underlying magic, but note here the way in which magic provides a useful scapegoat for a whole range of ill effects commonly ascribed to religion by Enlightenment thought. Through the use of a magical foil, Smith is able to segregate those ills in order to formulate a positive social role for religion.

Many scholars quickly agreed that totemic systems were prior in human cultural development to Tylor's notion of animism. The enthusiasm for totemism reaffirmed magic's central role in debates over religion's origins, as scholars argued that totemism and magic both preceded animism. The concept of totemism framed questions of the definition of magic and the functions of religion in a fundamentally sociological perspective. For example, in his widely circulated *Introduction to the History of Religion* (1896), Frank Byron Jevons argues that religion emerges through the development of social relationships with a clan god who arises and functions in a manner comparable to the totem. Jevons rejects the claim that magic and religion have a common origin or that religion develops out of magic, asserting instead that there are always essential differences between the two. Magic always appears as "a degradation or relapse in the evolution of religion."[48] In fact, in Jevons's view, magic can emerge only when religion is in place to provide its foil.

Jevons argues that the initial human concept of the supernatural takes shape as larger natural forces overturn human expectations, and thus intimate the existence of powers qualitatively different from any type of human capacity. These supernatural powers establish the proper bounds of human power, and only when those limits have taken root can magic emerge in the effort to trespass them. As Jevons explains, the earliest attempts to manipulate nature by means of sympathetic magic are actually based on poorly formed conceptions of the limits of human power. While some social groups come to recognize and accept these limits, their less civilized neighbors continue to attempt to manipulate phenomena in improper ways. The notion of magic arises from the juxtaposition of "the more and the less enlightened views of what man can effect"; more developed groups come to consider the machinations of the less enlightened as magical. The "pretension" that a human being can wield supernatural power becomes an impious offense to the evolving sense of the supernatural.[49]

In Jevons's view, religion is based on the relationship with the clan god, developing as spirits are invoked to augment the art of the priest or leader for the good of the community. In contrast, magic commonly seeks the aid of spiritual beings other than the god of the community, and it assumes clearer definition as practices are recognized as antisocial or injurious. In these situations, the objectives of magical practice are seen as offending the god of the community and are condemned by religion and morality. The proper distinction between magic and religion thus lies not in the means that are used but in the objectives of the practitioner. Magic is fundamentally malign at its core. Religion is always opposed to magic, and it is an error, Jevons asserts, for Frazer or other theorists to suppose that magic is somehow prior to religion. Magic can emerge only when the social bonds cemented by religion are in place: "There can be no magic save where there is religion to be opposed to it."[50]

By far the most prominent amplification of this sociological perspective on magic came in Émile Durkheim's *Elementary Forms of the Religious Life* (1912), in which Durkheim elaborates his theory of totemism. Durkheim begins by formulating what he identifies as the core principle of religion, the classification of the world between the sacred and the profane. Yet since religion and magic both appear to involve the sacred, Durkheim faces the additional task of distinguishing between these two phenomena; his goal, he asserts, is "to limit our researches to religion, and to stop at the point where magic commences." Like religion, magic consists of beliefs and rites, myths and dogmas. And magic often invokes the very beings and forces that religion addresses. Yet while it is tempting to see the two phenomena as so intermingled as to be indistinguishable, the fundamental difference between the two is demonstrated by their marked mutual repugnance. Magic remains "more elementary" than religion, because with its "technical and utilitarian" focus, "it does not waste its time in pure speculation." Further, "magic takes a sort of professional pleasure in profaning holy things."[51]

Durkheim finds the appropriate line of demarcation between religion and magic in the work of Robertson Smith and Mauss and Hubert. Smith had argued that when religion becomes too fully a matter of the clan or the state, people turn to magical superstitions for the resolution of their personal concerns. Public religion fails to meet every personal need, especially those needs that run counter to the interests of the community. In these situations, people turn to magical rites to invoke the assistance of demonic powers. These magical practices lie outside of religion, and since individuals are seen as having no right to enter into private relations with supernatural powers, in well-organized communities these practices are regarded as illicit. In contrast, as Smith had stated, true religious worship expresses "the idea that man does not live for himself only but for his fellows, and that this partnership of social interests is the sphere over which the gods preside and on which they bestow their assured blessing."[52]

Durkheim concurs in this assessment. Religious beliefs, he explains, be-

Magic as individualistic

long to the group and foster its unity. The very word "Church" denotes a society sharing beliefs about the sacred and the profane and translating those beliefs into common practices. Magic, on the other hand, fails to bind together its adherents or to unite them into a common life. In Durkheim's famous formulation, "There is no Church of magic." The magician never establishes the social bonds that would create a moral community with those who seek out magic; the magician has only a clientele. This, then, is the fundamental difference between magic and religion: "A Church . . . is a moral community formed by all the believers in a single faith. . . . magic lacks any such community." In this light, Durkheim defines religion as "a unified system of beliefs and practices relative to sacred things, that is to say, things set apart and forbidden," a system of beliefs and practices that unites its followers into a single community. Still, even with this definition in place, Durkheim acknowledges that there is no clear "break of continuity" between religion and magic: "The frontiers between the two domains are frequently uncertain."[53]

Durkheim objects to Frazer's analysis of sympathetic magic. Rather than seeing magical action as rudimentary science unrelated to religion, Durkheim argues that it is essential to understand magic as derived from religion. Religion is not born of the failure of magic; instead, it is only under the influence of religious ideas and rituals that magic takes shape. Religious principles are applied through secondary processes of extension to noncultic social relations in the practice of magic. Durkheim hesitates to claim that religion is chronologically prior to magic, but he affirms that the two systems "have a relation of definitive derivation between them." Thus the axioms of magic can only be understood in the context of their religious origins. As he asserts, "The faith inspired by magic is only a particular case of religious faith in general. . . . it is itself the product, at least indirectly, of a collective effervescence." In this view, sympathetic rites should be understood both as occurring within religion and as moving from religion into magic. Magic is permeated with conceptions and forces adapted from religion, because "it was born of religion." Durkheim concludes that Mauss and Hubert were correct in their assessment that magic should be understood as "nothing more nor less than crude industry based on incomplete science."[54]

Many scholars soon challenged central components of Durkheim's theory of totemism, particularly his claims that religion involved the worship of the social group and that magic was fundamentally antisocial.[55] But the concept of totemism proved extremely influential, particularly in the sociological analysis of the origins of religion. In various theories of totemism, magic plays a distinctive role in representing the interests of the individual in relation to the interests of the social group. While religion is communally adaptive, both expressing and meeting the collective needs of a social group, magic stands in opposition to those collective interests. It is individualistic and self-seeking. It stands on the margins of society as a mysterious and malignant forum for antisocial appetites. In this frame, the relation between magic and religion reflects the tensions between the individual and the collective.

Decline of the Search for Origins

Through the early decades of the twentieth century, the effort to seek the evolutionary origins of religion faltered. Georg Wobbermin argued in *Das Wesen der Religion* (1921) against the search for origins, claiming, first, that the questions of origin and essence were distinct and, further, that it was impossible to uncover information about prehistoric human life. As he pointedly stated, "The method of trying to grasp the nature of religion by tracing it to its origin means making that which is poorly known the basis for understanding that which is better known." By the 1920s and 1930s, increasing numbers of social scientists and scholars of religion were actively disclaiming the effort to determine the origins of religion and to map religious evolution, opting instead for new modes of analyzing the nature and function of religion.[56] Yet while the overt search for religion's origins fell into disfavor, many fundamental suppositions of the social evolutionary schema were firmly entrenched, particularly the notion that magic was characteristic of primitive peoples.

One of the primary effects of the early theories of religious evolution was to focus the scholarly analysis of magic on primitive societies. Thus, for example, while the sociologist Hutton Webster begins his 1948 text on magic by announcing that his study is aimed to encompass the entire subject, he quickly restricts his discussion to magic as found "among so-called preliterate peoples." Webster explains that the fundamental principles of magic are particularly "well exemplified in rude communities" and that the magic of more developed cultures is merely redundant of that found among the primitive.[57]

Earlier forms of evolutionary thought have continued to resound in the common association of magic with nonmodern culture and in the supposition that magical thinking declines as one comes closer to home. C. J. Bleeker provides a clear assertion of the ways in which the perspective of social evolution continued to shape the analysis of religion through the twentieth century even in the absence of overt evolutionary theory. As he stated in 1963:

> A gradual change in the trend of religious thinking can be noticed
> and thereby an increase of the discerning power. The magical world
> conception has given way to a more realistic outlook. The people of
> Antiquity for instance believed in the interrelation and in the mu-
> tual participation of religious symbols and ideas in a way which we
> hardly understand any longer. . . . Modern man has a clearer view of
> what is genuinely religious, is more able to distinguish the religious
> from the secular, and makes higher demands as to the quality of re-
> ligion.[58]

In Bleeker's confident assessment, modernity, the "genuinely religious," and the secular all go hand in hand. We learn the nature of one by knowing the nature of the others. And all three share an aversion to magical thinking. This association of magic with primitive antiquity has functioned as a type of cultural common sense among Western scholars.

Recent Accounts of Religious Development

As new forms of evolutionary thought have emerged within the study of religion in recent decades, magic has remained linked to early stages of cultural and religious development. In his influential essay "Religious Evolution" (1964), Robert Bellah evaluates religious systems based on their proximity to the norms of Christian monotheism and post-Christian modernism. While Bellah makes little overt reference to magic in his evolutionary scheme, his description of lower forms of religion is filled with echoes of earlier analyses of primitive magic. (Primitive religion is characterized by "identification, 'participation,' acting out," while historic religion is "transcendental and universalistic," built upon the notion of "a responsible self, a core self, or a true self.")[59] These links are made even more explicitly by the philosopher of religion John Hick, who has recently amplified Bellah's basic evolutionary scheme.

In his *Interpretation of Religion* (1989), Hick follows Bellah in dividing religious systems into pre-axial religions aimed at providing stability and post-axial world faiths concerned "with salvation/liberation as the realisation of a limitlessly better possibility." While disclaiming that this scheme should be seen as a clear-cut evolutionary sequence or that "archaic" religions should be stigmatized, Hick finds his prime examples of pre-axial religion among "the 'primal,' 'pre-literate,' or 'primitive' religions of stone-age humanity." In Hick's view, pre-axial religions are inherently conservative, aimed at preserving a social and cosmic status quo. These systems serve to hold the social group together within a common worldview and to reinforce the community's claim on the loyalties of its members. They thwart the development of personal autonomy and intellectual independence, and their concerns are not socially transformative in any respect but rather "conservative, a defense against chaos, meaninglessness and the breakdown of social cohesion." These "pre-literate forms of archaic religion" are filled with magical practices in which the supernatural interpenetrates the natural world.[60]

As Hick explains, rational criticism and science emerge only in axial religions (particularly those of ancient Greece, India, and China). In modern Western forms of rationalism, the "relation to the Real" is maintained by "a radical scepticism," while "in the archaic world the human mind was protected from an overwhelmingly direct presence of the Real by religion itself, functioning as a system for filtering out the infinite divine reality and reducing it to forms that could be coped with."[61] Modern rationality and skepticism facilitate a more developed relation to the Real, while the magical practices of more archaic religions serve as buffers interposed between humanity and ultimate reality. In the following chapter, I will return to this theme of the superior realism of modern religion, and in the final chapter, I will consider the claim of magic's fundamental conservatism. But for our purposes now, it is most relevant to note the ways in which Hick demonstrates the persistence of the traditional evolutionary link between magic and nonmodern culture. The magic of pre-axial religion is fundamentally incompatible with the rationality of the modern axial world.

Throughout these debates over the origin and development of religion, magic serves as a remarkably flexible rhetorical tool. Some scholars such as Frazer or King place magic at the roots of religion as a part of their broader attacks on religion. Religion can be portrayed as having a disreputable lineage or as being even more fundamentally misguided than primitive magical thought. Other theorists deploy an analytical distinction between religion and magic in order to establish and maintain the purity of religion. In these theories, magic is constructed as the foil against which religion is legitimated or even as the cause of religion's degeneration from a state of original monotheistic purity. Still other theorists use the analysis of magic as an opportunity to amplify and clarify their accounts of the various social functions served by religion. Throughout these theories of religious evolution, debates over magic served as an important site at which to articulate and contest the nature and role of religion in human society. As Tylor himself pointed out, theories concerning distant and ancient peoples provided a useful screen onto which scholars could project more contentious contemporary concerns.

As we turn to consider subsequent theoretical debates concerning the nature of religion, it is important to underscore the pervasive and persistent stigmatizing of magic in these theories. As Donate Pahnke has asserted, despite the efforts by various contemporary scholars of religion to disclaim the excesses of earlier theories of religious evolution, and despite the repeated recognition by various scholars of important commonalities between religion and magic, the traditional evaluative connotations of the terms remain secure in popular and academic discourses. As Pahnke concludes, "It is at least strongly to be doubted that any suggestion of renaming the science of religion as 'science of magic' would have any prospect of succeeding."[62]

The Essence of Religion

While efforts to uncover the origins of religion or to chart a concrete, unilinear path for its development have largely subsided, magic has continued to play an active role in scholarly attempts to define the nature and function of religion. Already in the theories discussed here, many of the major themes informing subsequent approaches have been sounded. Throughout the twentieth century in various academic disciplines and modes of analysis, magic served as an important tool in efforts to demarcate the limits of religion. The dominant theoretical formulations of magic articulated distinctive views of the nature of human identity and the proper reach of human agency, and they emphatically prescribed a notion of religious piety thoroughly informed by post-Reformation and post-Enlightenment rationalism.

A number of important scholars have followed Marett in rejecting the possibility that a clear boundary can be formulated between religion and magic. Theorists regularly acknowledge that the two phenomena seem so intertwined as to be indistinguishable. Others point out that the effort to formulate this boundary is thwarted by the ways in which the two phenomena appear quite often to transmute. As Alban Widgery put it in 1922, practitioners of magic sometimes abandon their addiction in favor of religion, and at the same time religious practices can easily mutate into magical forms.[63] These phenomena are so mobile and amorphous that it seems impossible to formulate a stable differentiation between them.

Yet also like Marett, despite the disclaimers that there can be no stable boundary between religion and magic, many of these very theorists then proceed to offer various distinctions between the two. For example, in his *Religion among the Primitives* (1951), William Goode begins by listing the important commonalities between religion and magic (both are concerned with "the nonempirical," both are "pervasively symbolic," both deal with nonhuman sacred forces, both involve ritual systems directed toward entities who are dealt with as though they had human mentalities, and so on), and concludes that it is impossible to draw a clear boundary between the two phenomena. But despite these similarities, Goode asserts that the traditional anthropological distinction between religion and magic has "gradually assumed conceptual clarity," and he proceeds to outline various characteristics that distinguish magic from religion and to formulate a continuum with magic and religion set at opposite poles.[64]

Goode is far from alone in continuing to seek some analytical differentiation between magic and religion. The aspect of this enterprise most relevant for our purposes here is the way in which this attempt to distinguish magic from religion provides scholars such a ready opportunity to reiterate modern norms for religion. As will become clear in what follows, the traditional efforts to distinguish magic from religion in the social sciences and religious studies have been thoroughly informed by post-Reformation views concerning the proper bounds of human agency and the proper position of religion within the social order. In this light, let us examine some of the most pervasive distinctions scholars have drawn between the two phenomena. In each case, religious values are defined in contrast to the fallacies of magic.

Transcendence

One of the central distinctions drawn between religion and magic in the scholarly literature involves their respective objects. Religion is configured as involving matters that are, in one or another sense, "ultimate," "transcendent," or "nonempirical." In contrast, magic is directed toward lesser, more immediate goals. The classic anthropological formulation of this claim is found in the work of Bronislaw Malinowski.

In his effort to account for the function that religion serves in human society, Malinowski asserts that a religious rite "is not a means to an end but an end in itself." The purpose of the rite resides solely within the action itself, not in any subsequent event or consequence. Malinowski points to the broad significance of tribal religious rituals (such as initiation) as creative and socially transformative: "The ceremony and its purpose are one. . . . the end is realized in the very consummation of the act." These ritual practices serve largely to create mental and social habits of great value to the group. The main sources of religious behavior are to be found in the strong interpersonal attachments among members of the group and in the ultimate fact of death; religion thus centers on "wider issues of personal and social integration than those arising out of the practical necessity of hazardous action and dangerous enterprise." Religious rites provide "mental integrity" to the individual and social reintegration to the group in times of crisis, thus assuring "the victory of tradition and culture."[65] In this view, religious rituals are undertaken for no reason other than the psychic and social integration the practices themselves create.

One of the more striking aspects of Malinowski's attempt here to explain the function of religion is the amorphous circularity of his claim. Religious rituals are defined in contrast to the normal flow of human purposive behavior, but religion itself still serves important purposes. Those purposes are to be identified only within the rituals themselves, but they have great value throughout the social system. Religious rituals are defined as ends in themselves, and rituals that are ends in themselves are defined as religious. Malinowski's claim here is extremely vague, and without greater clarity concerning the nature of these religious rites, his account of the function of religion would falter. Yet Malinowski is able to add content to his claims concerning religion by means of a time-honored strategy: he contrasts religion to magic. By explaining what religion is not, Malinowski bolsters his account of the nature of religion.

Unlike religion, Malinowski explains, magic is carried out as a means to an end with a specific practical purpose in view. Both religion and magic function as responses to situations of emotional stress, but magic is "a practical art consisting of acts which are only means to a definite end," an art with "limited, circumscribed technique." Religion opens onto "a whole supernatural world of faith: the pantheon of spirits and demons, the benevolent powers of totem, guardian spirit, tribal all-father, the vision of the future life," while the field of magic is "much more practical, definite, and circumscribed." The mythology of religion is more complex, varied, and creative than that of magic, and in primitive conditions religion is actually more democratic: "everyone takes an active and equivalent part" in religious rituals, while magic remains the province of specialists. Religion addresses the most fateful and significant events and a complex world of supernatural forces and beings. It fosters "all valuable mental attitudes, such as reverence for tradition, harmony with environment, courage and confidence in the struggle with difficulties and at the prospect of death." Thus, religion "creates values and attains ends directly, whereas magic consists of acts which have a practical utilitarian value and are effective only as a means to an end."[66]

With this contrast in place between transcendent religion and pragmatic magic, Malinowski elaborates on the various functions of magic. Magic offers a set of practical techniques that address situations where human knowledge or power is limited or inadequate. It demonstrates a certain functional or pragmatic truth, since it responds to individual and social psychological needs "under conditions where the human organism is disintegrated." Magic "enables man to carry out with confidence his important tasks, to maintain his poise and his mental integrity" in the face of limited capacity. The function of magic is thus "to ritualize man's optimism, to enhance his faith in the victory of hope over fear." We find in magic "the embodiment of the sublime folly of hope, which has yet been the best school of man's character."[67]

Numerous objections have been raised to Malinowski's distinction between religion and magic. Many scholars point out that his account of religion discounts the more pragmatic aspects of religious behavior; others reject his basic functionalist analysis of the two phenomena (pointing out, for example, that magic itself can cause rather than allay fear).[68] Perhaps the most obvious objection lies in the illusory differentiation Malinowski draws between ends and means—even within his own account both religion and magic seem to serve various utilitarian purposes (just as they both seem to foster "mental integrity" in comparable ways). Yet a large number of important theorists echo Malinowski in this contrast between the pragmatic focus of magic and the transcendent nature of religion.

So, for example, the sociologist J. Milton Yinger concurs with Malinowski that the essential difference between magic and religion is that magic is concerned with transitory objectives while religion is focused on ultimate concerns. As Yinger states, "Religion is concerned with salvation, with death, with the meaning of existence. Magic is concerned with immediate goals—control of the weather, assurance of a good crop, victory in battle, good health." Keith Thomas echoes this assertion in his claim that Christianity is characterized by "elaborate self-fulfilling rituals" that offer "a symbolism of human experience whose social and psychological relevance far transcended the limited and specific contexts in which its more purely magical aspects were invoked." Early modern popular magic, Thomas argues, was merely "a collection of miscellaneous recipes, not a comprehensive body of doctrine." Many other scholars have repeated the claim that religion focuses on the cosmic or the transcendent, while magic addresses only concrete or practical worldly objectives such as wealth, health, or power (in the words of historian Jean Delumeau, "the lower needs of domestic life").[69] In this view, religion is focused on transcendent matters through the use of self-fulfilling practices and rituals. Magic is attuned only to immediate and specific practical goals.

In *The Sociology of Religion* (1922), Max Weber frames this theme as one of intellectual systematization. Weber's initial elaboration of the difference between religion and magic comes in his consideration of the roles of the priest and the magician. One of the distinguishing features of a priesthood lies in the formation of a continuously operating cultic enterprise. With the development of a specialized priesthood, religion becomes characterized by "an ever-broadening rational systematization of the god concept and of the thinking concerning the possible relationships of man to the divine." In contrast, magic maintains a concern with "the original, practical and calculating rationalism." Thus, while religion expands in its focus and content, magic remains largely adaptive, seeking only to satisfy immediate and provisional goals. Weber offers various accounts of how magic comes to be defined as powerful cultic religions are established. He states, for example, that the historical development of a differentiation between religion and sorcery frequently occurred "when a secular or priestly power suppressed a cult in favor of a new religion, with the older gods continuing to live on as demons." As the process of religious rationalization proceeds, the significance of religious behavior is found less in worldly, economic advantages, and more in "otherworldly non-economic goals." This reduces the scope of religious irrationalism in ways that allow an unbridled immersion into worldly labor. The peak of this process of rationalization of the concept of the divine appears in the Protestant repudiation of all Catholic sacramental magical means of salvation: "Only ascetic Protestantism completely eliminated magic and the supernatural quest for salvation, of which the highest form was intellectual, contemplative illumination. It alone created the religious motivation for seeking salvation primarily through immersion in one's worldly vocation."[70] While magic remains focused on concrete and immediate needs, religious cults foster rational systematization and abstract intellection. This systematic elaboration of rationalized, transcendent, otherworldly concerns has the effect of cordoning the supernatural away from the world of mundane human needs, but this cordoning away of the supernatural ultimately facilitates the rational manipulation of the material world.

More recently sociologists William Sims Bainbridge and Rodney Stark have reiterated the claim that "magic does not concern itself with the meaning of the universe, but only with the manipulation of the universe for specific goals." As they explain, while religion deals in the most general compensators (beliefs that rewards will be obtained in ways that cannot be directly tested), magic deals in more specific compensators. Thus religion is relatively "immune to disconfirmation," while magic is more prone to disproof because it is more subject to empirical verification. This difference offers Bainbridge and Stark an explanation for the tendency of religion to become socially differentiated from magic and leads them to a further bold conclusion: "In our judgment, faiths suited to the future will contain no magic, only religion. This will not, of course, allow them to escape in the long run the forces of secularization—all successful faiths are fated to be tamed by the world. But faiths containing only religion will be immune to scientific attack and thus will avoid the accelerated secularization in effect during recent centuries." Religions cleansed of magic will have greater immunity from rational scrutiny, presumably because their claims are so abstract and otherworldly as to be devoid of significant testable content.[71]

Bryan Wilson has clearly elaborated the links between transcendent religion and secularization. Wilson concurs with the scholarly consensus that religion offers benefits that are "spiritual, general, and abstract," while magic "posits specific consequences and effects for particular action" and "offers more particular reassurance than that offered by the higher religions." This distinction raises problems for higher religions, Wilson points out, since even they must find ways to deliver reassurance in a local manner. The very processes of constraining local cults and magical practices and of developing and centralizing the intellectual and organizational structures of religion are "gestures in the direction of secularization." Thus, Wilson states:

> As doctrine and structure become centralized, hierarchized, and increasingly well co-ordinated, so religious power is conceived to operate essentially in formalized ways and through specified channels. Immanentism gives way to transcendentalism, which leads to a further removal of supernatural power from the lives of ordinary men in everyday situations. The world is disenchanted. . . . Local religion—now designated by urban man as the religion of the heath (heathen) or the village (pagan), and as "superstition"—demanded that wherever official religion existed, it should compromise and temporize with local need. When, however, men ceased to live in communities, when their lives, or the lives of the vast majority, were lived out in impersonal and functionally specialized contexts, so the locale in which religion had flourished best ceased to provide it with hospitality. However contemptuous the priestly or intellectual classes might become about the religion of local communities, it was in these communities that the demand for religion had been most sustained, no matter that they were disposed to eclecticism, syncretism, and superstition. It is to the passing of natural communities, in

which people lived virtually all their lives and undertook most of their activities, that we may look for a significant part of the explanation of secularization, when that term is used to refer to the transformation of religious consciousness.[72]

Wilson gives this issue of the transcendent nature of religion a decidedly geographic turn. Systematized and abstract urban religion is contrasted to the superstitious practices of the heath and the village. As he contrasts older immanent forms of magical and religious practice with newer transcendentalism that removes supernatural power from the ordinary world, Wilson points toward the ways in which heightened transcendentalism leads toward a disenchantment of the world and increasing secularization. There are important questions to be raised about Wilson's formulation, both in the ways his analysis turns on a questionable binarism between "natural communities" and secularized urbanism and in the ways his understanding of the nature and function of religion seems to turn on the very logic of secularization. But his fundamental claim that valorizing the transcendent aspects of religion at the expense of immanent concerns leads toward disenchantment and secularization echoes the most persuasive aspects of Weber's analysis.

Given these links between religious transcendentalism and the logic of modern secularism, it is striking to see the moralistic tone with which many scholars reiterate this distinction between religion and magic. Mircea Eliade asserts that while magic is involved only in the effort to achieve concrete and mundane objectives, religion is properly focused on the more lofty worship and adoration of supernatural beings. In a similar vein, Gregory Bateson states that magic is "a degenerate 'applied' form" of religion or science. Bateson believes that "in their primitive state" rituals such as rain dances or totemic rites are "true religious ceremonials," "ritual statements of unity, involving all the participants in an integration with the meteorological cycle or with the ecology of totemic animals." But from these pure beginnings, "the pathway of deterioration from religion to magic" is opened when the participants move from this "statement of integration in some often dimly recognized whole" toward "an appetitive stance": "[The practitioner] sees his own ritual as a piece of purposive magic to make the rain come or to promote the fertility of the totemic animal or to achieve some other goal. The criterion that distinguishes magic from religion is, in fact, *purpose* and especially some extrovert purpose." Bateson contrasts the degenerate extrovert purpose of magic with a properly religious "introvert purpose, the desire to change the self." Rejecting the supposition of theorists such as Frazer that religion is somehow a product of magic, Bateson concludes that magic is clearly "a product of decadence from religion." Religion involves lofty purposes such as unity, integration with the cosmos, "change of the self"; magic arises only with the emergence of an "appetite" for more mundane concerns such as rain or fertility.[73]

binaries [handwritten marginal note]

This theme recurs throughout the scholarly literature on magic, and in each version the claim turns on the reiteration of basic binaries between the immediate and the ultimate, the mundane and the metaphysical, the immanent and the transcendent. Given the inherent instability of such dualistic schemes, it requires enormous intellectual ingenuity to maintain these antinomies. The binaries inevitably begin to falter and deconstruct, particularly since the notion of transcendence is so dependent for its meaning on contrast with the mundane. In each of these variations, the worldly concerns consigned to the realm of magic seem to reinsinuate themselves in the transcendent religious realm. The most lofty purposes eventually offer a pragmatic payoff.

But even disregarding these inevitable tendencies toward deconstruction, the effort to impose a sharp bifurcation between the transcendent and the immanent turns on a strikingly narrow view of the objectives of religion. In his *Magic of Ritual* (1991), Tom Driver pointedly rejects Bateson's claim that magic is a degenerate form of religion because it seeks to accomplish particular purposes. Driver argues that this "vaguely Neoplatonic point of view" implies that "the application of knowledge for practical ends is a corruption." In contrast, Driver asserts that "the genius of religion" is always transformation, and in this transformation, "change in the self and change in the outer world are bound into an intimate connection." Thus, Driver asserts:

> It would be a poor anthropology, in the theological as well as the social-scientific sense, to categorize all desire as bad or corrupting. The better moral and theological question is not *whether* there is appetite or whether people perform rituals and other acts out of desire to change their situations, but *what* they desire, in what situations, and with what sense of responsibility for the common good. Bateson's assumption that an appetite for change in the external world makes religion degenerate flies in the face of the fervent desire present in many religions for transformation of the external world.

In support of this conclusion, Driver cites Arnold Van Gennep's famous assertion that religion dissolves when its theory and practice become separated: "the theory without the practice becoming metaphysics, and the practice on the basis of a different theory becoming science."[74]

Driver's perspective comports with the experience and expectations of innumerable religious believers, including those within modern secular culture. Given how persuasive Driver is here and how much more accurately he seems to reflect the role of religion within the contemporary world, the persistence of the scholarly claim that religion is properly transcendent, while only magic is concerned with mundane, worldly concerns, is all the more notable. Even as this claim appears to prescribe lofty ideals for religion, it has the paradoxical effect of enervating religion while serving the interests of modern secularization. As Bruno Latour succinctly states it, "A purely spiritual religion would rid us of the religious."[75]

Timothy Fitzgerald underscores this point. As he argues, despite all claims to the contrary, in the modern world "the secular is itself a sphere of transcendent values, but the invention of religion as the locus of the transcendent serves to disguise this and strengthen the illusion that the secular is simply the real world seen aright in its self-evident facticity." A rhetoric of religious transcendence serves a number of interrelated ideological functions. First, the configuration of what Fitzgerald calls "an interior private realm of supreme values and ultimate meaning in relation to God" deflects attention away from the significance of the human world, a world that in this scheme is seen "not as the deepest location of our social being but merely as a place in which we find ourselves."[76] This construction of a transcendent religious realm serves to mask or eclipse the moral significance of life in the mundane world, even as it aids in naturalizing the mute facticity of the secular realm. At the same time, the potency of religion to effect transformation within the social world is undercut, and dominion over empirical reality is more readily left to secular rationality and markets. Finally, even as this configuration of religion as transcendent serves to undercut the potency of religion, it also conceals the actual power exercised by (and within) modern religion institutions. Such matters are surely inconsequential in comparison to more lofty, supraempirical objectives. Transcendent religion readily conforms to the interests of liberal modernity.

Before proceeding, let me underscore the central role of magic in this scheme. The effort to provide a functionalist account of religion while simultaneously arguing that religion serves no concrete utilitarian purposes would be very difficult without the contrast provided by murky, pragmatic magic. "Transcendence" is a decidedly vacuous notion, one that can be given content only through juxtaposition with more mundane concerns. Magic has regularly filled that void. Nonutilitarian, self-generating, and self-fulfilling religious practices appear to take on more substantial form when contrasted to degenerate, instrumental magic. At the same time, the stigma of magic carries over to all forms of religious practice that fail to conform to this rarefied ideal. As we will see, the basic notion that religion must be insulated from concern with worldly interests is reiterated in various other contrasts drawn between religion and magic in the scholarly tradition.

Submission

The differentiation between magic and religion in terms of their respective objects is far eclipsed by the large number of scholars who have underscored that the primary distinction is located within the attitude of the practitioner. Efforts to define magic have long centered on questions of appropriate human relations to the spiritual world. A number of early scholars (Lub[...] and others) saw this as the defining difference between religion[...] While magic is characterized as self-seeking and rebellious in rel[...] itual powers, appropriate religion is marked by a pious submiss[...] powers.] *Early scholars = Magic/religion distinction attitude of Practitioner*

One of the classic assertions of this theme is found in Gerardus van der Leeuw's *Religion in Essence and Manifestation* (1933). As with many early phenomenologists of religion, van der Leeuw's analysis is shaped by Christian theological themes. He begins his consideration of magic by arguing that the contemporary Western antithesis between the supernatural and the natural is not applicable to the primitive mind; for the primitive, "all marked 'efficiency' is *per se* magical." Magic, he explains, is based on the effective arrogation of power. Thus the "magical attitude" should be seen as an attempt to influence the world in a manner that exceeds logic and that is driven by a desire to manipulate and dominate the world. This response is neither a survival from the past nor some kind of degeneration. It is, instead, "a primal attitude very deeply grounded in human nature, as vital among ourselves as it ever was, in fact an eternal structure."[77]

Science / Modernity as Magic?

With this view of magic, van der Leeuw rejects the notion of an abstract boundary between magic and religion, but he argues that the relevant distinction is to be located within the practitioner:

> It is, therefore, never legitimate to set "religion" and "magic" in any definitely adverse relationship, as though religion were the successor of magic, the latter being non-religious and the former never magical. Magic itself is religion simply because it is concerned with powers; certainly it requires no "god," but a "godless" act may very well be religious. Magic differs, however, from all other forms of religion in that the desire to dominate the world belongs to its essential nature. . . . Thus I can concede neither the antithesis between religion and magic as social-antisocial, nor as ethical-scientific, nor again that magic is anterior to religion: wherever there is religion there is magic, even though the magical stream does not always follow the main channel of religion; similarly, wherever there is magic there is religion, although it can be only one specific type of religion.

Van der Leeuw identifies the element that distinguishes magic from religion as "protest" against the fundamental order of nature, though of course such protest is doomed to sinful and solipsistic failure. Magic is a form of "presumption . . . [an] autocratic seizure of power . . . an almost wanton arrogance." The magical response to the world is the product of an inadequate set of boundaries between subject and object, an autistic focus on the inner human realm, an inadequate appreciation of reality to which children and primitives are particularly prone. The magical attitude depends on too great a sense of participation and appropriation of the world, but the attitude of science itself is characterized by an improperly heightened detachment from the world, a detachment that facilitates disinterested observation, but that fails to accept the given nature of the world. In contrast to magic and science, the appropriate faithful response to the material world is a form of "receiving," an obedience that rejects the fundamental presumption that human beings have control of the world.[78]

The distinction van der Leeuw draws between religion and magic is a venerable one, with roots far back in Western culture. One of the primary polemics used by Reformers against Catholic sacramental doctrine was the claim that priests improperly seek to manipulate and coerce the means of grace. Calvin argued that the doctrine of transubstantiation reduced the unconditional freedom and sovereignty of God by effectively placing God under the control of the priest. For hundreds of years, Protestants have argued that the Catholic sacraments operate "mechanically and indiscriminately," through the usurping actions of the priesthood. This distinctive Protestant inflection of religion as pious submission to divine prerogative stands at the heart of Schleiermacher's claim that the fundamental religious emotion is an attitude of "absolute dependence."[79]

Many of the most prominent theorists of religion of the late nineteenth and early twentieth centuries repeated this claim in their efforts to distinguish religion from magic. Tiele explains the primary difference between magic and religious worship by asserting that the aim of the magical cultus is to acquire power over spirits and thwart their influence, rather than pay homage to them. Only as higher conceptions of divine beings emerge do "these enchantments" give way to efforts to propitiate or calm the divine beings. Thus, in animistic and magical religions "fear is more powerful than any other feeling, such as gratitude or trust." According to the philosopher of religion Otto Pfleiderer, the patristic writer Lactantius properly defined religion as "the attachment to God by the bond of piety." In magic, Pfleiderer explains, "man does not act in the service of the god and for his purposes, but without the god and against him, man desires to achieve his own purposes by mysterious means." Jevons reiterates this basic claim as he concludes that the fundamental difference between prayers and spells lies in "the difference of the spirit inspiring them." When uttered in a pious spirit, words constitute a religious prayer, but in a different mode the identical words are "vain repetition and mere magic."[80]

This theme predominated among many important theologically and phenomenologically inclined scholars of religion. Rudolf Otto asserts that magic, which stands only as "the vestibule at the threshold of the real religious feeling," seeks "to appropriate the prodigious force of the numen for the natural ends of man," the "profane goods" of human desire. Georg Wobbermin states that the coercive attitude behind magic is "egoistic . . . pure caprice, and nothing but caprice." Magic is fundamentally self-contradictory, because while it is based on the notion of a higher realm of transcendent powers, it attempts to force these powers into the human sphere and to subordinate them to the human will. True religion emphasizes the necessity that human beings subordinate themselves and obediently surrender to this higher reality. Thus, religion is adamantly opposed to magic, and when magic intrudes into religion (as it has in Christianity), religion has fought it (as the Protestants have "deliberately waged war upon all magic"). Wobbermin affirms the fundamental presupposition that appears to have shaped much of this effort to distinguish religion from magic: "We can only find religion without magic in Christianity, and here also this is not at all completely realized." The Christian opposition to magic is most clearly demonstrated, Wobbermin explains, in the Lord's Prayer, which "presents the most concentrated summary of the whole religious attitude of Jesus." The very context of the prayer in the synoptic Gospels, "where it is contrasted with babbling and 'much speaking,'" implies also a contrast to magic, a contrast most emphatic in the central petition "Thy will be done."[81]

The Swedish phenomenologist Nathan Söderblom launches the discussion of magic in his 1931 Gifford Lectures by asserting that religion involves the submission and obedience to the deity, while in magic "man makes himself lord of the powers and employs them for his own purposes." Because of the mechanical laws on which sympathetic magic operates, magic has no need to invoke spirits or a deity. Thus, Söderblom asserts, "communion with superhuman powers" may occur in magic, but it is not indispensable for magic as it is for religion. In religion "man worships the deity" in submission and trust, while in magic "man employs the deity for his own ends." The characteristic feature of magic is that the divine force is invoked as an instrument or means to human ends, not as the power over humanity. Magic is essentially "an audacious self-glorification." In higher levels of religious development, magic is revealed as "the most dangerous adversary of religion." As Söderblom concludes:

> Magic knows no bounds to its power; it deems itself able to make rain and to change the course of the heavenly bodies. Religion, in the proper sense, begins when man feels his impotence in the face of a power which fills him with awe and dread. In magic man is the master. In religion the deity is lord. Magic denies and destroys the feelings of devotion and reverence which uplift the soul of man. To this very day, religion comes to life in a person only when the perception of shortcomings and limitations have forced him to his knees before the superhuman, only when he has gained a true dignity by submission to the elemental power of existence, God. Magic is thus in direct opposition to the spirit of religion.

In this respect, magic is no longer primarily an offense against the tribe or against the prerogative of the priesthood, but rather an offense against God, because it negates the proper trust and adoration due to God: "God is degraded into a means towards selfish ends."[82]

This theme is prominent in numerous important texts from a range of disciplines. In his *Origin and Development of the Moral Ideas* (1912), Edward Westermarck defines religion "as a belief in and a regardful attitude towards a supernatural being on whom man feels himself dependent and to whose will he makes an appeal in his worship." Westermarck acknowledges that the word "regardful" is rather vague, but he asserts that it is a necessary component of the religious act ("we do not call it religion when a savage flogs his fetish to make it submissive"). Magic, on the other hand, is characterized by "supernatural mechanical power": "he who performs a purely magical act utilises such power without making any appeal at all to the will of a supernatural being." The psychiatrist and ethnographer W.H.R. Rivers offers a comparable claim in his lectures published in 1924 as *Medicine, Magic, and Religion*. Rivers here distinguishes religion and magic based on the locus of the power adverted to by the practitioner. Religion, he explains, comprises "a group of processes, the efficacy of which depends on the will of some higher power, some power whose intervention is sought by rites of supplication and propitiation." In contrast, magic is "a group of processes in which man uses rites which depend for their efficacy on his own power, or on powers believed to be inherent in, or the attributes of, certain objects and processes which are used in these rites." Religion differs from magic in that religion "involves the belief in some power in the universe greater than that of man himself." Thus, Rivers explains, religious practices always "reveal an attitude of respect and appeal" to powers regarded as higher and more powerful than humanity. Magical actions assume that the powers responsible for misfortune are either human or less powerful than humanity, so these powers are approached with neither respect nor supplication.[83]

From the early years, of course, there have been various theorists who challenge this pervasive distinction between religion and magic. Mauss and Hubert reject the claim that spirits are always constrained in magic. While this aspect of magic is common, they explain, there are also examples of magic where spirits are independent and their aid is not inevitable. Other scholars have made related arguments. Many note the difficulty of attempting to distinguish coercion from worship, particularly in primitive societies where such a differentiation is alien. As Edwin Burtt states it, "A sharp distinction between coercing and persuading is a distinction not of the primitive but of the civilized mind" coming from "civilized religion, with its insistence on the appropriateness of humility on man's part when he stands before a divinity possessing superior perfection." Others emphasize the existence of magical rites (such as sacrifice) aimed at augmenting the power of the gods to enable them to comply with human desires, not at compelling a response. Jean Delumeau points out that magic can incorporate propitiatory elements such as sacrificial ceremonies, vows, prayers, and hymns, while religious rites can seek to exert coercive force over the divine.[84]

Yet the notion that the primary distinction between religion and magic can be identified within the will or attitude of the practitioner has been remarkably resilient in the analysis of magic throughout a range of academic disciplines. Social scientists have echoed Tiele and Wobbermin by citing the Lord's Prayer ("Thy will be done") as the benchmark of the religious attitude, and scholars with very different assessments of religion have rehearsed a common Reformation-inspired ideal of religious piety. The truly religious response to supernatural power is seen as humble, pietistic submission, a thoroughly non-utilitarian approach to the divine.[85] Some scholars frame this attitude as one of awe, worship, or reverence; others as supplication, surrender, or obedience. But in either case, the religious attitude is one that recognizes essential limits on human capacity to affect the divine and accepts the constraints of the natural order.

In contrast, magic is framed as an overinflation of the human will, a mode of arrogance, willfulness, or protest. It seeks to exert coercive power, to manipulate or dominate the world in ways that exceed human capacities and the prerogatives of the divine, to effect human desires in a manner that disregards the appropriate boundaries of the ego. As Hans-Joachim Schoeps succinctly states it, "The essence of magic is bold self-glorification. There is an element of megalomania in magic."[86] In this view, magic errs in seeking to exceed the appropriate limits on human agency. But this notion of religion as submission also turns on a distinctive construction of the nature of the divine will.

Divine Volition

Throughout these efforts to distinguish religion and magic on the basis of the attitude of their practitioner, we find the claim that magicians see the results of their actions as automatic or mechanical. One important aspect of this claim involves the view of the divine held by those who practice magic. As Keith Thomas states:

> A prayer had no certainty of success and would not be granted if God chose not to concede it. A spell, on the other hand, need never go wrong, unless some detail of ritual observance had been omitted or a rival magician had been practising stronger counter-magic. . . . Magic postulated occult forces of nature which the magician learned to control, whereas religion assumed the direction of the world by a

conscious agent who could only be deflected from his purpose by
prayer and supplication.

The magician is seen as claiming control over spiritual powers. As Adamson
Hoebel asserts, in the world of the magician "the supernatural power has no
volition or choice of its own. It must respond."[87]

This disregard of the agency and autonomy of spiritual or supernatural
powers is one of the prime ills that theorists attribute to coercive magic. As
scholars frame it, this disregard of divine volition can take one of two forms.
First, as we have seen previously in the theories of scholars such as Frazer and
Schmidt, some formulate magic as involving impersonal powers wielded by
the magician. Edmund Leach frames the distinction between magic and religion in the following terms: "If the power is treated as inherent in the rite
itself, the analyst calls the action magic; if the power is believed to be external
to the situation—a supernatural agency—the analyst says it is religious." In a
similar vein, Evans-Pritchard writes of the magical powers deployed by the
Nuer unrelated to spiritual forces, and Ninian Smart discusses the magic of
"mantra causation" in creating effects in the world through sacred formulae
directed at worldly forces rather than spiritual beings: "It supposes not that the
events influenced by the mantra are powered by a spirit but that natural objects
may jump to our commands."[88]

More commonly scholars frame magic as involving personal spiritual
powers that the magician claims to control. As Hutton Webster states it, the
proper distinction between a magical act and a petition or prayer is to be located in "the extent to which the object of the address is personified and endowed with human-like feelings and will": "If the spiritual being is supposed
always to grant a request or obey a command, then the speaker's words act
automatically and constitute a spell. If, on the other hand, the spiritual being
retains some freedom of action and may or may not accede to the speaker's
words, then these will take the form of a supplication or entreaty, that is, of
a prayer." Fritz Graf points out that this demarcation between religion and
magic has its roots in Plato, who "distinguishes magic and religion in that
magic makes every effort to persuade the gods, whereas the truly religious
behavior is to leave the gods a free choice, for they know better than we do
what is good for us." Many scholars reiterate the claim that magic seeks automatic results, while religion attempts to persuade the divine power. James
Leuba states that rites which act directly or automatically are magic, but that
"rites in which ideas, feelings, and volitions are supposed to be awakened in
personal agents, by means that are not mechanical or automatic, but which
may be called anthropopathic, that is to say, invocations, offerings, prayers,
and the like are called religion." The key to religion, in Leuba's view, is this
sense of a personal interaction. Raphael Karsten concurs that magic is "a relation only to supernatural mechanical powers," while religion is "a relation

to beings endowed with will and more or less personally conceived." In this scheme, religion involves the attempt to influence the will of these supernatural beings "by natural means—by offering them gifts, by flattering them, by humiliating himself, and so on," but in magic the influence occurs through "supernatural means, by using mechanical powers which they *cannot* resist."[89]

Some scholars go so far as to assert that any effort to influence the spiritual powers moves from religion into magic. To the extent that divine entities are seen as having autonomy and volition, any effort to persuade them quickly becomes suspect or morally ambiguous. So, for example, T. Witton Davies asserts that magic—not religion—depends on the beliefs "that the powers in the world on which human well-being depends are controlled by spiritual agents, and that these agents are to be conciliated and made friends of by words, acts, and so forth, which are thought to please them." And K.W.S. Kennedy states that any effort to cajole the deity into action constitutes a magical "libel on his power, a denial of his goodwill towards his dutiful servants."[90]

This notion of divine volition combines with the theme of religion as submission to promote a distinctively bourgeois discretion in religious fervor and comportment. To the extent that supernatural powers are personified, the cosmos is framed in vaguely congenial terms. But the appropriate response to worldly needs and desires is not the demonstrative enlistment of divine aid, but instead a passive submission to distant divine prerogative. The supernatural is framed as a transcendent object of dutiful reverence and obedience. While divine powers might be addressed through prayer or supplication, it is unacceptable to imagine that they might be influenced by human flattery.

But when the divine is insulated from human influence, the notion of divine volition is reduced to little more than a neutral cipher. In a recent exploration of nineteenth-century reformist efforts in Britain to extirpate popular superstition and magic, Maureen Perkins concludes that these efforts were driven by deep ideological concerns with the future. As she explains, "superstitious" notions of fate and determinism were feared to dampen industry and the drive to self-improvement, and the suppression of popular magic promised to instill a more serviceable sense of independence and individualism.[91] The notion of divine volition promulgated in these scholarly theories of magic serves much the same purpose. The divine is configured here as unresponsive to human entreaty, and the divine will is reflected primarily through the orderly operation of the natural world. In this light, pious submission comes to mean merely a stoic resignation to duty. With the divine so far removed from human influence and interaction and the world left to its own devices, the rhetoric of pious submission has the paradoxical effect of unbridling human willfulness in the mode of rationalized worldly action.

Morality

Related to the claim that religion is characterized by submission is the often repeated charge that magic is fundamentally immoral. Again the basic structure of this theme goes back far in Western thought. Ancient attacks on magic viewed it as a social threat, and Christian thinkers long viewed witchcraft and magic as sinful and evil. By the eighteenth century, Enlightenment thinkers saw magic and superstition not as sinful pacts with demonic forces but as dangerous impediments to social progress. Thus, for example, David Hume painted a broad array of religious practice as superstition and sought to delimit the proper scope of religion to a thinly rationalized notion of morality. As Robert Baird has recently detailed, through this move a narrow form of religious morality could be configured simultaneously as acceptably rational and as universal across human culture. Religion could be reduced to "a species of universal morality."[92]

This effort to reduce religion to morality is prominent among many Enlightenment thinkers. Kant provides a classic formulation of the claim that religion should be distilled to a fundamental sense of pious duty (a duty defined largely in contrast to magical rituals, prayers, and all other efforts to affect the divine). The sense that religious formalism and ritual stand in fundamental competition or conflict with morality goes very deep in important strands of Protestant thought, and this perspective has shaped the scholarly response to magic. Mary Douglas points out that this Protestant suspicion of external manifestations of religion, a suspicion that "any ritual is empty form," that "any external religion betrays true interior religion," has clear implications for the study of "primitive religions": "If they are formal enough to be reported at all, they are too formal, and without interior religion." (In the words of F.R.S. Raglan, magic is "ritual which has lost its theology.")[93]

This perspective has clearly informed the scholarly differentiation between rational religion and immoral magic. Scholars offer a number of variations on this theme. Some argue that the beliefs of primitive religious systems fail to lead to "right living"; the presence of magic in these belief systems leaves them with less concern for morality and ethics than more developed systems. Others point out that the formalism and automatic efficacy of magic mean that its results do not depend on the moral or ethical condition of the practitioner. As Keith Roberts states it, while religious systems involve such factors as "moral purification, confession, or some other transformation of the person involved," magic works "regardless of the moral righteousness" of the practitioner. Still other scholars assert that the automatic efficacy of magic indicates that magical systems hold the spiritual entities themselves in low ethical regard (often as simply greedy), and this again confirms the immoral nature of magic.[94]

In one of the more vivid expositions of this theme, Alexander Le Roy asserts in *The Religion of the Primitives* (1922) that one of the primary elements of religion is a "universal moral sense, based on the distinction between good and evil: a sense of shame, justice, responsibility, liberty, duty; explicit or implicit recognition of conscience." Magic stands in harsh contrast:

> Magical morality, if one may use the term, is purely and often brutally utilitarian. That is good which is serviceable and pleasant. Everything is sacrificed to personal interest; in that contaminated atmosphere, egoism reigns supreme, as a tyrannical master. *Vae victis!* The vanquished are the weak, the slaves, the women, the children. This is the barbarous morality which too often conceals and stifles true morality in the black country.

Magic is particularly prevalent because of its use by Africans in promoting the slave trade. The violence of African magic, a morass of "anthropophagy, infanticide, poisoning, and all the plagues of magic," represents "the depth of degradation to which humanity can fall." As Le Roy explains, cruel and immoral magic leads to the corruption of true religion, depopulation ("In the black continent fetishism has slain more victims than wars, disease, or slavery. It is a Moloch whose appetite is never sated"), social tyranny, and a breakdown of the basic human relations and trust that could lead to cultural progress.[95]

[margin handwritten note: Racism]

Max Weber offers an important development of this theme as he discusses the effects of the religious cultus. While religion is populated by gods to be worshiped, he explains, magical beliefs are characterized by demonic beings who are to be "coerced and charmed" through sorcery. Preaching, the basic form of collective instruction in religious and ethical matters, is common in prophetic religion. Thus, we find that "the importance of preaching stands in inverse proportion to the magical components of a religion": ethical instruction stands in inverse relation to magic. As human relations to the supernatural develop and a professional and independent class of priests emerges, priests receive forms of rational training different from the initiation of charismatic magicians. Religions come to develop "both a metaphysical rationalization and a religious ethic." In contrast, magicians lack a continuously operative cult and fail to develop a full-blown rationalization of their metaphysical views or a specifically religious ethic. As Weber concludes, the development of doctrine and a concomitant ethic is "the distinctive differential of prophecy and priestly religion, in contrast to pure magic."[96]

This theme of morality will circulate through the following chapters. Many scholars configure religion as properly representing human moral and ethical values, with magic standing either as a superstitious impediment to the development of those values or as an overt form of destructive and antisocial behavior. This theme has already appeared in the discussions of religion as submission, where magic was seen as involving various types of impiety in relation to the divine and the natural order. Here the impropriety of magic extends to harm against human moral interaction as well.

Conformity

Finally, one further major theme in this theoretical tradition is the claim that magic is inappropriately individualistic. This theme has already circulated through the discussions of magic as coercive and immoral. Many early scholars, such as Robertson Smith, stressed this aspect of magic, and it has been repeated regularly in the scholarly literature. For example, Sidney Hartland asserts that religion "binds the society together by raising the individual above himself, and teaching him to subordinate his desires and actions to the general good." In contrast, magic is focused only on the "wishes of the individual, though they may be contrary to the interests of the society as a whole." Hartland concludes that it is this tendency toward individualism that eventually gives rise to social hostility against magic. In a similar vein, James Leuba asserts that the fundamental immorality of magic arises because its practitioners seek their own benefit in disregard of the interests of the community or its gods.[97]

This claim assumed clarity and prominence in sociological accounts of the function religion serves in relation to the social group and its norms. As discussed previously, numerous scholars—Durkheim most famous among them—have argued that religion is fundamentally social, with magic relegated to the fringes of society. In this light, religion is almost tautologically configured as the embodiment of the system of social morality. Magic is reduced, in turn, to an inherently antisocial and unethical phenomenon, leading (in Frederick Schleiter's phrase) "a precarious career in the shape of disorganized rags and tags of practices within the body politic." Durkheim asserted that while religious transgressions are punished by misfortune and public condemnation, magical transgressions may entail misfortune but never indignation or condemnation. Because of the very nature of magic on the margins of the social group, "there is no sin in magic." The interests of the community are sanctioned by religion, with magic serving only the desires of self-seeking individuals.[98]

Magic is regularly portrayed by scholars from various disciplines as directed at the aims of the individual in opposition to the interests of the social collective. This theme remains prominent in recent accounts of the nature of magic. Thus, in *Stolen Lightning* (1982), as Daniel Lawrence O'Keefe sets out his broad general theory of magic, two of his fundamental postulates are that "magic tries to protect the self" and that "magic helped develop the institution of the individual."[99] Through these many configurations, magic is disruptively individualistic, while religion teaches conformity.

A concise summary of this range of distinctions between magic and religion was given by Henry Presler in 1971:

> Magic is often private, secret, closed; religion is generally public,
> commonly known, open, available. Magic is coercive, manipulative;

religion is propitiatory, petitionary, and provides communion, obedience, and praise. Magic is non-moral, useful for good or evil; complex religion . . . [gives] some place for morals . . . magic provides a
goal and the claim for achieving it; religion provides an experience.
Magic is mechanical; religion is spiritual. Magic has its own laws;
religion has the laws of wills of divinities.

Can insert
Science

As Presler concludes, the "main difference is that magic operates independently of any divine will; religion depends upon the wills of personalized supernatural beings."[100]

"Where Your Treasure Is"

A rarefied ideal for religion emerges through these distinctions between
religion and magic. Religion is configured as a phenomenon focused solely on
otherworldly objectives; any pragmatic or mundane concern is deemed magical. Religion is restricted to a narrow, pietistic submission to distant divine
powers; any effort to manipulate or deploy the supernatural in connection with
worldly concerns is magical. Religion is focused on a narrow sense of moralistic duty; any attempt to achieve ends benefiting the practitioner through the
use of supernatural power is immoral magic. This stridently Reformed view
of rationalized religion is well suited to a view of nature and system of economic relations from which the supernatural has been effectively expelled. We
are left with a generalized religious piety conforming to the liberal social order.

The final charge against magic discussed in the prior section is its individualism, which may seem at first an unusual target for attack by modern
liberal social theorists. But just as the form of submission advocated in this
construction of religion is a submission that leaves ample terrain for self-
assertion, only a particular variety of individualism is condemned in these
theories of magic. The individualism stigmatized here is individualism that
challenges rationalized social control. Within the limits of the dominant social
and economic order, self-assertion is appropriate and desirable. Only deterritorialized, disruptive forms of individualism are problematic, a disruption em-
blemized by the magical invocation of supernatural power to threaten the regularity of the natural order and economic relations.

Moving through all the norms for religion articulated in these theories of
magic is an abiding concern with the relation of religion to materiality.
Throughout the scholarly literature magic is commonly portrayed as predis-
posing human beings toward erratic and superstitious relations with material
objects (charms, amulets, fetishes, and so on). Max Weber, for example, underscores the persistent human need for "accessible and tangible" religious
objects that can exert magical power in concrete life situations. As he explains

it, this desire for tangible objects can impede the development of rationalized monotheism, because the manipulation and deployment of concrete magical objects provides far more immediate comfort and reassurance than the worship of a distant and often unresponsive deity.[101]

This theme is a common trope in social scientific accounts of magical practices. Scholars regularly include extensive catalogs of the exotic objects serving as the focus for magic and its manipulations, and they repeatedly advert to the fundamental materiality of magic. While some early theorists had argued that magic is aimed at an abstract natural force such as *mana*, Malinowski asserts instead that the focus of magic is the mediation of human relations with the concrete natural world. Magic, he concludes, functions as a quality of the relation between human beings and material objects. Many other scholars point to the role of objects in mediating the magician's relations with the magician's audience and with the spiritual and material worlds. Thus, as E. D. Soper concludes, while in "true religion . . . we trust God," in magic "we trust some contrivance or spell or charm."[102]

This aspect of magic fundamentally contradicts the logic of modernity. Magic idiosyncratically sets aside certain objects as having unique forms of efficacy and deserving special veneration. But this superstitious over-investment of particular objects interrupts the regularity and uniformity of the material world, a regularity on which modernity and its economic system depend. And magic is disruptive not only because of the particular material means it uses but also because of the location of the ends it seeks to effect. Magic uses material means to effect pragmatic results within the material world itself.

This is a common scholarly theme. Magic, Ruth Benedict asserts, is "technological and mechanistic, a compulsion of a passive universe to one's own ends," a desire for overt material consequences. In his *Structure of Social Action* (1949), Talcott Parsons provides a succinct statement of this defining aspect of magic: magic is "the application of ritual means to empirical ends." Parsons contrasts this magical ritual to religious rites aimed only at nonempirical ends (thus, he explains, Catholic baptism is aimed not at empirical objectives but only at salvation). The sociologist of religion Thomas O'Dea distinguishes magic from religion by pointing out that though both phenomena seek contact with the "supraempirical aspects of reality," religion "claims only to place men in relation to such forces and realities and expresses the human response to them," while magic "claims to offer ways of manipulating these forces to bring about changes and effect consequences in the empirical world itself." O'Dea thus defines religion as "the manipulation of non-empirical or supraempirical means for non-empirical or supraempirical ends," in contrast to magic as "the manipulation of non-empirical or supraempirical means for empirical ends."[103] Through its various formulations, this basic distinction simply amplifies the claims that religion is transcendent and submissive, while magic is pragmatic and coercive.

Usually the coercive effects alleged to be involved in magic are seen as relating to supernatural beings or some underlying reservoir of magical power, but at times this coercion appears to intrude directly into the stream of natural causation. Werner Stark explains that the essence of magic turns on the underlying idea that "a human being loaded with occult power can coerce nature, can, by his will, . . . impose himself on the forces of reality and make them do his imperious bidding." Underlying magic is the effort by the magician "to insert himself into the natural nexus of cause and effect, to introduce his wish, his subjective whim, into the objective texture of events. He regards himself as a new cause that will bring a specific new effect." Magic differs from religion in that magic remains enclosed in the physical universe, both in its "causative act and the anticipated emergent effect."[104]

Notice, of course, that in Stark's rather excessive formulation, all purposive human action in the material world of any sort would constitute magic. What could possibly be the shape of human life that did not seek to insert itself into the "natural nexus of cause and effect . . . into the objective texture of events"? But Stark is not alone in this excess. The role of human mental states (desires, intentions, and consciousness itself) in physical causality has long troubled modern scholars in a variety of disciplines, and many have been inclined to declare mental states nonphysical and therefore noncausal. Carried to its extreme, this conclusion easily renders all purposive action magical. So, for example, W. J. Perry offers the following explanation of the essence of magic: "By the aid of certain substances or objects, or by means of certain acts, men believe, in certain circumstances, that they can influence each other, and also natural phenomena, for their own advantage." More recently, in an effort to avoid imposing anachronistic distinctions between religion and magic onto contexts where the modern categories do not apply, Morton Klass defines magic in these extraordinarily broad terms: "For me, at any rate, magic simply refers to techniques employed by those who believe that in specific circumstances persons, powers, beings, or even events are subject to control or coercion."[105] In these formulations, all purposive human action in the material world seems to fall within magic. All that is left to religion is a vague, disembodied piety that is, in every sense of the word, immaterial. While these assertions might be explained as a product of carelessness (or, in Klass's case, a desire to minimize the stigma of magic), they have plausibility only because they carry to its logical conclusion a long scholarly tradition that configures religion as thoroughly passive and dematerialized.

Magic differs from religion, we are told, because magic seeks to effect changes in the flow of material objects and events. This improper action (alternatively stigmatized as pragmatic, coercive, impious, self-seeking) threatens the regularity of natural law and commerce. Any effort to employ the supernatural to effect material changes is magical; pious religion focuses its attention only on nonempirical, otherworldly ends. One of the prime objectives of these formulations is to constrict the permissible scope for any sort of human agency in relation to the supernatural. Religion is to steer away from any concern with materiality, focusing its attention only on vaguely personable supernatural forces. While it may supplicate those forces through prayer and entreaty, overt efforts to influence those forces in a way that curtails their absolute autonomy become immediately suspect. Any hint of efficacy or potency—in relation either to materiality or to the supernatural—raises the specter of magic. This form of transcendent religion is thin indeed.

This construction of transcendent religion is thoroughly gendered. As we will see in subsequent chapters, women are regularly portrayed as prone to magic. But even in the present more abstract formulations, the gendered basis of the differentiation between religion and magic is palpable. Religion is transcendent, metaphysical, ultimate, immaterial; magic is immanent, mundane, willful—and preoccupied with material effects. In this coding, religion is a decidedly masculine province, while magic is the realm of women (and sexually suspect men). At every turn the rhetoric of magic reverberates with the rhetoric of gender norms.

And yet again, even in this focus on the materiality of magic, the concept has proved remarkably pliable. While many scholars invoke these transcendent norms for religious behavior in an effort to purify religion, to insulate it from the pollution of materiality, this theme of the otherworldly nature of religion can quickly shift to demonstrate religion's ultimate irrelevance. Frazer, for example, claims that despite the folly of magic, the primitive magician at least maintains a dignified sense of industry and a focus on immediate, pragmatic, material problems. In contrast, the pious priest is engaged in vain speculation and a demeaning grovel thoroughly unbefitting the modern enlightened subject. Other scholars confirm that magic and religion are equally futile; as Frederick Schleiter states it, "So far as the productivity of results is concerned, both [religion and magic] are, and always have been, equally sterile and inefficacious in the accomplishment of real changes in the outer world or in the achievement of the purposes for which they are supposed to exist."[106]

This shifting valence demonstrates that scholars can deploy a similar theme to dramatically different ends. But it also demonstrates the ultimate trajectory of the rarefied, sublime zone constructed for religion in these modern theories of magic. Whether expounded by the pious van der Leeuw or the materialist Frazer, the abstract and dematerialized norms for religion articulated in these theories reduce religion to inconsequence. This is religion from which all power and efficacy have been drained. As Michael Buckley has argued, when harsh antinomies are framed between the natural and supernatural realms—when the dualism between immanence and transcendence is pressed to eliminate the divine from materiality—secularization thrives because religion is rendered irrelevant to life in the natural world.[107]

Disembodied religion quickly dissipates. Yet a fundamental suspicion of materiality persists among many modern religious thinkers. Within Protestant theology, this tendency has taken the form of what Philip J. Lee refers to as a type of Protestant gnosticism. Liberal and conservative Protestants alike have demonstrated discomfort with the role of materiality in Christianity, a discomfort most evident in their ambivalence toward religious ritual and sacraments. Let me conclude here by pointing to Horatio Dressler's effort to address this ambivalence in his *Outlines of the Psychology of Religion* (1929). Dressler adopts what he calls a "rationalist" distinction between magical effects (which involve some superstitious occult force) and religious values (which invoke "the highest objects of the spiritual life"). Magic, he explains, has promised that "the performance of certain motions or rites here on earth sufficed to invoke power from the unseen world, from its deities."[108]

Dressler acknowledges that magic is difficult to extirpate from religion, particularly since "many people expect magical effects from prayer, conversion, and the sacraments; to the neglect of those values which might withstand the test of criticism." While magic involves the faulty attempt to bend matter to the human will, religious values rest on the assumption of a fundamental "harmony between ourselves and the universe at large." This principle can serve to distinguish religion from magic (which casts us adrift "in the sphere of miracle and caprice"). Dressler thus concludes:

> If then as religionists we are in quest of peace and happiness, we cannot reasonably avoid the comparison between magic and religion, between the possible world-views, with the hope that we may find ground for believing that the universe is good. What can or what cannot be done with matter, for instance, is of great moment to us. . . . [Because of the pain inflicted by the material world] we are driven beyond matter and beyond materialism in quest of doctrinal reconstruction—by appeal, it may be, to the aspect of eternity, or to some view of the spiritual world affording belief in reconciliation.[109]

Dressler is correct in his assertion that many people who experience material suffering seek some sort of transcendent reconciliation with the spiritual world. Yet Dressler ignores another major response to suffering. That alternative is a thoroughly materialist science. If modern theories of magic have largely condemned the exercise of human agency with respect to the supernatural, these same theories have offered a very different lesson concerning human agency in regard to the rationalized, scientific manipulation of nature. With religion cordoned away in pious abstraction, the material world is ceded to the unbridled control of modern science. It is to science that we now turn.

3

Magic and the Regulation of Reason

> Science needs those who disobey it.

—Theodor Adorno

Historian David Lindberg opens _The Beginnings of Western Science_ (1992) with a deceptively straightforward query: "What is science?" Lindberg then lists eight distinct ways of responding to this question (science as systematic human behavior seeking to control the envi- ronment; science as a body of theoretical knowledge distinct from technology; science as a set of universal, lawlike propositions; sci- ence as particular procedures for exploration; and so forth). Lindberg undertakes this exercise to demonstrate the difficulty histo- rians, philosophers, and social scientists face in attempting to define such a broad and amorphous phenomenon. The range of practices and forms of knowledge grouped under this label are dispersed throughout the social field, assuming enormously divergent forms. Is science best understood as a worldview, or a form of logic, or a method of inquiry and observation, or a body of results, or a set of academic disciplines and broader social institutions? Most relevant for our purposes here is the final entry on Lindberg's list: " 'science' and 'scientific' are often simply employed as general terms of ap- proval—epithets that we attach to whatever we wish to applaud."[1]

The effort to understand science, to uncover its nature, is partic- ularly compelling because of the central role of science in modern society. Science stands as the determinative feature of developed modern economies, operating through an elaborate network of edu- cational and research institutions, government and defense funding, and business and technological interests. The influence of this scientific-industrial complex is felt in every aspect of modern life, penetrating and informing the most obscure reaches of the body and psyche, even as it propels its reach to the heavens.

But beyond its technical and economic importance, science is also central to the self-representations of the modern world. Science and scientific rationality have served as the definitive markers of precisely what it means to be modern. Science is, in large measure, who "we" are. It has been championed as the defining characteristic that separates us from our primitive and unenlightened forebears; it offers the allure of limitless potential and progress. Indeed, as many cultural historians have underscored, science began to fill these ideological functions in the West's self-representations long before scientists could boast extensive achievements.

But this modern identity—this "we"—is itself thoroughly ambiguous and contested. The story of scientific rationality and progress has always been plagued by detractors. A long tradition of Western thinkers has championed modernity and eagerly trumpeted the powers of science, but at least from the era of Rousseau and early Romanticism there have been prominent voices skeptical of the modern world and the social structures it fosters. Philosophers and social theorists have engaged in heated disputes over the nature of modernity and the implications of the modern race to the future. And because of the central role of science in the representational and ideological schemes of the modern world, these disputes have often taken the form of debates over the origin and essence of science, its capacity to mark the standard of truth, its effects both intended and unforeseen. Critics of modernity have repeatedly targeted the pretensions and presumptions of science and cold scientific rationalism. They have challenged many of the consequences of science, from destructive and dehumanizing technological developments, to the reordering of social and economic systems, to the implications of science for human self-perception and identity. These battles have taken on new vigor in recent years in conflicts over science studies and various critical approaches to traditional epistemology.[2]

As discussed in the first chapter, the effort to stake out what it means to be "rational" or "scientific" stretches back to the earliest days of modernity. Debates over the early modern witchcraft persecutions and the slow process of formulating and clarifying various grounds for opposing the persecution of witches were a formative episode in the self-constitution of modernity. Many of the early opponents of the witchcraft persecutions (Weyer, Scot, Bayle) were lauded by subsequent generations as harbingers of modern scientific rationality and critical thought. And one of the recurrent themes among the Western philosophers discussed in that chapter was an aversion to—and simultaneous fascination with—the superstitious or nonrational.

Magic has served as a principal weapon in these contests over modern identity. It has been configured, in Frazer's words, as "the bastard sister of science." As discussed in the prior chapter, there is a venerable tradition seeing magic as the illegitimate relation of religion, but there is also a long tradition mapping its bastardy in regard to science. While the precise nature of magic's filiation has remained ambiguous, there has been broad scholarly consensus in the West both that magic is illegitimate and that magic is gendered in decidedly feminine terms. As Alexander Le Roy framed it, "Magic is the perversion of science as well as of religion."[3]

In this chapter, I examine various aspects of the scholarly literature since the late nineteenth century in which magic is invoked in the effort to define science. Many social scientists of the late nineteenth and early twentieth centuries sought to uncover the essence of science by discovering its origin, and they regularly invoked magic in these efforts. A number of scholars (Tylor and Frazer, most famously) have seen magic and science as fundamentally continuous or related forms of practice (with science evolving in a relatively organic fashion out of magical thought). Others have rejected the claim that magic constitutes a primitive form of science and have attempted instead to formulate various essential distinctions between the two categories (to establish that science is sui generis and originated independently of magic). At stake in this debate are fundamental notions concerning the boundaries of modern science and scientific rationality.

This chapter begins with a section considering the nature of primitive thought. One of the most prominent sites of the debate concerning the relation between magical and scientific thought occurs in early theoretical constructions of the "primitive." Irrational (or prerational) magical thinking was seen by numerous early anthropologists, sociologists, and psychologists as the definitive index of the primitive mind. In this frame, many early theorists discussed magic in the course of debates concerning the origin of science. How did science, this decisively important phenomenon, take root? Did magic play a role in the emergence of science, or are the two types of activity fundamentally opposed?

These questions have served many thinkers as a means of bringing the nature of science into sharp relief; we can identify science through the contrast with what it is not—prescientific magic. And at the same time, other scholars have argued that science and magic are better understood as sharing some common line of descent. They assert that understanding this filiation actually offers a more nuanced assessment of science's pedigree: if science bears a family resemblance to its rather disreputable sibling, it can be placed in more organic relation with other forms of human thought.

Over time the rather fanciful scholarly conjecture concerning the prehistory of science began to subside, and social scientists turned from the search for origins to other themes. But magic remained a central component in later theoretical disputes over the nature of primitive thinking. It has also featured prominently in scholarly disputes concerning human cultural commensurability and the ability of modern scientific rationality to explain or "comprehend" irrational modes of thought.

The second section of this chapter considers another major arena of scholarly debate over the relation of magical thought to modern rationality, the history of early modern science. Intellectual and social historians and philosophers of science have long sought to account for the emergence of scientific thought in Europe in the early modern period and to explain the relation of this new science to prior modes of thought, particularly medieval and Renaissance traditions of hermetic magic and occultism. Again these debates involve questions of origin. Did modern science emerge in a "revolution," or is it better understood as continuous in significant respects with prior traditions of inquiry? Is scientific rationality a new and distinctive mode of thought, or does it share important links with earlier forms of occultism and natural magic? In these debates scholars not only have struggled to explain the defining characteristics of science and magic but also have engaged in a thinly veiled discussion of the role of science in the modern world. The competing accounts offered by historians concerning the emergence of science are shaped by the very categories used to formulate the accounts, and these categories are shaped in turn by the historians' valuations of science, their perspectives on the role of science in the modern world, and their fundamental assessments of modernity itself.

The concluding section of this chapter examines some of the important themes that emerge though these debates concerning the morality of scientific inquiry. Debates over the relation between magic and science have revolved around fundamental issues of the human relation to nature and technology. Does science epitomize the triumph of the rational control over nature, or does it rather represent the victory of a dehumanizing reductivism? Does science teach us an appropriate humility in the face of nature's laws, or is it the pinnacle of human hubris? Positioned at (or beyond) the boundary of rationality, magic has served both as the foil against which distinctive forms of modern science have been defined and as a tool for contesting the hegemony of those forms of rationalized thought.

Do Natives Think?

As we saw in the prior chapter, throughout late nineteenth-century and early twentieth-century social evolutionary theory dealing with the earliest stages of human cultural development, science was an integral component of theories concerning the relation between magic and religion. And just as magic was central in debates over the etiology of religion, so also magic served as a useful polemical tool in the effort to account for the origins and nature of

Origins of science?

science. Magic could be deployed variously as a device for portraying scientific thinking as a distinctive, sui generis phenomenon, or for humbling the pretensions of modern science by showing its debt to primitive thought, or for bolstering alternative developmental theories stressing various forms of human commonality.

Through these competing theories magic was configured as a defining characteristic of primitive or nonmodern peoples.[4] One of the major themes of these scholarly debates was the question of the relation between modern people and primitives. Do all human beings share fundamental mental operations, or are there differences in mental processes that create unbridgeable gulfs among peoples? What light do the intellectual and emotional lives of primitives shed on the nature of modernity?

Theories of the Primitive Philosopher

In *Primitive Culture*, Edward Burnett Tylor offers a thoroughly rationalist account of the nature of magical thought. He attributes the belief in magical, occult science to a misapplication of principle of "the Association of Ideas, a faculty which lies at the very foundation of human reason, but in no small degree of human unreason also." Human beings in a low intellectual condition come to associate in thought objects or events that in their experience have been associated in fact. Yet because of their low development, primitives conclude that there must be some inevitable connection between association in thought and association in reality. Events linked only by coincidence become joined in the primitive mind, and this mental connection comes to predominate primitive thought. Savage, barbaric, and civilized life all demonstrate, Tylor explains, that magic results from thus "mistaking an ideal for a real connexion." Cultural history is filled with examples in which the claimed connection between two objects or events is only a connection of analogy or symbolism. It is only the modern educated world that has come to recognize the folly of magical analogies that "would to this day carry considerable weight to the minds of four-fifths of the human race." As "progressive races" have learned to test their opinions and conclusions through various forms of experimentation, occult science has been reduced to the status of a cultural survival.[5]

The concept of the association of ideas comes to Tylor from ancient Greek philosophy mediated through Locke and Hume, both of whom stressed the fundamental role of association in human reasoning. Locke, for example, had explained that irrational or extravagant human thought could often be explained by erratic associations formed by chance or custom; Hume cited the superstitious devotions of Roman Catholicism as prime examples of credulous association. This notion was further developed by eighteenth-century British associationist psychologists such as David Hartley and Joseph Priestly. As Tylor explains, the processes of analogy and symbolism have often been systematized into "pseudo-sciences" that demonstrate the errant application of the principle of association. Tylor spends a great deal of his discussion of magical survivals analyzing the analogical and symbolic principles at their core.[6]

Faced with numerous examples of magical association, Tylor inquires whether "there is in the whole monstrous farrago no truth or value whatever?" His response reflects the evolutionist tone of his analysis: "practically none . . . the world has been enthralled for ages by a blind belief in processes wholly irrelevant to their supposed results." As discussed in the next chapter, Tylor attributes the persistence of these massive magical errors largely to conservative social forces—particularly magicians—who promote magical beliefs. Yet the manipulation of the magician is not solely fraud and imposture; magic has its origins not merely in deception but also in "a sincere but fallacious system of philosophy, evolved by the human intellect by processes still in great measure intelligible to our own minds." Magic develops as "an elaborate and systematic pseudo-science," which then benefits from the rhetorical skills and "brazen impudence" of magicians eager to hide the failures of the magical system. This "pseudo-science" differs from true science only on the basis of the misapplication of the basic principle of association. As proper associations are formulated, true science emerges. Tylor offered a succinct (if tautological) summary of this theme in his 1883 entry on "Magic" in the ninth edition of the *Encyclopaedia Britannica:* "The very reason why magic is almost all bad is because when any of it becomes good it ceases to be magic."[7]

Tylor's intellectualist view of magic as pseudoscience was greatly amplified by Frazer, who argues that the magician recognizes the fundamental associationist principles of similarity and contact as components of a universal scheme of natural law. In this scheme, nature is viewed as consisting of events that occur "in an invariable order without the intervention of personal agency." Magic thus constitutes "a false science" (to the extent that it is framed as theoretical knowledge about the operations of the world) and "an abortive art" (to the extent that it is deployed as practical knowledge concerning the effects of human effort). In its most primitive manifestations, magic is always practical, since the primitive magician never rises to the level of analysis or abstract reflection on the principles involved in magic. This magician "reasons just as he digests his food in complete ignorance of the intellectual and physiological processes which are essential to the one operation and to the other." Only the student of philosophy comes "to discern the spurious science behind the bastard art."[8]

Frazer argues that the two great principles of magic are merely two basic misapplications of the association of ideas. Homoeopathic magic mistakenly assumes that items resembling one another operate in similar fashion, and contagious magic mistakenly assumes that items having been in contact maintain a connection. These errors can be found in "the crude intelligence not only of the savage, but of ignorant and dull-witted people everywhere," since magic has an "extraordinary hold . . . on the human mind in all ages and all countries." The essence of false magical beliefs is the notion that "sympathetic influence" can be exerted by persons or objects at a distance.[9]

The error of magic lies not in its basic assumption that nature consists of a series of of events determined by law but in its fundamental misconception of the actual laws in question. From the earliest stages of culture, human beings have searched for general rules allowing them to manipulate the natural order in advantageous ways. The principles of association of ideas are essential to the operation of all human thought. When legitimately applied, these principles yield science; "illegitimately applied they yield magic, the bastard sister of science." Frazer concludes with an emphatic assertion of Tylor's basic distinction between the two phenomena: "It is therefore a truism, almost a tautology, to say that all magic is necessarily false and barren; for were it ever to become true and fruitful, it would not longer be magic but science."[10]

As Frazer himself acknowledges, his scheme turns on a fundamentally tautological definition of magic. Magic is "next of kin to science," but it is defined by its illegitimacy, a pseudoscience that is erroneous and impotent. As he states, "Every single profession and claim put forward by the magician as such is false; not one of them can be maintained without deception, conscious or unconscious." For example, the feared consequences of taboos never actually result from violation of the prohibitions. Were the taboo actually effective, it would no longer be a taboo but merely "a precept of morality or common sense." Thus it is not a taboo to warn against the effects of fire; "it is a rule of common sense, because the forbidden action entails a real, not an imaginary evil." In this light Frazer asserts that all "those simple truths, drawn from observation of nature, of which men in all ages have possessed a store," fall soundly within the ambit of science.[11]

Yet it is also central to Frazer's evolutionary scheme to underscore the ways in which magic, despite its errors, sets the stage for science. In higher levels of social evolution, as the religious notion of nature as animated by spiritual beings begins to give way to a scientific recognition of natural law, magic reemerges from obscurity. By promoting investigation of the causal principles of nature, magic "directly prepares the way for science." The more intelligent members of society become dissatisfied with the religious conception of the world in which nature is fundamentally variable and irregular, a notion conflicting with the empirical observation of "the rigid uniformity, the punctual precision" of the laws of nature. "The keener minds . . . revert in a measure to the older standpoint of magic by postulating explicitly . . . an inflexible regularity in the order of natural events." Through this reversion to the precepts of magic, religion can be displaced by science. The new science differs from magic, of course, in that science deduces the true order of nature through the patient and painstaking observation of phenomena. We can be confident in the scientific method because of "the abundance, the solidity, and the splendour of the results already achieved."[12]

Thus for Frazer, while religion presupposes that nature is subject to erratic, personal intervention by divine beings, magic and science share the view that nature is regular and mechanistic. As he states, "Wherever sympathetic magic occurs in its pure unadulterated form it assumes that in nature one event follows another necessarily and invariably without the intervention of any spiritual or personal agency." In this respect, the fundamental conception of magic is "identical with that of modern science; underlying the whole system is a faith, implicit but real and firm, in the order and uniformity of nature." Magic and science both see nature as "rigid and invariable" and unmoved "by persuasion and entreaty . . . by threats and intimidation." Religion is fundamentally antagonistic to magic and science in its assumption that the natural world can be "directed by conscious agents who may be turned from their purpose by persuasion." Magic and science, in contrast, see the course of the natural world determined "not by the passions or caprice of personal beings, but by the operations of immutable laws acting mechanically." In magic as in science, humanity relies on its own strength to deal with difficulties and dangers through seeking to manipulate these immutable laws.[13] From this perspective, religion appears to be a rather unfortunate, if inevitable, detour in human cultural evolution. Even before human beings could fabricate the notion of spirits and gods, they had a rudimentary sense of natural law. Only when that primordial seed is rejuvenated can religion be overcome.

Frank Byron Jevons offered a widely circulated elaboration of this intellectualist understanding of the "primitive philosopher." For primitive people, he explains, sympathetic magic does not involve the supernatural; it is instead "the applied science of the savage." "The foundation, the principle, and the methods of savage logic and scientific logic are identical." This foundation is the belief in the uniformity of nature, "the inherent tendency of the human mind to expect similar sequences or coexistences in similar conditions." Thus, "the principle of induction, again, is the same in the logic of the savage and the *savant*":

> The point of resemblance between what [the savage] does and what he wishes to effect seem to the savage to be the essential points for his purpose: the man of science deems otherwise. Doubtless the man of science is right; but the savage is not therefore superstitious in this matter. He applies a principle of logic—to the wrong things perhaps, but still the process is one of logic, savage if you like, but not superstitious.

Jevons argues that the "savage theory of causation" is only an "incomplete and exaggerated" from of scientific causation. While the modern *savant* forms hypotheses, the savage forms myths. This leads Jevons to a striking conclusion:

The uniformity of nature, the principle of induction, the theory of causation, the inductive methods, form the common framework of both logics: the savage would probably be able to give his assent to all the principles of Mill's logic. . . . The errors of the early logician were extra-logical, and therefore were such as could be remedied by no process of logic but only by wider experience.

Early humans come to the more or less conscious conclusion that "like produces like" through observation and logic. In its original form, there is nothing magical about this fundamentally practical maxim; as Tylor and Frazer have explained, magic results only when the maxim is applied beyond its proper bounds.[14]

Jevons explains how these bounds are demarcated by returning to Tylor's assertion that magic is commonly attributed to less civilized neighboring tribes. In Jevons's version of this theme, a more civilized race determines that certain natural phenomena are due to divine agency and thus beyond human influence or control. Their less civilized neighbors continue to attempt to manipulate these phenomena (through the old principles of induction). Magic arises from the juxtaposition of "the more and the less enlightened views of what man can effect" and the survival among the less enlightened of efforts to produce effects that their more enlightened neighbors consider supernatural. The more enlightened group comes to believe that members of the lower group possess magical powers, an attribution that the lower group often eagerly accepts: "At times it is gratifying to the despised 'nigger' or 'barbarian' to excite the terror of his owner or his superior in civilization." (This theme of ethnic and class conflict will return in the following chapter.) In the end an uncommon practice is marked off as "an idea not generally known, a thing not commonly done, a proceeding not generally approved of," and that practice comes to be regarded as a form of magic. A final stage in this evolution occurs when, as in the present, magic is no longer accepted by educated people. Even in the modern world the belief in magic persists (particularly among sailors), but social evolution points toward the ultimate rejection of magic. Indeed, belief in the efficacy of magic is "rotten before it is ripe," because by its nature it is generally applied only where it is false.[15]

These intellectualist accounts of magic were highly influential, and various of their themes were echoed by other important theorists. The American scholar of comparative religion Morris Jastrow concurred in the claim that magic is "thoroughly logical":

So far from being due to caprice or accident, magic represents a primitive form of real science, based as is modern science upon experimentation and observation. Its fallacy or its weakness is due merely to the limited scope of the observation and experience upon which it rests; and the greater value of modern science results, primarily, from the infinitely wider scope of our experience and observation.

Jastrow concluded that the primitive belief in the efficacy of magic is precisely equivalent to the modern confidence in science. Salomon Reinach echoed Tylor and Frazer in asserting that when magical techniques begin to have actual effect, science is born. And W. H. R. Rivers also reiterated this intellectualist perspective as he argued that a concept of medicine separate from magic or religion emerged only with "the gradual substitution of the concept of physical causation for the spiritualistic agencies of the animism which formed the early attitude toward nature." Thus, Rivers asserted, the development of medicine is bound up with the emergence of a clear differentiation between the natural and supernatural worlds. Early animistic interpretations of the universe become increasingly replaced by materialist explanations as cultures evolve.[16]

Theories of a Primitive Mentality

These intellectualist accounts of the operations of magical thought were soon attacked from a number of directions. Many theorists complained that Frazer, in particular, overestimated the extent of primitive rationality. Some argued that the foundations of primitive thought should be sought in instinct or other basic physiological processes, while others stressed the social and emotional elements of primitive thinking. Alfred Haddon, for example, pointed to the "nervous instability" of primitive peoples and explained that magic was prevalent among them because "the mental equilibrium of many backward peoples is very unstable," making them particularly prone to the power of suggestion and fascination. Irving King also rejected the intellectualism that Frazer and Jevons attributed to primitive peoples, arguing instead that the origins of primitive associations should be understood through "the almost physiological processes of habit and of association." While King concurred that magic could be seen as the science of the primitive, he explained that primitive magical activities should be understood largely as the product of "half-instinctively recognized necessities of the life-process," as "primarily the natural reaction of the psychophysical organism, almost its mechanical reflex, in situations of strain or relaxation." In his view, primitives respond to stimuli in an instinctive and physiological manner, not one partaking of intellection.[17]

Mauss and Hubert also attacked the inordinate stress on abstract, impersonal representations that, in their view, led theorists such as Frazer and Jevons to the conclusion that magic functioned as a kind of science. Mauss and Hubert agree that in certain circumstances magic can function as a type of science or fill the place of undeveloped scientific abilities (thus sorcerers are the first poisoners, the first surgeons, and the first experts in fields such as metallurgy). But, they argue, in performing most magical or religious rites "the individual does not reason," because the rite is received socially and its practice requires no logical justification. While Frazer found a similarity between magic and science in the abstractions of sympathetic natural relations, Mauss and Hubert are willing to accord magicians the title of scientist only because primitive magicians' speculation concerning the properties of natural objects can sometimes lead to "rudiments of scientific laws." Otherwise, the principles of magic are "a series of empty, hollow forms" involving only inchoate laws of causality.[18]

In magic, Mauss and Hubert explain, the creative and critical mental operations demonstrated by practitioners of science and the arts are missing. Scientific beliefs are formed a posteriori, "constantly submitted to the scrutiny of individuals and dependent solely on rational evidence." In contrast, magic is based only on a priori belief that has such authority that it can resist contradictory experiences. Even failures can be turned to the advantage of the magical system, since they can be attributed to countermagic or to flaws in the performance of the ritual. Just like the belief in religion, belief in magic is obligatory, "unanimous and collective." Only as magic comes over time to be justified by reference to individual experience does the role of the collective decline, and only then can magic come to resemble and approximate the sciences and technology as it increasingly claims to be based on individual experimentation and deduction. Magic assumes the aura of technology "as it becomes more individualistic and specialized in the pursuit of its varied aims."[19]

Thus there is a "genealogical link between techniques and magic," since they share similar aims. Under the cloak of magical authority, Mauss and Hubert state, magician-craftsmen take small, practical steps in the development of techniques in areas such as medicine, pharmacy, alchemy, and astrology. While magic stands as "the domain of pure production, ex nihilo," using only words and gestures, over time techniques emerge that involve actual meaningful labor. Magic facilitates this development through its great stress on ideas and knowledge. While religion tends toward metaphysics, magic is often concerned with understanding concrete nature and can develop a repertoire of reliable information in the physical and natural sciences. Finally, in primitive societies sorcerers and magicians are the only people with the leisure to engage in observation and reflection on nature. Thus it is possible that it was in schools of magic that scientific traditions and intellectual methods first emerged.[20]

Yet as Mauss and Hubert reiterate, the basic operations of magic must not be understood from the perspective of individualistic, intellectualist psychology. Where magic is believed, the basic principles of magical judgments exist before any magical experience. Such experience serves only to confirm the prior judgment and belief (which remains impervious to refutation). Magic exists as a type of a priori synthetic judgment imposed on the believer through social convention. The most remarkable (almost, it appears, magical) feat is that "the same association should necessarily be reproduced in the minds of several individuals or rather of a mass of individuals." These magical judgments form the conditions of possibility for magical experience, and the judgments are so central to the operations of magic that contrary experience can rarely dislodge them. Magic has this persistence because it is a product of massive and collective social consensus. Thus, Mauss and Hubert conclude, "group sentiments will always be found at the origin of all magical manifestations, whether the magic was borrowed from an earlier religion or an outside religion, or whether they sprang from the world of magic itself."[21]

Many aspects of this account of magic are quite baffling, particularly Mauss and Hubert's vague account of the processes through which magical judgments take root within a social group and through which magic then becomes more individualized. For our purposes here, note simply that when speaking about religion, Mauss and Hubert argue that magic stands in fundamental opposition to the interests of the collective. It is fundamentally antireligious and unauthorized, taking place outside of organized social cults. In relation to science, however, magic is portrayed as too much in the thrall of the collective. Rational scientific innovation can occur only when the individual breaks free from the group sentiment. The problem with magic would seem not to be its general individualism but rather specific forms of antisocial individualism; at least in relation to science, Mauss and Hubert see individual agency as essential to innovation.

The German psychologist Wilhelm Wundt also rejected Frazer's claim that magical or mythological thought among primitive peoples represents a "naïve attempt at an interpretation of the phenomena which man encounters in nature or in his own life," "a sort of primitive science, or, at any rate . . . a precursor of philosophy" that imperfectly applies causal laws. Wundt argued that primitive man feels no need to explain regularly occurring phenomena: "For him everything is as it is just because it has always been so." Only phenomena that arouse emotions and elicit fear come to be the object of magical beliefs. Wundt thus asserted that it is emotion that must be seen as central to the operation of magic. It is "not intelligence nor reflection as to the origin and interconnection of phenomena that gives rise to mythological thinking, but emotion; ideas are only the material which the latter elaborates." As he stated:

> We utterly confuse primitive thinking with our own scientific standpoint when we explain it by the need for the interpretation of phenomena. Causality, in our sense of the word, does not exist for primitive man. If we would speak of causality at all on his level of experience, we may say only that he is governed by the causality of magic. This, however, receives its stamp, not from the laws that regulate the connection of ideas, but from the forces of emotion. The mythological causality of emotional magic is no less spasmodic and

irregular than the logical causality arising out of the orderly sequence of perceptions and ideas is constant.

While magical causality prepares the way for natural causality, the latter arises only when human beings direct their attention away from unusual phenomena and toward "the orderly, the regular, and commonplace." Thus, Wundt concluded, Galileo made his great scientific advance only when he looked to explain the commonplace of gravity; older physics had followed Aristotle in merely asserting that a body falls because "it must behave as it does because it has always done so."[22]

These various challenges to intellectualist psychology share a presupposition that primitive thought is fundamentally different from modern thought, based on instinct, nervous instability, collectivity, or emotion rather than intellection. This claim received its most prominent articulation in the work of the French anthropologist and philosopher Lucien Lévy-Bruhl. In his early writings on the "primitive mentality," Lévy-Bruhl argues that primitive people do not demonstrate logical or causal thought but rather remain in a mystical, "prelogical" stage characterized by affectational participation (between subject and object, cause and effect). This notion of participation, which traces back to Rousseau, forecloses the possibility that primitives can grasp even the rudiments of scientific rationality. Magic plays little role as a discrete phenomenon in Lévy-Bruhl's analysis, largely because in his view all primitive thought is permeated with magical, prelogical thinking. For example, he asserts that "the primitive, whether he be an African or any other, never troubles to inquire into causal connections which are not self-evident, but straightway refers them to a mystic power." In Lévy-Bruhl's view, the primitive prelogical mentality thoroughly mistakes the nature of causality, forming fallacious cause-and-effect links and ignoring relevant intermediate phenomena.[23]

E. E. Evans-Pritchard explains Lévy-Bruhl's position as turning on two fundamental propositions: "that there are two distinct types of thought, mystical thought and logical thought; and that of these two types of thought the mystical type is characteristic of primitive societies and the logical type is characteristic of civilized societies."[24] Lévy-Bruhl's formulations frame an emphatic bifurcation of humanity into the primitive and the civilized. As he explains, primitives are influenced by the communal and highly emotional atmosphere surrounding totemism, and, as we saw in Mauss and Hubert, they lack a developed sense of individuality. Primitive life is permeated by notions of magical force, while more sober scientific thought can emerge only among the civilized.

Of course this thesis of a "primitive mentality" was extremely controversial. Evans-Pritchard offers a succinct summary of the major arguments raised against Lévy-Bruhl's theory: "Firstly, he makes savage thought far more mystical than it is; secondly, he makes civilised thought far more rational than it is; thirdly, he treats all savage cultures as though they were uniform and writes of civilised cultures without regard to their historical development." Later in his career, Lévy-Bruhl himself came to severely constrain his hypothesis concerning the prelogical nature of primitive thought. He explained that he arrived at this theory in the effort to account for "mental habits different from ours" among primitive peoples. On further consideration, he determined that it is possible to render the "incomprehensible and amazing" facts of primitive culture intelligible without invoking the notion of a prelogical mentality. Thus the differences between primitive and modern thought should not be understood as differences of a logical nature. He concluded that the surviving "core of the truth" of his hypothesis is simply that for primitives the necessity of orderly laws of nature and the fixity of the forms of natural objects are not separable from the concepts of objects and relations. Because of their lower mental orientation and their confidence in mystical experience, primitives "do not accept that there is anything physically impossible, that is to say that the supernatural powers may at any moment intervene in, interrupt or modify the normal course of things."[25]

Presumably even civilized notions of laws of nature and the fixity of natural objects are inseparable from fundamental concepts of objects and relations. Yet despite these subsequent modifications, Lévy-Bruhl's notion of primitive participatory thought proved extremely influential. Jean Piaget built on this notion to argue that up to the age of six or seven years, all human beings live in a magical world comparable to the worldview of primitive peoples. Piaget argues that young children constantly blend and assimilate internal and external events, thought and reality, and thus lack a capacity for distinguishing between the self and the outside world or between psychological and physical phenomena. In the child's view, the external world is animated with will and consciousness. Piaget explains that the development of magic is related to the development of language:

> Signs begin by being part of things or by being suggested by the
> presence of the things in the manner of simple conditioned reflexes.
> Later, they end by becoming detached from things and disengaged
> from them by the exercise of intelligence which uses them as adapt-
> able and infinitely plastic tools. But between the point of origin and
> that of arrival there is a period during which the signs adhere to the
> things although already partially detached from them. . . . What the
> magical stage itself shows, in opposition to the later stages, is pre-
> cisely that symbols are still conceived as participating in things.
> Magic is thus the pre-symbolic stage of thought.

Magical actions appear effective only because the subject has not yet reached the symbolic stage and because the subject has not yet differentiated the self from external objects.[26] Magic would appear to recede, then, only when human consciousness is formally detached from any connection to the world of objects, only when culture is successfully bifurcated from nature. This trope, echoing Freud's analysis of the "omnipotence of thoughts" discussed in the following chapter, is common among modern scholars—it seems central to what Latour calls the "modern constitution." But it is built on a sustained repression of the direct ways in which human will and consciousness actually do interact with material objects.

Numerous other social scientists invoked Lévy-Bruhl's fundamental distinction between the primitive and logical mentality. For example, in 1942 the medical historian and anthropologist Erwin Ackerknecht adapted Lévy-Bruhl's theory to assert that while primitive medicine contains some nascent rational elements, it remains in essence magical. Ackerknecht argues that primitive theories of illness (based on such notions as mystical object intrusion, loss of the soul, spirit intrusion, and witchcraft) can occur only in a world that is the inverse of "ours," "a magical world where the natural is supernatural but the supernatural quite natural, where causality in our sense does not exist, but things, animals, and plants, are tied together by mystical participations and moved by occult forces." The "logic" (Ackerknecht's quotation marks) behind such primitive medicine can give rise only to "pseudo sciences."[27]

As Ackerknecht explains, primitive people are governed by emotions that create illusions (thus they remain in "the world of the poet or the dreamer"). Even in situations where primitives actually uncover natural causes for disease, that knowledge is so interwoven into the magical system that the primitive cannot grasp the difference. The primitive persists in searching for the cause of disease in "contact with the dead, the spirits, and the mystic ancestors. What for us is mere hallucination is for him a privileged experience." In all this, the primitive is wedded to "extreme traditionalism, conservatism, and conformity," a traditionalism that makes the primitive person "surprisingly insensible to experience."[28]

In light of this morass of error, Ackerknecht faces the problem of accounting for the persistence and, in fact, success of primitive medicine. First, he denies that there is any empiricism to be found in primitive medicine. Even when drugs known to primitives are actually effective, "the strange fact" remains that there is still no primitive empiricism within the magical system. As he asserts, "Magic is not built on experience; sensual experience never furnished the proofs of a magical judgment." Primitive people find successful drugs only by "animal instinct"; just as animals perform "reflex-like healing measures," so "in the same way man or pre-man chooses his herbs." But in subsequent stages of development, magic replaces these useful instincts with useless conjecture. Indeed, magic is responsible for a wide range of ills: "It counteracted surgery by mystical fears, perhaps introducing cannibalism, paralyzed growing empiricism by its traditionalism, entangled the materially effective measures in an enormous body of materially useless acts and beliefs."[29]

Ackerknecht offers other reasons beyond instinct for the successes found in primitive medicine, including the psychosomatic effects of socially reinforced action, the role of magic in sustaining the social order (and concomitant prestige of the magician), and a certain "metaphysical need" in human beings, an "irrational tendency." (The study of these issues, he says, can shed light on various contemporary manifestations of these same tendencies.) Ackerknecht concludes that it is absolutely erroneous to see the medicine man as the forerunner of the modern physician: "The conservative medicine man plays his role as the most irrational man in an irrational pattern. The critical modern doctor gains social leadership by expressing the rational tendencies in society, rationalizing even the irrational as for instance the psychoanalyst, and invading in this way the oldest domain of the priest." Rather than a predecessor of the physician, the medicine man is rather "the ancestor of the priest, the antagonist of the physician for centuries."[30]

Claude Lévi-Strauss sought to ameliorate the stridency of such theories of primitive mentality, but he concurred that there were important differences in thought between the "savage" and the modern. Lévi-Strauss defines this savage mind as characterized by the effort simultaneously to analyze and synthesize, as "definable both by a consuming symbolic ambition such as humanity has never again seen rivaled, and by scrupulous attention directed entirely towards the concrete, and finally by the implicit conviction that these two attitudes are but one." Savage thought is marked by its relentless effort "to grasp the world as both a synchronic and a diachronic totality" and by its focus on analogical connection in an effort to understand and represent the world. In this vein, Lévi-Strauss asserts that magic should be distinguished from science not because magic lacks an awareness of causal determinism but because it actually demonstrates "a more imperious and uncompromising demand for it" that ultimately leads to unreason. Magic is not primitive science but a parallel mode of acquiring knowledge.[31]

The debate over the distinctive nature of primitive thought has persisted in recent decades. For example, Jack Goody argues against the rigid bifurcation of civilized and primitive, rational and irrational, that long characterized much of the scholarly literature in favor of more specific attention to particular cultural formations and their change over time. But C. R. Hallspike, in his *Foundations of Primitive Thought* (1979), describes "the primitive milieu" as characterized by a form of thinking that is "context-bound, concrete, nonspecialized, affective, ethnocentric, and dogmatic," in contrast to "the generalizable, specialized, abstract, impersonal, objective, and relativist" modern mode of thought.[32] Most recent theories are much milder than the formulations of earlier decades, but as will be discussed later, many scholars persist in seeing nonmodern thought as fundamentally distinct from modern rationality.

Theories of Psychic Unity

Despite its wide influence, Lévy-Bruhl's theory of primitive mentality was strongly attacked, particularly along the lines laid out by Evans-Pritchard. One of the most interesting strands of criticism came from theologically inclined scholars who wished to defend the notion of fundamental human common-ality, often in the interest of Christian missionizing. For example, in *Le non-civilisé et nous* (1927), the Protestant theologian Raoul Allier sets out to clarify and correct Lévy-Bruhl's hypothesis of the fundamental difference between the civilized and uncivilized mentalities. Surveying information from missionaries and other observers, Allier acknowledges that these reports support the claim that "the chief characteristic of the uncivilized man is his amazing incapacity for attention, and more especially his disconcerting inability for logical think-ing."[33] Yet Allier wants to defend the fundamental psychic unity of humanity, and he actually finds magic a useful tool in his argument.

Allier argues that the "arrest of the intelligence" of primitive man can best be explained not by the notion of a distinct primitive mentality but by the pervasive, insidious influence of magical thought in primitive culture. Magic is fixated on tradition and stymies individual innovation and the development of new technical knowledge, since any change threatens the efficacy of tradi-tional magic rites. When aspects of "our logical mentality" emerge in the prim-itive mind, magic overwhelms and stifles those seeds. Magic does profound harm to the primitive: "The mind is warped, and the intelligence is thereby prevented from making real conquests, from profiting by those conquests; in a word, its development is stopped." The logic of magic is totally fallacious and renders uncivilized peoples "indifferent to truth." The evils that magic foments reinforce one another, leaving the primitive in a world governed by the un-foreseen, which, in turn, breeds even more uncertainty and fear.[34] Magic thus thwarts the birth of rational thought.

Allier explains that all human groups begin at the same starting point, but various groups progress differently. While remnants of the belief in magic persist in civilized culture, this belief stands in tension with the weight of modern intellectual and moral life, making its persistence "a mystery, almost a scandal." The uncivilized man, on the other hand, is "magic-bound every moment of his life. . . . the belief in magic determines the essentials of his inner life." For reasons not yet understood, the process of development has led humanity down two divergent paths, producing an "irreducible" difference between the two levels of culture. In this light, Allier calls for more humane colonial administration aimed at ameliorating the pitiable state of the super-stitious savages (a task best accomplished with the aid of the gospel).[35]

Wilhelm Schmidt also rejects the claims of Lévy-Bruhl, the intellectualists, and other evolutionary theorists that primitives lack logical capacities, and like Allier, Schmidt does so from a theological concern to defend the psychic unity of humanity. Schmidt gives great stress to the logical and rational capacities of primitive peoples because, he argues, it is this primitive rationality that leads these people to the notion of a monotheistic, personal Supreme Being:

> The prehistoric tools and weapons and those of the ethnologically oldest peoples of to-day are alone enough to show that he was a vigorous and daring man of action. To begin with, his mental powers made their way through nature and analyzed her phenomena; his synthetic activities mastered her by forming generalizing and classificatory ideas; he grasped the conception of cause and effect, and then adapted that to the relationship of means to end. His means, to effect the ends he desired, were his tools, which he invented and used. Now all this sufficed to lead him to a real religion, to the recognition of a personal Supreme Being; for he was able to apply these same mental powers to the contemplation of the universe as a whole.[36]

In defense of the theory of the primitive high god, Schmidt valorizes the reasoning capacities of primitive peoples.

Perhaps the most notable aspect of these arguments for the basic psychic unity of humanity from theorists such as Allier and Schmidt is the explicit theological objectives that drive the claims. Only if all human beings are fundamentally linked can they share a common religious perspective. Other theorists in the middle decades of the twentieth century debated the parallels between primitive and modern thought on the more pedestrian terrain of primitive ingenuity.

Theories of Primitive Ingenuity

Frazer insisted on parallels between primitive sympathetic magic and modern natural science in his argument that a stage of magic preceded religion and science in human development. But this argument was rejected by subsequent scholars who, paradoxically, had a much higher regard for primitive ingenuity than did Frazer. These theorists wanted to argue that scientific thinking appears in the very earliest stages of human development and that even in the earliest stages, magic is always seen as distinct from science. In these theories, the reification of magic actually served as a valuable tool in bringing primitive science into sharper relief. These debates provided an important site for clarifying the nature of modern modes of thought and an equally important occasion for exploring the relations between modern scholars and the nonmodern peoples they analyze.

"The savage," says R. R. Marett, "is perfectly aware of the difference between killing his enemy by striking him and killing him by striking at him through his image." Magic derives not from primitive intellectualism but from the primitive sense of magico-religious *mana*. Thus, Marett argues, the spell that accompanies magic operates not according to a formula resulting from induction or an assertion of mechanical causation but from symbolic actions of wish or will, a "projection of will, a psychic force, a manifestation of personal agency, *mana*." The magical act is a response to emotional tension, a form of cathartic or expressive action that should properly be regarded as a species of the occult and supernatural, not the mechanistic. As Marett explains, the magician never mistakes magic for mundane experimental action; the efficacy of magical action is always sought in a hidden spiritual link between incommensurable cause and effect. The techniques of the magical hierophant and the craftsman are thus fundamentally distinct. Marett rejects Frazer's argument that magic is primitive science and that magic develops from elementary processes of reasoning through the law of association on the ground that Frazer's claims (like those of Tylor and Jevons) are based on faulty and outdated associationist psychology. Instead, Marett asserts, in developed magic the rite is known to the "savage" as "the very antithesis of 'natural.' "[37]

In his essay "Magic, Science and Religion" (1925) Malinowski expands this theme as he explores the distinct functions served by magic and science in primitive society. He rejects Frazer's claim that science is not present in the earliest stages of human development, arguing instead that no primitive art or craft (such as hunting, fishing, or tilling) could have emerged without "the rudiments of science," "the careful observation of natural process and a firm belief in its regularity." These primitive accomplishments require both reasoning capacities and confidence in the reasoning process. In Malinowski's view the advent of tools and language must have depended on the existence of "primitive knowledge of an essentially scientific character." In normal productive activities the primitive is readily capable of making exact observations and sound generalizations and of engaging in logical reasoning. Malinowski thus also rejects Lévy-Bruhl's claims concerning the mystical and prelogical nature of primitive thought. Even the most primitive communities possess "a considerable store of knowledge, based on experience and fashioned by reason." So, for example, the Trobrianders demonstrate a wealth of agricultural knowledge (including knowledge of weather and seasons), and they also possess confidence in the accuracy and reliability of this knowledge. Primitives not only have a practical form of science ("a body of rules and conceptions, based on experience and derived from it by logical inference, embodied in material achievements and in a fixed form of tradition") but also possess theoretical forms of scientific knowledge "open to control by experiment and critique by reason" and even elements of "the really scientific attitude, the disinterested search for knowledge and for the understanding of causes and reasons."[38]

As Malinowski explains, among primitive peoples there is an emphatic difference between the ordinary realm of technical knowledge and the realm of "unaccountable and adverse influences"; the former are "coped with by knowledge and work, the second by magic." In his most famous example, Malinowski recounts that in the relative safety of lagoon fishing, Trobrianders rely solely on knowledge and skill, and magic is nonexistent. But in the danger and uncertainty of open-sea fishing, there is an extensive resort to magic to ensure safety and success. "Primitive man recognizes both the natural and the supernatural forces and agencies, and he tries to use them both for his benefit." There is active recourse to magic only when the primitive actor is compelled to recognize "the impotence of his knowledge and of his rational technique": "Forsaken by his knowledge, baffled by his past experience and by his technical skill, he realizes his impotence." In the face of this realization, the primitive is driven by basic and instinctive forms of anxiety, fear, and hope to substitute forms of magical activity that come from "a universal psycho-physiological mechanism." Thus for Malinowski magic does not arise from abstract notions of supernatural power or from purely intellectual cogitation but from anxiety and emotion that become manifested in external behavior.[39]

Malinowski thus argues that magic and science are based on essentially different mental attitudes and serve fundamentally different cultural functions. The basic feature of all magical beliefs is a sharp distinction between the traditional powers of magic and the other forces and powers shared by humanity and nature, a distinction between "supernatural efficiency" and "physical force." Malinowski summarizes the relation between magic and science in their respective relations to definite practical aims:

> Science, even as represented by the primitive knowledge of savage man, is based on the normal universal experience of everyday life, experience won in man's struggle with nature for his subsistence and safety, founded on observation, fixed by reason. Magic is based on specific experience of emotional states in which man observes not nature but himself, in which the truth is revealed not by reason but by the play of emotions upon the human organism. Science is founded on the conviction that experience, effort, and reason are valid; magic on the belief that hope cannot fail nor desire deceive. The theories of knowledge are dictated by logic, those of magic by the association of ideas under the influence of desire.

Malinowski also specifically rejects Freud's notion of magic as the "omnipotence of thoughts," arguing instead that magic expresses a constructive hope aimed at overcoming doubt and anxiety. Magic persists in large measure because of the emotional relief it provides in assuaging anxiety.[40]

In response to those who would create a wide chasm between primitive and modern peoples, Malinowski asserts that "the savage is not more rational than modern man nor is he more superstitious"; rather, the savage is only "more limited, less-liable to free imaginings and to the confidence trick of new inventions." Yet savage magic is thoroughly disappointing to the rational observer. It is nothing more that "an entirely sober, prosaic, even clumsy art, enacted for purely practical reasons, governed by crude and shallow beliefs, carried out in a simple and monotonous technique." As every field anthropologist knows, primitive magic is "extremely monotonous and unexciting, strictly limited in its means of action, circumscribed in its beliefs, stunted in its fundamental assumptions." As he states, "Follow one rite, study one spell, grasp the principles of magical belief, art and sociology in one case, and you will know not only all the acts of one tribe, but, adding a variant here and there, you will be able to settle as a magical practitioner in any part of the world yet fortunate enough to have faith in that desirable art." Primitive magic is hedged in by strict and invariable conditions: "exact remembrance of a spell, unimpeachable performance of the rite, unswerving adhesion to the taboos and observances which shackle the magician."[41]

There have been numerous critiques of Malinowski's functionalist analysis of magic. Some scholars point to the fallacy of Malinowski's simplistic distinction between magic and practical knowledge, arguing that magical practices often produce more anxiety than they alleviate or that magic is regularly invoked to complement practical skill. In 1948 A. L. Kroeber rejected the basic functionalist supposition that there is some straightforward relation between organic physical or mental needs and human cultural activities such as magic.[42] But Malinowski's approach also had many proponents. J. H. Driberg concurred with Malinowski's assessment that magic serves to provide emotional satisfaction when "embryonic science" leaves gaps of ignorance and uncertainty. Magic does not demonstrate the irrationality or prelogic of the primitive or any fundamental mental difference from modern thinkers; instead, it is "the sign of a questing mind, of a disturbed mind, of an anxious mind, of a mind desirous of probing further than it has yet reached." Magic provides primitive people with an indispensable element of confidence in the face of the unknown. It has now been established, Driberg states, that the primitive has forms of empirical science and a store of accurate knowledge derived from experiment, observation, and deduction, but this body of knowledge is distinct from magic. Magic steps in only when science fails, and the two forms of practice are kept "rigidly apart." In more primitive cultures there will be more magic, since there is "less knowledge to take its place."[43]

Evans-Pritchard and Ruth Benedict concur that primitive culture contains both systems of magical technique and bodies of knowledge equivalent to science. Evans-Pritchard praises Lévy-Bruhl for acknowledging that mental processes (both primitive and nonprimitive) are shaped by social conditioning and that "primitive mystical thought" actually operates according to its own coherent system of logic, yet he argues that Lévy-Bruhl underestimates the variety in primitive thought. "Savages" often have interests in objects that are not mystical, but are instead "entirely utilitarian and empirical," and "patterns of thought of a mystical kind are never exclusively mystical." These two modes of knowledge differ in regard to the experimental standpoint: "Science experiments and is open to experience and ready to make adjustments in its notions of reality whereas magic is relatively non-experimental and the magician is impervious to experience." Benedict also sees primitive magic as coexisting with primitive scientific knowledge, but unlike Malinowski and Evans-Pritchard, she argues that this primitive science is limited to a far more narrow set of "routine procedures" for such activities as felling trees and tempering pottery:

> Although both magic and science are bodies of techniques, they are
> techniques directed to the manipulation of two incompatible worlds.
> Science—and in primitive life the corresponding factual knowledge
> and command of procedure—is directed toward the manipulation of
> natural phenomena operating according to cause and effect. Magic
> is directed toward another world operating according to another set
> of sequences, toward the world of the supernatural.

In Benedict's view, magic is "the consequence of a blindness to the essential disparateness of techniques that can be used in dealing with the various aspects of the natural world. . . . the assumption of a mystic sympathy in the external universe by which techniques applied at one point are efficacious at another point." Progress in human instrumental control of the world is made only by abandoning this broad "pantheistic" procedure and by focusing techniques on a narrow set of ends.[44]

A different tack in the broad approach stressing parallels between modern and nonmodern thought came from the American anthropologist Alexander Goldenweiser. In contrast to the theories of Tylor, Frazer, and Malinowski, Goldenweiser underscores the continuing significance of magical thought in modern life. In his *Anthropology: An Introduction to Primitive Culture* (1937), Goldenweiser valorizes supernaturalism as "perhaps the most outstanding and certainly the most historically significant achievement" of the human faculty of imagination. Like Malinowski, he underscores the positive functions served by magical practices, particularly in connection with economic, industrial, and technical endeavors. Magic supplements technical efforts, increasing human confidence and even control. Yet Goldenweiser sharply contests the notions of theorists such as Frazer and Lévy-Bruhl, who would place magical practices in a primitive past or mentality or only amid the lower classes of modern society. As Goldenweiser argues, aspects of primitive magic have been eclipsed by modern technology, and magical practices are more prevalent among primitives than moderns, but magic remains common even among educated citizens of the modern world. He cites a range of examples of superstitious and magical beliefs prevalent in modern society, particularly in schools and universities and even within institutionalized Christianity. Goldenweiser argues that magic arises from the very nature of human life in which people find themselves lacking control and facing the unknown. Even when moderns try to be most scientific, they often prove to be "furthest removed from rationality." So, for example, technological achievements such as film produce great magical pleasure. As he states concerning "movies of the Mickey Mouse variety":

> These pictures represent the magical universe in its most undistilled form. We have here the same disregard of space and time; the typical magical shifts in size and shape; humanizing of animals, birds, and other natural features; transformation of men into animals and vice versa; accomplishment of impossible feats of speed and strength. And what is our reaction? When a huge monster hides his portly figure behind the trunk of a sapling, or when a cow smashed to bits by bullets presently becomes whole again, we are not outraged but delighted. The whole performance does not impress us as either ludicrous or absurd, but as fascinating and, for the moment, convincing. Apparently our minds follow this tabloid magic without any effort whatsoever, delighted to travel along these ancient trails. In such moments we are ourselves magicians, or magical devotees, pure and simple.[45]

When Goldenweiser turns to consider the relations among magic, science, and religion, he contests Frazer's assertion that magic and science share a comparable, mechanistic view of the world. While agreeing with Frazer's claim that magic seeks to produce specific results automatically through the use of uniform mechanisms, Goldenweiser argues that Frazer disregards "the essence of magic, namely the belief in the transcendent or supernatural power of the magical act, and, behind it, of the will that controls it, that is, the will of the magician." Further, the magician does not learn from adverse experience in the same way as the scientist. The magician's precision is "nothing but a sanctified routine," while the scientist aims at accuracy and readily alters hypotheses and experiments in the face of experience. While industry represents "common sense, knowledge, skill, objective matter-of-fact achievement," religion and magic stand at an opposite pole, representing "mysticism, a subjective translation of experience, a substitution of mental states for external realities." As he concludes, supernaturalism succumbs to the lessons of reason and experience only when the human being has learned "through measurement and inquiry and criticism and the detachment of the individual, to evade the pitfalls of myth and ritual, the shrewdness of the priest and the magician, and his own craving for the impossible."[46]

These theories of primitive ingenuity and its limits provided an important occasion for debate concerning the nature of modern rationality and concerning the relations between modern social theorists and the nonmodern peoples they analyze. Some scholars used this discussion as an opportunity to stress the fundamental continuities between modern and nonmodern peoples, while others were more focused on a need to account for discontinuities and differences. But whether the emphasis was on continuity or difference, the reification of magic and the process of clarifying exactly how it differed from primitive practical knowledge provided a valuable strategy for bringing primitive science into sharper relief. Various forms of nonscientific thinking could be segregated away as aspects of magic, and this cleared a space in which primitive science could emerge as a distinct entity.

Theories of Primitive Expressiveness

In recent decades, a large number of philosophers and social theorists have moved to new modes of analyzing the nature of magical thinking. One of the important themes in these theories has been to identify magical thought as fundamentally symbolic, a factor stressed by such figures as John Beattie, Edmund Leach, and Stanley Tambiah. This approach builds on Radcliffe-Brown's distinction between expressive and technical modes of thought and Evans-Pritchard's between the mystical and the empirical. The effort to account for magical practices as primarily symbolic action has, in turn, been subjected to critique from "neo-Tylorian" and other quarters, where scholars such as Robin Horton stress the various types of rationality underlying magic. But despite their differences over whether the accent should be placed on magic's expressiveness or its rationality, both sides of this debate share a fundamental common concern. For both, this dispute turns on the question of the proper definition of rationality itself. Magic serves as an important catalyst for debate concerning the boundaries of rational thought.

Dispute over the degree to which magic should be understood as primarily symbolic diverges into two interesting directions, both of which show the polemical utility and pliability of magic. First, for some scholars the debate over the coherence of magic has become an important site for debating fundamental issues of cultural commensurability. This issue is sometimes framed as a dispute concerning the degree to which truth claims that arise within particular cultural systems can be meaningfully evaluated outside of those specific systems, whether there is some position of scholarly objectivity that permits an evaluation of diverse cultures. For other scholars, this debate primarily involves the question of whether symbolist approaches to the study of magic adequately capture its rational structure. Does the invocation of magic's symbolic or expressive aspects expand our capacity to understand it, or does that move serve instead to forestall certain types of rational analysis? Underlying both forms of this dispute is a fundamental question concerning the extent to which modern rational analysis can comprehend the "nonrational." This area of debate over magic thus ultimately turns on whether magic might escape the limits of Western scholarly rationality.

A prime example of the first branch of this argument is provided by the philosopher Kai Nielsen. Nielsen strongly rejects what he sees as a fideist form of cultural relativism exemplified by scholars such as Peter Winch. In the essay "Understanding a Primitive Society" (1964), Winch challenged Evans-Pritchard's ultimate assessment of Azande witchcraft. Evans-Pritchard had concluded that while witchcraft beliefs cohere within the Azande system, the system itself is ultimately illusory. In Evans-Pritchard's view, the Western scientific perspective conforms to objective reality in a way that the Azande system does not. Winch rejects this conclusion, arguing that Evans-Pritchard is "wrong, and crucially wrong, in his attempt to characterize the scientific in terms of that which is in accord with objective reality." Winch argues that the scientific perspective does not have some ultimate privileged access to reality over the system of the Azande. In a similar manner, Winch asserts, the reality of God "can only be seen from the religious tradition in which the concept of God is used." Nielsen summarizes Winch's point here as follows: "As the concept of what is real or what is unreal *vis-à-vis* magic is only given within and only intelligible within the Azande form of life in which the Azande magical practices are embedded, so the concept of God's reality is only given within and only intelligible within the religious form of life in which such a conception of God is embedded."[47]

Nielsen labels this claim a bald version of "Wittgensteinian Fideism," a position that truth claims can be evaluated only from within the cultural contexts in which they arise. The problem with Winch's relativism, in Nielsen's view, is that it leaves us with "no extralinguistic or context-independent conception of reality in accordance with which we might assess or evaluate forms of life." Nielsen rejects Winch's conclusions concerning both Azande magic and contemporary religious belief. He argues, instead, that it is improper to cordon off contemporary religious discourse from evaluation in light of other contemporary discourses, particularly science; in the contemporary world we do not have "two *different* conceptual structures exemplifying two different ways of life. . . . we do not have two cultures but only one." Nielsen maintains that it is necessary to be able to state that particular forms of life are "illogical, irrational, unintelligible or incoherent"; he would do this, whether assessing Azande witchcraft or medieval Christendom, using "conceptual resources within each culture and conceptual resources that may cut across cultures" such as fundamental inconsistency or incoherence.[48]

In this debate and in other disputes concerning the limits of cultural relativism, magic is regularly invoked as the eponymous "Other." As scholars contest what types of cross-cultural communication or evaluation might be desirable or practically possible, the prime exemplar of the alien Other is magical thought. This leads to the second major focus of debates over the rationality of magic that have occupied social scientists in recent decades, the question of whether magic should be understood as demonstrating basic aspects of "rationality" or whether it should be understood primarily as "symbolic" or "expressive."

A recurrent theme in ethnographic literature has long been the difficulty of translating non-Western concepts into Western terms. For example, in his discussion of sorcery in Bunyoro, anthropologist John Beattie underscores the complexities of trying to translate the Nyoro word *kuroga*, which generally means "to injure somebody by the secret use of harmful substances or techniques." Beattie explains that such practices usually include "a magical element, in the sense that they generally have a symbolic, 'expressive' quality and are not ordinarily tested or varied experimentally like practical everyday techniques." But, he continues, the Nyoro do not distinguish between "magical" and "non-magical" forms of harm as do Westerners, and *kuroga* (which Beattie translates as "sorcery") does not necessarily involve magic. Beattie highlights the symbolic and expressive qualities of magic, arguing that magical systems have a coherence distinct from modern thought (which is built on the fundamental distinction between practical and expressive modes). The belief in magic, he asserts, is not practical or protoscientific but is instead thoroughly informed by the needs of symbolic expression. In fact, Beattie explains, many of the problems that Western scholars face in their efforts to comprehend magic arise from the difficulty of understanding systems in which practical and expressive thought are so inextricably intermingled.[49]

A number of important scholars have followed Beattie in emphasizing the symbolic aspects of magic (as opposed to its rational or functional aspects).[50] Theorists inclined toward this approach stress various hermeneutic methods of analyzing the operations of magic. Edmund Leach, for example, is a strong proponent of the effort to comprehend magic as symbolic action. Rejecting Malinowski's effort to understand magic primarily from a functionalist perspective, Leach seeks to account for the symbolic nature of magical objects and action. In his essay "Magical Hair" (1958), Leach focuses on the symbolic significance of hair, which had played a prominent role in early debates concerning animism and magic as a sign of personal power or *mana*. He argues that magical power is regularly seen as residing in symbols (such as hair) that can be detached from individuals in ritual situations. These circumcision symbols are invested with magical potency, a symbolization that is particularly effective because the ritual situation can signify castration. In putting forward this symbolic analysis, Leach states that his objective is to find a deeper consistency between the sociological analyses of magic and symbolism (exemplified by Durkheim, Mauss, and Radcliffe-Brown) and psychological analyses of these phenomena (from Frazer and Freud). And in this process he also hopes to justify the types of symbolic interpretations that anthropologists commonly make in their analysis of other cultures.[51]

Yet the symbolic and expressive interpretations of magic exemplified by scholars such as Beattie and Leach have been challenged by other important theorists. The most prominent critique of Beattie's approach comes from Joseph Agassi and Ian C. Jarvie, who argue that the effect of Beattie's analysis of magic is to construct two different modes of rationality, one instrumental and the other symbolic. In contrast, Agassi and Jarvie concur with Frazer that magical action is protoscientific in the sense of being "goal-directed and belief-dependent." They claim that the effort to identify the significance of magical acts primarily in their "symbolic" or "expressive" content is an application of modern prejudices that deny rationality to actions that look unusual to the scholarly observer. Instead Agassi and Jarvie underscore the ritualistic aspects of modern science and the intrasystemic nature of magical rationality. Primitive peoples resort to magic, they claim, not for the purpose of symbolic or expressive fulfillment but for the achievement of concrete aims. Agassi and Jarvie distinguish various modes of rationality depending on the degree of explicit belief attached to the action and the degree of social acceptance of those beliefs.[52]

Robin Horton is another prominent opponent of the "symbolist" approach to magic. In an influential 1967 essay, Horton analyzes the continuities and differences between traditional African thought and Western scientific thought. In this essay (aspects of which will be discussed in more detail in the following section of this chapter), Horton seeks to account for the differences between the two modes of thought by focusing on the "small-scale relatively self-contained communities" within which African thought takes shape. These small, closed communities lack alternatives to traditional beliefs. Despite his acknowledgment of important differences between traditional thought and modern scientific thought, one of Horton's prominent themes in this essay is that these two forms of thought share a fundamental continuity in structure and intention. Horton rejects the efforts by representatives of the "symbolist" approach to formulate various essential distinctions between traditional and modern thought. In his view these scholars seek to reduce traditional religious action (and, ultimately, all other forms of religious action) to "a species of poetic jollification rather than . . . a system of theory and practice guided by the aims of explanation, prediction and control." Horton sees this desire to bifurcate traditional religious action and practical instrumental action as an attempt to shield religion from rational scrutiny, serving the dubious ideological objective of placing "traditional religious thought beyond the range of invidious comparison with Western scientific thought in respect of efficiency in the realms of explanation, prediction and control."[53]

Horton is correct in his assessment that many of the participants in this debate seem intent on protecting magical (and, by implication, religious) thought from basic kinds of rational scrutiny. By configuring magical thought as primarily symbolic or expressive, certain types of rational evaluation are ruled out of bounds. But this means, in effect, that the ultimate focus of this debate is not so much about the status of magic but about the scope of rationality itself. Horton (together with Agassi and Jarvie and others) argues for a fundamental continuity among various forms of human thought, but the way he constructs this continuity serves to give a properly framed notion of "rationality" full sway over all forms of meaningful human conduct. (When Agassi and Jarvie wish to insult what they see as Beattie's conceptual sleight of hand, they declare his assertions "a ritual invocation of Oxford philosophy-magic."[54] Just as they believe their approach can give a meaningful account of magic in general, they also believe that their analysis can explain Beattie's particular form of scholarly magic.)

Despite their differences over whether the focus should be placed on magic's expressiveness or its rationality, both sides of this debate share a fundamental common concern. For both, this debate turns on the question of the proper definition and scope of rationality and the proper scope of scholarly analysis. Even those scholars stressing magic's symbolic or expressive qualities are eager to offer various types of analysis of that symbolism; they simply prefer modes of analysis either that challenge the capacity of a narrowly defined "rationality" to serve as the ultimate arbiter of meaningful human action or that expand the sense of "rationality" to include broader forms of meaning. For all the participants in this debate, magic is particularly tantalizing because of its position in relation to the boundaries of rational thought. Magic stands as a deep challenge to rationality because of the ambiguity as to whether it stands at or beyond the boundaries of the rational. Any answer to that question requires deliberate reflection on the meaning of rationality itself. Important variations of this theme will emerge as we turn to debates concerning the history of science.

Medieval Magic and Modern Science

One of the decisive characteristics of modernity has been the emergence of new forms of scientific thought. Intellectual and social historians have long sought to account for the origins of modern science and to explain its relation to prior modes of thought, particularly medieval and early modern magic. This dilemma persists in recent history of science, as scholars struggle to account for the relation between ancient and medieval scientific practices and modern forms of science. As David Lindberg explains, this issue focuses on the basic question of whether medieval and early modern science are better understood as fundamentally continuous with one another or as fundamentally discontinuous. Was there a "Scientific Revolution," and, if so, what was the nature of that intellectual and cultural shift?[55]

Scientific Triumphalism

For generations of historians under the sway of Enlightenment theories of social evolution and progress, there was widespread acceptance of the claim that modern scientific thought represented a fundamental and decisive break with prior schemes of inquiry. The thesis of discontinuity has its roots in condemnations of the ignorance and violence of the medieval period from figures such as Bacon, Voltaire, and Condorcet, and this view became particularly prominent in the later half of the nineteenth century in the work of historians such as Jacob Burckhardt. While historians of this perspective might acknowledge that early modern science benefited from the thought or method of classical antiquity, they insisted that the new science stood in sharpest contrast to the benighted stagnation of the Dark Ages and the medieval period.[56]

In this view, the Scientific Revolution was sparked by the emergence of a distinctive form of rationality that ignited in direct opposition to all forms of medieval and Renaissance occultism and magic. As Floris Cohen points out, historians of this perspective commonly assert that the rationality that distinguished the Scientific Revolution arose in open conflict with "various brands of mysticism, magic, supernaturalism, and the like, which early modern science conquered and gradually outgrew." Cohen summarizes this view: "The emergence of early modern science comes down to a general process of purification, to which the three undistinct sisters 'magic, mysticism, and superstition' contributed in an essentially negative way by allowing themselves to be gradually eliminated by science."[57]

In this tradition, the advent of science was a true revolution. These historical accounts commonly invoke Europe's benighted past as a foil that heightens, by contrast, the revolutionary luster of the new rationality. So, for example, in his 1958 account of the emergence of modern science, Charles Singer declares that knowledge in the Middle Ages was perverted, corrupt, and minimal. The early modern witchcraft persecutions (contemporaneous, of course, with the emergence of early modern science) are configured as the final great paroxysm of medieval superstition, and Renaissance traditions of high magic and hermetic occultism are depicted as an unfortunate outbreak of folly soon squashed by the enlightened insight of heroic scientific innovators. Historian Marie Boas provides a clear example of this viewpoint, as she writes concerning the era around 1630: "The sheer success of science and the steady advance of rationalism generally meant the end of the magical tradition. Mathematician no longer meant astrologer; the word chemistry replaced alchemy as a new science was born. . . . natural magic was about to be replaced by experimental science and the mechanical philosophy."[58]

The triumphalism of this account of the thoroughgoing antipathy between incipient scientific thought and the occultism and magic of the Renaissance is vividly captured in Preserved Smith's *History of Modern Culture* (1930). Smith asserts that the belief in witchcraft in Europe and America was destroyed by "the spirit of science with its revelation of a new world of law and of reason in which there is no place for either magic or devil." As he states: "The noxious germ of superstition can no more flourish in a world flooded with the light of science than can the germ of tuberculosis flourish in the beams of the sun, even though a few germs linger on and develop sporadically." The greatest achievements of science are not its material advances but "the diffusion of the bright light of knowledge and the consequent banishment of ghosts and bugaboos created by man's fear of the dark." "As the light of science brightened and diffused itself among the public," he explains, "some minds [such as Spinoza] had become completely rational." Smith concludes that even if superstition and magic were not thoroughly extirpated by Enlightenment rationalism, they suffered "a decisive defeat": "The devil . . . and his army of spirits still skulked in the backward parts of the world, in lonely country houses or in the chambers of the inquisitors or in the alchemical laboratories of the idle and uneducated rich. . . . yet, a vast change in public opinion had taken place. The sun had pierced the clouds, but not wholly dispelled them."[59] This newly enlightened "public" thus emerges in Smith's account in contrast to the "backward" country people, Catholic inquisitors, and the idle rich.

Smith is joined in the basic outlines of his account by many other prominent philosophers and historians of science. Bertrand Russell was a strong opponent of those who would find any place for magic in the emergence of modern science. Russell condemns those who would seek "to discredit modern science by suggesting that its discoveries were lucky accidents springing by chance from superstitions as gross as those of the Middle Ages." Russell argues that the decisive difference between science and superstition is not the content of beliefs but the nature of those beliefs: the beliefs of "the man of science" are "tentative, not dogmatic; they are based on evidence, not on authority or intuition." With this faith in the scientific mentality, Russell explains that the advent of science in the seventeenth century successfully banished magic and sorcery; by 1700 "the mental outlook of educated men was completely modern."[60]

Karl Popper follows a similar line in his account of the essential difference between medieval magic and emerging forms of modern science. Magical beliefs, he says, are essentially impervious to refutation. One of the basic differences between medieval astrologers and alchemists and their contemporaries who were developing forms of applied scientific knowledge was a lack of "intellectual optimism" on the part of the astrologers and alchemists. They were looking to the past for mysterious, lost secrets. In sharp contrast, prototypical scientists such as Francis Bacon were looking toward the future in the confidence that they could find new forms of wisdom, that they could "unveil the mysteries of nature without having to be initiated into the secret wisdom of the ancients." Relying on powers "independent of divine revelation, and in-dependent of the disclosure of mysteries in the secret writings of ancient sages," the new scientific approach to investigation encouraged enterprise and self-confidence. This independence from revelation and tradition set modern science decisively apart from older modes of inquiry.[61]

Throughout the many versions of this story of revolutionary progress, we see various efforts to insulate the new mode of scientific inquiry and rationality from contamination by what has preceded it. Yet the ignorance, superstition, and depravity of the past can be invoked in these accounts in various ways that heighten the contours of science and bring it into sharper and more flattering relief. The greater the darkness of the past, the more lustrous the victory of scientific innovation.

The Role of Religion

Through the course of the twentieth century, a dissenting view gained prominence challenging fundamental aspects of this traditional perspective. In contrast to the triumphalist account of the victory of modern rationalism over the superstitions of the past, a number of historians came to argue that, far from being discontinuous with earlier modes of inquiry, early modern sci-ence actually emerged as a more organic or continuous development from those systems of thought. Many important advocates of this thesis stressed the formative role of Christianity in the emergence of early modern scientific thought. Historians such as Pierre Duhem came to argue that the foundations of modern science lie in the theories of medieval natural philosophers and in the interaction between Christian theology and scholastic natural philosophy in medieval universities. Similarly, Alfred North Whitehead asserted that sci-ence arose in Europe only because of "the inexpugnable belief that every de-tailed occurrence can be correlated with its antecedents in a perfectly definite manner, exemplifying general principles." Whitehead argued that this convic-tion became implanted in "the European mind" because of "the medieval in-sistence on the rationality of God, conceived as with the personal energy of Jehovah and with the rationality of a Greek philosopher." He concluded that "faith in the possibility of science . . . is an unconscious derivative from me-dieval theology." Duhem and Whitehead were joined in this assertion by many other historians, such as M. B. Foster, who argued that the Christian doctrine of God as a personal and creative force transcended the limitations of Greek rationality to give rise to modern scientific empiricism.[62]

Other historians seeking to find a place for religion in the emergence of science have stressed the role not so much of Christianity in general but of its distinctly Protestant forms. This view emphasizes the novelty of Protestantism in its break with the traditions of the past (and is thus more attuned to some of the themes of discontinuity). A long historical tradition argues that the origins of modern science are to be found in the religious ethos of the Reformation. For example, Robert Merton builds on Weber's *Protestant Ethic and the Spirit of Capitalism* (1904–1905) to claim that specifically Puritan values "of a scarcely disguised utilitarianism; of intramundane interests, methodical, unremitting action, thoroughgoing empiricism; of the right and even the duty of *libre examen;* of anti-traditionalism—all this was congenial to the same values in science." A number of subsequent scholars have followed Merton in seeking to assess the precise role of Christianity—and particularly Protestantism—in the rise of modern science.[63]

The Role of Magic

Scholars have differed over the degree to which modern science should be understood as continuous with the traditions of the past or as a decisive break from those traditions. While some historians have rejected the triumphalism of the discontinuity thesis by stressing the role of medieval natural philosophy and Christian theology in the emergence of modern Western science, other historians have moved to examine the development of science within the broader social and intellectual milieu of the early modern period. This has led many to conclude that there were important links between Renaissance natural magic and early modern scientific thought.[64]

In the 1960s Frances Yates elaborated the argument that the Neoplatonic magic and hermetic occultism of the Renaissance played a significant role in the emergence of early modern science. While Yates acknowledged that there were important differences between hermetic magical thought and "genuine science," she argued that various strands of hermetic thought served to "stimulate the will towards genuine science and its operations" by encouraging new attitudes toward the natural world. Yates concluded that the "Hermetic attitude toward the cosmos" provided "the chief stimulus of that new turning toward the world and operating on the world which, appearing first as Renaissance magic, was to turn into seventeenth-century science."[65]

While many of the specifics of Yates's claims have been challenged, the basic outlines of her argument have attracted widespread support. Subsequent historians have highlighted the contributions of the hermetic and natural magic traditions (and various other forms of spiritualism) to the rise of science and offered nuanced appraisals of the relation between hermeticism and modern modes of thought.[66] One of the significant adaptations of Yates's line of argument has come from Brian Easlea, who analyzes the gender and class framework within which modern science emerged in the seventeenth century to formulate a materialist account of the rise of the mechanical philosophy. Modern science developed in opposition both to the traditional Aristotelian-Thomistic worldview and to the various magical cosmologies thriving during the early modern era. But, Easlea asserts, the success of the new mechanical philosophy over the magical systems "cannot be understood in terms of the relative explanatory successes of each basic cosmology but rather in terms of the fortunes of the social forces identified with each cosmology."[67]

As Easlea explains, early modern natural magicians and mechanical philosophers shared a common desire to exercise power over the natural world, and many of them also agreed that the "experimental philosophy" was the appropriate mode of inquiry. In seeking to account for the success of the mechanical philosophy over the natural magic of the seventeenth century, Easlea focuses on the connections of various Continental hermetic and natural magicians (such as Paracelsus, Bruno, and Campanella) with subversive religious thought and movements for social and political reform. In late sixteenth-century England, natural magic was seen as a threat to religious orthodoxy, and particularly during the English civil war and the decade that followed, natural magic became associated with radical populist politics. Easlea concludes that "not only did natural magic have atheistic connotations, it had socially subversive ones as well, a dual threat to the privileged that gave the mechanical philosophy its eventual cutting edge over those traditions and practices too closely associated with the beliefs of 'the people.'"[68]

In response to these social threats, orthodox Christianity came to attack natural magic by stressing that the material world lacked occult or extraordinary properties that could be tapped by the magician without recourse to demons, an argument easily harmonized with the new mechanical philosophy. Mechanical philosophy also had the further advantage of opening the way for the unfettered appropriation of the material world, making human beings, in Descartes's phrase, "the lords and masters of nature." As Easlea states, "If matter is characterized solely by the property of extension then it necessarily becomes mere stuff. Its mechanical appropriation by men is not merely legitimate, it is the only sensible course of action." Thus in England Cartesian mechanical philosophy seemed to offer a stable middle ground between the twin threats of atheism and popular sectarian enthusiasm. This philosophy also conformed with the immediate economic interests of the propertied classes in the spread of the mercantile economy. Easlea argues that the mechanical philosophy became the predominant cosmology, despite its limitations, in large measure because of the degree to which it served the political and economic needs of influential social classes.[69]

As Easlea frames it, the end of the witchcraft persecutions and the acceptance of mechanical and experimental philosophies both stem from the growing confidence by "male members of ruling classes in their potential ability to control events and an almost obsessive desire to impose such control":

> If nature is to be mechanically appropriated, then the course of nature itself (or "herself") must be regular and orderly, in no way whimsical or capricious, so that causes of effects can be identified

and reproduced at will. . . . no interference in the (regular) course of nature must be allowed that is not sanctioned or commanded by the (male) ruling elite; the Devil must consequently be dismissed as a reality or as an active agent in human affairs while God Himself, although Divine Creator of the cosmos, must be relegated to the position of benign spectator and supporter of the affairs of Europe's (male) ruling elites.

The belief in God need not be rejected, since that belief could be deployed in support of the powers of the ruling elites. As Easlea concludes, the resultant mechanistic cosmology rendered human labor more pliable and appropriable for the ends of the emerging capitalist class.[70]

Science as Sui Generis

Despite its many defenders and the work of subsequent historians who have adapted and refined Yates's thesis of the continuity between modern science and earlier hermetic traditions, Yates's claim has remained a subject of debate among historians of science for over thirty years. Her fundamental argument that hermetic magic and other occult traditions had a positive role in the emergence of modern science proved unacceptable to a number of historians intent on discounting the role of hermeticism and other occult traditions in the emergence of science.[71]

These debates over Renaissance natural magic and occultism offer a valuable demonstration of the political potency of analytical categories. If modern science is configured as a distinctive, sui generis phenomenon, this definition leads to historical accounts in which science is rigorously contrasted to the modes of inquiry that preceded it. Renaissance magic is left with only a negative role in the story of the origins of science, as an antithetical mode of thought that was decisively superseded. If, on the other hand, science is not reified as sui generis, historians can formulate accounts in which modern scientific inquiry shares important commonalities with prior modes of investigation or evolves from them in a more organic fashion. Renaissance magic might then be seen, for example, as displaying new forms of attentiveness toward the material world that could contribute to the emergence of new scientific modes of thought. The definitions of these basic categories—science and magic—and the ways in which the categories are deployed play a decisive role in shaping the various historical accounts.

The processes through which these categories are constructed and deployed, and the politics that animate them, come into clearer focus if we examine a particular text. One of the most prominent opponents of Yates's thesis of the continuity between Renaissance magic and early modern science has been Brian Vickers. In his introduction to the essays collected in *Occult and*

Scientific Mentalities in the Renaissance (1984), Vickers rejects the fundamental premises of Yates's argument, even in milder versions that would assert only that the occult had a minor influence on the development of the new science.[72] Vickers's arguments here are notable particularly because of the extraordinary efforts he makes to formulate and maintain a rigid and fixed boundary between scientific and occult thought as two mutually incompatible traditions. As his arguments build, Vickers demonstrates the rhetorical power of using this occult Other to reify and idealize the nature of science. His arguments are instructive in the present context not so much because of the originality of his claims but because of the vivid manner in which he sets out this compendium of arguments. Vickers provides a valuable example of the power of scholarly categories to shape a distinctively moralizing theoretical project.

Vickers begins by stressing that the distinction between occult and non-occult science was clear even in the sixteenth and seventeenth centuries, and he rejects any historical model in which modern science might be seen as emerging out of an occult or magical view of nature or in which the occult work of various early modern scientists (most notably Newton) might be harmonized with their non-occult science. It is erroneous, he asserts, either to seek any connection between these two distinct systems of thought or to claim that Renaissance occultism had any kind of positive role in the production of scientific ideas or techniques. Vickers proceeds to offer a catalog of what he sees as the fundamental distinctions that must be drawn between science and magical occultism.[73]

The first important difference between science and occultism is that occult science is marked by resistance to change. In Vickers's view, the scientific mentality depends on an ability to reflect and to abstract and, in turn, to assimilate the results of this reflection and abstraction (leading ultimately to an awareness of the very process of theorizing itself). In this regard, he quotes Robin Horton on the key difference between traditional African thought and Western science: "In traditional cultures there is no developed awareness of alternatives to the established body of theoretical tenets; whereas in scientifically oriented cultures, such a awareness is highly developed. It is this difference we refer to when we say that traditional cultures are 'closed' and scientifically oriented cultures 'open.'" In Vickers's view, the closed system of the occult is "self-contained, a homogeneity that has synthesized its various elements into a mutually supporting relationship from which no part can be removed."[74] Thus, the occult system (like "African" and all other "traditional" systems) is fundamentally conservative, blind to alternatives, and improperly holistic in the synthetic sweep of its worldview.

Next Vickers asserts that magical thought fails to acknowledge the proper boundaries between language and reality, between human minds and materiality, between humanity and the nonhuman world. While the scientific worldview clearly differentiates literal and metaphorical meanings, in the occult tradition metaphors are mistaken for realities, "words are equated with things, abstract ideas are given concrete attributes." Magical occultism thus demonstrates a tendency to think in nebulous and self-referential images rather than appropriate forms of abstraction. Far from constituting "a disinterested study of nature," the magical system is built on "a self-centered concern" for human welfare. As Vickers states:

> Much of occult science, if I may sum up the conclusions of my own researches, is built out of purely mental operations, the arrangement of items into hierarchies, the construction of categories that become matrices for the production of further categories. Far from being a science of nature, or even of man, it comes to seem more and more like a classification system, self-contained and self-referring.

Science maintains clear differentiation between words and things and between literal and metaphorical meanings, but occultism fails to acknowledge these boundaries. In distinction to the magical confusion of words and objects, "modern science has dismissed such ideas because they would imply that reality did not exist independently of language and that human whim could control the world." The scientific worldview is based on a recognition that "ideas and reality exist on different levels."[75] Modern science is thus superior to magical thinking both because science views human thought (and "whim") as fundamentally immaterial and because science maintains important analytical boundaries between humanity and other aspects of the natural world.

Third, science and magical occultism also differ in their responses to the failure of their predictions. Again Vickers quotes Robin Horton: "In the theoretical thought of the traditional cultures, there is a notable reluctance to register repeated failures of prediction and to act by attacking the beliefs involved. Instead, other current beliefs are utilized in such a way to 'excuse' each failure as it occurs, and hence to protect the major theoretical assumptions on which prediction is based." Traditional and occult minds lack the fundamentally scientific ability to question one's basic beliefs on the basis of predictive failures. In Vickers's view, this recognition of success and failure enables the scientific tradition to modify or even discard its theories because a scientist knows that theory is always provisional and subject to change. In contrast, the occult never disposes of even the most absurd components; instead, even as the occult assimilates new discoveries with the old, the occult sciences remain fundamentally unchanged.[76]

The progressivism of science stands in sharp contrast to the stasis of the occult, and the two modes of thought thus demonstrate radically divergent attitudes toward the past. While traditional and occult thought holds the past in relatively high regard (with the past often seen as a golden age of pure knowledge or simplicity), the scientific view is dramatically different:

The scientific tradition . . . sees the first age as . . . a state of deprivation out of which we have painfully emerged, thanks to inventors,
technologists, scientists. As Horton puts it: "Where the traditional
thinker is busily trying to annul the passage of time, the scientist" is
"trying frantically to hurry time up. For in his impassioned pursuit
of the experimental method, he is striving after the creation of new
situations which nature, if left to herself, would bring about slowly if
ever at all."

This scientist has "his" eyes on the future, envisioning and striving for new
creations that dawdling nature "herself" might neglect. Yet despite this enthu-
siastic affirmation of the instrumental capacities of the masculine scientific
will, Vickers immediately stresses that a further difference between science
and the occult is to be found in the fundamental humility of science. While
occult sciences "claimed to be omniscient, able to account for all phenomena,
and were, as a result, strictly irrefutable," modern science has demonstrated a
willingness "to admit the limits of its knowledge, to state clearly what it does
not know." In fact, this mature acknowledgment of limits further facilitates
scientific innovation, as science focuses more on questions than on answers.[77]

Vickers next turns to anthropologist Ernest Gellner's "The Savage and the
Modern Mind" (1972) to trace a further set of differences between occult and
scientific thought. The occult system, Vickers explains, lacks abstraction; it
relies too much on the concrete properties of the objects rather than a more
general, second-order focus on the properties of explanation itself. Further, the
occult is by its nature secretive or hidden, cultivating obscurity. While scientific
thought is designed to be public and repeatable, the occult seeks to restrict
knowledge to adepts or initiates, and the knowledge it generates is personal
and idiosyncratic. And again, while the occult persists in using "anthropo-
morphic, socioreligious, or ethical categories" and characterizations, modern
science is "socially neutral" and "ill suited for the underpinning of moral expectations, of a status- and value-system."[78] Science is superior to magical occultism because science disclaims parochial social interests.

Further, in its effort to account for the world in "homocentric, symbolic,
and religious terms," the occult seeks to form "totalities in which everything
mutually coheres." Science, on the other hand, "depends on a classification of
knowledge and language into various types" and into separate components,
and then applies different criteria of validity to these respective domains. Thus,
Vickers explains, "Primitive thought systems are able to tolerate logical contradictions that would be unthinkable to a modern European."[79] Europeans
avoid these contradictions, it appears, by segmenting the world and various
forms of knowledge into differentiated components and by keeping these differences firmly in place.

As he concludes, Vickers cites Gellner for two last distinctions between occult and scientific thought. First, according to Gellner, traditional societies are unable to distinguish between concepts "which have an empirically operational role, and those whose reference is transcendent"; they use "concepts that are, so to speak, semioperational, which have both empirical and transcendent reference."[80] In contrast, the scientific tradition has worked to define a boundary between the testable and the nontestable and has worked to inhibit improper crossing of this boundary. Again science is superior to magic because of its superior forms of differentiation and boundary maintenance.

Finally, according to Gellner, in traditional thought systems the network of fundamental beliefs is so widespread and mutually reinforcing that challenges to one belief reverberate throughout the system. Thus, in a traditional system the notion of "the sacred or the crucial" is "more extensive, more untidily dispersed, and much more pervasive" than in the modern worldview, where this notion is "tidier, narrower, as it were economical," less "diffused among the detailed aspects of life."[81] Science surpasses magic because the scientific worldview has successfully delimited the realm of the sacred. With the sacred cordoned away into a more "economical" zone, the world is rendered more readily subject to scientific manipulation.

Many aspects of Vickers's account of the difference between magical occultism and modern science are relevant for our purposes here. Perhaps the most striking feature of his enterprise is that the effort to reify certain categories requires that a whole range of other distinctions collapse. So, on the one hand, we find "the occult," "traditional thought," "traditional belief-systems," "African thought," "African magic," members of "primitive societies." Juxtaposed to this seemingly uniform mode of thought, there is "modern science," "scientific thought-systems," "Western science," "Western modes of thought," "the Western scientific tradition." In keeping with a lengthy tradition in European and American social thought going back through Lévy-Bruhl and beyond, Vickers configures a sharp, Manichean division between the magical and the scientific, the irrational and the rational, the nonmodern and the modern, a division in which all the related components seamlessly align. This aspect of Vickers's argument is particularly apparent in his deployment of evidence from the anthropological study of "primitive" cultures to further his claims concerning early modern European history. It would appear from the structure of his argument that there is little relevant difference in worldview between the high magicians of the European Renaissance and Robin Horton's "Africans" or Ernest Gellner's "savages."[82] The differences among these diverse peoples (chronological, geographic, cultural) evaporate as Vickers contrasts them with the scientific modern Westerner. And yet the principal effect of this rhetorical structure is not so much to submerge the identities of these practitioners of magic as it is actually to consolidate the identity of this modern Western thinker (appropriately rationalized and scientific), a figure who emerges in heightened contrast to all that has gone before and all that exists elsewhere.

Vickers uses this bifurcation of two antithetical modes of thought not only to consolidate the identity of the modern scientist but also to consolidate a single form of proper scientific thought. (Note, of course, that even as the differences among various forms of magic collapse, the differences among various forms of science also disappear.) The singular nature of scientific thought can then be used to bolster the claim that modern science is ontologically distinct from all preceding forms of "traditional" thought. Through this process, the conclusions of Vickers's argument are largely determined by his reification of a singular mode of scientific thought.

Yet this rigid contrast between science and magic serves even more significant functions in Vickers's argument. This abstract notion of science has little definition or content until it is brought into contrast with its magical foil. It is actually by means of his extended account of magic that Vickers is able to demarcate the precise contours of science and to explain its nature. He here provides a vivid example of the use of magic for the purpose of giving shape to a concept of science. Echoing innumerable earlier theories of magic in philosophy and the social sciences, Vickers explains to us that magic (of whatever cultural provenance) demonstrates a uniform and consistent set of features (it is resistant to change, closed, unresponsive to failure, traditionalist, inflexible, obscure, arrogant, morally biased). In fact, magic epitomizes everything that science is not—or should not be.

This leads to a further aspect of Vickers's argument that is worth underlining. While he has explained that modern science is "socially neutral" and ill suited to serve as a tool in ethical or moral debates,[83] the same cannot be said of Vickers's own account. In fact, his catalog of the contrasts between science and magic is characterized by a strident, and often moralizing, tone. Science, he tells us, should relativize the content of its theories (recognizing that this content is always contingent), but science's own relativizing method appears to be beyond question. Vickers uses the discussion of magical occultism as an opportunity to formulate and promote a distinctive set of scientific values and ideals, and he spells out those ideals and gives them rhetorical force through the deployment of magic as a foil. His account of magical thought demonstrates an overriding concern with policing human relations toward nature and technology. He offers a broad array of normative declarations concerning the proper mode of scientific inquiry, the appropriate shape of human engagement with the material world, and important limits on human efforts to manipulate nature.

As an example of Vickers's moralizing, let me turn to one final issue raised in his discussion of the distinctions between science and magic. On one hand, Vickers valorizes the capacity of the scientific will to intervene in the natural world in order to reshape the world to human intentions and desires. Yet on the other hand, he underscores the fundamental humility of science in recognizing the limits of human knowledge and human power.[84] Science is more effective—and, it appears, more moral—than magic because science acknowledges limits that magic arrogantly disregards. This aspect of Vickers's argument leads us to the concluding section of this chapter, a consideration of the ways in which scholarly disputes over the relation between magic and science have provided a forum for debate over scientific values and the value of science.

The Morality of Inquiry

Historians and philosophers of science continue to grapple with the degree to which modern science represents a break with prior theological, philosophical, and hermetic traditions or to which it is better understood as emerging organically from those traditions. As David Lindberg concluded in 1992, "At this point the question of the Renaissance and its scientific achievement remains something of a muddle."[85] Yet more relevant for our purposes here than the resolution of this debate are the important subtexts underlying the dispute.

In *The Scientific Revolution* (1994), Floris Cohen argues that one of the principal reasons that scholars of science have been so exercised by questions surrounding hermetic magic is that this topic opens onto broader questions concerning the role of science in shaping the modern world. Should the Scientific Revolution be seen as "the beneficial triumph of rational thought about nature" or as "the agent chiefly responsible for the destructive handling of nature"?[86] Does science epitomize the triumph of rational control over nature, or does it rather represent the victory of a dehumanizing reductionism? Does science teach us an appropriate humility in the face of nature's laws, or is it the pinnacle of human hubris?

On one hand, as Cohen explains, we find historians holding the traditional, Enlightenment-inspired view of early modern science as surmounting a premodern fear of nature with "the quiet certainty that we know, and can predict, nature's operations." Scholars in this tradition not only see science as a profoundly liberating force but also view it as decisively distinct from earlier forms of inquiry.[87] Such scholars are eager to construct sharp boundaries between science and magic. A rigid separation of these categories bolsters the distinctive and singular nature of modern science.

On the other hand, we find theorists and social critics more ambivalent in their assessment of the consequences of science, an intellectual tradition prominent at least since the era of Rousseau and early Romanticism. These scholars have been less persuaded by the Enlightenment reifications of scientific rationality and more inclined to stress the continuities between science and various forms of magical thinking (including the traditions of Renaissance hermetic magic and occultism). They have even at times invoked magic as an alternative to the dominant rationalist modes of relation to nature. Thus, Cohen argues, historians such as Frances Yates emphasize the links between early modern science and magical thought because this very relation underscores that the new technical insights of science came only through the suppression of alternative perspectives on human identity and the human relation to nature. As Cohen explains:

> The persistence of Hermetic patterns of thought throughout much of the 17th-century adventure in science betrays an acute awareness, among many though not all of the pioneers of the Scientific Revolution, that their new science, however irresistible in its intellectual sweep, causes an attendant loss of insight into the endlessly complex makeup of the human personality—not without consequences for man's future handling of nature. . . . Throughout the history of western European culture a dual attitude toward science can be discerned: the enthusiastic embrace of science as the embodiment of our triumph over nature, accompanied by bitter denunciations of science for its dehumanizing reductionism.[88]

Historians of the latter perspective configure the boundaries between science and magic as far more porous than do those of the first. A more organic relation between the two categories undercuts the reification of science and opens up a conceptual terrain with more resources for critique of the excesses of modernity.

At the core of these scholarly debates over the role of hermetic magic in the emergence of early modern science are competing visions of the nature and effects of science in the modern world. This broader context helps explain the tenacity of these disputes, and it also illuminates the particular role that magic plays in these conflicts. Magic is readily invoked by partisans of differing positions as the antithesis of modern rationality. As we have seen, one of the long-standing strategies for delineating the nature of modern rationality is to juxtapose rationality with magical thought. In this contrast, scholars have found a ready mechanism for articulating and contesting the nature and implications of science and scientific rationality.

This strategy shaped debates over the relation between magic and science in primitive society. Discussions of the nature of primitive society and primitive thought provided an invaluable site for social theorists to delineate the nature of rationality and to sound its limits. Primitive peoples provided a ready foil against which modernity could be defined, serving as a central component in scholarly efforts to map the boundaries of modern rationality. At the same time, the study of primitive peoples also provided useful resources for critiquing the pretensions of modernity. To the extent that these peoples were configured as demonstrating various forms of scientific, technical, or instrumental rationality, "rationality" as such was no longer exclusively modern; to the extent that these peoples demonstrated productive forms of interaction with their environment, they offered alternatives to the sterile and disenchanted rationality of modern science. Finally, primitive thought also served as a decisive test for various scholars eager to explore the ability of rationality to comprehend or explain the irrational.

One of the persistent undercurrents in these disputes over the relation between the primitive and the modern, the magical and the scientific, has been the morality of scientific inquiry. Just as the debates on the relation between magic and religion discussed in the prior chapter have been informed by moralizing views of appropriate religious piety, so also the debates on the relation between magic and science have been shaped by a concern with policing human relations with nature and technology.

Brian Vickers provided a useful example of these moralizing tendencies. At the conclusion of the prior section, I examined Vickers's argument that, on the one hand, science properly wields enormous power in reshaping the natural world to human intention and desire, while on the other hand, science is fundamentally humble in recognizing the limits of human knowledge and human power.[89] Science, he asserts, is morally superior to magic because science acknowledges limits that magic blindly disregards.

Vickers is alone neither in his ambivalence on this issue (is science assertive, or is it submissive?), nor in ultimately accenting what he sees as the fundamental humility of science. While many scholars valorize modern science as a tool of profound, liberating power that immeasurably enlarges "the bounds of human empire,"[90] many also join Vickers in stressing the fundamental humility of science. As a particularly vivid example, W. C. Dampier echoes this theme when he states that the spirit of magic is fundamentally opposed to that of science because the scientific spirit is shaped by "a slow, cautious and humble-minded search for truth." As Dampier explains, magic is arrogant and willful in ways far removed from the quiet path of science: "Science, with clearer insight than is possessed by magic, humbly studies nature's laws, and by obeying them gains that control of nature which magic falsely imagines itself to have acquired."[91] Science humbly submits in order to master.

There is a significant element of irony to this claim that science is fundamentally humble, not only because of the enormous social and economic capital of the scientific establishment but also because of the innumerable ways in which scientific "humility" has licensed unimaginable transformation—and destruction—of the human and nonhuman world. Yet this rhetorical contrast between humble, submissive science and willful, arrogant magic is a recurrent trope in the literature of the social sciences. Science is configured as respecting the appropriate bounds of both reason and desire. This notion of the fundamental humility of science mirrors the theme of the fundamental submissiveness of appropriate religious piety discussed in the prior chapter. In contrast to religion and science, magic is constructed as arrogant, willful, self-seeking. As Carol Urquhart-Ross stated it, "Magic requires that the will must be cultivated and nurtured until it dominates all aspects of being and awareness."[92] Practitioners of magic (primitive, nonmodern, or antimodern) are regularly depicted as dominated by improper and inordinate desires that lead them to magical irrationality. But the modern theories of magic themselves demonstrate complex networks of desire. In the following chapter, I will examine more explicitly the place of desire in these theories.

4

Magic and the Regulation of Desire

What men want to learn from nature is how to use it in order
wholly to dominate it and other men. That is the only aim.
—Max Horkheimer and Theodor Adorno

Magic and superstition make a notable appearance in David Hume's
Enquiry concerning the Principles of Morals (1751). Hume's discussion
of this topic is striking particularly because it occurs in the midst of
a consideration of the rules of private property. In order to determine the rules governing the distribution and control of property,
he explains, human societies have recourse to various social conventions (expressed in statutes, customs, precedents, and innumerable
other forms). Yet given the inevitable degree of caprice in these conventions, "nothing can appear more whimsical, unnatural, and even
superstitious, than all or most of the laws of justice and of property."[1]

Human society is filled with superstitions concerning a wide
range of matters ("meats, days, places, postures, apparel"), and
Hume acknowledges that the rules governing the distribution of
property might easily appear to be just one more form of superstition:

I may lawfully nourish myself from this tree; but the fruit of another of the same species, ten paces off, it is criminal for me to
touch. Had I worn this apparel an hour ago, I had merited the
severest punishment; but a man, by pronouncing a few magical
syllables, has now rendered it fit for my use and service. Were
this house placed in the neighbouring territory, it had been im-

moral for me to dwell in it; but being built on this side the river, it is subject to a different municipal law, and by its becoming mine I incur no blame or censure. The same species of reasoning it may be thought, which so successfully exposes superstition, is also applicable to justice; nor is it possible, in the one case, more than in the other, to point out, in the object, that precise quality or circumstance, which is the foundation of the sentiment.

As Hume asserts, "All regard to right and property, seem entirely without foundation, as much as the grossest and most vulgar superstition."[2]

Of course it is unacceptable for a matter as important to the burgeoning mercantile economy of the eighteenth century as the distribution of property to be so fundamentally arbitrary, and Hume searches for a definitive distinction between property rights and superstition. But he can find only a rather thin line of demarcation. Superstition differs from property rights, he tells us, because superstition is in its very nature "frivolous, useless, and burdensome." The rules of law and property, on the other hand, are "absolutely requisite to the well-being of mankind and existence of society."[3] Hume thus offers the rather tautological distinction that, despite their pervasive similarities, superstitions differ from property laws in that the one set of conventions is burdensome and socially maladaptive, while the other serves the central interests of society (or at least its propertied classes). We know a convention is superstition because it is disruptive; it is disruptive because it is superstitious.

A few pages later, Hume finds a further contrast between the pragmatic and socially useful rules of law and the murky principles of superstition. He explains that in the legal system (particularly in rules dealing with the creation of legal obligations), individual intention is regularly overshadowed by an emphasis on standard (and conventional) external words and signs. This rationalized legal focus on external conventions must be differentiated from the obsession with externals that characterizes superstition, an obsession demonstrated most vividly in Roman Catholic sacramentalism:

> It is a doctrine of the Church of Rome, that the priest, by a secret direction of his intention, can invalidate any sacrament. This position is derived from a strict and regular prosecution of the obvious truth, that empty words alone, without any meaning or intention in the speaker, can never be attended with any effect. If the same conclusion be not admitted in reasonings concerning civil contracts, where the affair is allowed to be of so much less consequence than the eternal salvation of thousands, it proceeds entirely from men's sense of the danger and inconvenience of the doctrine in the former case: And we may thence observe, that however positive, arrogant, and dogmatical any superstition may appear, it never can convey any thorough persuasion of the reality of its objects, or put them, in any

degree, on a balance with the common incidents of life, which we learn from daily observation and experimental reasoning.[4]

Thus, Hume would have it, while issues of subjective (and sometimes nefarious) intention lie at the core of religion and superstition, such amorphous and capricious factors must be exorcised from the pragmatic world of empiricism and commerce. Thin ironies aside, there is little doubt how Hume weights the relative value of these two realms.

In these brief comments, Hume sets out the themes that will dominate this final chapter. My discussion here will explore the central role of social and economic relations in scholarly theories of magic. As we will see, on one level, Hume is precisely correct in his assessment of the place of superstition and magical thought in modernity. He provides a valuable synopsis of many of the foundational elements of the common sense shaping the modern economy. Modern economic relations are built on rules governing the distribution of private property, and as prior chapters have shown, one of the recurrent themes in academic theories of magic has been a desire to regulate human relations with material objects.

Hume underscores the profound and uncanny resemblance between the rules of private property and magical superstition (a resemblance amplified by Marx's discussion of commodity fetishism and, later, by Mary Douglas's assessment of money itself as an example of magical ritual).[5] Yet Hume also demonstrates that modern economic relations are founded on the twin principles that these different modes of practice must be distinguished and that their resemblance must be repressed. And as Hume further shows, when all other distinctions fail, the boundary between the two realms can be enunciated tautologically: one group of practices—those under the control of the market system—are lauded as socially salutary (modern, rational, productive), while the other—those threatening the hegemony of the market or exposing its mystifications—are configured as a social threat (primitive, irrational, subversive). Scholarly debates over magic have often revolved around concern with the proper human relations to nature, commodities, and technology, and the boundaries drawn to demarcate magic have regularly turned on a distinction between practices that conform with the interests of the dominant classes and practices that threaten those interests.

Yet Hume's effort to distinguish between market and magic also demonstrates, despite his protestations, that this boundary is far less—and far more—hermetic than he might imagine. The boundary between market and magic is less hermetic than Hume acknowledges in that it often proves to be quite permeable—the subversive play of magic threatens at every turn to surface at the heart of the capitalist economy. Throughout modern theories of magic, we find scholars underscoring the degree to which marketing and advertising actively partake of magical associations and, at the same time, the degree to which magic remains a potent menace to the orderly operations of modern social interchange. Despite Hume's attempt to characterize matters of subjective intent as the concern of religion and superstition, not the pragmatic market, the very forms of subjective desire, intention, and antagonism expressed through magic are pervasive within the market system—indeed, they are constitutive of it. While, as Hume asserts, liberal property law might claim to prefer pragmatic rationalization to murky, subjective intention, willfulness and desire animate the capitalist market. Despite the voluminous scholarly efforts to circumscribe magical thinking in favor of more circumspect, rationalized interchange, it seems that the market inevitably reverts to magic.

At the same time, the boundary between market and magic is also far more hermetic than Hume acknowledges. The repeated and insistent scholarly gesture of demarcating that boundary is itself a hermetic, magical act. Hume's tautological effort to distinguish the two is an apt display of this magic. Like subsequent generations of liberal social theorists, Hume seeks to contain and marginalize unregulated forms of desire. His analysis assumes the form of detached rationalism, and in assuming this posture he is able to disclaim both the complex web of material spirits on which such rationalism relies and the potent—and uncontrollable—material transformations it can effect. There is magic in this theory-making.

This chapter opens with an examination of one of the major sites at which modern theorists have considered the role of subjective desire in the practice of magic. As we have already seen, magic has regularly been configured as impious and irrational, governed by improper or inordinate desires. With these associations of irrationality and desire, magic has been a significant concern in psychoanalytic theory. The first section explores various psychoanalytic perspectives on magic and the ways in which those perspectives have been adapted in other social scientific approaches. Psychoanalytic theorists have regularly defined the norms of mature, modern subjectivity through contrast with forms of consciousness attributed to magically inclined primitives, children, and other deviants. Yet even in psychoanalytic theory, we find important dissenting voices that affirm various forms of magical thought as constitutive of meaningful human life.

The claim that disruptive individual desires lie at the core of magic has been a recurring theme in scholarly theories of magic, but this notion has not remained an abstract principle. The theme has assumed a very concrete form as social theorists have invoked the figure of the magician, the embodiment of magic. The magician plays a central role in theories of magic, standing as the epitome of a distinctive complex of magical desires. Throughout the scholarly tradition, this figure is configured as quintessentially exotic and alien, a transgressive "Other" contrasting with the stable modern subject. The second section of this chapter examines the scholarly portrayal of the magician and the particular threat to social norms posed by the magician's desires.

The following section moves to consider more directly the relation between magical desire and social order. While many early evolutionary theorists ceded magic an important (if ambivalent) role in the development of human society, magic has more commonly been seen as a profound social threat, an impediment to progress and innovation. Scholars have differed over the precise nature of the threat posed by magic: some have argued that magic is socially conservative and authoritarian, while others claim that it is antisocial and anarchical. But despite these differences magic has regularly been aligned with groups on the periphery of social power (the feminine, the alien, the marginal), and scholars have commonly attributed the persistence of magic to the inappropriate and disruptive desires of these groups. Even scholars claiming to analyze the process through which magic is associated with the social margins themselves often replicate that very process. Through these various formulations, debates over magic have provided theorists with an important venue for articulating fundamental notions of social order.

The final section of this chapter turns to explore the ways in which modern theories of magic have reflected concrete political and economic struggles over territory and social control. Colonialism played a profound role in shaping these theories, with scholarly constructions of magic forming an important component of the Euro-American "imagination of empire."[6] In the context of immediate disputes over territory, the dominant theories of magic have configured distinctive modern norms for proper relations to space and location. Central to modernity are fundamental ideals of deterritorialization and universality, and theories of magic have regularly stigmatized desires and practices that challenge those ideals by inordinately privileging particular locations and objects.

The dominant scholarly theories of magic have legitimated two distinct channels through which human needs are to be constructed and resolved: a spiritualized religious realm (constrained to increasingly marginal and tenuous abstraction) and a rationalized scientific realm (given unbridled control over the manipulation of the material world). With magic deployed as the stigmatized mediator between religion and science, the separation between these two channels is reinforced, and capitalism and Western science are relegated broad instrumental control over the material world. Deviant desires and behavior resisting this channeling of social power (and thus transgressing liberal piety and capitalist rationality) are labeled magical and denounced as futile, irrational, and primitive.

Yet the debates over magic have also been far more mobile and polyvalent than this dominant discourse would acknowledge. Theories of magic have also provided an important ground for the critique of modernity and the articulation of alternative modes of social relation. Even within debates over social control, we can find magic redeployed as a tool for social critique. Turning the fundamental logic of modernity against itself, various social critics and activists have formulated magic as a line of subversive flight. Despite so much theorizing about magic—so many attempts to contain and circumscribe it—magic maintains remarkable potency as the "unthought" of modernity.

Desire and the Subject

Throughout the prior chapters, we have seen the central role of psychology in social scientific efforts to analyze magic. Many of the prominent opponents of the early modern witchcraft persecutions (most notably Weyer and Scot) turned to psychological explanations to account for the hysterical delusions of confessed witches. The British intellectualists and later psychological theorists such as Lévy-Bruhl and Piaget sought to account for the thought processes or mentalities underlying magical thinking. Functionalists and symbolists alike placed human emotions at the center of their discussions of magic. Various scholars have sought to explain the persistence of magic by recourse to the subjective desires of magical practitioners, and many different aspects of desire have assumed prominence in these theories—intellectual curiosity, emotional participation with the environment, self-centered gratification, thwarted needs. One of the most important arenas in which scholars have thematized the role of subjective desire in the practice of magic has been psychoanalytic theory.

Magic and the Omnipotence of Thoughts

The most influential psychoanalytic discussion of magic comes in Freud's consideration of the omnipotence of thoughts. Freud expressed overt contempt for the occultism of his day, calling it, in Jung's report, "the black tide of mud." But as Alex Owen has recently explored, Freud demonstrated a deep fascination with occultism even as he worked to distance himself from it. Early in his career he had significant professional relationships with various figures connected to spiritualist and occult movements, but he later came to have great discomfort with the occult connotations of certain aspects of his work, fearing that his early connections to spiritualism might besmirch the legitimacy of the psychoanalytic method.[7] Freud's discussion of the omnipotence of thoughts illustrates both his fascination with the workings of occultism and his desire to surmount it.

While Freud explores the primary process thinking that underlies magic in a number of contexts, he addresses magic most prominently in *Totem and Taboo* (1913). He responds here to contemporary debates over the origins of religion, arguing that animism (the precursor stage of social evolution to religion and science) is itself not yet religion. Freud rejects the claim of the British intellectualists that primitive people formulate belief systems merely on the basis of speculative curiosity; instead, he asserts, primitives are motivated as well by practical needs to manipulate and control the natural world. In response to these needs, human beings evolve a body of knowledge that allows them some degree of mastery over the natural world and human society, magical practices that (following Mauss and Hubert) Freud calls the "technique" of animism.[8]

Freud concurs with Tylor's basic view that magic derives from mistaking mental or "ideal" connections for real ones, but Freud seeks to carry this theory further in order to uncover the fundamental mechanism through which psychological drives can so effectively eclipse the laws of nature. The central error in magic derives from the inordinate degree to which primitive people believe in the power of their wishes, a tendency demonstrated also in the psychological makeup of children. As Freud frames it, even prior to developing a notion of spirits (the doctrine at the heart of animism), primitives engage in magical processes through which they create representations of the satisfaction of desires. This process allows them to experience gratification "by means of what might be described as motor hallucination." The satisfaction afforded by these representations leads to "a general over-valuation . . . of all mental processes—an attitude towards the world, that is, which, in view of our knowledge of the relation between reality and thought, cannot fail to strike *us* as an over-valuation of the latter." He concludes: "The principle governing magic, the technique of the animistic mode of thinking, is the principle of the 'omnipotence of thoughts.'"[9]

Turning to the scheme of human evolutionary development, Freud explains that in the prereligious, animistic stage human beings ascribe omnipotence largely to themselves. Freud concurs with Marett that magic predates the doctrine of spirits; in magic omnipotence is reserved for human thought, while in animism important aspects of power are attributed to spirits (laying the groundwork for the religious stage). As religion takes shape, omnipotence is transferred onto the gods (with human beings reserving for themselves various means of influencing the gods). Frederick Schleiter describes the Freudian view in his *Religion and Culture* (1919): "In the magical stage man ascribes '*Allmacht*' to himself. In religion, however, he abdicates this power in favor of the gods, but only in a somewhat imperfect way with a string tied to it, as it were, because he still considers himself able to wheedle or constrain them to encompass his wishes by means of manifold influences." As Freud explains, the ultimate scientific stage dispenses almost entirely with the notion of human omnipotence: "Men have acknowledged their smallness and submitted resignedly to death and to the other necessities of nature." Residue of the primitive belief in omnipotence can be found principally in the arts and in "men's faith in the power of the human mind, taking account, as it does, of the laws of reality." The process of social evolution leading to the scientific stage is paralleled by comparable processes of individual psychosexual development (with the stage of animism corresponding to narcissism, the religious stage to the phase of object-choice directed toward the parents, and the scientific stage to its "exact counterpart in the stage at which an individual has reached maturity, has renounced the pleasure principle, adjusted himself to reality and turned to the external world for the object of his desires").[10]

The magical mode of thought is fundamentally unscientific, because science emerges only after a recognition of the limits of human knowledge and power and an overt, conscious search for means to address those limits. The primitive sense of the omnipotence of thoughts can be witnessed with particular clarity in its survival among obsessional neurotics (though all neurotics share this same overvaluation of mental processes). Modern neurotics, Freud explains, resemble "savages who believe they can alter the external world by mere thinking." Freud thus understands magic as a fundamentally primitive or immature response to life situations in which appropriate boundaries are not maintained between desire and result, between thought and action. As Edward Benson states it, "Freud saw magic as seeking to deny mediation, to equate desire and realization as if the word incarnated the thing instead of representing it."[11] People prone to magic (primitives, children, neurotics) are under the inordinate sway of emotions and desires and fail to acknowledge realistic means for the satisfaction of those desires. Only with the development of an appropriate sense of limits and a mature surrender to the reality principle can the magical stage be surmounted. Freud echoes the scholars discussed in chapter 2 who argue that magic is characterized by improper rebellion, but while those theorists prescribe submission to appropriately transcendent forms of religion, Freud prescribes submission to the necessities of nature and the developmental principles of the psyche. In either case, the modern subject must learn to submit.

Freud's theme of magical thought as a psychologically immature response to untempered desire proved extremely influential on subsequent psychoanalytic theorists. Many scholars repeat his claim that magical thinking is characteristic of primitives, children, and various forms of psychopathology. For example, Alfred Storch asserts that primitive magic and schizophrenia are both the product of "a still undifferentiated will" failing to distinguish "real acts and mere wishes." The primitive lacks "definite ideas of things and of self as a circumscribed entity," and this failure leads to the magical objectification of various parts of the self and of others. As Storch explains, modern schizophrenics share these tendencies in their futile efforts to protect the ego from menacing external influences. In a similar manner, the French psychiatrist and psychoanalyst Charles Odier contrasts the "normal anxiety" leading to efficient action with "pathological anxiety" disrupting action and inducing magical thinking; anxiety can serve productive and adaptive functions, but inordinate feelings of anxiety and powerlessness lead to magical responses. Erich Fromm argues that the appropriate acceptance of reality involves an adequate sense of individual autonomy and power. Emotionally immature individuals lacking the fundamental ability to function independently and to address their needs through direct expression and action are prone to direct their feelings of dependence on external "magical helpers"—gods, parents, analysts.[12]

In his *Comparative Psychology of Mental Development* (1957), developmental psychologist Heinz Werner builds on the theme that magic disregards boundaries and limits essential to the modern, scientific worldview. Werner argues that the core of magical thinking (exemplified in primitives, children, and the pathologically disturbed) is to be found in a type of syncretic and diffuse perception in which human emotion or affect distorts sense perception. Objects are not understood as appropriately passive and neutral but rather appear to be "foci of dynamic powers." The world becomes filled with "magical entities that are the reflections of the interplay of human fears and desires." In this primitive syncretic mode, abstract thinking is not yet differentiated from "imaginative-perceptual activities," and thought is "limited to and enclosed within concrete, picture-like forms," with ideas materializing only in activities and objects. It is only "for us at a more advanced level" to recognize the actual contours of objects as "a thoroughly formal, objective quality."[13]

This syncretic, magical mode of perception has many detrimental effects. First, Werner explains, it prevents appropriate demarcations between subjective and objective phenomena. Because of the similarities between the subjective world of dreams and visions and the external world of objects, primitives come to believe that human wishes and thoughts are "reality itself." The world and the ego are so intermingled that perception operates primarily "in terms of the emotional needs of the self." Moreover, the inability to differentiate affect and perception means that the content of perception is often highly contradictory—disparate notions and objects are brought into indiscriminate contact, just as gods and demons are often imbued with contradictory attributes. And further, in this syncretic mode meaning itself remains fundamentally fluid. Perception and significance can change based on new circumstances or moods; a single idea can "invade the entire world . . . everything susceptible to this idea suffers a transformation."[14]

The primary effect of this syncretic perception is that primitive thought is dominated by a "diffuseness" in which "the totality overrules the differentiation into elements." In conceptually advanced modes of perception, objects are characterized by "having a constant, immutable substratum to which are attached essential properties" and by a "strict delimitation and closure." But in the magical view, objects are not seen as objective or constant but as "labile, pliant" entities that can change in character and in attribute. Neither their essence nor their properties remain constant. In magic the structure of objects is "diffuse and homogeneous," with essential and nonessential properties intermingling indiscriminately; "the part is seen as the representative of the whole, and the whole consists of a diffuse union of global properties." This primitive, magical sense also means that objects may acquire the properties of other entities—"the connection between persons and things, or between things and other things can be so intimate and syncretized that the properties become transferable." Magic thus renders reality inherently unstable.[15]

In a more recent version of this theme of the omnipotence of thoughts, Leonard Zusne and Warren H. Jones argue in their 1989 study of anomalistic psychology that magic turns on "a confusion of semantic and physical relationships, a confusion between one's interpretive categories and the events they refer to." Magic fails to acknowledge the distinction between physical and psychological causes, the difference between "energetic and informational processes." As Zusne and Jones state it, "When meaning, instead of the physical processes of energy transfer or information transmission, is taken to be causal, when meaning is externalized or reified, magical thinking enters into this picture." The notion of "participation" as used by Piaget and Lévy-Bruhl designates "the mystical belief that everybody and everything form part of each other, with no strict boundaries drawn between one being and another, between beings and things, and between the subjective and the objective." From this perspective, magic turns on the "reification of subjectivity," a process centering on the omnipotence of thoughts.[16]

This fundamental Freudian conception of magic has been a subject of extensive debate among social scientists. Some anthropologists, such as Alexander Goldenweiser, quickly rejected the notion that the omnipotence of thoughts should be viewed primarily as characteristic of primitive societies, pointing instead to its prevalence in the modern world. Other theorists cited ethnographic data to challenge various aspects of Freud's developmental arguments. For example, Ruth Benedict asserted that while the parallel Freud draws between magic and obsessional neuroses might seem to indicate that magic is used to give a sense of security and to promote wish fulfillment, in practice magic often serves only to underscore and institutionalize fear and insecurity. As Benedict concluded, beliefs in magic and sorcery operate largely "through the institutionalizing of a fear neurosis."[17]

Other social scientists were more favorably inclined toward Freud's notion. Anthropologist Paul Radin argues that the original human postulation of the supernatural was an evolutionary development in which human beings sought "to adjust the perceiving ego to the things outside" by absorbing those external objects into the ego and preventing them from exercising independent power, a process rooted in human animal nature. In this early developmental stage, magical thinking ascribes coercive power to humanity alone or to the coercive interaction of the ego and external objects. Radin asserts that "in the extended learning process called civilization, magic constitutes the first application of the principle of causation, the first explanation of the interaction of the ego and the object." In fact, he explains, this magical process actually predates humanity, since apes and monkeys both face the same circumstances confronting early humanity and respond in similar ways. In the course of evolution from magic toward religion, we find "a progressive disentanglement of the ego from an infantile subjectivism; the freeing of man, as Freud has correctly observed, from the compulsive power of thought." Over time, religious innovators socialize and objectify the procedures of magic and, in that process, "mitigate the rigorousness of the coercion exercised by the ego upon the object." External objects are thus ceded independent powers. The concept of a supreme deity begins to take hold, which in time comes to dominate a passive humanity.[18] In Radin's view, magic is a productive stage of human development, but in this stage human beings are unable to recognize the appropriate limits of the ego in relation to the material world.

Underlying these different versions of the Freudian theme of magic as the omnipotence of thoughts is a constellation of normative views of mature and rational human identity. An appropriately differentiated and mature modern individual exercises autonomous and externally directed action in which emotion and desire are kept distinct from perception and cognition. The external world is to be seen as stable, objective, and orderly. Clear boundaries are to be maintained between the individual and the world, among individuals, and among objects in the world. Any modes of action or agency that exceed those directives, through either an overinvestment of desire or a blurring of conceptual boundaries, lapse into magic. Subjectivity must be kept within the bounds of a reified notion of "reality."

But there are a number of questions to be raised about this fundamental formulation of magic as the omnipotence of thoughts. Pamela Thurschwell has underscored the deep level at which Freudian psychoanalytic theory turns on simultaneously "inviting and disavowing magical thinking." As she explains, psychoanalysis claims to master magical thinking both in identifying it with psychic immaturity and in subjecting it to rational analysis. But at the same time psychoanalysis is drawn to magical thinking because the notion is so essential to explaining the basic workings of the unconscious: "At crucial moments [psychoanalysis] relies on [magical thinking] as a bridge between unconscious desire and worldly effects."[19] Without a basic sense of the omnipotence of thoughts, unconscious desires would never be manifested in worldly action; meaningful human action would not be initiated without a deep sense that the will can effect change in the world. In seeking to banish the omnipotence of thoughts from mature modern subjectivity, Freudian psychoanalytic theory wildly overestimates the potential for objective perception and dispassionate action. At the same time, this approach has great difficulty in specifying exactly what might constitute an overinvestment of mental processes or how the precise limits of the ego should be drawn in relation to materiality. Defining magic as the "omnipotence of thoughts" is a rather vacuous assertion without an analytical frame permitting an assessment of the social and economic factors that give the boundaries of subjectivity and individual autonomy their aura of "realism"—and that give the thoughts of some subjects so much more omnipotence than those of others. But that assessment would turn us toward the very type of material factors that Freud was so poorly equipped to acknowledge.

Magic and Realistic Action

The psychoanalyst and anthropologist Géza Róheim addressed certain of these issues in his posthumously published essay "The Origin and Function of Magic" (1955). Róheim here argues that the basic forms of magic spring from the same root as schizophrenic fantasy. But Róheim distinguishes "schizophrenic magic" (which eschews all realistic action) from "magic in general" (which can promote active response to difficulties). Róheim states that magic is "located somewhere half-way between the pure pleasure principle and the reality principle," in that it involves more than pure hallucinatory wish fulfillment and less than simple instrumental labor. Even Malinowski, he asserts, overestimated the degree to which magic is unrealistic. Magic is invented in the autoerotic libido as "the infant obtains mastery over the separation situation by finding pleasure in its own body." In this way the infant reidentifies with the mother as a source of pleasure and in fantasy assumes mastery of the world.[20]

Róheim concurs with Freud and Piaget that all human beings "grow up via *magic*":

> We pass through the pregenital to the genital phases of organization, and concurrently our mastery of our own body and of the environment increases. This is our own "magic". . . . The child deals with the threat of object loss either by identification or by calling on the sources of pleasure within its own body. Magic may thus be oral, anal, urethral, narcissistic, or phallic. It is our great reservoir of strength against frustration and defeat and against the superego.

This growth through the stage of magic is essential for human development in teaching a productive response to the frustrations of reality. Without the belief in magic and in its own magical abilities, a child cannot learn to withstand the challenges of the environment and the superego. Yet given the logic of this developmental progression, "magic in the hands of an adult means a regression to an infantile fantasy." Childhood magical thought involves a denial of appropriate human dependency on the parents; it is thus also "a revolt against the gods."[21]

While Róheim accepts Freud's claim that the magical attitude can be found in all neuroses, he differs from Freud in seeing magic as a centrally important component of every human personality. All human beings tend to repeat certain actions, believing that the repetition will serve to avert danger and promote success, and this repetitive behavior clearly constitutes an unconscious form of magic. Repetition "keeps us true to ourselves and prevents the loss of our infantile introjects or love objects." In all its forms magic involves the effort of the ego to direct "id strivings toward the environment" in the effort to reunite with the lost object.[22]

Róheim thus postulates that between Freud's pleasure principle ("wish fulfillment in imagination") and the reality principle ("the ability to weight the pros and cons of a situation") lies a third magical principle that "deals with the world outside as if it were governed by our wishes or drives or emotions." While this middle principle is unrealistic in a number of fundamental respects, it is "at the same time the only way in which we can achieve something in reality." The belief that it is possible to satisfy desires—the belief that satisfaction is possible because of the desires—is an essential adjunct to "realistic action" in the effort to meet human needs. Thus Róheim concludes, "We might therefore say that mankind functions mainly according to the magical principle." The goal of analysis should never be the elimination of magical thinking: "We cannot transform a species with a prolonged infancy into a calculating machine."[23]

In a lengthy 1969 examination of the psychology of superstitions, Gustav Jahoda follows on Róheim's theory by asserting that superstition might well have positive effects on individual psychology. For example, it can provide a subjective sense of power, predictability, and control, thereby reducing forms of anxiety that could hinder effective responses to danger. In addition, superstition can serve to support beneficial social norms and to encourage the repetition of behavior that has proved to have no harmful effects. In Jahoda's view superstition takes hold as "an inevitable by-product of the constant scanning for patterns in which we are engaged." Scientific thought and magic both seek patterns in the natural world: "The search for order, regularity and meaning is a general characteristic of human thought processes." Jahoda concludes that superstition is "intimately bound up with our fundamental modes of thinking, feeling and generally responding to our environment . . . an integral part of the adaptive mechanisms without which humanity would be unable to survive."[24]

We see in psychological theorists such as Róheim and Jahoda the attempt to affirm the role of subjective desire and a sense of power in meaningful human action. While acknowledging that aspects of magical thinking are fundamentally unrealistic, Róheim and Jahoda both see magical thinking as a basic constituent of all human action and as demonstrating positive adaptive value. Freud's notion of magic as the omnipotence of thoughts configures magical thinking as flouting an essential boundary between desire and realistic action. In a related gesture, various scholars discussed in preceding chapters have defined magic so broadly that it seems to encompass all willful, purposeful action. In response, Róheim and Jahoda underscore that factors such as expectation, desire, and a sense of control are essential to any meaningful notion of human identity and to any type of human action. Yet their conclusion that these aspects of magical thinking are essential elements in all human action raises, in turn, important questions concerning the basic effort to reify "magical thought" in the first place. When we see Róheim asserting both that magic is characteristic of schizophrenic and neurotic behavior and that magic is an essential component of every human activity based on wish or desire, we might rightly question the analytical utility of such a concept. In the hands of these psychoanalytic theorists, magic seems to have both too much and too little content to provide useful conceptual clarity.

Magic and Intersubjective Power

This question of the utility of magic as a psychoanalytic concept leads us once again to the issue of the phantasmatic powers exercised by scholars themselves. In deploying magic as a conceptual tool, psychoanalytic theorists are engaged in the production of potent intersubjective effects. In his *Eros and Magic in the Renaissance* (1987), Ioan Couliano identifies this mode of intersubjective power as itself a form of magic.

Couliano argues that rather than diagnosing magic as schizophrenia (in the manner of Freud and even Róheim), we are better served by understanding magic as a form of psychoanalysis. Medieval magic, Couliano explains, functioned as a "science of the imaginary," "a means of control over the individual and the masses based on deep knowledge of personal and collective erotic impulses." Couliano affirms a principle he attributes to Marsilio Ficino: "Magic is merely eroticism applied, directed, and aroused by its performer." The medieval magician served as "psychoanalyst and prophet . . . the precursor of modern professions such as director of public relations, propagandist, spy, politician, censor, director of mass communications media, and publicity agent." Magicians and prophets have not fallen in decline; instead they have become "camouflaged in sober and legal guises, the analyst being one of them. . . . Nowadays the magician busies himself with public relations, propaganda, market research, sociological surveys, publicity, information, counterinformation and misinformation, censorship, espionage, and even cryptography." Couliano thus asserts, "Nothing has replaced magic on its own terrain, that of intersubjective relationships. To the extent that they have an operational aspect, sociology, psychology, and applied psychosociology represent, in our time, indirect continuations of magic revived."[25]

Couliano attributes the Marxist notion of religion as the opium of the people to Neoplatonic magicians such as Giordano Bruno, who saw religion as a powerful tool for controlling and manipulating the masses. In fact, Bruno's ideal of the magician was a "prototype of the impersonal systems of mass media, indirect censorship, global manipulation, and the brain trusts that exercise their occult control over the Western masses." Historians are wrong to conclude that magic faded with the arrival of quantitative science, since these sciences actually serve to extend the reach of magic by means of technology: "Technology, it can be said, is a democratic magic that allows everyone to enjoy the extraordinary capabilities of which the magician used to boast."[26]

Couliano's claims here echo themes sounded earlier by Sartre. In his study of the emotions, Sartre argues that emotions themselves are the manifestation of a magical response to the world. When other avenues of effective action through practical means are blocked, emotions seek magically to alter the quality of external objects. Because of the fundamental unreality of the response, magic commonly represents a degraded form of consciousness. Yet there are situations in which the magical is not "an ephemeral quality which we impose upon the world as our moods dictate"; instead, the magical reflects the fundamental existential quality of central aspects of the world itself. As Sartre states it, "The category 'magical' governs the interpsychic relations of men in society and, more precisely, our perception of others." The magical is

> an irrational synthesis of spontaneity and passivity. It is an inert activity, a consciousness rendered passive. But it is precisely in this form that others appear to us, and they do so not because of our position in relation to them, not as the effect of our passions, but out of essential necessity. . . . Thus, man is always a wizard to man, and the social world is at first magical. It is not impossible to take a deterministic view of the interpsychological world nor to build rational superstructures upon this magical world. But this time it is they which are ephemeral and without equilibrium; it is they which cave in when the magical aspect of facts, of gestures, and of human situations is too strong. What happens, then, when the superstructures laboriously built by reason cave in and man finds himself once again abruptly plunged into the original magic? It is easy to guess; consciousness seizes upon the magical as magical; it forcibly lives it as such.

Determinism and rationality are ephemeral superstructures erected over the fundamentally magical realm of interpersonal relations. Thus, Sartre concludes, there are ultimately two forms of emotion, one in which we seek to exercise magic in lieu of thwarted practical action and a second in which the world abruptly and accurately "reveals itself as being magical."[27]

Like Sartre, Couliano affirms the essentially magical quality of human relations. Through the skillful manipulation of eroticism, deception, and desire, practitioners of intersubjective magic are able to effect potent material changes. In fact, Sartre and Couliano seem to indicate that intersubjective relations are most appropriately understood through the mode of magical thinking. Yet this notion of magic as intersubjective power leads once again to questions concerning the viability of magic as a useful analytical concept. If magic is seen as permeating human relations, as saturating the world of human interaction, this amorphous sense of intersubjective manipulation offers little in the way of conceptual illumination. If magic is everywhere, it is nowhere. In an effort to clarify the surreptitious social and psychological power exerted in these forms of intersubjective magic, a number of scholars have directed their attention to the most prominent practitioner of magic, the magician.

The Desires of the Magician

The dominant psychoanalytic theories of magic presuppose a distinctive set of norms for modern subjectivity. The modern subject is to have a mature respect for reified notions of material reality and a clear sense of the boundaries of the ego. This subject should demonstrate appropriately individuated and autonomous forms of action, but this action should conform with socially sanctioned modes of industry. This subject should exhibit a fundamental stability in its regularized relations with the material world and the political order.

These norms for the modern subject are brought into clearer relief in contrast to one of the prime archetypes of the nonmodern subject, the magician. The magician is important to systems of magic, but the magician also assumes a central role in theories of magic. As the active promulgator of magical belief and practice, the embodiment of magical desire, the magician has fascinated—and perplexed—social theorists seeking to comprehend magic. As we will see, a number of important themes underlying the scholarly debates concerning magic coalesce in discussions of the magician.

The "Impostor Who Is His Own Dupe"

One of the major questions that has preoccupied theorists seeking to uncover the nature of magic involves the sincerity or deceit of the magician. Is the magician a dupe who believes his own magical claims? Or is he a duplicitous fraud seeking to augment his personal status? Or, given the imponderable difficulties surrounding the resolution of these questions, is the magician better understood, as Raoul Allier concludes, to be an "impostor who is his own dupe"?[28] Numerous scholars have addressed this issue. Some stress the fundamental gullibility of magicians, while others highlight the elements of fraud and trickery involved in the practice of magic.

This theme features prominently in Tylor's effort to explain the persistence of the belief in magic. According to Tylor, magic is too pervasive and resilient to depend solely on deceit and imposture. Magic has its origins not in mere fraud but in "a sincere but fallacious system of philosophy, evolved by the human intellect by processes still in great measure intelligible to our own minds."[29] Magic follows its own form of logic, and it persists because many of its adepts sincerely believe its claims.

A number of theorists have joined Tylor in stressing the sincerity of the magician. Mauss and Hubert reject the claim that magicians and sorcerers act primarily by fraud. While they acknowledge that there is a necessary element of dissimulation in magic, Mauss and Hubert assert that the faith of the magician "is sincere in so far as it corresponds to the faith of the whole group." Magic is "a condition of the collective soul, a condition which is confirmed and verified by its results. Yet it remains mysterious even for the magician." In a similar vein, Malinowski argues that the originator of new magical performances must be "a man of genius" who acts "in perfect good faith." Followers who transmit and develop the magical rite "must have been always men of great intelligence, energy, and power of enterprise." Malinowski concludes that it is "an empirical fact that in all savage societies magic and outstanding personality go hand in hand. Thus magic also coincides with personal success, skill, courage, and mental power." Indeed, he asserts, "the first profession of mankind is that of a wizard or witch." E. O. James offers the same conclusion: "The magician is a genuine 'medicine-man' who unquestionably believes firmly in his own creative powers."[30]

But many theorists stress not the sincerity underlying magic but the elements of deceit involved in its promulgation. As Tylor affirms, the professional magician or cunning man commonly doubles as a priest, with the prestige and authority of religion behind him, and he is "often a man in power, always an unscrupulous intriguer" who shrewdly manipulates the ignorance and uncertainty of the masses, most often for personal gain. Because of the self-interests of the magical profession, magic depends on more than mere success to maintain its power. According to Frank Byron Jevons, while magicians among the least evolved cultural groups might actually have a degree of belief in their magical powers, they still practice a great deal of magic that they know to be fraudulent. Particularly among the most cunning magicians, the belief in magic begins to give way "before the scientific observation of fact," but magicians hide the truth in order to protect their own power. And these magicians become even more insidious, Jevons asserts, as they combine their magical nonsense with arcane forms of knowledge.[31]

Numerous scholars emphasize the magician's deceit. In *Magic and Grace* (1929), Lindsay Dewar argues that magic results from a hypnotic relation that develops between the magician and his audience. Assertive individuals come to exercise hypnotic power over their more submissive neighbors, particularly through the use of spells, and the audience falls under the sway of the magician's dominant and duplicitous personality. Primitives and the uneducated are distinctly prone to hypnotic suggestion, and the magical spell should be understood as "the phenomenon of hypnosis pure and simple." Ignorance and submission are central to the power of magic, Dewar explains, as demonstrated vividly in the influence of Lenin and Mussolini over the uneducated masses.[32] The magical personality can exercise nefarious power over its ignorant followers.

In his 1931–32 Gifford Lectures, R. R. Marett echoes the themes of Mauss and Durkheim as he addresses the relation between the magical "charlatan" and the social group of which he is a member:

> The charlatan, then, must be sought outside the ranks of the recognized groups that serve as ministers of the social tradition. Thus at the level of savagery the typical impostor is the dabbler in black magic, because he is an individualist. . . . the wizard is not entirely a myth, but forms one of those sporadic types which at every stage of society provide a criminal element. Casually recruited and continually harried as it is, such an underworld can have no cohesion. . . . the black or anti-social branch of occultism, to which the name of magic should be confined, has at no time any settled doctrine or meaning behind it; but is a jumble of mock rites, cribbed from the established religion of the day, and altogether caricatured and perverted in the process.

This view of the magical charlatan standing outside the social order conforms with Marett's stress on the communal nature of primitive culture and on the institutional mechanisms for the transmission of socially cohesive religious knowledge. The criminal charlatan can persuade his "dupes" only because they also are "such base folk as have never known serious study or training in any form" and who "remain at the mercy of appearances . . . incurious of truth, curious of gossip and idle tales."[33]

According to sociologist Hutton Webster, even magicians who have doubts concerning their own power rarely question the powers of other practitioners. To assume that they would engage in such questioning would be "to make of every medicine man or shaman a rationalistic freethinker far in advance of his age." Yet while the magician might not be a total impostor, elements of fraud constitute a central feature of magic. As Webster asserts, "Trickery and deceit, the production of bizarre and astonishing effects by means of ventriloquism, prestidigitation, and conjuring in all its branches characterize the magical art everywhere." Indeed, "the more intelligent the magician the greater charlatan he will be." These magical frauds prey upon the "primitive minded, whether savage or civilized," who mistake chronological coincidences for causal connections. The "primitive minded" ignore the true principles of causality: "Not for them a meticulous inquiry into the laws of chance, the power of the human imagination, and the psychology of suggestion." The magician deludes his benighted followers through recourse to trickery, deceit, a battery of excuses, and, finally, the "hoary antiquity" of tribal tradition. One of the prime sources of the power of the shaman or medicine man is a skill in manipulating mental factors such as unconscious suggestion: "The doctor impresses his personality upon the very susceptible patient by his outlandish trappings, grotesque gestures, unintelligible utterances, and a 'bedside manner' which radiates calm confidence in his ability to relieve or cure."[34]

The degree of the magician's duplicity has been a recurrent theme in modern theories of magic, and many aspects of this issue are relevant for our purposes here. While most theorists from Tylor forward have acknowledged the difficulty of determining the subjective beliefs of the magician, and while many have also acknowledged the complex and undecidable mixture of motives that appears to be at issue, scholars return to the topic again and again, only to offer opinions based on the most transparent conjecture. The very persistence of such concern with an issue that seems so fundamentally unresolvable might lead us to ask why the motives of the magician would be such a scholarly preoccupation. But before addressing this question, let us turn to another of the central themes in the discussions of the nature of magicians. Here we find the fundamental ambiguity of the magician shifting from duplicity to deviance.

Magicians and Their Deviance

Beyond the question of the magician's deceit lie more fundamental phantasmatic concerns with the nature of the magician's desires themselves, and here the focus turns quickly to issues of sexuality. The literature of the early modern witchcraft persecutions discussed in the first chapter demonstrates the long-standing resonance of the claim that practitioners of magic are socially deviant. In that literature the deviance of witchcraft was linked to various other forms of antisocial behavior, including heresy, cannibalism, sexual licentiousness, and sodomy.

While the social scientific discourse on magic moved away from the rhetorical extremes of earlier demonological literature, echoes of those earlier formulations of magic still resound. One of the most striking aspects of scholarly discussions of the magician since the late nineteenth century has been the preoccupation that innumerable theorists have shown with respect to the sexual identity and behavior of this figure (configured almost universally as male). Perverse sexuality has remained a persistent marker of magic.

Magic has long been linked in the European cultural imagination to perverse or deviant sexual practices, particularly sodomy.[35] Magicians are regularly portrayed in scholarly literature as sexually suspect. Indeed, magic is commonly constructed as incorrigibly queer (in every sense of the term). The analysis of magic has ready recourse to tropes of perversity, compulsiveness, sterility—a rhetoric with decidedly queer connotations. Transvestitism, homosexuality, transsexuality, and other violations of modern heterosexual norms regularly appear as significant concerns in the scholarly literature on magic.

In numerous nineteenth-century ethnographic accounts, the religious and magical practitioners of various non-European societies were described as sexually suspect or deviant. For example, ethnographic reports of various indigenous North Americans often stressed the prevalence of cross-gender and same-sex behavior among these groups and linked this behavior with religious rituals and shamanic practices. As Rudi Bleys recounts, many early ethnographers "emphasized the ambiguous sexual status of shamans as being constitutional to their power and status," a power often seen as threatening local colonial authorities. Various nineteenth-century reports from Africa linked same-sex practices to shamanism or initiation rites and identified native priests as hermaphrodites. Bleys notes that in 1911 Ferdinand Karsh-Haack published a lexicon of 106 indigenous terms used to label male cross-gender roles, many of which simultaneously referred to shamanistic or divinatory functions.[36]

One of the formative texts in the development of this theme came from the ethnographer Waldemar Bogoras, a central figure in the 1900 Jesup North Pacific Expedition mounted by the American Museum of Natural History and directed by Franz Boas. After extensive fieldwork among the Chukchi of northeastern Siberia, Bogoras published a classic ethnographic account of Chukchi culture in 1907. In this text, Bogoras offers a lengthy discussion of shamanism that focuses particular attention on the sexual anomaly demonstrated by Chukchi shamans. Bogoras begins by explaining that it is "nervous and highly excitable temperaments" that are most likely to be drawn into shamanism; he found Chukchi shamans "as a rule extremely excitable, almost hysterical, and not a few of them were half crazy." The call to shamanism can regularly be detected in the "peculiar . . . combination of cunning and shyness" that characterizes the gaze of a prospective young shaman.[37]

Bogoras is fascinated by the aspects of Chukchi shamanism involving "shamanistic transformation of men and women in which they undergo a change of sex in part, or even completely." Such transformation is demanded by the spirits and is so dreaded by youthful adepts, he explains, that some of the young shamans prefer death to obedience to this call. Transformation takes a number of forms, beginning with men impersonating female hairstyles and adopting female dress. Yet to obtain more magical power, there are further, more comprehensive transformations:

> A young man . . . leaves off all pursuits and manners of his sex, and
> takes up those of a woman. . . . Even his pronunciation changes
> from the male to the female mode. At the same time his body alters,
> if not in its outward appearance, at least in its faculties and forces.
> He loses masculine strength, fleetness of foot in the race, endurance
> in wrestling, and acquires instead the helplessness of a woman.
> Even his psychical character changes. The transformed person loses
> his brute courage and fighting spirit, and becomes shy of strangers,

even fond of small-talk and of nursing small children. Generally speaking, he becomes a woman with the appearance of a man.

Such transformations are baffling for Bogoras; he questions whether some of these changes are a product of "auto-suggestion" or are merely feigned to impress the community.[38]

Yet there is still a further stage in the process of shamanistic transformation:

> The most important of the transformations is, however, the change of sex. The "soft man" begins to feel like a woman. He seeks to win the good graces of men, and succeeds easily with the aid of "spirits." Thus he has all the young men he could wish for striving to obtain his favor. From these he chooses his lover, and after a time takes a husband. The marriage is performed with the usual rites, and I must say that it forms a quite solid union, which often lasts till the death of one of the parties. The couple live much in the same way as do other people. The man tends his herd and goes hunting and fishing, while the "wife" takes care of the house, performing all domestic pursuits and work. They cohabit in a perverse way, *modo Socratis*, in which the transformed wife always plays the passive rôle. In this, again, some of the "soft men" are said to lose altogether the man's desire and in the end to even acquire the organs of a woman; while others are said to have mistresses of their own in secret and to produce children by them.

But despite this perplexing surface harmony, the family relations of these transformed shamans invert once again in a further unexpected perversion: because the transformed shaman (male to female) often has a special spirit protector who plays the role of "supernatural husband" and who acts as the actual head of the family by communicating through the transformed wife, "the voice of the wife is decidedly preponderant" within the household.[39] Gender roles are confounded time and again, as these men become women who seek husbands, only to dominate those husbands in the name of supernatural masculine powers.

Bogoras reports that "the state of the transformed man is so peculiar that it attracts much gossip and jests on the part of the neighbors," yet people are extremely fearful of the powers of these transformed shamans. Bogoras himself demonstrates an extraordinary level of voyeuristic fascination in his attempt to inspect these shamans. He recounts his efforts to uncover the secrets of one particular transformed shaman, "tall and well developed," with "large rough hands" exhibiting "no trace of womanhood":

> I staid for two days in his tent, and slept in his small inner room, which was hardly large enough to accommodate four sleepers. Thus I had a chance to observe quite closely the details of his physique,

which, of course, were all masculine. He refused obstinately, however, to permit himself to be fully inspected. His husband . . .
tempted by the offered price, tried to persuade him, but, after some
useless attempts, was at last silenced by one scowling look from his
peculiar "wife." He felt sorry, however, that I had been baffled in
gratifying my curiosity, and therefore offered me, to use his own
words, his eyes in place of my own. He described the physique of
[the transformed shaman] as wholly masculine, and well developed
besides. He confessed that he was sorry for it, but he hoped that in
time . . . [the shaman wife] would be able to equal the real "soft
men" of old, and to change the organ of his sex altogether, which
would be much more convenient than the present state. . . . [The
shaman's face] was something like a female tragic mask fitted to a
body of a giantess of a race different from our own. All the ways of
this strange creature were decidedly feminine. He was so "bashful,"
that whenever I asked a question of somewhat indiscreet character,
you could see, under the lay of its usual dirt, a blush spread over his
face, and he would cover his eyes with his sleeve, like a young
beauty of sixteen. I heard him gossip with the female neighbors in a
most feminine way, and even saw him hug small children with evident envy for the joys of motherhood.

Bogoras reports his encounters with a variety of other transformed shamans,
including one who boasted that with the aid of the spirits he had borne two
sons from his own body, another who was widowed from both his wife and a
male lover, and another "nimble young fellow" accused of "perverting all his
young companions, who beset him with their courtship, to the great detriment
and offense of the lawful beauties of the camp."[40]

Female shamanistic transformation is much less frequent, Bogoras explains, and his only accounts of it are indirect. For example, he reports stories
of one middle-aged widow who was directed by the spirits to transform into a
man. When the transformed woman wanted to marry, she "easily found a quite
young girl who consented to become her wife"; as Bogoras explains, "the transformed one provided herself with a gastrocnemius from the leg of a reindeer,
fastened to a broad leather belt, and used it in the way of masculine private
parts." Eventually, this transformed shaman entered into a "mutual marriage"
with a neighbor in order to have children with the young wife.[41]

Bogoras's account of the sexual transformations of Chukchi shamans is
remarkable on many levels, and it proved extremely influential in the development of subsequent theories of magic. Numerous scholars would return to
this theme, citing Bogoras as a proof text of the sexually anomalous nature of
magic and magicians. One of the first theoretical developments of Bogoras's
report appears in Edward Westermarck's 1908 treatise on human moral de-

velopment. Westermarck's portrayal of magicians underscores many aspects of their perverse behavior (he explains, for example, that in some cultures magicians gain power by cannibalizing human flesh), but sexuality is a central component of the magician's anomalous status. Westermarck explains that magicians are sometimes prone to more sex than is common, sometimes to less. But despite such variation, one aspect remains constant: magicians are "addicted to homosexual practices."[42]   MAGICIANS ARE GAY ✗

In Westermarck's survey of same-sex behavior among various peoples of the world, he recounts numerous examples of magicians and shamans (or prospective shamans) adopting female dress, hairstyles, and activities and seeking in various ways "to be transformed physically into women." He cites Bogoras's account to explain that among the Chukchi of Siberia "nearly all the shamans were former delinquents of their sex." The shaman becomes a "disclaimer of his sex," submitting to a "most unnatural and voluntary subjection" to a husband. Further, Bogoras's account confirms that "in some cases at least there can be no doubt that these transformations were connected with homosexual practices." Shamans engage in this "change of sex" in the belief that this transformation leads to great magical power. As Westermarck explains:

> We have seen that the effeminate men are frequently believed to be versed in magic; their abnormalities readily suggest that they are endowed with supernatural power, and they may resort to witchcraft as a substitute for their lack of manliness and physical strength. But the supernatural qualities or skill in magic ascribed to men who behave like women may also, instead of causing hatred, make them honoured or revered.[43]

Many aspects of Westermarck's text are notable, but of particular interest here is the way in which the discussion of magical practices provides him an opportunity to explore human sexual diversity. Arnold Van Gennep's *Les rites des passage* (1908) follows a similar course. Citing Westermarck's analysis, Van Gennep discusses the prevalence of homosexual practices in various initiation rituals, though Van Gennep downplays the social and symbolic significance of these practices (seeing them instead as primarily amusements and means of social incorporation). Speaking of ritual pederasty among the Pueblo Indians and the Arunta, Van Gennep asserts that such acts might be called a "magical lubricant" serving the interests of social unity.[44]

The sexual proclivities of the magical and religious practitioners of primitive society are also a significant theme in *Intermediate Types among Primitive Folk* (1914), from the prominent early sexual reformer Edward Carpenter. Carpenter asserts in this text that homosexuals "of a more effeminate and passive sort" have a distaste for "the ordinary masculine occupations and business of the world" and "an inclination to retire into the precincts of the Temples." In primitive society these inclinations lead them not only to religious service but also "to such things as Magic, learning, poetry, music, prophecy, and other occupations not generally favoured by the normal man, the hunter and the warrior." Carpenter argues that primitive homosexuals develop "faculties like divination, clairvoyance, ecstasy, and so forth, which are generally and quite naturally associated with religion." Carpenter cites the evidence collected by scholars such as Frazer, Westermarck, and Elie Reclus of the "most marked and curious" connection between homosexuality and cross-dressing (on the one hand) and magic and shamanship (on the other). Thus, Carpenter asserts, sorcerers are often known to adopt women's clothing, and this cross-dressing can be taken as an indication of homosexuality.[45]

Like Westermarck before him, Carpenter configures a culturally venerable lineage for same-sex behavior by linking these practices to visible and prominent members of non-Western cultures. This strategy became common among early sexual liberationists. In his effort to explain the "world-wide attribution of magic powers to homosexuals," Carpenter posits a connection between "the homosexual temperament and divinatory or unusual psychic powers." But, he argues, magical power is attributed to homosexuals not simply because of their divergent sexuality but because of their distinctive character as intermediates positioned between the dominant gender roles. By combining feminine emotionality with masculine practicality, "intermediates . . . would undoubtedly be greatly superior in ability to the rest of the tribe . . . and . . . become inventors, teachers, musicians, medicine-men and priests." Further, since old religions are labeled with the charge of magic as they are superseded, and since many primitive religions were "largely sexual, even homosexual," earlier same-sex rites become associated with sorcery and occult powers. Carpenter concludes that while the "normal sex types" provided the foundations of society, "it was largely the intermediate types who developed the superstructure. The priest or the medicine-man or shaman was at first the sole representative of this new class, and we have seen that he was almost invariably, in some degree or other, of Uranian temperament."[46]

This theme of the link between magic and sexual nonconformity has been widespread in the scholarly literature. Ruth Benedict again repeats Bogoras's account of Siberian shamans. Potential initiates, she explains, are identified in their youth from among "various unstable types of individuals," and further changes occur when initiates assume the role of shaman:

Especially powerful shamans change their sex. There are many degrees. Some men only assume women's dress and continue to live with their wives and children. Some add women's occupations to the assumption of women's dress; they are thought to learn these quickly and well because of their instruction by the spirits. The final stage is that of the assumption of femininity. The body outlines change, and the shaman is supposed to marry another man. He has now a spirit husband in the supernatural world, a control who is more powerful than the spirit wife he could have had as a man.[47]

Chukchi shamans reappear in mid-century discussions of magic by American anthropologists Alexander Goldenweiser and Hutton Webster. Goldenweiser quotes Bogoras concerning the "extremely excitable, almost hysterical" nature of these shamans. During shamanic rituals, Goldenweiser tells us, the shaman is "extremely sensitive ('bashful')" and typically "neurotic." Goldenweiser cites Max Schmidt's list of characteristics on the basis of which Arawak-speaking peoples selected shamans from young boys: "epilepsy, various physical peculiarities, such as hemorrhages of the breast, and general nervousness." Webster stresses that medicine men and shamans sometimes cross-dress and engage in feminine behavior, abnormalities that confirm their occult power. Webster vacillates as to whether this transvestitism is linked to homosexuality; he notes that while transvestitism is not necessarily a sign of homosexual practices, homosexuality is commonly found in groups prone to cross-dressing. He offers a range of examples of the ways in which tribal magicians are "sexually disabled" before commencing their roles, how they are treated as women and engage in feminine activities, and how often the "soft" or effeminate are selected for these roles. Speaking of the Chukchi shaman, Webster states, "His body alters, if not in outward appearance, at least in its faculties and forces, and his mental characteristics become more and more those of a woman." The transformed shaman goes so far as to marry another man "with whom he leads a regular married life." Webster concludes that while many people become sorcerers out of the hope for easy, unlawful gain, "it is also true that men will take up its practice out of sheer perverseness and depravity."[48]

This notion of the shaman as sexually suspect gained even greater currency through its reiteration in Mircea Eliade's influential *Shamanism* (1951). Eliade once again repeats Bogoras's account of the "change of sex" among Chukchi shamans who engage in transvestitism and marry other men (Eliade here also repeats the aside that "some, rather than carry out the command, have chosen suicide, although pederasty is not unknown among the Chukchee"). Eliade then cites examples of similar "transvestitism and ritual change of sex" among the Kamchadal, the Asiatic Eskimo, and the Koryak and in Indonesia, South America, and among certain North American tribes. To account for this phenomenon, he offers the rather enigmatic hypothesis that it is "probably explained by an ideology derived from the archaic matriarchy."[49]

This trope of magic and shamanism as sexually anomalous remains pervasive in recent texts, with Bogoras and similar ethnographers cited particularly by contemporary theorists seeking to disrupt traditional gender dualisms.[50] And even when overt images of cross-dressing and same-sex behavior are omitted, theorists often describe magicians in thinly veiled codes. Marcel Mauss and Henri Hubert, for example, assert that the magician is most often set apart by a society because of "physical peculiarities" or suspect personality traits:

> All over the world there are people who have a peculiarly cunning look, who appear odd or untrustworthy, who blink at one strangely. . . . They are all lumped together as magicians, along with nervous and jumpy individuals or subnormal peoples in those backward areas where magic still has a hold. Violent gestures, a shrill voice, oratorical or poetic gifts are often taken to be attributes of magicians. They are all signs betraying a kind of nervous condition, which in many societies may be cultivated by magicians.

Magicians may even come to believe in their special powers because of "oversensitivity to the reactions of normal people, a persecution complex or delusions of grandeur." These magicians come to actualize their magical powers not so much because of their individual particularities, but as a result of the social attitudes they elicit.[51]

Anthropologist Robert Lowie asserts that "shamans are often nervously unstable persons" who work themselves into a frenzy that is interpreted as spirit possession. Paul Radin concurs that the medicine man and shaman are selected because of "some form of emotional instability and well-marked sensitivity"; "they must be disoriented and they must suffer." Adamson Hoebel repeats the claim that shamans are "as a rule excitable and hysterical," prone to "suggestibility and a greater or lesser degree of emotional instability." In fact, Hoebel asserts, "to be a spirit-endowed shaman the odds favor those who belong to the 'lunatic fringe.'" Carleton Coon provides a vivid and suggestive description of shamanism (which Coon again describes as "the oldest profession") in his discussion of prehistoric healing:

> A shaman is usually a man, though sometimes women who have passed the age of childbearing take over these functions. As a boy he is different from his companions. Dreamy, crotchety, ill-adjusted, he may fall ill about the time when he is supposed to show his prowess as a hunter; during these illnesses he has attracted the attention of shamans, who recognize a recruit in him. Instead of, or in addition to, the regular course of higher education which the other boys go through, the novice receives special treatment from the specialists, who hide him out in some retreat of their own.

Joachim Wach also argues that magicians share with seers and prophets "the same nervous susceptibility and sensitiveness, the same disposition to trances and ecstasy, and the same inclination to vision, audition, and 'clairvoyance.'" Wach concludes that while many religions have antipathy to the magical attitude, "in most of the world religions where there was no place for them, magicians have crept in through the 'back door.' "[52]

Through all of these rhetorical turns, magicians are regularly configured as sexually suspect. And the violation of gender norms is not the only sexual deviance attributed to magicians. The psychologist Renée Spitz, for example, asserts that magical cults are generally orgiastic and that magical practices probably derived from orgiastic sexuality: "Sexual intercourse is the basis of the magical ceremonial." William Graham Sumner and Albert Galloway Keller argue in *The Science of Society* (1927) that nakedness is "often regarded as essential to the production of magical effects." Arturo Castiglioni stresses the magician's inordinate control over the sexual activities of the social group, and Hutton Webster notes that magical potency is sometimes acquired through the deliberate commission of incest. Magical practices themselves are regularly described as prone to various types of sexual deviance and obscenity.[53]

Gender and sexual deviance stands as the epitome of the magician's social disruption. But through these various formulations, there is great ambiguity as to the precise nature of that deviance. What exactly is meant by the often quoted phrase that the shaman "changes his sex"? Is this "change of sex" attributable only to the localized and particular group of shamans that Bogoras described, or does it apply more broadly (as appears in subsequent amplification) to all shamans, even all practitioners of magic? Is the magician merely prone to "excitability," or does he have more fundamental and more suspect proclivities? Does the magician have too much sex or too little? Is the magician a transvestite or a transsexual, a homosexual or a violator of still other gender norms?

The rhetorical slippage demonstrated in this broad network of texts indicates that the specifics of the claims are not nearly as important as is their underlying logic.[54] The magician may be a fraud or a dupe, a cross-dresser or a homosexual, dreamy or hysterical, but the logic of his deviance is clear. In the dominant scholarly articulations of this theme the magician is deformed in his fundamental nature; in fact, he serves to embody deviance at its most generalized level. He violates the basic norms of modern, rationalized, masculine, and heterosexual subjectivity. Regardless of the precise nature of his offense, the magician is, in a word, queer. Whether duplicitously mimicking perversity or acting on it in vaguely unspeakable ways, the magician stands as an archetype of the nonmodern—or antimodern—subject. No rhetorical shorthand better captures this deviance than Westermarck's trope of the magician as a "disclaimer of his sex." In this phrase we have the inversion of gender, the renunciation of proper sexual function, even the obsessive declamation of gratuitous sexuality itself.

Finally, let me also underscore the remarkable rhetorical mobility of this theme of the perverse magician. For many theorists, the queer magician stands

Magic is queer

as a clear marker of everything suspect in magic. The magician embodies the perversity of magic. Yet even for scholars most eager to denounce magic, this figure and his deviance are a source of intrigue, the object of voyeuristic fascination. And devoting such attention to perversity has the (often unintended) effect of making more perversity; these scholars acknowledge, if implicitly, that magicians obtain great power through their polymorphous sexuality. But at the same time other theorists can deploy this theme to a very different end. Scholars such as Westermarck and Carpenter can invoke the queer magician to amplify the theme of human sexual diversity in a direct challenge to the gender and sexual norms on which modern society is founded.[55] The magician—and magic itself—can be enlisted either to affirm or to subvert the rigid limits of modern subjectivity.

Desire and Social Order

This examination of the ways in which the magician personifies a fundamental—if tantalizing—perversion of modern social norms points us toward the basic preoccupation with social order underlying these theories of magic. While the theories often focus on subjective desires and individualized notions of piety and rationality, they are informed by far broader social and economic concerns.

Magic and the Birth of Order

Despite magic's suspect nature, many social theorists have given it a prominent role in their accounts of the emergence of social order. Herbert Spencer argues that the medicine man plays a significant part in the evolution of political leadership because of the importance of the medicine man's magical powers. When the belief in spirits of the dead emerges (the originary stage of religion in Spencer's account), "the medicine-man, professing ability to control them, and inspiring faith in his pretensions, is regarded with a fear which prompts obedience." Citing various reports of the cunning and deceitful nature of primitive medicine men and their great influence within their tribes, Spencer concludes that the rise of belief in ghosts and the concomitant expectation that certain leaders can enlist their aid are major factors in the development of political order. Spencer sees all such supernatural power as fundamentally conservative, profoundly resistant to change. As he frames it, every form of ecclesiasticism (embodying "the rule of the dead over the living, and sanctifying in its more advanced forms the authority of the past over the present") stands as support for the social status quo.[56]

Frazer follows Spencer in arguing that the development of a class of public magicians is of great importance for the political and religious evolution of early social groups. Because of the prestige, wealth, and power that magicians can amass, Frazer explains, they draw to their ranks the most capable and ambitious members of the tribe. While some magicians might actually believe in the power of their magic, the most acute and capable members of the profession tend to end up as "more or less conscious deceivers" who "dupe their weaker brother and . . . play on his superstition for their own advantage." At this point in social evolution, "the supreme power tends to fall into the hands of men of the keenest intelligence and the most unscrupulous character." In Frazer's view this concentration of power is fortuitous, because the shift of power from the "democracy" or "oligarchy" of the traditional tribal structure into the hands of the most capable member of the group (a monarch or sacred king) is "on the whole very beneficial," "an essential condition of the emergence of mankind from savagery." The shift of power to the monarch pulls society from its cultural stagnation and facilitates social process "by opening a career to talent and proportioning the degrees of authority to men's natural abilities." Through magic's role in increasing respect for monarchical government and social hierarchy, it has made vital contributions to the establishment of civil order.[57]

In this manner, Frazer asserts, the social group progresses socially, industrially, and intellectually. In fact, "all the first great strides towards civilisation have been made under despotic and theocratic governments. . . . at this early epoch despotism is the best friend of humanity and, paradoxical as it may sound, liberty." Magic has functioned as "one of the roads by which the ablest men have passed to supreme power," and it has served to emancipate humanity from "the thraldom of tradition and to elevate them into a larger, freer life, with a broader outlook on the world." So, if magic has done evil, it has also been "the source of much good . . . the mother of freedom and truth." With a special class of magicians set apart and relieved from the daily tasks of subsistence labor, new social leaders are free to begin the systematic investigation of nature. Thus magicians were the direct predecessors of physicians and surgeons, the investigators and discoverers in all the natural sciences. Further, not only has the belief in superstitious magic promoted the investigation of nature, it has also served to deter theft and promote the stability of private property, "contributed to a stricter observance of the rules of sexual morality both among the married and the unmarried," and strengthened respect for human life.[58]

In his *Elemente der Völkerpsychologie* (1912), the psychologist Wilhelm Wundt concurs that medicine men and magicians emerge as the precursors of the first professional classes as they develop countermagic to ward off the evils of death and illness. The medicine man is thus the ancestor of both the physician and the priest. From this original preoccupation with death and disease, forms of protective magic radiate throughout the lives of primitive peoples. This magic, Wundt explains, likely gave rise to the earliest forms of clothing and bodily adornment, which arose less for decoration than for magical protection. Further, like a number of other important scholars, Wundt claims that magic played a central role in the development of various forms of art (dancing, music, and other representational arts).[59]

Long after the eclipse of overt evolutionism, scholars continued to assert the claim that magicians played a central role in the emergence of social order. Hutton Webster stresses that magic is a lucrative profession attracting the ambitious and the greedy. As Webster explains:

> It is evident that, the world over, the profession of a medicine man or a shaman is lucrative and that those who engage in it often con-trive to live comfortably at the expense of their fellows. . . . The large incomes which magicians receive and the special privileges which they enjoy tend to raise them above the common herd and thus be-come a potent factor in the differentiation of social classes within a community.

Webster notes that magicians form "the intelligentsia of primitive society," demonstrating both keen wits and some degree of understanding of natural phenomena. The profession attracts the most able members of the group, who use it as a path to wealth and privilege. In Africa governmental and magical functions are often united, and in some parts of the "Dark Continent" chiefs develop from the ranks of magicians. Magic thus commonly serves "as the prop of absolutism."[60]

Magic and the Stagnation of Culture

Webster's assertion that magic can become a "prop of absolutism" shows how easily a stress on magic's role in the development of social order can shift to an emphasis on magic as a socially regressive and authoritarian force. The theories discussed in the prior section granted magic a degree of grudging (if ambivalent) respect as a factor in the emergence of social order. But far more commonly scholars have stressed the threat that magic poses to the orderly and productive operation of society. Historian Charles Singer expresses a widely held conclusion when he asserts that "few realize the degradation in-volved when the mind becomes saturated with such material and deluded with such hopes."[61]

Many theorists have echoed Spencer's claim that magic is fundamentally conservative, an impediment to social progress. For Tylor, the study of survivals such as magic demonstrates the profound power of "stupidity and unpractical conservatism and dogged superstition" in shaping human life. The savage is "firmly, obstinately conservative," appealing with unquestioning confidence to wisdom of the ancestors that can overwhelm even the most obvious evidence. In the face of the blind conservatism of magic, members of modern culture, particularly modern scientists, demonstrate a far nobler response to the past: "to honour the dead without grovelling before them, to profit by the past without sacrificing the present to it."[62]

As discussed earlier, Frazer also saw magic as fundamentally authoritarian (though Frazer appears rather favorably disposed to such concentration of power). Other theorists agree with Tylor and Frazer concerning the authoritarian nature of magic. Malinowski asserts that in all cases "sorcery is either in the same hands as political power, prestige and wealth or else it can be purchased or demanded by those who can afford to do so." Thus, he concludes, sorcery is "invariably a conservative force used at times for intimidation but usually for the enforcement of customary law or of the wishes of those in power." It stands as a constant "safeguard for the vested interests, for the organized, established privileges." Alexander Goldenweiser also stresses the fundamental conservatism of supernaturalism and ritual. Through the form of ritual, conservative social forces reinforce their hold by means of the crowd. Further, Goldenweiser concurs with Malinowski's argument that magic tends to become rigidified and centralized in the hands of technical experts or professionals, while religion remains more fluid and accessible, "free to all and for all." Religion stands open to "subjective elaboration and reinterpretation" in an essentially democratic mode, he asserts, while magic is authoritarian, under the rigid control of the magician.[63]

The theme that magic stifles social progress has as its prime corollary the often repeated claim that magic serves as an impediment to technological innovation. In his *Lectures on the Religion of the Semites* (1889), W. Robertson Smith argues that while religion places restrictions on "individual license" that actually promote social progress and moral order, magic thwarts such progress by cultivating more slavish forms of fear. Sidney Hartland asserts that since magic is used largely for private gain, the fear of accusations of witchcraft leads to the suppression of individual initiative and innovation in primitive societies. Hartland quotes John H. Weeks in this regard: "To know more than others, to be more skillful than others, more energetic, more acute in business, more smart in dress, has often caused a charge of witchcraft and death. Therefore the native, to save his life and live in peace, has smothered his inventive faculty, and all spirit of enterprise has been driven out of him."[64]

Hutton Webster repeats this claim that the belief in sorcery is a particularly strong check on initiative and leads to cultural stagnation, but his emphasis is not only on the fear of witchcraft accusations but also on the fear of witchcraft as a tool for retaliation against innovators:

> The belief in sorcery, when an obsession, destroys individual initiative and numbs the desire for self-advancement, thus becoming a potent cause of the stagnation of culture. . . . In the Trobriand Islands . . . great success of a man in love making, unusual personal

> beauty, exceptional skill as a dancer, inordinate desire for wealth,
> recklessness in the display and enjoyment of worldly goods—these
> arouse resentment and lead to punishment by the chief. He does
> not use violence to enforce the golden mean of mediocrity, but re-
> sorts to a sorcerer . . . for spells and charms which will bring the cul-
> prit low. Sorcery thus forms a support of vested interests; it is al-
> ways a conservative force.

The people of Dobu, Webster says, feel great resentment toward successful members of their group and use black magic to maintain mediocrity; various South American tribes hold back their agricultural efforts in order to avoid the suspicion of using magic to increase their crops. The fear of witchcraft among the Tarahumara Indians of Mexico breeds artificial forms of property sharing and secretiveness, which lead in turn to conflicting obligations, mistrust, and suspicion. Webster claims that the fear of accusations of magic has the stulti-fying effect of suppressing invention, initiative, creativity, and social progress. In all these circumstances, the belief in sorcery serves as a potent mechanism of social control, but one repressing inventiveness and economic development. Webster concludes that "considered in the large, magical beliefs and practices have operated to discourage intellectual acquisitiveness, to nourish vain hopes that can never be realized, and to substitute unreal for real achievement in the natural world."[65]

Fear, either of accusation or of countermagic, is not the only mechanism through which magic retards innovation. Sumner and Keller argue that in teaching that results depend on "the unpredictable whims of the supernatural," magic has the effect of "reducing confidence in labor and economy and fur-nishing subterfuges to those who shun them," leading to a life of "ignorance and sloth." The anthropologist John Honigmann elaborates this claim as he argues that the very thought processes of magic inhibit progressive change. Smaller social groups, he explains, demonstrate a "magical attachment to ex-isting procedures," but larger societies can develop "a relativistic attitude to-ward truth" as they search for new ways of doing things. In Honigmann's scheme, magical dogmatism is juxtaposed to a mode of relativistic thinking that understands facts as built on probability, consensus, and contingency. While magic may ensure social consensus and group equilibrium, it also op-erates to limit the scale of the society: "It holds people back from contact with the new and prevents intense relations with people who follow a different way of life or possess different physical features." Magical dogmatism thwarts pro-gressive relativism.[66]

In these theories, magic represents a blind attachment to the past, a rigid addiction to fallacious procedures, a superstitious reluctance to innovate. And as a cultural survival—a residue from the past persisting into the present—magic stands as a clear threat to progressive development and social change.

This theme persists in recent theories of social and religious development, such as that of John Hick discussed in chapter 2. There Hick, following Robert Bellah, argues that pre-axial, magical religions are fundamentally conservative and aimed at preserving the cosmic and social status quo. In a future-oriented frame of social progress, magic epitomizes the forces of social and cultural stagnation.[67]

Magic and the Threat of Anarchy

Yet while numerous scholars portray magic as a force of social stagnation, many others—particularly those of a more sociological bent—argue that magic poses a very different threat to the productive operation of society. The sociological theories discussed in chapter 2 (represented by such figures as Mauss and Durkheim) based their distinction between magic and religion on the notion that magic is fundamentally individualistic and antagonistic to the mechanisms promoting social cohesion and preserving social order. In this regard Nathan Söderblom could assert that black magic is "the sin of sins— sin against the tribe, the community."[68] From this sociological perspective, magic is seen not as socially regressive and authoritarian but as fundamentally antisocial and anarchical. Rather than retarding social progress by a dogged clinging to the past, magic is portrayed as a menace to social unity and the communal good through its excessive self-seeking, individualism, and disruption.

The sociological view of magic as fundamentally individualistic has been a major theme in theories of magic. Hutton Webster asserts that while sorcery or witchcraft can sometimes be used for public ends (particularly in situations where it is aimed against antisocial members of a community or external enemies), black magic is essentially private and individual, practiced in disregard of public opinion and in order to bring misfortune. Its practitioners are thus viewed with fear and suspicion. As Irving King states it:

> There is, we believe, no generalization concerning savage practices which may be made with greater assurance than this, that magic is relatively individualistic and secret in its methods and interests, and is thus opposed fundamentally to the methods and interests of religion, which are social and public. This individualistic and secret character of magic makes it easy for it to become the instrument of secret vengeance. . . . There is no primitive society, as far as our accounts have gone, which does not dread the sorcerer.[69]

Throughout these formulations, magic is a tool of individual interests running counter to those of the social group.

In his study of the Dinka tribes of the Sudan, Godfrey Lienhardt offers a particularly impassioned explanation of the social threat lurking within the individualism of witchcraft beliefs:

> So we may see in the night-witch a representation of the hidden na-
> ture of the relationships which give rise to suspicions of witchcraft,
> of the behaviour of one man to another unregulated by their recog-
> nition of membership in a community, of the breaking-up of com-
> munity where such unregulated hostilities exist, and of the individu-
> alism, the aggressiveness, malice, selfishness, and resentment,
> which work against the maintenance of orderly relationships be-
> tween men as persons, according to their status. The night-witch is
> an outlaw because he embodies those appetites and passions in every-
> man which, if ungoverned, would destroy any more law. The night-
> witch may thus be seen to correspond to the concealed intention,
> the amorality, and hence the opposition to those shared moral values
> which make community possible, of the unique individual self, ex-
> isting and acting as such.[70]

In this view, the antisocial passions underlying magic threaten the core unity of social life. Magic is a threat because it gives vent to unsocialized desire.

Max Weber's thesis as to the precise harm posed by magic differs from the standard Durkheimian approach. In Weber's view, magic is largely adaptive, mediating conflicts between individuals and their groups. Yet precisely because it provides this type of mediation, magic can serve as an impediment to social change. By assuaging social antagonisms, magic reduces the impetus for more fundamental change. Further, Weber asserts, the ideas and institutions supported by magic (such as social castes and sacred spaces) can serve to hinder the emergence of rationalized social structures such as the distinctive Western polis or capitalist modes of economic exchange. Thus, as Weber concludes, even the individualistic tendencies of magic can serve the interests of the social status quo.[71]

There is, of course, an apparent contradiction between those who see magic as socially reactionary and authoritarian and those who see it as individualistic and anarchical. But, as Weber demonstrates, these competing contentions can be resolved because the forms of magic that scholars are considering and the social position of the various magical practitioners differ so widely. What is most relevant for our purposes here, however, is not so much the specific nature of the social threat posed by magic as the broad degree of consensus that magic is indeed a threat. An array of theorists concur that whatever form magic takes, it poses a danger to the productive operation of the social order. And there is also broad agreement not only that magic is a threat to social order in general but also that magic is a particular threat to modern society.

Magic as Contemporary Menace

As discussed in the introduction, Edward Burnett Tylor was deeply concerned by the persistence of magic in modernity. As Tylor framed it, magic "belongs in its main principle to the lowest known stages of civilization, and the lower races, who have not partaken largely of the education of the world, still maintain it in vigour."[72] Yet while magic belongs in its essence to the chronological and geographic distance, it has an insidious power to resurface within the modern world. Magic threatens to swamp social progress.

Frazer also sees magic as belonging primarily to earlier stages in human social development and primitive cultures, but like Tylor, Frazer is also concerned about the intrusion of magic close to home. Frazer cites numerous examples of magic and superstition from the folklore and practices of contemporary peasants of Europe, Scotland, and Wales, from the laborers and lower-class "wiseacres" and "rustics" of contemporary England, and even among Europeans who appear "outwardly civilised." As Frazer laments, superstitions can be found "almost at our own door" in nearby English counties. The mode of thought operating within sympathetic magic "commends itself to English and German rustics," just as to the savages of Melanesia and America and the aborigines of central Australia. The primitive system of magical superstition has had "an extraordinary hold . . . on the human mind in all ages and all countries."[73]

Frazer offers a remarkable metaphor to describe the lurking, tectonic dangers of magic. There are relatively superficial differences, he tells us, in the religious practices of various groups (mainly affecting the "intelligent and thoughtful part of the community"). But lurking beneath this surface is a pervasive and ominous "menace to civilization":

> We shall find underlying them all a solid stratum of intellectual agreement among the dull, the weak, the ignorant, and the superstitious, who constitute, unfortunately, the vast majority of mankind. One of the great achievements of the nineteenth century was to run shafts down into this low mental stratum in many parts of the world, and thus to discover its substantial identity everywhere. It is beneath our feet—and not very far beneath them—here in Europe at the present day, and it crops up on the surface in the heart of the Australian wilderness and wherever the advent of a higher civilization has not crushed it under ground. This universal faith, this truly Catholic creed, is a belief in the efficacy of magic. . . . We seem to move on a thin crust which may at any moment be rent by the subterranean forces slumbering below. From time to time a hollow murmur underground or a sudden spurt of flame into the air tells of what is going on beneath our feet.[74]

Note the layers of Frazer's metaphor here. On the surface, at least in Europe, we have what he describes as the "intelligent and thoughtful part of the community," the bearers of "civilization." Right below, and encroaching from abroad, we have a sulfurous mass of "the dull, the weak, the ignorant . . . the superstitious . . . the vast majority of mankind." Frazer speaks with a contempt (even paranoia) concerning the superstitious masses that is difficult to equal. But the fundamental structure of his claim, juxtaposing an elite educated class over against the unreflective and gullible masses, is a recurrent trope throughout the tradition of Western theories of magic. As Tylor asserted, it is only the elite educated class that has learned the folly of magical beliefs holding sway among the great majority of the human race.

Subsequent generations of scholars have concurred in this assessment. Malinowski laments the "morbid interest" in magic commonly ministered to by "stale revivals of half-understood ancient creeds and cults, dished up under the names of 'theosophy,' 'spiritism' or 'spiritualism,' and various pseudo-'sciences,' -ologies and -isms." Despite minor changes in its specific manifestations, Malinowski concludes, magic exists in all human societies. Tenacious and dangerous forms of magical practice can be found particularly in the slums of London and among the European peasantry; Roman Catholic saints are enlisted in popular practice as "passive accomplices of magic." Magic thrives wherever there is danger and uncertainty (particularly in areas such as gambling, sailing, and aviation), and even among intellectuals various forms of magical thought persist (most notably in the faith in psychoanalysis). As Malinowski concludes (stating perhaps more than he intended), "It is very difficult to discover where common sense ends and magic begins."[75]

Ruth Benedict also underscores the prevalence of magic in contemporary society. In fact, she asserts, modern processes of secularization have had far greater success in suppressing religion than magic. Magical thought thrives, as evidenced in the popularity of various divinatory cults and astrology, various contemporary debates over sexuality (which seem to exude superstition), and numerous other aspects of modern life (even the American educational system, which seems to elevate education itself into a form of "power in the non-naturalistic sense"). Industrial relations and international trade are beset by magical thinking (demonstrated in the failure to acknowledge that "good results . . . follow only from intelligent and specific procedures accurately adjusted to specific problems"). But there is an even more prominent and immediate example of modern magic, one pointing back to the discussion of Hume that opened this chapter:

> The most characteristic magic of present western civilization is that which centers around property; the violent sense of loss that is experienced by the typical modern in the loss of a sum of money, quite

irrespective of whether he and his family will be housed and clothed and fed, is as much a case of magical identification of the ego with externals as any of Lévy-Bruhl's examples of prelogical mentality.[76]

Sociological theorists have also been extremely concerned with the threat posed by magical thought in modern society. Mauss and Hubert assert that the magical beliefs persisting in various corners of the modern world are "the most alive, the most real indications of a state of social unrest and social consciousness, in which float a whole crowd of vague ideas, hopes and vain fears." Magic has far greater endurance than a mere set of false ideas or primitive science. Instead, it survives because it expresses "the expectations of successive generations, their tenacious illusions, their hopes in the form of magical formulas." Magic persists because it provides an expression of social antagonisms and vain hopes.[77]

Scholars studying twentieth-century fascism have often asserted that the German people were susceptible to Hitler because of an aberrational tendency toward magical thinking. This theme appeared as early as Franz Neumann's *Behemoth* (completed just as World War II began and published in 1944). In this work, Neumann attempts to account for the appeal that fascism exerted over the German masses by recourse to the notion of charisma, the same social force seen as providing the basis for primitive kingship. Neumann explains that in times of great social and economic anxiety people will embrace superstition and that the "least rational strata of society turn to leaders. Like primitive men, they look for a savior to fend off their misery and deliver them from destitution." The charismatic leader, supposedly possessing superhuman gifts, demands obedience and submission, which in turn "foster helplessness and hopelessness among the people." As Neumann explains:

> Magic becomes the major concern of National Socialist culture. The world can be manipulated by techniques and formulas; in fact, if properly used these techniques and words automatically change things. And the secret is in the possession of the National Socialist leadership. Magical ceremonies are celebrated on many occasions, reminiscent of the practices of primitive tribes. . . . The words used at mass meetings carry in themselves means for changing nature and society. . . . The emphasis on magic has even changed the language. The noun tends to supersede the verb. Things happen—they are not done. Fate, providence, objective natural forces produce things: German victories.

This theme of the magical nature of fascism recurs in a number of scholarly texts. For example, Arturo Castiglioni asserts that fascists and authoritarians commonly vitiate the critical reasoning of their followers through use of a magical mode of collective suggestion (involving "toxic, mechanical, rhythmical, or otherwise suggestive elements" producing a collective state of consciousness). Louis Pauwels and Jacques Bergier's *Morning of the Magicians* (1963) stresses the preoccupation of Hitler and various Nazi intellectuals with occultism. As Pauwels and Bergier conclude, the Nazis "had a magical conception of the world and of man, to which they had sacrificed all the youth of their country and offered to the gods an ocean of human blood." Nicholas Goodrick-Clarke's *Occult Roots of Nazism* (1985) contains a valuable account of popular literature attributing the success of the Nazi movement in Germany to its supposed inspiration and direction by occult agencies.[78]

Two aspects of this theme are particularly relevant for our purposes. First, these scholarly texts sometimes vacillate, often in very subtle ways, between accounts of Nazi enthusiasm for the occult and accounts of ways in which that enthusiasm contributed to the success of Nazism. These two issues are quite different from one another, but even when discussing the former, scholars often find themselves inadvertently drawn to the latter, particularly given the urgency and complexity of accounting for the rise of Nazism. Second, this theme fits seamlessly both into scholarly traditions emphasizing the authoritarian nature of magic and into traditions stigmatizing occultism as reprehensibly antimodern. If the Nazis were prone to magic or if the German people were drawn to Nazism because of a tendency to magical thinking, fascism can be understood as a problem of mass regression, an occult survival fundamentally at odds with modernity.

Theodor Adorno builds on this theme of the contemporary menace of authoritarian magic in his analysis of twentieth-century superstition. Adorno approaches the study of modern superstitions such as astrology within the context of his broader effort to understand fascism and anti-Semitism. He argues that while superstitions might appear relatively benign, they are actually indicative of broad, reactionary social tendencies toward authoritarian irrationalism. In these superstitions, irrational elements are fused with "pseudo-rationality" in a manner that tends toward totalitarianism.[79]

Echoing the broad range of social theorists who claim that magic is fundamentally reactionary, Adorno argues that modern astrology is permeated with authoritarianism. As he explains, astrology serves to breed and exploit dependency in its audience. It offers its followers "an *ideology for dependence*" and caters to their flight from responsibility for their lives or the social conditions within which they live. Astrology preaches social conformity, a complacent acceptance of hierarchical social and economic relations, and contentment with the status quo: "The stars seem to be in complete agreement with the established ways of life and with the habits and institutions circumscribed by our age." Through these tendencies, superstitions such as astrology stand as an ominous barometer of totalitarian impulses lurking in the contemporary world. As Adorno asserts, "The bent little fortune-tellers terrorizing their clients with crystal balls are toy models of the great ones who hold the fate of mankind in their hands."[80]

The manipulative, mass-culture aspects of contemporary magic also emerge in Raymond Williams's famous essay "Advertising: The Magic System" (1961). Williams here argues that modern advertising works to invest materiality with inordinate social and personal meanings. This system constitutes a form of magic, "a highly organized and professional system of magical inducements and satisfactions, functionally similar to magical systems in simpler societies, but rather strangely coexistent with a highly developed scientific technology." Advertising magic serves both to facilitate and to mask the material forces shaping human beings as consumers. Through a mode of magical association, the consumption of various goods is associated with the satisfaction of disparate desires. "You do not only buy an object: you buy social respect, discrimination, health, beauty, success, power to control your environment. The magic obscures the real sources of general satisfaction because their discovery would involve radical change in the whole common way of life." And the great irony, of course, is that this magic actually succeeds. The very mass circulation of these magical associations gives them a type of efficacy: "The fantasy seems to be validated, at a personal level, but only at the cost of preserving the general unreality which it obscures."[81] Our desires are created, manipulated, and satisfied through magical means that can work even when we perceive their artifice.

This theme of magic as dissembling manipulation remains prominent, but it is not only authoritarian dictators and advertising moguls who are labeled as magicians in contemporary polemics. The charge of "magical thinking" remains a powerful rhetorical weapon, one amply coded with echoes of duplicity, perversity, and disruption. In his *Mysteries of Religion* (1986), Stephen Clark directs this charge against various forms of postmodern thought. In a section of his text entitled "Anti-realists and Magicians," Clark targets contemporary scholars who have moved down the "the anti-realist road" by abandoning older correspondence theories of truth. These antirealists, Clark explains, claim that changing human discourse has the effect of changing reality. But this assertion is pure magic:

> Magical rituals are founded on the implicit assumption that if we all speak differently about something, the real world changes, not because any power moves (as it might or might not) in response to our pleas, but because the words themselves, our words, are the real constitutive powers of the universe. If we *say* that a cucumber is an ox, or a wafer is the Christ, or a feather is a knife at our enemy's throat, it is, since its being so just consists in what we say of it, and

do with it. What is clearly true of many things (as that this piece of paper is worth a sovereign if enough people say it is) the magician reckons true of everything.

Thus, Clark asserts, where early anthropologists saw "an ignorant and childish confusion between words and the world, late modern reasoners must see a sophisticated anti-realism on a level with their own." Particularly in the 1960s and 1970s, some radical antirealists went so far as to argue that " 'science' and 'scholarship' are magical in effect." Yet this magical "total relativism, in the mouths of anti-establishment gurus or a few 'hermeneutical philosophers' " of the "continental fashion," is wrongheaded and dangerous. Cultural relativism is fatally self-contradicting, and "the magical conclusion is indeed a product of unreason and naive hopefulness." Clark concludes that magic, "the brash and foredoomed assertion of the will to control all things by the way we speak of them, is the very opposite of religious piety, which recognizes an established Order as the root of Truth."[82] For Clark magic remains a marker of subversive, antimodern irrationality. Good order can only be maintained by submission to a well-established regime of truth.

Magic and the Margins

While many theorists concur that magical thinking poses a threat to modern society, they are often rather vague about the specific nature of this threat. As we saw in the prior section, thinkers such as Mauss and Hubert underscore the significance of magic as an index of social unrest. But the nature of the danger posed by magic becomes more overt when we turn to consider the specific peoples to whom magic is attributed. While Adorno and Raymond Williams assay the magic of the dominant classes, magic is far more commonly seen as characteristic of those with little access to legitimate forms of social power. Beneath the surface of theories of magic often lies a tacit preoccupation with the power of those on the social margins.

According to Tylor, the "modern educated world" rejects occult science as contemptible superstition and "has practically committed itself to the opinion that magic belongs to the lower level of civilization." As he explains, this judgment is confirmed even among less developed peoples where education has not yet succeeded in eradicating the belief in magic. Even in these settings it is predominantly "an isolated or outlying race, the lingering survivor of an older nationality," that is most liable to a reputation for sorcery or magic. As Tylor states, "The usual and suggestive state of things is that nations who believe with the sincerest terror in the reality of the magic art, at the same time cannot shut their eyes to the fact that it more essentially belongs to, and is more thoroughly at home among, races less civilized than themselves."[83]

Tylor cites numerous examples of peoples who attribute frightening and powerful magic to "lower tribes," "the slave-caste below them," or various out-casts. For example, in speaking of the Malay fear of the Mintira, he notes that the strongest weapon available to the Mintira is the fact that the Malay are cautious to avoid Mintira magic. Similarly, while the Malay despise the Jakuns, the Malay also live in extreme fear of the Jakuns' supernatural powers and thus often refrain from acting on their hostility. And again, the magical powers of the Finns and Lapps are feared by their more developed Scandinavian neigh-bors. This dynamic, Tylor explains, conforms with the survival of magical ideas among less developed groups within the civilized world. Even in Europe pow-ers of sorcery are ascribed "to despised outcast 'races maudites,' Gypsies and Cagots." Protestants in Scotland have been known to revere the power of Cath-olic priests to cast out demons or cure madness, and "the vulgar" are said to think the Church of England clergy weak in comparison to the power of "pop-ish priests" to lay spirits (a circumstance that with "unconscious irony" dem-onstrates the relation of the Roman church to modern civilization).[84]

Many scholars join Tylor in this theme. As noted previously, Frazer attrib-utes magic to the uneducated peasants and lower social classes of Europe. Mauss and Hubert offer extensive discussion of the processes through which magic is attributed to various groups. They assert, for example, that throughout the world women are viewed as particularly prone to magic, not so much because of their physical characteristics as because of the social attitudes and responses those characteristics elicit. Women are seen as "the font of myste-rious activities, the sources of magical power"; since women are largely ex-cluded from most religious cults, "the only practices left to them on their own initiative are magical ones." A type of self-fulfilling prophecy sets in, as women are denied access to legitimate forms of power and accused of magic, and then turn to magic as the most readily available means of empowerment. Children, Mauss and Hubert continue, are also seen as having important magical pow-ers. As older religions are supplanted by new faiths, the priests of the old religions are considered magicians. Similarly, strangers in a community are regularly considered prone to sorcery. And since strangers are often defined by reference to their foreign place of origin, magical powers come to be "de-limited topographically." Magic is also attributed to nomads, gypsies, and less developed cultures (such as the Dasyus by the Hindus, the Finns and Lapps by the Scandinavians, and forest dwellers in Melanesia and Africa by more advanced tribes of the plains, coasts, and rivers). Mauss and Hubert thus assert that magicians are characterized by an essentially abnormal social status: "It is public opinion which makes the magician and creates the power he wields." As they conclude, "The magical value of persons or things results from the relative position they occupy within society or in relation to society." It is in-sufficient to say that *mana* is attributed to certain things because of the position they occupy in relation to society; the very idea of *mana* is "none other than the idea of these relative values and the idea of these differences in potential."[85]

In this light, magical power is itself the product of an underlying differential in social power.

Chantepie de la Saussaye stresses the dynamic through which magic is attributed to foreign cultures: "The more highly developed nations look with contempt, if not without fear, on the older, lower, or foreign nations and their gods, as magicians." Westermarck underscores the ways in which magic is attributed to the outsider and the socially marginal. He discusses, for example, how the visiting stranger is often considered a "quasi-supernatural character" with fearful magical powers and how the magical potency of West African slaves is feared by their masters. In a similar manner, magic is attributed to the elderly, particularly to elderly women. In fact, Westermarck asserts, all women are prone to the attribution of supernatural powers, since they are seen not only as better skilled in it but also as having ample opportunities for practicing it.[86]

One of the most developed accounts of the role of social class in the attribution of magic comes from Max Weber, who asserts that magic is "the most widely diffused form of mass religion all over the world," with nonprivileged social groups such as peasants and the lowest of the proletariat more inclined to magical practices. These classes focus their religious concerns on salvation from immediate, external dangers, while more privileged intellectual classes have the luxury to consider inner needs for meaning that are "remote from life." Thus it is only with the rise of intellectualism that disenchantment spreads and "the world's processes . . . lose their magical significance." While the bureaucratic classes usually scorn all forms of irrational religion, they tolerate irrationalism when it can serve as a means of maintaining social control. Rationalized religion is a privilege of the elite—and a tool they wield in their efforts to control the lower classes. In applying these principles to the contemporary European scene, Weber argues that only among the lowest and most vulnerable of the proletariat (and the permanently impoverished lower-middle-class groups at greatest risk of falling into the proletariat) is there a susceptibility to religious indoctrination. The religious propaganda most effective among such groups has "a distinctively magical form or, where real magic has been eliminated, it has certain characteristics which are substitutes for the magical-orgiastic supervention of grace."[87]

This theme remains prominent. Keith Thomas notes that those accused of witchcraft in early modern England were most often the powerless and desperate, a condition that leads Thomas to conclude that "like most forms of magic, [witchcraft] was a substitute for impotence, a remedy for anxiety and despair." By their very nature, he explains, English witchcraft accusations usually depended on the accused being socially and economically inferior to the victim; if the accused had more social power, she would have more direct methods to act out her hostilities. In this frame, Thomas states, witchcraft stands as "an inarticulate but dramatic form of protest against the hopelessness of [the accused witch's] condition," but a form of protest that remains ineffective and politically naive.[88]

As we proceed, note a subtle form of rhetorical slippage at work here. On the one hand, scholars claim to be explaining the ways in which the people they are describing attribute magic to socially marginal groups (foreigners, strangers, women). We see people from various cultures identifying their inferiors as prone to magic, as possessing unexplained, potentially disruptive powers. At the same time, the scholars themselves echo this attribution. The suspect or illicit practices of those on the margins of social power seem to constitute magic, since magic is defined as the province of the powerless. Scholars thus replicate the very gesture they claim to be recounting. Perhaps, as Mauss and Hubert frame it, magic is indeed produced by this differential in social power.

The first chapter began with Hume's assertion that "it is natural, that superstition should prevail every where in barbarous ages, and put men on the most earnest enquiry concerning those invisible powers, who dispose of their happiness or misery."[89] Happiness and misery often depend on invisible powers, but this is not a feature only of barbarous ages. The dynamic of attributing magic to those on the margins of society—those faceless masses whose suppression underwrites the material well-being of the socially dominant and who would gain the most from disrupting the status quo—confirms Hume's basic claim, though not in the sense in which he might have intended it. Stigmatizing the practices of socially marginal groups as magical can itself serve as a form of countermagic, one aimed at suppressing the disruptive potential of these groups and at containing latent subversion. Thus we come to the final section of this chapter, a consideration of the ways in which modern theories of magic have functioned as a magical mechanism of social control.

Magic and the Channeling of Power

In a vivid and often quoted declaration concerning the links between supernaturalism and the mercantile economy, Voltaire states in a 1772 entry for his *Philosophical Dictionary*: "One does not hear about vampires in London nowadays—I can however see merchants, speculators, tax-collectors, who have sucked the blood of the people in broad daylight, but who were definitely not dead, although they had been corrupted quite enough. These real bloodsuckers do not live in cemeteries but in very pleasant palaces."[90] The most dangerous vampires are to be found, Voltaire tells us, not among the dead, but rather among thriving economic elites. So also the most potent magic may well be found not where we have been told to expect it—the social margins—but rather among the intellectual and cultural elites, even among scholars of magic.

Magic and Colonial Control

One of the recurrent themes we have encountered in modern theories of magic has been the deep interrelation between these theories and the concrete needs of European and American colonialism and imperialism. Early modern theories of cultural and religious evolution emerged in the context of widening European economic and political power, and the modern social sciences themselves developed in the era of Europe's most extensive colonial conquests. Numerous recent cultural theorists have explored the complex ways in which anthropological and sociological theory conformed with the interests of European colonialism. So also the dominant theories of magic demonstrate a deep concern with controlling non-European populations.

This theme has appeared repeatedly in the preceding pages. The colonial context of these scholarly debates is overt in discussions of "primitive mentalities" and "African modes of thought," where theorists attempt to determine the distinctive forms of reasoning characterizing various populations. As we saw in the prior chapter, more recent discussions of this topic have questioned whether human cultures are commensurable—can meaningful translation and comparison occur among different cultures, or are cultures fundamentally alien from one another? But in a context of wildly unequal economic and material power, debates over cultural commensurability are profoundly double-edged. If cultures are commensurable, cultural difference is a trivial impediment to the spread of modern markets, one that can be ignored or commodified according to market needs; if cultures are incommensurable, that very difference can be readily invoked to confirm the superiority of the dominant powers and to give license for suppression and exploitation.

Colonialism is often an explicit concern in these theories. For example, in *At Home with the Savage* (1932), J. H. Driberg examines the difficulties colonial administrators face in their attempts to control and eradicate magic. In Driberg's assessment, magic is one of the most pressing problems confronting colonial governments. While white magic can have beneficial effects in spurring productive and harmonious social interaction, black magic is thoroughly detrimental. Colonial authorities have disrupted traditional methods of suppressing black magic, but this has made black magic a far greater problem. "Witchcraft Ordinances" put into place by European administrators against practitioners of black magic are difficult to enforce and ineffective (since death is the only adequate solution to witchcraft). And even in recognizing black magic as a social problem, these ordinances have given tacit support to native witchcraft beliefs.[91]

Driberg questions whether the entire effort by colonial governments to eradicate magic might be misplaced, since in many native societies magic serves useful social functions. Black magic and white countermagic work together, and if black magic were to be eliminated, the social forces creating group cohesion and providing an impetus to productive activity might falter. Subversive threats actually serve to keep social integration at a high level, and the repression of subversion can have the unintended effect of reducing integration. But despite these concerns, Driberg concludes that colonial governments must find more effective means for eradicating primitive magic. In the end, the only solution he can offer for this dilemma is a more intensive program of colonial education.[92]

Driberg is one of many scholars concerned with how colonial administrators can better manage indigenous populations, particularly with respect to traditional belief systems. In another vivid example, near the conclusion of his 1948 sociological study of magic Hutton Webster offers an explanation of how his analysis can be used by colonial governments. Webster acknowledges that beliefs in magic are extremely difficult to eradicate and disappear only slowly as traders, missionaries, and colonial administrators introduce European culture. Still, there is hope that these eradication efforts can succeed, particularly with respect to white magic:

> Religious and moral teaching, together with instruction in elementary science, may be counted upon, slowly but surely, to get rid of much white magic among primitive peoples, or to reduce it, as among ourselves, to pale and inconsequential survivals. Even the weapon of ridicule may be usefully employed to undermine faith in the efficacy of magic. . . . In Central Australia, for instance, the aborigines often have their magical notions shattered as the result of the contemptuous attitude toward them displayed by white settlers.

Like Driberg, Webster acknowledges the particular difficulties European administrators face with respect to black magic, difficulties that are "a part of the much larger problem of the relations of the 'higher' races to the 'lower' throughout much of the world." "The white man's law" punishing charges of witchcraft or reprisals against suspected witches actually has unintended consequences "from the native point of view." This new law serves to encourage black magic by removing social constraints on the activities of magicians and sorcerers and by suppressing the operations of beneficial witch doctors. Again like Driberg, Webster argues that before measures against sorcerers and witch doctors can be effective, a colonized population must be educated away from their beliefs in sorcery by knowledge of the true causes of sickness and misfortune.[93]

As Driberg and Webster demonstrate, one of the major undercurrents of Western theories of magic has been concern with administering non-European populations. This theme emerges in numerous social science texts, and it is also particularly prominent in texts popularizing social scientific theory for use by European and American missionaries and administrators.[94] Western theories of magic formed an important component of the broader efforts to subjugate and manage populations under imperial control. Magic marked non-Western peoples as culturally and developmentally inferior, and in this light colonialism could be framed as a compelling civilizing mission.

Magic and the Domestic Terrain

Social and economic elites within the West were not merely concerned with controlling non-European populations; they also faced important needs to regulate and control their domestic populations. As Rudi Bleys states in his study of modern discourses on perversion, there has been a "complex and self-validating interrelationship between attempts to categorize and regulate colonial subjects of imperialism 'abroad' and the potentially rebellious, politically seditious subjects of the social underclass . . . 'at home.' "[95] Magic has regularly been configured by scholars as predominantly linked to nonmodern cultures, but it has also remained a major domestic concern. Groups within Europe and America that fail or refuse to conform to the norms of modern life, to the dominant standards of identity and agency, have regularly been portrayed as prone to magic. And members of these marginalized groups have, in turn, often embraced various forms of magic as a mechanism of social subversion.

Concern with regulating the domestic population has taken numerous forms. In her recent study of efforts to suppress popular superstitions and magical beliefs in late nineteenth-century Britain, Maureen Perkins has focused on the importance of the issue of time in the production of modern subjectivity. As Perkins argues, many reformers saw superstition and magic as immured within a deterministic worldview fostering a fundamentally pessimistic or fatalistic sense of the future. These reformers understood their efforts to extirpate superstition as opening the way for a modern sense of optimism that would promote industrious action and social progress.[96] As we have seen in prior chapters, modern polemics against magic have also focused on regularizing human relations with material objects—at least to the extent that commodity fetishism and the type of advertising magic that Raymond Williams discusses could supplant other modes of overinvestment. In addition to these themes of time and materiality, another major preoccupation of modern efforts to suppress magic has been a concern to regularize human relations to space and location.

A number of recent cultural theorists have explored the central role the construction and regulation of space have played in the organization of Western modernity. The mapping and quantification of space were prominent concerns of nineteenth- and twentieth-century Western colonialism. As Edward Said states it, "At some very basic level, imperialism means thinking about, settling on, controlling land that you do not possess, that is distant, that is lived on and owned by others." The power to quantify and regulate geography marks a potent form of cultural power. But this preoccupation with space and geography has not been limited to the colonial periphery; it has also been a major theme in the management of the domestic populations of Europe and America. Just as the meaning of time is central to the organization of modern society, so also the meaning of space is a fundamental concern. The operations of modern economies depend on increasingly complex mechanisms for controlling the timing and spacing of the behavior of large numbers of human agents across great distances. The regulation of space plays a crucial role in the management of human behavior.[97]

This focus on geography has been a prominent undercurrent in modern theories of magic. Tylor's *Primitive Culture*, a founding text in this tradition, provides a valuable illustration of the relation between magic and geography. At the same time Tylor's formulation of this relation also demonstrates the significance that geography and location can assume in efforts to prescribe a distinctively modern notion of human identity. In his consideration of magical survivals, Tylor catalogs a large number of magical practices persisting in the modern world. One of the most striking aspects of Tylor's catalog is the way in which he specifies—even circumscribes—the identities of the contemporary magicians he cites by their specific geographic locations. Thus, for example, he points to "the Tatar necromancer, the Highland ghost-seer, and the Boston medium," "the German cottager," the "Hessian lad," and "the Cornishman."[98] Tylor sees these figures and their magic as linked to the past through the dynamic of cultural survivals, but he also sees them as bounded in fundamental respects by geographic origin and location.

This emphasis on the geographic specificity of magic predates Tylor. In his *Lectures on the Philosophy of Religion* (1827), Hegel addresses magic in the context of the "determinate, particular, and hence finite religions, the *ethnic religions* generally." In Hegel's configuration, magic is a feature of determinate and bounded ethnic religions.[99] Throughout the scholarly tradition that has followed Tylor, magic is regularly configured as displaying murky, superstitious relations to specific locations. Nonmodern magic has been configured as archetypically "indigenous," a phenomenon to be found, as the title of J. H. Driberg's text indicates, *At Home with the Savage*. Scholarly accounts regularly portray magic in a florid, exotic mode that highlights this fundamentally indigenous nature.

As Tylor frames this issue in *Primitive Culture*, it is only members of the modern educated world who are able to transcend such specific geographic boundedness. Only the modern subject can aspire to universality, with an abstract rationality detached both from the specificity of a local identity and from magical relations to the material world. As Marshall Berman describes, the notion of the modern is infused with ideals of dislocation and deterritorialization in which geographic boundaries are relentlessly overcome.[100] Scholars have configured nonmodern magic as fixed in particularity—as inherently local, bounded, and constrained. But in the same gesture, they have affirmed idealized notions of modern science and religion that promise to surmount the limits of spacial particularity. Space is effectively desacralized, and the cosmological significance of local territory is overcome. Through the contrast with magical particularity, modernity presses a strident deterritorialization of space, time, and materiality that renders the world uniformly subject to Western science and uniformly open to commodification by modern markets. As Deleuze and Guattari would explain, this scholarly discourse reflects capitalism's drive to configure a deterritorialized, smooth—and universal—space that breaks from local, territorialized, striated configurations.[101]

From this perspective magic lurks as a specter threatening unassimilated and uncommodified relations to the physical world. Magical thinking is seen as overinvesting particularity—spaces, objects, even affects—with inordinate significance. Yet such subversive magic can still serve an invaluable function as the foil against which modes of religion and rationality more readily conforming to the needs of the modern economy can be articulated. In order to accommodate the deterritorializing drive of capitalism and render the world free for unconstrained commodification, religion must be configured as breaking its ties to specific sites and locations, as becoming quite literally "nowhere." As Roger Friedland and Deirdre Boden have explored, the formulation of new religious cosmographies and cosmologies was a central feature in the emergence of modern social structures. We see this particularly in the relation between Protestantism and the formation of the early nation-state:

> In Protestantism God was neither immanent in the natural world
> nor in history, thereby providing a cleaner ground on which the
> state could resacralize its territory in terms of its own historicity.
> The imagining of an undifferentiated space, where no location was
> ontologically privileged, may have opened the way for the world to
> be divided up into putatively equal sovereign pieces, thereby destroy-
> ing the cosmographical nature of local territory in the process but
> making it possible to imagine a world of beings just like us.[102]

Magical practices—modes of thought and behavior that maintain murky links to specific locations and identities, that invest particular geographies and objects with supernatural significance—are the practices of beings decidedly not "just like us." Nonmodern magic provides a ready foil for the relentless deterritorializing of modern capital.

Magic and the Subversion of Markets

The dominant scholarly theories of magic have prescribed two distinct channels for the construction and resolution of human needs. On the one hand, they have constructed a rarefied, abstract, and unlocalized model of religion. The supernatural is cordoned away from the material world, and believers are prompted to limit their religiosity to a restrained and pietistic sense of duty and submission to the inexorable workings of the cosmos (and the market). At the same time, these theories of magic prescribe a notion of modern rationality that, through the workings of science and capital, is ceded unbridled control over the material world. Magic is deployed as the stigmatized mediator between these modes of religion and scientific rationality, reinforcing their separation. Deviant desires and behavior that resist this channeling of social power, that seek to intermingle the spiritual and material realms or to enlist other forms of nonrationalized or surreptitious power, are condemned as magical and irrationally primitive.

Yet the notion of magic is far too amorphous and pliable, far too potent, to remain under any type of hegemonic control. In fact the modern scholarly debates over magic have been so cacophonous that it is perhaps suspect even to speak of a "dominant" perspective at all. There has been a broad consensus among scholars in positioning magic in opposition to Western modernity, and the majority of scholars have invoked this contrast in order to define and affirm the values of the modern world. But through the prior chapters we have encountered a number of important scholars who reject the axiological presuppositions of this tradition, who find in the notion of magic valuable resources for contesting the presuppositions and presumptions of modernity. Some thinkers enlist magic in order to question the alienating effects of modern disenchantment. Others point to the magic of the socially powerful in an effort to uncover how that power is wielded and maintained through dissimulation. And still others invoke the magic of the social margins as a tool with which to challenge the inequities of Western economic and social structures.

A number of important social theorists have explored the role of magic as a mode of subversion and cultural critique. For example, in his response to Keith Thomas's *Religion and the Decline of Magic* (1971), E. P. Thompson underscores the ways in which religious systems can be used to render people docile and obedient to their economic masters. But in this light Thompson points out that the magical practices of the poor can constitute an "anti-culture," a mode of resisting both the dictates of religious authority and the will of the masters. In Thompson's reading, Keith Thomas pays inadequate attention to issues of social class in the early modern suppression and decline of magic; Thomas can thus express surprise at the persistence of "popular ignorance" among the uneducated masses. Instead, as Thompson argues, ignorance itself may serve as a powerful political tool, particularly in the hands of the dispossessed: "ignorance may indicate evasion, or translation, irony in the face of the Church's homilies, or, very often, active intellectual resistance to its doctrines." Thompson rejects Thomas's assertion that changes in the belief structures of social elites necessarily seep down into communities of the poor and illiterate. Indeed, Thompson indicates, the differentiation between magic and religion that took shape during the early modern period may well have served as a marker of cultural dissociation and differentiation between "the polite and the vulgar cultures."[103] A more compelling account of the early modern era might focus not so much on the decline of magic as on the ideological efforts of social elites to formulate a heightened differentiation between religion and magic and thus to exert their own forms of surreptitious power.

The political potency of modern magic as an "anti-culture" has depended on the underlying logic of the cultural and scholarly paradigm stigmatizing magic as nonmodern and condemning it to the margins. The effort to valorize magical practices as subversive of the norms of modernity adopts the logical structure of this paradigm but then turns the paradigm against itself. This move has been important to various countercultural groups that have adopted magic as a trope for social critique. As we saw in the introduction, Starhawk claims that magic is a potent resource for feminist spirituality because of magic's unsettling political valence. Donate Pahnke concurs that one of the reasons feminists were drawn to magic is that magic and feminism share a similar countercultural pull. In "spiritual feminism," Pahnke explains, magic is given a positive role, while its contents are transformed and revalued. Magic is configured not as a form of "power-over" various spiritual forces, but as a form of "power from and with" those forces through which feminists seek to challenge pervasive modern notions of individuation, hierarchy, and instrumental control. As Pahnke frames it, this notion of spiritual magic is profoundly contrary to traditional Christianity; magic has "an explosive political dimension" in its radical rethinking of the notion of power.[104]

Other proponents of modern magic join Pahnke in seeking to overcome what they see as the constrictions of modern religion and rationality, in seeking to reintegrate human life into a more organic unity with the natural and spiritual worlds. David Farren has invoked magic as an alternative to the sterility of modern religion and science. In contrast to religious and scientific efforts to transcend the specificity of human culture and identity, he explains, magic remains firmly rooted in history, community, and tradition. Magic holds out a promise of escape from the cold instrumentalism of modernity: "If there is magic, then man is not just a tool of society for ends that he can barely recognize." In a related vein, Ariel Glucklich has stressed magic's potential as a resource for overcoming the fragmentation of modern life and for promoting new forms of human consciousness. In Glucklich's account, magical thinking fosters a distinctive form of consciousness, an "awareness of the interrelatedness of all things in the world." Glucklich sees magic as a means of restoring a fundamental "experience of relatedness" and re-creating empathetic bonds among human beings and other aspects of the nature world.[105]

These themes are quite prominent among a wide range of modern practitioners of magic. In his study of New Age religion Wouter Hanegraaff explains that one of the defining features of the modern neopagan advocacy of magic is "a rejection of the 'cold world of cause and effect' in favor of an 'enchanted world'" of the sort described by scholars such as Lévy-Bruhl. Neopagan magic is configured "as a means of invoking and reaffirming mystery in a world which seems to have lost it." This magic differs from the magic of traditional societies in that it is *"purposely adopted* as a reaction to the 'disenchanted' world of modern western society." These modern forms of magic give vent to various types of alienation and social discontent, but the very degree to which such magic is self-consciously adopted points to the deep level at which it is shaped by the modernity it is reacting against, particularly modern forms of individualism. As Hanegraaff and other scholars underscore, such talk of magic can quickly degenerate into affectation or eccentricity, another consumer preference to be commodified. Modern magic can readily supplant productive action and distract from more pragmatic and productive forms of collective action.[106]

Yet despite this constant reterritorializing, magic maintains its aura as a potent threat to the operations of modern capital. Positioned in stark counterpoint to the norms of modernity, magic holds great allure for cultural theorists with its intimations that the subterranean operations of modernity might be uncovered. Magic tantalizes with the possibility that some forms of identify and desire might escape the assimilation and commodification of modern forms of knowledge and power, and in its brazen display of the machinations through which objects are invested with meaning, it stands as an overt threat to the mystifications of the commodity form. At the core of magic we find the prospect of other possible relations to materiality, relations that threaten both to expose the fetishism of the commodity and to disrupt its hegemony.

In all these respects magic maintains a profoundly disruptive potential as the "unthought" of modernity, the very condition of possibility that must be repressed in order for modernity to maintain its hold. One of the most valuable scholarly explorations of this disruptive potential comes from Michael Taussig. In *Shamanism, Colonialism, and the Wild Man* (1987), Taussig offers a lengthy and elusive consideration of the colonial terror imposed on the Indian population of the Putumayo region of southwest Colombia in the early decades of the twentieth century and of shamanistic and magical healing among the contemporary Indian and peasant populations of the region. Magic is a dominant theme of his text, both the magic of the Indian shaman and the magic of the social analyst.

Taussig argues that the magic of shamanistic rituals has great power in giving voice to the social antagonisms shaping the lives of the oppressed inhabitants of the Putumayo and in providing lines of empowerment and subversion for these peoples. The disruptive visions that animate the shaman's healing rituals offer both a critical window onto the operations of colonial power in the lives of its victims and a mechanism through which "that power provides a view of its inner constitution." Just as the shamanistic rituals feed lisorder and disjunction to excavate social antagonisms, so also colonial terror maintained its hold through the production of a potent mode of "epistemic murk."[107] The wild rupture of these rituals provides a palpable medium for the analysis and critique of the historical and political construction of subjects and their experience.

Taussig extends this theme to include the modern social analyst. Georg Lukács pointed to the phantom objectivity on which capitalist cultural structures are based, and throughout *Shamanism* Taussig builds on Lukács's theme to demonstrate the ways in which "the magic of academic rituals of explanation" is itself complicit with efforts by the ruling class to retain authority. A rhetoric of objectivity, order, and explanation masks the tangible (and often violent) social power that makes some people subjects—and others objects—of knowledge. Seeking "to devise ways of freeing imagery from the deadening hand of tradition and the stronghold of the ruling classes," Taussig works to illuminate and destabilize "the contrived manner by which objectivity is created" and, more pointedly, to demonstrate the subtle ways in which the fiction of objectivity depends on a "magic of style to make this trick of truth work."[108]

Taussig's focus on stylistic magic has a potent political objective. In line with his broader critique of the anthropological search for order and of the rituals of academic text-making, Taussig frames *Shamanism* as "a book of *magia*," one that can demonstrate both the magic of shamanic healing and the magic of social analysis. He argues that the path to productive political opposition—to imagining the world otherwise—lies in a representational mode that resists sterile logic yet contests remystification. This is a mode that seeks *"to penetrate the veil while retaining its hallucinatory quality,"* "to see the myth in the natural and the real in magic, to demythologize history and to reenchant its reified representation."[109] Taussig's account of colonial and imperial terror is built on a double movement of demythologization and reenchantment, a movement that invokes rational interpretation while simultaneously destabilizing the categories of that interpretation and the position from which analysis is undertaken, a movement that deploys concepts of history and experience while pointing to the magical nature of their construction. Through the destabilization of his own text, Taussig seeks to uncover the magic and myth at work in the reified representation of the real.

Just as he underscores the political potency of shamanistic magic, Taussig also points us toward the magic of text-making, the conjuring powers that underlie all forms of social analysis. Modern theories of magic have themselves exercised great power as they have fit into broad, and often unacknowledged, networks of cultural and material force. The social theorists examined in this book have themselves operated as magicians, but, as in all magical economies, the complex webs of magic and countermagic have served to obscure the ultimate vectors of their power. Magical power always surpasses the intentionality of even the most potent magicians. Spirits refuse to be contained, always re-emerging at some unanticipated site, assuming some unimagined form, performing some unthinkable feat.

The scholarly effort to contain and circumscribe magic always falters, falling prey to self-contradiction, ambiguity, and incoherence. But perhaps the greatest challenge to this effort comes from capital itself. Even as the dominant scholarly theories of magic have configured ideals that resonate with the ideological interests of the modern economy, capital itself has continued to permutate. As many recent cultural theorists have explored, global capitalism is dramatically reconfiguring its relations to space and location. Lawrence Grossberg, for example, has suggested that a new globalizing order is emerging in which capitalism is not merely reproducing itself as—or across—space, but is operating through "a stratification in which differences proliferate in a highly reterritorialized world. . . . It is a question of the global becoming local and the local becoming global."[110] The material particularity of local magic has long been seen as an impediment or threat to the spread of the modern capitalist order, but new forms of capitalism will require new forms of subjectivity and new relations to space, time, and materiality. Many of these new structures appear to be materializing around us in this very moment. These emerging structures may come to displace the dominant cultural understandings of magic as they move us beyond the limits of Western modernity.

Conclusion

A knowledge which is divorced from cultural reality is in itself a
symptom of witchcraft.

—J. H. Driberg

We have come to Michael Taussig's assertion that the most productive strategy for illuminating contemporary scholarly constructions
of magic and supernaturalism is through a double movement of demythologization and reenchantment, a movement that invokes rational interpretation while simultaneously destabilizing the categories of that interpretation. This strategy, Taussig argues, can serve to
unmask the contrivance and mystification through which scholarly
objectivity itself is constructed. This type of double movement circles back to an important theme raised in the introduction. There
we considered Emily Apter's analysis of the appeal that fetishism
has held for modern scholars—scholars have fetishized the concept,
seeing it as a key to religion, psychology, and culture. In seeking to
account for this scholarly preoccupation, Apter points to the power
of the fetish to destabilize normal modes of thought and representation. The very extravagance and excess of fetishism serve to manifest
the fundamental artifice of all human representation. Through this
play of fixation and estrangement, meaning is simultaneously rein-
scribed and transgressed.

The operations of the type of double gesture toward which
Taussig and Apter allude become more apparent as we consider one
of the central themes we have encountered throughout the scholarly
literature on magic, the claim that magic is fixated on the power of

words. This issue has appeared in numerous contexts through the course of this book, from scholars who argue that magic derives from an inordinate belief in the efficacy of mere words, to scholars who assert that magic turns on an overinvestment of mental representations, to scholars who argue that magical thinking fails to recognize essential differences between representation and reality. The German philosopher Ernst Cassirer provides an emphatic formulation of this theme in the second volume of his *Philosophy of Symbolic Forms* (1925). Cassirer argues that a decisive characteristic of the magical worldview is belief in the objective nature and efficacy of signs. As he explains, magic is commonly understood as seeking to animate the material world, but in a paradoxical manner this mythic drive is "directed with particular intensity toward what is most unreal and lifeless . . . the shadow realm of words, images, and signs." This paradox can be explained only when we recognize that in the mythical world "the two factors, thing and signification, are undifferentiated, because they merge, grow together, concresce in an immediate unity." In the magical worldview "there is no such thing as *mere* mimesis, *mere* signification," since objects and signs are undifferentiated and intermingled. Magical thinking fails to recognize the fundamentally illusory nature of language, and therefore interposes language and desire indiscriminately into the world of material reality. The practitioner of magic seeks to subject all outward being to the practitioner's desire, and external reality is thus deprived of autonomy and independent existence. In Cassirer's view we move away from magic only as the subjective realm of representation and desire is decisively segregated from the world of material objects and language is understood as "unreal and lifeless . . . the shadow realm."[1]

Cassirer here interweaves a view of language common among many modern scholars and a recurring theme in the scholarly construction of magic. Variations of this basic perspective can be found in numerous texts. For example, as we saw in the prior chapter, psychologists Leonard Zusne and Warren H. Jones claim that magic turns on a basic confusion of linguistic and physical relationships, a confusion between interpretive categories and external reality. Magic, they explain, disregards the distinction between physical and psychological causes, the difference between energy and information: "When meaning, instead of the physical processes of energy transfer or information transmission, is taken to be causal, when meaning is externalized or reified, magical thinking enters into this picture." In their view this confusion is symptomatic of the broader error of magic, its blindness to the strict and proper boundaries "between one being and another, between beings and things, and between the subjective and the objective."[2]

This scholarly disavowal of the magical power of words has a long history. As Thomas M. Greene has recently explored, debates over the nature and power of signification go back as far as Plato and Herodotus. In *The Discoverie of Witchcraft* (1584), Reginald Scot rejected the claim that words can exert magical power. Excepting only the decrees of God, he explained, "by the sound of the words nothing commeth, nothing goeth." Greene also cites Scot's contemporary, the theologian William Perkins, who sought to counter Scot's position on the illusory nature of witchcraft but offered a similar assessment of the power of language: "That which is in nature nothing but a bare signification, cannot serve to worke a wonder, and this is the nature of all words; for as they be framed of mans breath, they are naturall, but yet in regard of forme and articulation they are artificall and significant . . . for the first significations of words, depended upon the will and pleasure of man that framed and invented them."[3]

Modern scholars of magic have amplified this theme, repeatedly affirming that language is inert and powerless. There are a number of significant layers to this scholarly disavowal of the magical power of words. First, it configures a sharp and impermeable boundary between nature and culture, a natural world subject to nonhuman causality and the artificial, transitory world of human language, meaning, desire, and value. As Bruno Latour has shown us, this rhetorical divide between nature and culture is a formative component of the modern constitution. To be modern is to recognize this essential binary. In this light, magical thinking is most fundamentally nonmodern in its refusal to acknowledge the firm boundary between nature and culture (as well, of course, as the cognate boundaries between objects and subjects, the objective and the subjective). As Cassirer, Zusne and Jones, and numerous theorists from the preceding pages have argued, magical thinking brazenly disregards the modern configuration of this antinomy.

Further, in this scheme language is seen as functioning only as a medium of passive representation, a neutral, transparent—and powerless—reflection of stable natural processes (processes that are fundamentally more "real" than language). "Mere mimesis," "mere representation," "bare signification"—the construction of meaning and assertion of desire are portrayed as lacking all causal efficacy. Instead, as Cassirer frames it, language should be understood as "unreal and lifeless." The potency of representation—either in serving to constitute the phenomena represented or in exerting other causal effects—is aggressively disclaimed. And in its most extreme formulations, this argument has the effect of removing human purposiveness entirely from the chain of natural causality. Any visible manifestation of human desire, agency, or purposive action can become tainted with the aura of magic.

Numerous scholars discussed in the preceding chapters have argued that magic involves willful, assertive action—a failure to submit to the inexorable divine and natural order. Particularly at the conclusion of chapter 2, we encountered theorists who frame this claim so broadly that all purposive human action seems to be subsumed within magic. For example, W. J. Perry explains the essence of magic as follows: "By the aid of certain substances or objects, or by means of certain acts, men believe, in certain circumstances, that they can influence each other, and also natural phenomena, for their own advantage." In *The Science of Society* (1927), William Graham Sumner and Albert Galloway Keller assert that the basis of magic is the belief that personal longings and discontent prove that some satisfaction is possible, "that some change in conditions, instead of adjustment to them, is called for." In 1948 William Howells argued that "magic, properly, means all the formulas for doing things which are beyond one's personal powers." Werner Stark asserts that magic is based on the effort of the magician "to insert himself into the natural nexus of cause and effect, to introduce his wish, his subjective whim, into the objective texture of events. He regards himself as a new cause that will bring a specific new effect." And in his 1995 text on the anthropology of religion, Morton Klass asserts that in order to avoid applying the modern distinction between religion and magic onto peoples who do not function within those categories, he prefers to define magic simply as "techniques employed by those who believe that in specific circumstances persons, powers, beings, or even events are subject to control or coercion."[4]

Note the astounding breadth of these formulations. According to these scholars, any sense that human desire or behavior can influence other human beings or the natural world, that changes in circumstance are possible, that human techniques can exert control over other persons, powers, or events—any such sense falls into magic. We might reasonably attribute this type of hyperbole to carelessness or inadvertence. But the ease with which scholars can lapse into this astonishing claim—that all purposive human action is magical—demonstrates a central feature of the cultural logic undergirding modernity that is manifest throughout these theories of magic, a preoccupation with power that is at the same time strenuously disavowed.

Throughout the literature reviewed here, one of the recurring themes has been a deep scholarly ambivalence—often suspicion—concerning any overt attempt to exercise power. In the view of the dominant voices of this scholarly tradition, religion must be limited to transcendent or supraempirical objectives; any attention to materiality or pragmatic worldly ends veers into magic. At the same time, the material basis and effects of modern rationality and science fade from view in contrast with the extravagance and futility of the magical search for efficacy, and the rhetoric of magic's overinvestment of material objects provides ideological cover for the preoccupation with materiality on which capitalism depends. As Timothy Mitchell states it, within modernity "the appearance of order means the disappearance of power. Power is to operate more and more in a manner that is slow, uninterrupted and without external manifestation."[5] A broad range of scholars configure magic as the epitome of a self-seeking and emotionally laden will to power. Through contrast with magic, the material effects of religion are disclaimed, and the massive power of modern science and rationalized social control is naturalized.

This same logic of disavowal is also used to stigmatize the practices of groups on the margins of social power. As we have seen, scholarly debates over magic regularly turn on questions of social order. Issues of class, authority, and social control have been central components of theoretical formulations of magic, with magic commonly configured as the province of women, children, foreigners, primitives, and other deviants. The rhetoric of magic's self-seeking, irrationality, and futility reverberates with broader gender and racial ideologies, both lending its weight to those ideologies and taking on greater resonance through them. Magic is invoked as a marker of social difference, and by highlighting magic's preoccupation with power, the efforts of socially marginal actors to obtain or exert power is overtly stigmatized. At the same time, with the theme of power deflected onto magic, the forms of control exercised by the dominant classes are eclipsed and naturalized. As the prior chapters have shown, modern theories of magic have regularly conformed with the interests of dominant groups, both in configuring an unruly and benighted colonial periphery and in stigmatizing marginal groups within the domestic population.

A further effect of this logic of disavowal is to mask the power of the scholar. Despite the array of theorists who reiterate the claim that it is magical to believe in the power of words, scholars themselves have exerted substantial power with their theories of magic. While Cassirer or Zusne and Jones might assert that meaning and signification have no causal efficacy, the very labor they expend in producing meaning and signification belies their claim. As Latour states, "If magic is the body of practice which gives certain words the potency to act upon 'things,' then the world of logic, deduction, and theory must be called 'magical': but it is *our* magic."[6] Scholarly words enter into the flow of material causation, producing unpredictable and unintended effects to be sure, but demonstrating great potency nonetheless. Theorists of magic exercise the very magical power of words they so disclaim.

There is no more vivid display of this scholarly magic than the effort to conjure magic itself as a stable, reified phenomenon. We saw this tendency with particular clarity in the work of Brian Vickers, but the basic gesture underlies much of Western scholarship on magic through the nineteenth and twentieth centuries. Alexander Le Roy expresses an assumption that has shaped innumerable theorists: magic is "found everywhere, and everywhere is very nearly the same. . . . It is a fact." William Howells concurs that "magic is world-wide, by which I mean that it is the property not only of all primitive people but also of ourselves and all our ancestors, and it is the same thing precisely wherever it is found."[7]

"It is the same thing precisely wherever it is found." In these words and in innumerable similar formulations, scholars set about the process of making magic—culling diverse forms of behavior, modes of knowledge, social practices, and habits from an indiscriminate range of cultural systems and historical epochs and transmogrifying them into a unified phenomenon. As long as the spell can last, as long as this range of disparate practices can be held together as a distinct and stable phenomenon, magic can serve the scholars' ends. Instead of a multiplicity of overlapping human logics, practices, and social relations, we are offered a narrow, rigidly demarcated contrast between the magical and the modern. In this configuration, magic has served as a potent tool for the self-fashioning of modernity. Modern modes of religion, rationality, and social order have been given a distinctive clarity in contrast to the magical foil. Such a move functions so effectively because of the widespread agreement with Frank Byron Jevons's fundamental assertion that magic "is, always and everywhere, an error." Or, in Howells's redolent phrasing, magic "is not quite cricket."[8]

This production of magic has proved particularly valuable for scholars seeking to articulate modern norms for religion. As we have seen, numerous scholars have invoked the contrast with magic in order to configure an idealized model of religion as private, intellectual, spiritualized—a norm thoroughly insulated from any consideration of social power. This configuration has had two complexly intertwined effects. On the one hand, it serves to drain power from religion, to render religion an ineffectual and harmless abstraction with minimal consequences and thus increasingly extraneous to liberal modernity. As Max Weber has shown, a disenchanted world is more effectively subject to exploitation by capitalism and rationalized modern science. For good or ill, religious institutions remain one of the few social forces capable of challenging the unbridled power of the nation-state and the alienation and commodification of capitalist economic structures. As the sacred evaporates into a dematerialized fog, all objects, locations, and identities are rendered equally subject to the regimentation of the market.

In this light, modern theories of magic provide a particularly valuable window into the constitution of capitalist modernity. When religion is no longer grounded in the material world—when it becomes unlocalized and ethereal—it can easily become irrelevant to the basic concerns of human life. Such rarefied forms of religion can readily breed disbelief, a specter that visibly haunts liberal Christianity but that also permeates the aggressive incoherence of many contemporary conservatives. Modern theories of magic have often served to rearticulate and heighten these fundamental antinomies, promoting an ideal of religion that is vaporous and impotent. This study of magic demonstrates the deep level at which the very notion of religion, the process of differentiating the religious from the secular, is inextricably shaped by modern processes of social control. It is extraordinarily difficult—likely impossible—to invoke the term without reference to these normalizing processes, processes aimed at constraining the scope of religion in order to expand the range of secular modernity.

But at the same time, in keeping with the underlying modern logic of disavowal, this configuration also serves to mask the power actually exerted within and by religious institutions. With all overt concern with power deflected onto magic, this ideological structure diverts attention from the material effects of religion within the modern world. Bruno Latour declares that the very notion of modernity has always been an illusion, that despite the modern insistence on binary logics—the obsessive reiteration of purifying norms and ideals—this insistence has served only to mask the proliferation of potent hybrids transgressing those boundaries. Despite the massive scholarly literature reiterating modern norms for religion (and the efforts by modern liberal social structures to enforce those norms), these ideals have only masked a powerful religious hybridity. Religious institutions exercise potent cultural and material force, but the multiple, often conflicting effects of this power have been cloaked in an ideology of transcendence.

But the scholarly spell seeking to reify magic has always faltered. The dominant theories of magic often move into self-contradiction or incoherence. At the same time there have also always been dissenting countermagicians, scholars eager to resist the alienation and disenchantment of modern social and economic structures, to foster the proliferation of human logics and new modes of social relation. For over a century there have been important scholars overtly contesting the effort to reify magic, whether by demonstrating the futility of efforts to subsume divergent cultural practices into a single mode of thought or by underscoring the ways in which Western modernity itself depends on the very processes it has sought so desperately to externalize. While we have seen many modern scholars of magic engaged in a duplicitous disavowal of power, exercising it more effectively through that very duplicity, we have also found other thinkers such as Taussig and Apter invoking magic to engage in a very different double gesture. The instability of magic as a scholarly category, the palpable artifice required to conjure it, serves to illuminate the contrivance through which all rational objectivity is maintained.

We have also seen numerous modern scholars of magic seeking to segregate human representation and desire from the workings of the natural world, but again the very extravagance of magic seems to destabilize this effort. In 1935 Ruth Benedict asserted that "the province of magic in human societies is as wide as human desires," and subsequent social theorists have elaborated this theme to reject the modern rhetoric seeking to impose some firm differentiation between nature and culture, reason and desire, objectivity and subjectivity. As Tom Driver has shown, magic draws much of its appeal from the overt insistence that human beings inhabit a world in which nature and culture are fused in a unity, that "not all power is physical and material." While the logic of modernity seeks to impose stark boundaries among the psychological, the sociopolitical, and the material, magic works instead to disrupt those boundaries, to affirm the complex ways in which these realms interpenetrate one another. Desire is constitutive of all human signification, meaning, and behavior, and human subjectivity plays a formative role both within the array of circumstances to be transformed and as a causal force contributing to transformation. As Driver asserts, magic aims at the transformation of a multifaceted situation including human subjectivity together with a range of external subjects and objects; it constitutes the "reordering of a totality."[9] Despite so much scholarly insistence that subjectivity and desire must be cordoned away from the world of material causality, magic illuminates the potency of their intermingling. And in this display, magic also points us toward what has been taking place behind the modern logic of disavowal: never before has human desire intervened so powerfully within the workings of material causality.

Magic has held great appeal for scholars because of its capacity both to reinscribe and to subvert the self-representations of the modern world. The dominant modern constructions of magic have configured a disenchanted world prone to commodification by rationalized markets. But critics of this configuration have turned the paradigm against itself, invoking magic to resist the fundamental play of power within modernity. I opened with Bruno Latour's warning of the duplicity of those who analyze magic. It is fitting, then, to turn to him once again:

> Fortunately, the world is no more disenchanted than it used to be, machines are not more polished, reasoning is no tighter, and exchanges are not better organized. How can we speak of a "modern world" when its efficacy depends upon idols: money, law, reason, nature, machines, organization, or linguistic structures? We have already used the word "magic". . . . Since the origins of the power of the "modern world" are misunderstood and efficacy is attributed to things that neither move nor speak, we may speak of magic once again.[10]

With the illusory—and hypnotic—hold of Western modernity increasingly exposed both in material culture and in social theory, philosophers, cultural theorists, and political activists have moved forward in their efforts to think beyond the dualisms and binary logics on which modernity has been founded toward new configurations of knowledge and power. By contesting these reifications and binary logics, by unmasking the charade of a disenchanted world, by seeking to reanimate decayed and lifeless abstractions of religion with new spirit and power, we might confront modernity and imagine it otherwise. There is potent magic in that imagining.

Notes

INTRODUCTION

1. Bruno Latour, *The Pasteurization of France*, trans. Alan Sheridan and John Law (Cambridge, Mass.: Harvard University Press, 1988), 212.

2. Gustavo Benavides, "Modernity," in *Critical Terms for Religious Studies*, ed. Mark C. Taylor (Chicago: University of Chicago Press, 1998), 186–204, particularly 187–88. See also Stephen Toulmin, *Cosmopolis: The Hidden Agenda of Modernity* (New York: Free Press, 1990), 5–44.

3. See Jonathan Z. Smith, "Religion, Religions, Religious," in *Critical Terms for Religious Studies*, 269–84; and Attila K. Molnár, "The Construction of the Notion of Religion in Early Modern Europe," *Method and Theory in the Study of Religion* 14 (2002): 47–60.

4. See Robert J. Baird, "How Religion Became Scientific," in *Religion in the Making: The Emergence of the Sciences of Religion*, ed. Arie L. Molendijk and Peter Pels (Leiden: Brill, 1998), 205–29, particularly 218.

5. See Wilfred Cantwell Smith, *The Meaning and End of Religion* (Minneapolis: Fortress, 1991), particularly 15–50. See also Michel Despland and Gérard Vallée, eds., *Religion in History: The Word, the Idea, the Reality* (Waterloo, Ont.: Wilfrid Laurier University Press, 1992); Talal Asad, *Genealogies of Religion: Discipline and Reasons of Power in Christianity and Islam* (Baltimore: Johns Hopkins University Press, 1993); Tomoko Masuzawa, *In Search of Dreamtime: The Question for the Origin of Religion* (Chicago: University of Chicago Press, 1993); David Chidester, *Savage Systems: Colonialism and Comparative Religion in Southern Africa* (Charlottesville: University Press of Virginia, 1996); Russell McCutcheon, *Manufacturing Religion: The Discourse on Sui Generis Religion and the Politics of Nostalgia* (New York: Oxford University Press, 1997); Richard King, *Orientalism and Religion: Postcolonial Theory, India and "The Mystic East"* (London: Routledge, 1999), 35–61; Timothy Fitz-

gerald, *The Ideology of Religious Studies* (New York: Oxford University Press, 2000); and Hans G. Kippenberg, *Discovering Religious History in the Modern Age*, trans. Barbara Harshav (Princeton, N.J.: Princeton University Press, 2002).

6. See, for example, Ninian Smart, *The Philosophy of Religion* (London: Sheldon Press, 1979), 3–39; Donald Ploch, "Methods for the Time Being," *Sociological Analysis* 47 (March 1987): 43–51; Barbara Hargrove, *The Sociology of Religion: Classical and Contemporary Approaches*, 2d ed. (Arlington Heights, Ill.: Harlan Davidson, 1989), 19–31; and Andrew M. McKinnon, "Sociological Definitions, Language Games, and the 'Essence' of Religion," *Method and Theory in the Study of Religion* 14 (2002): 61–83.

7. E. Bolaji Idowi, *African Traditional Religion* (London: SMC Press, 1973), 191, quoted by Patrick F. Gesch, "Magic as a Process of Social Discernment," in *Powers, Plumes, and Piglets: Phenomena of Melanesian Religion*, ed. Norman C. Habel (Bedford Park, S. Aust.: Australian Association for the Study of Religions, 1979), 137.

8. Latour, *Pasteurization of France*, 216.

9. See Wouter J. Hanegraaff, "The Emergence of the Academic Science of Magic: The Occult Philosophy in Tylor and Frazer," in *Religion in the Making*, 253–75; R. R. Marett, "Pre-animistic Religion," *Folk-Lore* 11 (June 1900): 162–82; and Claude Lévi-Strauss, *The Savage Mind* (Chicago: University of Chicago Press, 1966), 220–21.

10. Erland Ehnmark, "Religion and Magic—Frazer, Söderblom, and Hägerström," *Ethos* 21, nos. 1–2 (1956): 9 (emphasis in original); Olof Pettersson, "Magic—Religion: Some Marginal Notes to an Old Problem," *Ethnos* 22, nos. 3–4 (1957): 119 (emphasis deleted); and Edmund Leach, *Social Anthropology* (Oxford: Oxford University Press, 1982), 133. See also Murray Wax and Rosalie Wax, "The Notion of Magic," *Current Anthropology* 4 (1963): 495–518; Dorothy Hammond, "Magic: A Problem in Semantics," *American Anthropologist* 72 (1970): 1349–56; David Pocock, "Foreword," in Marcel Mauss, *A General Theory of Magic*, trans. Robert Brain (London: Routledge and Kegan Paul, 1972), 2; and Marcello Truzzi, "Definition and Dimensions of the Occult: Towards a Sociological Perspective," in *On the Margins of the Visible: Sociology, the Esoteric and the Occult*, ed. Edward Tiryakian (New York: Wiley, 1974), 243–55.

11. Daniel Lawrence O'Keefe, *Stolen Lightning: The Social Theory of Magic* (New York: Continuum, 1982), xv, xvii; and Stanley J. Tambiah, *Magic, Science, Religion, and the Scope of Rationality* (Cambridge: Cambridge University Press, 1990), 82–83. For other recent examples, see Jacob Neusner, Ernest S. Frerichs, and Paul Virgil McCracken Flesher, eds., *Religion, Science, and Magic: In Concert and in Conflict* (New York: Oxford University Press, 1989); Stewart Elliott Guthrie, *Faces in the Clouds: A New Theory of Religion* (New York: Oxford University Press, 1993); and Ariel Glucklich, *The End of Magic* (New York: Oxford University Press, 1997).

12. Benavides, "Modernity," 197–200; and Stuart Clark, *Thinking with Demons: The Idea of Witchcraft in Early Modern Europe* (Oxford: Clarendon, 1997), 525–45. See also Bernard Leeming, *Principles of Sacramental Theology* (Westminster, Md.: Newman Press, 1956); and George S. Worgul, *From Magic to Metaphor: A Validation of Christian Sacraments* (New York: Paulist Press, 1980).

13. H. L. Mencken, *Treatise on the Gods* (New York: Knopf, 1930), vi, 30–31.

14. E. E. Evans-Pritchard, *Theories of Primitive Religion* (Oxford: Clarendon, 1965), 14–15.

15. John Milbank, *Theology and Social Theory: Beyond Secular Reason* (Oxford: Basil Blackwell, 1991), 100–143. See also in this regard Michael J. Buckley, *At the Ori-*

gins of Modern Atheism (New Haven, Conn.: Yale University Press, 1987), particularly 363.

16. See Fitzgerald, *Ideology of Religious Studies*, 3–32, particularly 6, 9, 20.

17. Ibid., 9; and McCutcheon, *Manufacturing Religion*, 3–26.

18. Charles Taylor, *Sources of the Self: The Making of the Modern Identity* (Cambridge, Mass.: Harvard University Press, 1989), 192.

19. See Lyndal Roper, *Oedipus and the Devil: Witchcraft, Sexuality, and Religion in Early Modern Europe* (London: Routledge, 1994), 5–7.

20. See Clark, *Thinking with Demons*, 509–25; and David Ray Griffin, "Introduction," in *The Reenchantment of Science*, ed. David Ray Griffin (Albany: State University of New York Press, 1988), 2. See also Maureen Perkins, *The Reform of Time: Magic and Modernity* (London: Pluto Press, 2001).

21. See Hutton Webster, *Magic: A Sociological Study* (Stanford, Calif.: Stanford University Press, 1948), ix.

22. See Alice B. Child and Irvin L. Child, *Religion and Magic in the Life of Traditional Peoples* (Englewood Cliffs, N.J.: Prentice-Hall, 1993). See also Hargrove, *Sociology of Religion*, 89, where a chapter entitled "Primitive and Civil Religion" begins with the explanation that "the social manifestation of religion known as 'primitive' is not given that name because it applies only to preliterate peoples, but rather because it appears to be present to some degree in all religious behavior. It may be understood as the basic structure from which all religious phenomena have developed."

23. Edward Said, *Culture and Imperialism* (New York: Vintage, 1994), 9 (emphasis in original).

24. See Frank Byron Jevons, *An Introduction to the Study of Comparative Religion* (New York: Macmillan, 1920), 102–4. See also ibid., 2, asserting that the "business of the applied science [of religion] is, in our case, to use the discovered facts as a means of showing that Christianity is the highest manifestation of the religious spirit."

25. Webster, *Magic*, 504–5; and Said, *Culture and Imperialism*, 12, 14, 78, 170.

26. Edward Burnett Tylor, *Primitive Culture: Researches into the Development of Mythology, Philosophy, Religion, Language, Art and Custom*, 3rd American ed., vol. 1 (New York: Henry Holt, 1889), 112, 116, 136–37.

27. Ibid., 1:116–19, 123–33, 156.

28. See Marc Manganaro, *Myth, Rhetoric, and the Voice of Authority: A Critique of Frazer, Eliot, Frye, and Campbell* (New Haven, Conn.: Yale University Press, 1992), 9–10; and Jacob Gruber, "Forerunners," in *Main Currents in Cultural Anthropology*, ed. Raoul Naroll and Frada Naroll (Englewood Cliffs, N.J.: Prentice-Hall, 1973), 39.

29. See Rudi C. Bleys, *The Geography of Perversion: Male-to-Male Sexual Behaviour Outside the West and the Ethnographic Imagination, 1750–1918* (New York: New York University Press, 1995), 10, 89.

30. Bruno Latour, *We Have Never Been Modern*, trans. Catherine Porter (Cambridge, Mass.: Harvard University Press, 1993), 10, 12, 34 (emphasis deleted).

31. Ibid., 12, 34. See also Robert J. C. Young, *Colonial Desire: Hybridity in Theory, Culture and Race* (London: Routledge, 1995), 1–28; and Catherine Hall, "Histories, Empires and the Post-colonial Moment," in *The Post-colonial Question: Common Skies, Divided Horizons*, ed. Iain Chambers and Lidia Curti (London: Routledge, 1996), 70.

32. See Robert Fraser, *The Making of* The Golden Bough: *The Origins and Growth of an Argument* (New York: St. Martin's, 1990), 119; and Wouter J. Hanegraaff, *New*

Age Religion and Western Culture: Esotericism in the Mirror of Secular Thought (Leiden: Brill, 1996), 84, on the role of more recent academic texts in the emergence of neopaganism.

33. Alex Owen, "Occultism and the 'Modern' Self in *Fin-de-Siècle* Britain," in *Meanings of Modernity: Britain from the Late-Victorian Era to World War II*, ed. Martin Daunton and Bernhard Rieger (Oxford: Berg, 2001), 71–96, particularly 73–74, 88; and Pamela Thurschwell, *Literature, Technology and Magical Thinking, 1880–1920* (Cambridge: Cambridge University Press, 2001).

34. See Simon During, *Modern Enchantments: The Cultural Power of Secular Magic* (Cambridge, Mass.: Harvard University Press, 2002), 2, 39–41; and James W. Cook, *The Arts of Deception: Playing with Fraud in the Age of Barnum* (Cambridge, Mass.: Harvard University Press, 2001).

35. Starhawk, *Dreaming the Dark: Magic, Sex and Politics* (Boston: Beacon Press, 1982), 13 (emphasis in original). And see Charlene Spretnak, ed., *The Politics of Women's Spirituality: Essays on the Rise of Spiritual Power within the Feminist Movement* (Garden City, N.Y.: Doubleday, 1982); Margot Adler, *Drawing Down the Moon: Witches, Druids, Goddess-Worshippers, and Other Pagans in America Today*, rev. ed. (Boston: Beacon Press, 1986); Howard Eilberg-Schwartz, "Witches of the West: Neopaganism and Goddess Worship as Enlightenment Religions," *Journal of Feminist Studies in Religion* 5 (1989): 77–95; Theophus H. Smith, *Conjuring Culture: Biblical Formations of Black America* (New York: Oxford University Press, 1994); James R. Lewis, ed., *Magical Religion and Modern Witchcraft* (Albany: State University of New York Press, 1996); Paul Heelas, *The New Age Movement* (Oxford: Blackwell, 1996); Graham Harvey, *Contemporary Paganism: Listening People, Speaking Earth* (New York: New York University Press, 1997); Erik Davis, *Techgnosis: Myth, Magic and Mysticism in the Age of Information* (New York: Harmony Books, 1998); Bengt Ankarloo and Stuart Clark, eds., *Witchcraft and Magic in Europe: The Twentieth Century* (Philadelphia: University of Pennsylvania Press, 1999); and Sarah M. Pike, *Earthly Bodies, Magical Selves: Contemporary Pagans and the Search for Community* (Berkeley: University of California Press, 2001).

36. See, for example, Anthony Mansueto, "Religion, Solidarity and Class Struggle: Marx, Durkheim and Gramsci on the Religion Question," *Social Compass* 35 (1988): 261–77; Vatro Murvar, "Integrative and Revolutionary Capabilities of Religion," in *Religious Change and Continuity*, ed. Harry M. Johnson (San Francisco: Jossey-Bass, 1979), 74–86; and Benjamin B. Page, ed., *Marxism and Spirituality: An International Anthology* (Westport, Conn.: Bergin and Garvey, 1993).

37. Michael Taussig, *Shamanism, Colonialism, and the Wild Man: A Study in Terror and Healing* (Chicago: University of Chicago Press, 1987); and Taussig, "Why the Nervous System?" in *The Nervous System* (New York: Routledge, 1992), 8. See also Taussig, *The Devil and Commodity Fetishism* (Chapel Hill: University of North Carolina Press, 1980); and Taussig, *The Magic of the State* (New York: Routledge, 1997).

38. John M. MacKenzie, *Orientalism: History, Theory and the Arts* (Manchester: Manchester University Press, 1995), xiv–xviii, 10–12, 211.

39. See Reina Lewis, *Gendering Orientalism: Race, Femininity and Representation* (London: Routledge, 1996), 237.

40. See Maurice Olender, *The Languages of Paradise: Race, Religion, and Philology in the Nineteenth Century*, trans. Arthur Goldhammer (Cambridge, Mass.: Harvard University Press, 1992).

41. Emily Apter, "Introduction," in *Fetishism as Cultural Discourse*, ed. Emily Apter and William Pietz (Ithaca, N.Y.: Cornell University Press, 1993), 3, 6. See also During, *Modern Enchantments*, 61–66.

42. Manganaro, *Myth, Rhetoric, and the Voice of Authority*, 2.

CHAPTER 1

1. Gustavo Benavides, "Magic, Religion, Materiality," *Historical Reflections/Réflexions Historiques* 23 (1997): 302.

2. Lyndal Roper, *Oedipus and the Devil: Witchcraft, Sexuality, and Religion in Early Modern Europe* (London: Routledge, 1994), 21. Parts of the material in this section build on the discussion in Elizabeth Clark and Herbert Richardson, eds., *Women and Religion: A Feminist Sourcebook of Christian Thought*, rev. ed., assistant ed. Gary Brower and Randall Styers (San Francisco: HarperSanFrancisco, 1996), 119–43.

3 See Robin Briggs, *Witches and Neighbors: The Social and Cultural Context of European Witchcraft* (New York: Penguin, 1996), 8, 260. See also H. R. Trevor-Roper, *The European Witch-Craze of the Sixteenth and Seventeenth Centuries* (Harmondsworth, England: Penguin, 1969), 24–28; and Brian Levack, *The Witch-Hunt in Early Modern Europe* (London: Longman, 1987), 19–22.

4. See D. P. Walker, *Spiritual and Demonic Magic from Ficino to Campanella* (London: Warburg Institute/University of London, 1958); Frances Yates, *Giordano Bruno and the Hermetic Tradition* (London: Routledge and Kegan Paul, 1964), 84–116, 360–97; Brian Easlea, *Witch Hunting, Magic and the New Philosophy: An Introduction to Debates of the Scientific Revolution, 1450–1750* (Brighton, England: Harvester Press, 1980), 100–106; Mordechai Feingold, "The Occult Tradition in the English Universities of the Renaissance: A Reassessment," in *Occult and Scientific Mentalities in the Renaissance*, ed. Brian Vickers (Cambridge: Cambridge University Press, 1984), 73–94; Ioan P. Couliano, *Eros and Magic in the Renaissance*, trans. Margaret Cook (Chicago: University of Chicago Press, 1987), 24–52, 146; Stuart Clark, *Thinking with Demons: The Idea of Witchcraft in Early Modern Europe* (Oxford: Clarendon, 1997), 214–311; and Roelof van den Broek and Wouter J. Hanegraaff, eds., *Gnosis and Hermeticism from Antiquity to Modern Times* (Albany: State University of New York Press, 1998).

5. See Thomas J. Schoeneman, "The Witch Hunt as a Culture Change Phenomenon," *Ethos* 3 (1975): 540; J. P. Davidson, *The Witch in Northern European Art, 1470–1750* (Freren: Luca Verlag, 1987); and Jean-Michel Sallmann, "Witches," in *A History of Women in the West: III. Renaissance and Enlightenment Paradoxes*, ed. Natalie Zemon Davis and Arlette Farge, trans. Arthur Goldhammer (Cambridge, Mass.: Harvard University Press, 1993), 444.

6. G. R. Quaife, *Godly Zeal and Furious Rage: The Witch in Early Modern Europe* (London: Croom Helm, 1987), 35. For a discussion of the difficulty of distinguishing witchcraft from other forms of early modern magic, folk healing, and religious practice, see Keith Thomas, *Religion and the Decline of Magic* (New York: Scribner, 1971), 435–46. For critiques of Thomas, see E. P. Thompson, "Anthropology and the Discipline of Historical Context," *Midland History* 1, no. 3 (spring 1972): 41–55; Natalie Zemon Davis, "Some Tasks and Themes in the Study of Popular Religion," in *The Pursuit of Holiness in Late Medieval and Renaissance Religion*, ed. Charles Trinkaus and H. A. Oberman (Leiden: Brill, 1974), 307–36; Easlea, *Witch Hunting, Magic and the*

New Philosophy, 40–42, 196–98; and Willem de Blécourt, "On the Continuation of Witchcraft," in Witchcraft in Early Modern Europe: Studies in Culture and Belief, ed. Jonathan Barry, Marianne Hester, and Gareth Roberts (Cambridge: Cambridge University Press, 1996), 335–39.

7. See Trevor-Roper, European Witch-Craze, 12–14; Couliano, Eros and Magic in the Renaissance, 152–53; Julio Caro Baroja, "Witchcraft and Catholic Theology," in Early Modern European Witchcraft: Centres and Peripheries, ed. Bengt Ankarloo and Gustav Henningsen (Oxford: Clarendon, 1990), 19–43; and Gratian, "A Warning to Bishops: The Canon Episcopi 1140," in Witchcraft in Europe 1100–1700: A Documentary History, ed. Alan C. Kors and Edward Peters (Philadelphia: University of Pennsylvania Press, 1972), 28–31. On Augustine's views of magic and the miraculous, see Joseph Houston, Reported Miracles: A Critique of Hume (Cambridge: Cambridge University Press, 1994), 8–20.

8. See Thomas, Religion and the Decline of Magic, 177–231; Norman Cohn, Europe's Inner Demons: An Inquiry Inspired by the Great Witch Hunt (New York: Basic Books, 1975), 145–63; George Mora, "Reification of Evil: Witchcraft, Heresy, and the Scapegoat," in Evil Self and Culture, ed. Marie Coleman Nelson and Michael Eigen (New York: Human Sciences Press, 1984), 43; and H. C. Erik Midelfort, "Social History and Biblical Exegesis: Community, Family, and Witchcraft in Sixteenth-Century Germany," in The Bible in the Sixteenth Century, ed. David C. Steinmetz (Durham, N.C.: Duke University Press, 1990), 13–14.

9. See Thomas, Religion and the Decline of Magic, 48–49, 255–56. See also Jean Delumeau, Catholicism between Luther and Voltaire: A New View of the Counter-Reformation, intro. John Bossy, trans. J. Mosier (London: Burns and Oates, 1977), 166–68; Joseph Klaits, Servants of Satan: The Age of the Witch Hunts (Bloomington: Indiana University Press, 1985), 14–15, 65; Jane Schneider, "Spirits and the Spirit of Capitalism," in Religious Orthodoxy and Popular Faith in European Society, ed. Ellen Badone (Princeton, N.J.: Princeton University Press, 1990), 43–44; and Valerie I. J. Flint, The Rise of Magic in Early Medieval Europe (Princeton, N.J.: Princeton University Press, 1991).

10. See Margaret A. Murray, The Witch-Cult in Western Europe: A Study in Anthropology (Oxford: Clarendon, 1921); Murray, The God of the Witches (London: Faber and Faber, 1952); and Murray, The Divine King of England (London: Faber and Faber, 1954). On the roots of Murray's argument and her influence, see Cohn, Europe's Inner Demons, 99–125.

11. Mircea Eliade, Occultism, Witchcraft, and Cultural Fashions: Essays in Comparative Religions (Chicago: University of Chicago Press, 1976), 91–92. See also Jules Michelet, Satanism and Witchcraft, trans. A. Allinson (New York: Citadel Press, 1963); Jeffrey Russell, Witchcraft in the Middle Ages (Ithaca, N.Y.: Cornell University Press, 1972); Emmanuel Le Roy Ladurie, The Peasants of Languedoc, trans. John Day (Urbana: University of Illinois Press, 1974), 203–10; and Carlo Ginzburg, The Night Battles: Witchcraft and Agrarian Cults in the Sixteenth and Seventeenth Centuries (Baltimore: Johns Hopkins University Press, 1983).

12. See Cohn, Europe's Inner Demons, 107–9; Pennethorne Hughes, Witchcraft (Harmondsworth, England: Pelican, 1952); John P. Demos, Entertaining Satan: Witchcraft and the Culture of Early New England (New York: Oxford University Press, 1982); and Ronald Hutton, "Modern Pagan Witchcraft," in Witchcraft and Magic in Europe:

The Twentieth Century, ed. Bengt Ankarloo and Stuart Clark (Philadelphia: University of Pennsylvania Press, 1999), 1–79. For examples of the appropriation of witchcraft traditions in contemporary sexual subcultures, see Arthur Evans, *Witchcraft and the Gay Counterculture: A Radical View of Western Civilization and Some of the People It Has Tried to Destroy* (Boston: Fag Rag Books, 1978); and Mark Thompson, "This Gay Tribe: A Brief History of Fairies," in *Gay Spirit: Myth and Meaning*, ed. Mark Thompson (New York: St. Martin's, 1987), 260–78.

13. See H. C. Erik Midelfort, "Recent Witch Hunting Research, or Where Do We Go from Here?" *Papers of the Bibliographical Society of America* 62 (1968): 374–75; E. William Monter, "The Historiography of European Witchcraft: Progress and Prospects," *Journal of Interdisciplinary History* 2 (1972): 51–53; H. C. Erik Midelfort, "Were There Really Witches?" in *Transition and Revolution: Problems and Issues of European Renaissance and Reformation History*, ed. Robert M. Kingdon (Minneapolis: Burgess, 1974), 189–205; Cohn, *Europe's Inner Demons*, 99–125; Christina Larner, " '*Crimen Exceptum'?* The Crime of Witchcraft in Europe," in *Witchcraft and Religion: The Politics of Popular Belief*, ed. Alan Macfarlane (Oxford: Basil Blackwell, 1984), 46–48; and Jeffrey Richards, *Sex, Dissidence and Damnation: Minority Groups in the Middle Ages* (London: Routledge, 1991), 76–86.

14. See Cohn, *Europe's Inner Demons*, 16–125, particularly 124; Russell, *Witchcraft in the Middle Ages*, 86–93; and Richards, *Sex, Dissidence and Damnation*, 11–14, 50–51, 58–63, 80.

15. See Cohn, *Europe's Inner Demons*, 178, 192–97; E. William Monter, "French and Italian Witchcraft," *History Today* 30 (1980): 31; Ginzburg, *Night Battles*, 40–47; Klaits, *Servants of Satan*, 38–40; Henry Kamen, "Notes on Witchcraft, Sexuality, and the Inquisition," in *The Spanish Inquisition and the Inquisitorial Mind*, ed. Angel Alcalá (Boulder, Colo.: Social Science Monographs, 1987), 237–47; and Levack, *Witch-Hunt in Early Modern Europe*, 46, 170–71.

16. See E. William Monter, *Witchcraft in France and Switzerland: The Borderlands during the Reformation* (Ithaca, N.Y.: Cornell University Press, 1976), 193–94; Thomas, *Religion and the Decline of Magic*, 442–49; Merry E. Wiesner, *Women and Gender in Early Modern Europe* (Cambridge: Cambridge University Press, 1993), 228–33; and John Tedeschi, "Inquisitorial Law and the Witch," in *Early Modern European Witchcraft*, 83–118.

17. See Trevor-Roper, *European Witch-Craze*, 24–39, 112–22; Delumeau, *Catholicism between Luther and Voltaire*, 129–202, particularly 172; and Jean Delumeau, "Les réformateurs et la superstition," in *Actes du colloque L'Amiral de Coligny et son temps* (Paris: Société de L'Histoire du Protestantisme Français, 1974), 451–87. For critiques of Trevor-Roper's argument, see E. William Monter, "Patterns of Witchcraft in the Jura," *Journal of Social History* 5 (1971): 8–12; Geoffrey Scarre, *Witchcraft and Magic in Sixteenth- and Seventeenth-Century Europe* (Atlantic Highlands, N.J.: Humanities Press International, 1987), 38–39; and Richards, *Sex, Dissidence and Damnation*, 14–15.

18. See Irving Kirsh, "Demonology and Science during the Scientific Revolution," *Journal of the History of Behavioral Sciences* 8 (1980): 359–68; Nachman Ben-Yehuda, "Problems Inherent in Socio-Historical Approaches to the European Witch Craze," *Journal for the Scientific Study of Religion* 20 (1981): 326–38; Leland Estes, "The Medical Origins of the European Witch Craze: A Hypothesis," *Journal of Social History* 17 (1983): 271–84; Stuart Clark, "The Scientific Status of Demonology," in *Occult*

and Scientific Mentalities in the Renaissance, 351–74; Larner, " 'Crimen Exceptum'?" 48–67; Quaife, *Godly Zeal and Furious Rage*, 199–208; Ankarloo and Henningsen, eds., *Early Modern European Witchcraft*; Sallmann, "Witches," 448–51; and Anne Llewellyn Barstow, *Witchcraze: A New History of the European Witch Hunts* (San Francisco: Pandora/HarperCollins, 1994), 93–105.

19. See Schneider, "Spirits and the Spirit of Capitalism," 24–54, particularly 26; and Thomas, *Religion and the Decline of Magic*, 555–56.

20. Robin Briggs, "Witchcraft and Popular Mentality in Lorraine, 1580–1630," in *Occult and Scientific Mentalities in the Renaissance*, 339, citing Nicolas Rémy, *Daemonolatreiae libri tres* (Lyon, 1595), bk. I, chaps. ii–iii, and bk. II, chaps. vii–viii; and Thomas, *Religion and the Decline of Magic*, 278, quoting Francis Bacon, *Works*, 3:381, and John Cotta, *A Short Discoverie of the Unobserved Dangers of Severall Sorts of Ignorant and Unconsiderate Practisers of Physicke* (1612), 35.

21. See Briggs, *Witches and Neighbors*, 8, 260. See also Barstow, *Witchcraze*, 23–25; and Elaine G. Brelaw, ed., *Witches of the Atlantic World* (New York: New York University Press, 2000), 283–354. For a discussion of regional variation in the relative persecution of women and men, see Gustav Henningsen and Bengt Ankarloo, "Introduction," in *Early Modern European Witchcraft*, 13; and on the ways in which the persecutions reflected broader cultural understandings of gender, see Clark, *Thinking with Demons*, 106–33.

22. Larner, " 'Crimen Exceptum'?" 65; Briggs, *Witches and Neighbors*, 284; Monter, *Witchcraft in France and Switzerland*, 118–24, 136–41, 197; John Boswell, *Christianity, Social Tolerance, and Homosexuality: Gay People in Western Europe from the Beginning of the Christian Era to the Fourteenth Century* (Chicago: University of Chicago Press, 1981), 269–302; Christina Larner, *Enemies of God: The Witch-Hunt in Scotland* (London: Chatto and Windus, 1981), 51, 92–93, 102; Richards, *Sex, Dissidence and Damnation*, 13–14, 116–31, 142–43; and Roper, *Oedipus and the Devil*, 22–26, 47, 137–38, 149, 171–98.

23. See Heinrich Kramer and Jacob Sprenger, *Malleus Maleficarum*, trans. Montague Summers (London: Pushkin Press, 1948); and Clark, *Thinking with Demons*, particularly viii, 92, 152–64.

24. See Clark, *Thinking with Demons*, 214–33; William Monter, *Ritual, Myth and Magic in Early Modern Europe* (Athens: Ohio University Press, 1983), 33, 82, 155–56; Feingold, "The Occult Tradition in the English Universities," 73–94; Martin Bernal, *Black Athena: The Afroasiatic Roots of Classical Civilization*, vol. 1, *The Fabrication of Ancient Greece 1785–1985* (New Brunswick, N.J.: Rutgers University Press, 1987), 158–64; Couliano, *Eros and Magic in the Renaissance*, 58–84; Yates, *Giordano Bruno and the Hermetic Tradition*; and Thomas, *Religion and the Decline of Magic*, 283–385.

25. See Trevor-Roper, *European Witch-Craze*, 97–111; Robert Mandrou, *Magistrats et sorciers en France aux XVIe et XVIIe siècles* (Paris: Plon, 1968), 539–64; H. C. Erik Midelfort, *Witch Hunting in Southwestern Germany 1562–1684: The Social and Intellectual Foundations* (Stanford, Calif.: Stanford University Press, 1972), 121–63; and Klaits, *Servants of Satan*, 159–76. But see also Keith Thomas, "The Relevance of Social Anthropology to the Historical Study of English Witchcraft," in *Witchcraft Confessions and Accusations*, ed. Mary Douglas (London: Tavistock, 1970), 69–71; Monter, *Witchcraft in France and Switzerland*, 37–41; and Carol F. Karlsen, *The Devil in the Shape of a Woman: Witchcraft in Colonial New England* (New York: Norton, 1987), 254–55.

26. See Owen Davies, *Witchcraft, Magic and Culture 1736–1951* (Manchester: Manchester University Press, 1999), 287–93; Schoeneman, "Witch Hunt as Culture Change Phenomenon," 545–46; James L. Brain, "An Anthropological Perspective on the Witchcraze," in *The Politics of Gender in Early Modern Europe*, ed. Jean R. Brink, Allison P. Coudert, and Maryanne C. Horowitz (Kirksville, Mo.: Sixteenth Century Journal Publishers, 1989), 15–27; Karlsen, *Devil in the Shape of a Woman*, 255–57; Christina Larner, "Witchcraft Past and Present," in *Witchcraft and Religion*, 87–89; Levack, *Witch-Hunt in Early Modern Europe*, 227–29; and Thomas, *Religion and the Decline of Magic*, 453. See also Sallmann, "Witches," 457; Jeanne Favret-Saada, *Deadly Words: Witchcraft in the Bocage*, trans. Catherine Cullen (Cambridge: Cambridge University Press, 1980); and Monter, *Witchcraft in France and Switzerland*, 191–92.

27. See Benavides, "Magic, Religion, Materiality," 316–17; Clark, *Thinking with Demons*, 437–545, particularly 530; Robert Scribner, "Witchcraft and Judgment in Reformation Germany," *History Today* 40 (April 1990): 12–19; and Christina Larner, "James VI and I and Witchcraft," in *Witchcraft and Religion*, 3–22. See also Wiesner, *Women and Gender in Early Modern Europe*, 218; Sigfrid Brauner, "Martin Luther on Witchcraft: A True Reformer?" in *Politics of Gender in Early Modern Europe*, 29–42; and Delumeau, *Catholicism between Luther and Voltaire*, 175–202.

28. Thomas, *Religion and the Decline of Magic*, 51, quoting H. S. Cronin, "The Twelve Conclusions of the Lollards," *English Historical Review* 22 (1907): 298; Noel L. Brann, "The Proto-Protestant Assault upon Church Magic: The 'Errores Bohemanorum' according to the Abbot Trithemius (1462–1516)," *Journal of Religious History* 12 (June 1982): 9–22; and Joannis Hus, *De Sanguine Christi*, Nach Handschriften Herausgegeben von Wenzel Flajshans, in Mag. Jo. Hus, *Opera Omnia*, tom. 1, fasc. 3 (Osnabrück: Biblio-Verlag, 1966).

29. Roper, *Oedipus and the Devil*, 181, 191–92. On the development of Protestant sacramental theology, see Francis Clark, *Eucharistic Sacrifice and the Reformation*, 2d ed. (Oxford: Basil Blackwell, 1967), 56–176; and Paul H. Jones, *Christ's Eucharistic Presence: A History of the Doctrine* (New York: Peter Lang, 1994), 117–95.

30. Martin Luther, "The Babylonian Captivity of the Church," in *Luther's Works*, vol. 36, ed. Abdel Ross Wentz, general ed. Helmut T. Lehmann, trans. A. T. W. Steinhäuser (Philadelphia: Muhlenberg Press, 1959), 41; Jean Calvin, *Institutes of the Christian Religion*, 4.14.15, trans. John Allen, 6th ed. (Philadelphia: Presbyterian Board of Christian Education, 1935), 538; ibid., 4.17.36, 570–71; Calvin, "Short Treatise on the Supper of Our Lord," in *Tracts and Treatises on the Doctrine and Worship of the Church*, vol. 2, trans. Henry Beveridge (Grand Rapids, Mich.: Eerdmans, 1958), 193; W. T. Davison, *Lord's Supper: Aids to Its Intelligent and Devout Observance* (London: Charles H. Kelly, 1895), 83 n. 1; Ulrich Zwingli, "On the Lord's Supper," in *Zwingli and Bullinger: Selected Translations*, trans. G. W. Bromiley (Philadelphia: Westminster Press, 1953), 176–238; and Thomas, *Religion and the Decline of Magic*, 25 (quoting William Perkins, *A Golden Chaine* [1591]), 68–69, 75–76.

31. See Davison, *Lord's Supper*, 83–86; and John W. Nevin, *The Mystical Presence: A Vindication of the Reformed or Calvinistic Doctrine of the Holy Eucharist*, intro. Richard E. Wentz (Hamden, Conn.: Archon Books, 1963), 184 (where the German Reformed Nevin argues that the Lutheran doctrine of consubstantiation can only be understood as "mere blind magic"). See also John Locke, *An Essay concerning Human Understanding*, ed. Peter H. Nidditch (Oxford: Clarendon, 1975), 713; David Hume,

"The Natural History of Religion," in *Writings on Religion*, ed. Antony Flew (La Salle, Ill.: Open Court, 1992), 154–55; Hume, *Enquiries concerning Human Understanding and concerning the Principles of Morals*, 3d ed., ed. P. H. Nidditch (Oxford: Clarendon, 1975), 109–10; and Voltaire, "Eucharist," in *A Philosophical Dictionary*, vol. 4, in *The Works of Voltaire*, vol. 7, trans. William F. Fleming, intro. Oliver H. G. Leigh (Paris: E. R. DuMont, 1901), 276–80.

32. H. C. Erik Midelfort, "Witchcraft and Religion in Sixteenth-Century Germany: The Formation and Consequences of an Orthodoxy," in *Archiv für Reformationsgeschichte* 62 (1971): 266–78. And see Thomas, *Religion and the Decline of Magic*, 78–112, 256–57, 483–86; Stuart Clark, "Protestant Demonology: Sin, Superstition, and Society (c. 1520–c. 1630)," in *Early Modern European Witchcraft*, 45–81; Edmund Kern, "Confessional Identity and Magic in the Late Sixteenth Century," *Sixteenth Century Journal* 25 (1994): 323–40; Margaret J. Osler, *Divine Will and the Mechanical Philosophy: Gassendi and Descartes on Contingency and Necessity in the Created World* (Cambridge: Cambridge University Press, 1994), 83–84.

33. See Thomas, *Religion and the Decline of Magic*, 51–77, 113–24, 469–77, 497, 638–39; Monter, *Ritual, Myth and Magic*, 45–53; Allison P. Coudert, "The Myth of the Improved Status of Protestant Women: The Case of the Witchcraze," in *Politics of Gender in Early Modern Europe*, 61–89; and Robert W. Scribner, "The Reformation, Popular Magic, and the 'Disenchantment of the World,'" *Journal of Interdisciplinary History* 23 (winter 1993): 483–94.

34. Martin Del Rio, *Investigations into Magic*, ed. and trans. P. G. Maxwell-Stuart (Manchester: Manchester University Press, 2000), 32.

35. Clark, "Scientific Status of Demonology," 356, 361–63, 368–69.

36. See Midelfort, "Recent Witch Hunting Research," 383; Baroja, "Witchcraft and Catholic Theology," 19–43; and Clark, "Protestant Demonology," 45–81.

37. See Quaife, *Godly Zeal and Furious Rage*, 28–30; Midelfort, *Witch Hunting*, 30–66; James Hitchcock, "George Gifford and Puritan Witch Beliefs," *Archiv für Reformationsgeschichte* 58 (1967): 90–99; Alan D. Macfarlane, "A Tudor Anthropologist: George Gifford's *Discourse and Dialogue*," in *The Damned Art: Essays in the Literature of Witchcraft*, ed. Sidney Anglo (London: Routledge and Kegan Paul, 1977), 140–55; and Dewey D. Wallace, "George Gifford, Puritan Propaganda, and Popular Religion in Elizabethan England," *Sixteenth Century Journal* 9 (1978): 27–49.

38. See Friedrich von Spee, "*Cautio Criminalis*," in *Witchcraft in Europe 1100–1700*, 351–57; and Clark, *Thinking with Demons*, 118 (quoting *Cautio Criminalis*), 205–7. See also Baroja, "Witchcraft and Catholic Theology," 41–42; and Quaife, *Godly Zeal and Furious Rage*, 30–31.

39. See William L. Hine, "Marin Mersenne: Renaissance Naturalism and Renaissance Magic," in *Occult and Scientific Mentalities in the Renaissance*, 166–76; Peter Burke, "Witchcraft and Magic in Renaissance Italy: Gianfrancesco Pico and his *Strix*," in *Damned Art*, 32–52; Osler, *Divine Will and the Mechanical Philosophy*, 61–66, 82–83, 96; and Wayne Shumaker, *The Occult Science in the Renaissance: A Study in Intellectual Patterns* (Berkeley: University of California Press, 1972), 1–59.

40. See Richard H. Popkin, *The History of Scepticism from Erasmus to Spinoza* (Berkeley: University of California Press, 1979), particularly 19, 33; Desiderius Erasmus, *Ten Colloquies*, trans. Craig R. Thompson (Indianapolis: Bobbs-Merrill, 1979), 37–55; and Michel de Montaigne, "Of Cripples," in *Witchcraft in Europe 1100–1700*, 332,

337. See also Peter Burke, "Montaigne," in *Renaissance Thinkers*, ed. James McConica, et al. (Oxford: Oxford University Press, 1993), 301–85, particularly 328–30; Easlea, *Witch Hunting, Magic and the New Philosophy*, 25–29; and Popkin, *History of Scepticism*, 42–65, 84–109, 130–50.

41. See Clark, *Thinking with Demons*, 117–18, 198–203; Gerhild Scholz Williams, "The Woman/The Witch: Variations on a Sixteenth-Century Theme (Paracelsus, Wier, Bodin)," in *The Crannied Wall: Women, Religion, and the Arts in Early Modern Europe*, ed. Craig A. Monson (Ann Arbor: University of Michigan Press, 1992), 119–37; Willem Frijhoff, "Witchcraft and Its Changing Representation in Eastern Gelderland, from the Sixteenth to Twentieth Centuries," in *Witchcraft in the Netherlands from the Fourteenth to the Twentieth Century*, ed. Marijke Gijswijt-Hofstra and Willem Frijhoff, trans. Rachel M. J. van der Wilden-Fall (Rotterdam: Universitaire Pers Rotterdam, 1991), 170–74; and Charles Webster, *From Paracelsus to Newton: Magic and the Making of Modern Science* (Cambridge: Cambridge University Press, 1982), 85–86.

42. Reginald Scot, *The Discoverie of Witchcraft*, ed. Montague Summers (1930; reprint, New York: Dover, 1972), bk. XIII, chap. 19, 179; bk. I, chap. 5, 7; and bk. VIII, chap. 1, 89–90. See also ibid., bk. XV, chaps. 21–42, 251–72; Leland L. Estes, "Reginald Scot and His *Discoverie of Witchcraft*: Religion and Science in the Opposition to the European Witch Craze," *Church History* 52 (December 1983): 444–67; Sydney Anglo, "Reginald Scot's *Discoverie of Witchcraft*: Skepticism and Sadduceeism," in *Damned Art*, 134; and Thomas, *Religion and the Decline of Magic*, 579.

43. Scot, *Discoverie of Witchcraft*, bk. XIII, chap. 3, 164–65; bk. XVI, chap. 2, 274; bk. III, chaps. 7–13, 28–35; and Clark, *Thinking with Demons*, 211–12.

44. Monter, *Ritual, Myth and Magic*, 84; and see Jonathan L. Pearl, "French Catholic Demonologists and Their Enemies in the Late Sixteenth and Early Seventeenth Centuries," *Church History* 52 (December 1983): 457–67.

45. See Quaife, *Godly Zeal and Furious Rage*, 32; Monter, *Ritual, Myth and Magic*, 114–29; and Thomas, *Religion and the Decline of Magic*, 577, quoting John Webster, *The Displaying of Supposed Witchcraft* (1677), 68.

46. See Balthasar Bekker, "The Enchanted World (1691)," in *Witchcraft in Europe 1100–1700*, 369–77; and G. J. Stronks, "The Significance of Balthasar Bekker's The Enchanted World," in *Witchcraft in the Netherlands*, 149–56.

47. See Pierre Bayle, "Réponse aux questions d'un provincial (1703)," in *Witchcraft in Europe 1100–1700*, 360–68; Pierre Bayle, "On Superstition and Tolerance," in *The Portable Enlightenment Reader*, ed. Isaac Kramnick (New York: Penguin, 1995), 75–81; Howard Robinson, *Bayle the Skeptic* (New York: Columbia University Press, 1931), 224–31; and Monter, *Ritual, Myth and Magic*, 118–20.

48. See Quaife, *Godly Zeal and Furious Rage*, 32; Monter, *Ritual, Myth and Magic*, 121–26; Jean Meslier, *Superstition in All Ages*, trans. Anna Knoop (1889; reprint, New York: Arno Press/New York Times, 1972), particularly 38–43, 49–53; and Michael J. Buckley, *At the Origins of Modern Atheism* (New Haven, Conn.: Yale University Press, 1987), 268–72.

49. Clark, *Thinking with Demons*, 205, 249; Levack, *Witch-Hunt in Early Modern Europe*, 218–19, 223; Frijhoff, "Witchcraft and Its Changing Representation in Eastern Gelderland," 174–75; Monter, *Ritual, Myth and Magic*, 116–17; and Klaits, *Servants of Satan*, 161–68.

50. Francis Bacon, *Novum Organum*, bk. ii, aphorism 29, in *The Works of Francis*

Bacon, vol. 4, ed. James Spedding, Robert Leslie Ellis, and Douglas Denon Heath (London: Longman, 1858), 169; Bacon, *De Augmentis Scientiarum*, bk. ii, chap. 2, in *Works of Francis Bacon*, 4:296; Bacon, "Of Superstition," in *The Essays, the Wisdom of the Ancients, and the New Atlantis* (London: Odhams Press, n.d.), 69–70; Bacon, *Sylva Sylvarum*, in *Works of Francis Bacon*, 2:339–680; and Clark, *Thinking with Demons*, 221–24, 252–53. See also Lynn Thorndike, "The Attitude of Francis Bacon and Descartes towards Magic and Occult Science," in *Science, Medicine, and History: Essays on the Evolution of Scientific Thought and Medical Practice Written in Honour of Charles Singer*, vol. 1, ed. E. Ashworth Underwood (London: Oxford University Press/Geoffrey Cumberlege, 1953), 451–54; Paolo Rossi, *Francis Bacon: From Magic to Science*, trans. S. Rabinovitch (Chicago: University of Chicago Press, 1968); and Daniel Becquemont, "Le rejet de la causalité magique dans l'oeuvre de Bacon," in *La magie et ses langages*, ed. Margaret Jones-Davie (Lille: Université de Lille III, 1980), 71–82.

51. René Descartes, "First Meditation," in *The Philosophical Writings of Descartes*, vol. 2, trans. John Cottingham, Robert Stoothoff, and Dugald Murdoch (Cambridge: Cambridge University Press, 1995), 12–15; Descartes, "The Search for Truth," in *Philosophical Writings of Descartes*, 2:404; and Popkin, *History of Scepticism*, 210.

52. See Popkin, *History of Scepticism*, 180–81; and Michel de Certeau, *The Possession at Loudun*, trans. Michael B. Smith (Chicago: University of Chicago Press, 1996).

53. See Osler, *Divine Will and the Mechanical Philosophy*, 3–11, 118–52, 177–78; and Descartes, "Sixth Meditation," in *Philosophical Writings of Descartes*, 2:55–56. See also Keith Hutchison, "Supernaturalism and the Mechanical Philosophy," *History of Science* 21 (1983): 297–333; Ron Millen, "The Manifestations of Occult Qualities in the Scientific Revolution," in *Religion, Science, and Worldview: Essays in Honor of Richard S. Westfall*, ed. Margaret J. Osler and Paul Lawrence Farber (Cambridge: Cambridge University Press, 1985), 185–216; and Brian P. Copenhaver, "Natural Magic, Hermeticism, and Occultism in Early Modern Science," in *Reappraisals of the Scientific Revolution*, ed. David C. Lindberg and Robert S. Westman (Cambridge: Cambridge University Press, 1990), 270–75.

54. Osler, *Divine Will and the Mechanical Philosophy*, 8–11, 36–117, particularly 96–101, citing Gassendi's 1658 *Syntagma philosophicum*, in *Opera omnia*, vol. 2 (Stuttgart-Bad Connstatt: Friedrich Frommann Verlag, 1964).

55. Descartes, "Discourse on the Method of Rightly Conducting One's Reason and Seeking the Truth in the Sciences," in *Philosophical Writings of Descartes*, 1:131; Descartes, "The World," in *Philosophical Writings of Descartes*, 1:97; Descartes, "Principles of Philosophy," pt. 2, in *Philosophical Writings of Descartes*, 1:243; and Osler, *Divine Will and the Mechanical Philosophy*, 206–7.

56. Buckley, *At the Origins of Modern Atheism*, 97.

57. Benedict de Spinoza, *A Theologico-Political Treatise*, in *A Theologico-Political Treatise and A Political Treatise*, trans. R. H. M. Elwes (New York: Dover, 1951), 82–83.

58. Thomas Hobbes, *Leviathan*, ed. Richard Tuck (Cambridge: Cambridge University Press, 1991), bk. 1, chap. 2, 18–19; bk. 3, chap. 32, 255–56; and bk. 4, chaps. 45–46, 440–74 (particularly 442–45, 458). See also Thomas, *Religion and the Decline of Magic*, 518–19.

59. Hobbes, *Leviathan*, bk. 1, chap. 6, 42. See also ibid., bk. 1, chap. 12, 82–86; and David Berman, *A History of Atheism in Britain: From Hobbes to Russell* (London: Routledge, 1990), 57–69.

60. Joseph Glanvil, "Sadducismus Triumphatus, Or full and plain Evidence concerning Witches and Apparitions," in *Witchcraft in Europe 1100–1700*, 300; and Clark, *Thinking with Demons*, 296–303. And see Briggs, *Witches and Neighbors*, 99–100; Popkin, *History of Scepticism*, 84, 237; and R. M. Burns, *The Great Debate on Miracles: From Joseph Glanvill to David Hume* (Lewisburg, Pa.: Bucknell University Press, 1981), 19–69.

61. Thomas, *Religion and the Decline of Magic*, 643.

62. Isaac Newton, *Opticks, or A Treatise of the Reflections, Refractions, Inflections and Colours of Light* (New York: Dover, 1952), 403–4. See also Buckley, *At the Origins of Modern Atheism*, 106, 135–43, 347; Osler, *Divine Will and the Mechanical Philosophy*, 76–77, 149–51; Easlea, *Witch Hunting, Magic and the New Philosophy*, 136–37, 205–7; Richard S. Westfall, *Science and Religion in Seventeenth-Century England* (New Haven, Conn.: Yale University Press, 1958), 87–93; and Marie Boas Hall, *Robert Boyle on Natural Philosophy* (Bloomington: Indiana University Press, 1965).

63. See Easlea, *Witch Hunting, Magic and the New Philosophy*, 171, quoting John Maynard Keynes, *Essays in Biography* (London: Hart-Davis, 1951), 311; and Monter, *Ritual, Myth and Magic*, 34. See also Easlea, *Witch Hunting, Magic and the New Philosophy*, 180–87, 200; Richard S. Westfall, "Newton and Alchemy," in *Occult and Scientific Mentalities in the Renaissance*, 315–35; and Betty Jo Teeter Dobbs, *The Janus Faces of Genius: The Role of Alchemy in Newton's Thought* (Cambridge: Cambridge University Press, 1991).

64. Gottfried Wilhelm Leibniz, "Necessary and Contingent Truths," in *Philosophical Writings*, ed. G. H. R. Parkinson, trans. Mary Morris and G. H. R. Parkinson (London: J. M. Dent, 1973), 99; Leibniz, "Correspondence with Clarke (Selections) (1715–16)," in *Philosophical Writings*, 205–6; Leibniz, "New Essays on the Human Understanding," in *Philosophical Writings*, 158, 163, 169; Leibniz, "Discourse on Metaphysics," art. 16, in *Philosophical Writings*, 28–29; and Easlea, *Witch Hunting, Magic and the New Philosophy*, 183–87.

65. See Clark, *Thinking with Demons*, 157, quoting G. MacDonald Ross, "Occultism and Philosophy in the Seventeenth Century," in *Philosophy: Its History and Historiography*, ed. A. J. Holland (Dordrecht: D. Reidel, 1985), 107; Osler, *Divine Will and the Mechanical Philosophy*, 235; and Buckley, *At the Origins of Modern Atheism*, 324–26.

66. Easlea, *Witch Hunting, Magic and the New Philosophy*, 193–94; and see David Bohm, "Postmodern Science in a Postmodern World," in *The Reenchantment of Science*, ed. David Ray Griffin (Albany: State University of New York Press, 1988), 60–62.

67. Timothy Fitzgerald, *The Ideology of Religious Studies* (New York: Oxford University Press, 2000), 28–29.

68. See, for example, Bacon, "Of Atheism," in *Essays, the Wisdom of the Ancients, and the New Atlantis*, 65–66; and Edward, Lord Herbert of Cherbury, *De Veritate*, trans. Meyrick H. Carré (1937; reprint, London: Routledge/Thoemmes Press, 1992), particularly 289–307.

69. Spinoza, *A Theologico–Political Treatise*, 3–7, 25, 83–89, 99. See also Popkin, *History of Scepticism*, 229–48; and Manfred Walther, "Spinoza's Critique of Miracles: A Miracle of Criticism?" trans. Graeme Hunter, in *Spinoza: The Enduring Questions*, ed. Graeme Hunter (Toronto: University of Toronto Press, 1994), 100–112.

70. See Locke, *An Essay concerning Human Understanding*, bk. II, chap. 23, 297–

98, 305–17; bk. IV, chap. 3, 557–58; bk. IV, chap. 10, 619–30; bk. IV, chap. 18, 691–96; and Easlea, *Witch Hunting, Magic and the New Philosophy*, 236.

71. Locke, *An Essay concerning Human Understanding*, bk. IV, chap. 19, 704.

72. John Locke, *The Reasonableness of Christianity*, ed. I. T. Ramsey (Stanford, Calif.: Stanford University Press, 1958), 33, 37, 57–59, 67–68; and John Locke, "A Discourse of Miracles (1702)," in *Reasonableness of Christianity*, 80.

73. See D. P. Walker, *The Decline of Hell: Seventeenth-Century Discussions of Eternal Torment* (Chicago: University of Chicago Press, 1964); Burns, *Great Debate on Miracles*, 70–95; Anthony Collins, "A Discourse of Free-Thinking (1713)," in *Portable Enlightenment Reader*, 103–4 (emphasis in original); and Jonathan Z. Smith, *Drudgery Divine: On the Comparison of Early Christianities and the Religions of Late Antiquity* (Chicago: University of Chicago Press, 1990), 1–35.

74. David Hume, "Letter to William Mure of Daldwell (1743)," in *Writings on Religion*, 17; and Gilles Deleuze, *Empiricism and Subjectivity: An Essay on Hume's Theory of Human Nature*, trans. Constantin V. Boundas (New York: Columbia University Press, 1991), 76–77 (emphasis deleted).

75. Hume, "Of Superstition and Enthusiasm," in *Writings on Religion*, 3–4, 7; and Hume, "Natural History of Religion," 117–19, 133.

76. Hume, "Natural History of Religion," 120, 178; and Hume, *Enquiries*, 114–19, 127.

77. Hume, "A Note on the Profession of Priest," in *Writings on Religion*, 5–8, 11–12; and Hume, "Dialogues concerning Natural Religion," in *Writings on Religion*, 283.

78. Hume, *Enquiries*, 182; and Hume, "Dialogues concerning Natural Religion," 290–91.

79. Voltaire, "Superstition," in *A Philosophical Dictionary*, vol. 10, in *Works of Voltaire*, 14:30–32.

80. Voltaire, "Magic," in *Philosophical Dictionary*, vol. 7, in *Works of Voltaire*, 11:163; and Voltaire, "Enchantment," in *Philosophical Dictionary*, vol. 4, in *Works of Voltaire*, 8:228–29.

81. Voltaire, "Miracles," in *Philosophical Dictionary*, vol. 7, in *Works of Voltaire*, 11:273, 288–96; Voltaire, "Goat–Sorcery," in *Philosophical Dictionary*, vol. 5, in *Works of Voltaire*, 9:212; and Voltaire, "Superstition," 14:27–28. And see Voltaire, "Divinity of Jesus," in *Philosophical Dictionary*, vol. 6, in *Works of Voltaire*, 8:144–45; and Voltaire, "God-Gods," in *Philosophical Dictionary*, vol. 5, in *Works of Voltaire*, 9:242–43.

82. Jullien Offray de La Mettrie, "Man a Machine," in *Portable Enlightenment Reader*, 208.

83. Diderot to Voltaire, 11 June 1749, published in Arthur M. Wilson, *Revue d'Histoire littéraire de la France* 51 (July–September 1951): 258–60; Buckley, *At the Origins of Modern Atheism*, 38, 194–250 (particularly 225), 258–67; Baron d'Holbach, "Common Sense, or Natural Ideas Opposed to Supernatural (1772)," in *Portable Enlightenment Reader*, 140–50; and Baron d'Holbach, *Christianity Unveiled; Being an Examination of the Principles and Effects of the Christian Religion*, trans. W. M. Johnson (New York: Gordon Press, 1974).

84. Immanuel Kant, *Critique of Pure Reason*, trans. Norman Kemp Smith, unabridged ed. (New York: St. Martin's, 1965), 500–524, 528; Kant, *Critique of Judgment*, trans. J. H. Bernard (New York: Hafner Press, 1951), 286–92, 318.

85. Kant, *Critique of Judgment*, 298–312, particularly 310–11; and Kant, *Religion*

within the Limits of Reason Alone, trans. Theodore M. Greene and Hoyt H. Hudson (New York: Harper Torchbooks, 1960), 78–79, 158–62 (emphasis in original).

86. Kant, *Religion within the Limits*, 165–67 (emphasis deleted).

87. Ibid., 180–82 (emphasis in original); and Paul Tillich, *Perspectives on Nineteenth and Twentieth Century Protestant Theology*, ed. Carl E. Braaten (New York: Harper and Row, 1967), 48.

88. Friedrich Schleiermacher, *The Christian Faith*, ed. H. R. Mackintosh and J. S. Stewart (Edinburgh: T. and T. Clark, 1989), 429–30, 434–35.

89. Ibid., 71–73, 179–83, 417–30, 448–50.

90. See Giambattista Vico, *The New Science of Giambattista Vico*, trans. Thomas Goddard Bergin and Max Harold Fisch (Ithaca, N.Y.: Cornell University Press, 1984); and Margaret T. Hodgen, *Early Anthropology in the Sixteenth and Seventeenth Century* (Philadelphia: University of Pennsylvania Press, 1964), 488–97.

91. Marquis de Condorcet, *Esquisse d'un tableau historique des progrès de l'esprit humain*, intro. Alain Pons (Paris: GF Flammarion, 1988), 80, 94–95, 115, 213–69, 282, 296.

92. Monter, *Ritual, Myth and Magic*, 98–113, particularly 101–6; and Clark, *Thinking with Demons*, 79. See also Hodgen, *Early Anthropology*, 375–76, 405; and Wiesner, *Women and Gender in Early Modern Europe*, 229–30.

93. Edward Said, *Culture and Imperialism* (New York: Vintage, 1994), 8; Raymond F. Betts, *Europe Overseas: Phases of Imperialism* (New York: Basic Books, 1968), 21–35, 46–60; and George Lichtheim, *Imperialism* (New York: Praeger, 1971), 42–80.

94. See Bernal, *Black Athena*, 28, 201–4; Hodgen, *Early Anthropology*, 276–90, 485–87; W. D. Jordan, *White over Black: American Attitudes toward the Negro: 1550–1812* (Baltimore: Penguin, 1969), 235–36, 253; and Harry Bracken, "Philosophy and Racism," *Philosophia* 8 (1978): 241–60.

95. See Hodgen, *Early Anthropology*, 407–13; Londa Schiebinger, "The Anatomy of Difference: Race and Sex in Eighteenth-Century Science," *Eighteenth Century Studies* 23 (summer 1990): 387–94; Maurice Olender, *The Languages of Paradise: Race, Religion, and Philology in the Nineteenth Century*, trans. Arthur Goldhammer (Cambridge, Mass.: Harvard University Press, 1992), 44–46; and Rudi C. Bleys, *The Geography of Perversion: Male-to-Male Sexual Behaviour outside the West and the Ethnographic Imagination, 1750–1918* (New York: New York University Press, 1995), 87–89, 91–95.

96. See Bleys, *Geography of Perversion*, 87–89, 110–22, 129, 152; Philip D. Curtin, "Introduction," in *Imperialism*, ed. Philip D. Curtin (New York: Harper and Row, 1971), xv–xvi; excerpts from Cuvier and Knox in *Imperialism*, 4–12, 12–22; and Stephen J. Gould, *The Mismeasure of Man* (New York: Norton, 1981), 30–72.

97. Bleys, *Geography of Perversion*, 96, quoting Cristoph Meiners, *Grundriss der Geschichte der Menschheit* (Lemgo, 1793), 93. And see George W. Stocking Jr., *Victorian Anthropology* (New York: Free Press, 1987), 186–237, 302–4.

98. See John Westlake, "Chapters on the Principles of International Law," in *Imperialism*, 45–63; R. Rashed, "Science as a Western Phenomenon," *Fundamenta Scientiae* 1 (1980): 7–21; Betts, *Europe Overseas*, 64–68; Lichtheim, *Imperialism*, 81–99; and Richard Koebner and Helmut Dan Schmidt, *Imperialism: The Story and Significance of a Political Word, 1840–1960* (Cambridge: Cambridge University Press, 1964), 81–134.

99. See, for example, Marianna Torgovnick, *Gone Primitive: Savage Intellects,*

Modern Lives (Chicago: University of Chicago Press, 1990); Torgovnick, *Primitive Passions: Men, Women, and the Quest for Ecstasy* (Chicago: University of Chicago Press, 1996); and John M. MacKenzie, *Orientalism: History, Theory and the Arts* (Manchester: Manchester University Press, 1995).

100. Eric J. Sharpe, *Comparative Religion: A History*, 2d ed. (La Salle, Ill.: Open Court, 1986), 1–26; Hodgen, *Early Anthropology*, 375–76; David Pailin, ed., *Attitudes to Other Religions: Comparative Religion in Seventeenth- and Eighteenth-Century Britain* (Manchester: Manchester University Press, 1984); and Jonathan Z. Smith, "Religion, Religions, Religious," in *Critical Terms for Religious Studies*, ed. Mark C. Taylor (Chicago: University of Chicago Press, 1998), 269–84.

101. See Sharpe, *Comparative Religion*, 17–19; Morris Jastrow Jr., *The Study of Religion* (London: Walter Scott, 1901), 23–57; F. E. Manuel, *The Eighteenth Century Confronts the Gods* (Cambridge, Mass.: Harvard University Press, 1959); and Smith, *Drudgery Divine*.

102. Sharpe, *Comparative Religion*, 20–24; Richard M. Dorson, *The British Folklorists: A History* (Chicago: University of Chicago Press, 1968); Jastrow, *Study of Religion*, 29–37, 147–49; and Olender, *Languages of Paradise*, 40–50.

103. See G. W. F. Hegel, *Lectures on the Philosophy of Religion: The Lectures of 1827*, ed. Peter C. Hodgson, trans. R. F. Brown, P. C. Hodgson, and J. M. Stewart (Berkeley: University of California Press, 1988), 109, 391–92; and Peter C. Hodgson, "Editorial Introduction," in Hegel, *Lectures on the Philosophy of Religion*, 25–26.

104. Hegel, *Lectures on the Philosophy of Religion*, 201–7, 223–26.

105. Ibid., 220, 224–26.

106. Ibid., 227–29.

107. Ibid., 228.

108. Ibid., 229–30, 233–38, 243, 249; and Hegel, *The Philosophy of History*, trans. J. Sibree (Buffalo, N.Y.: Prometheus Books, 1991), 93–96.

109. Ludwig Feuerbach, "Twenty-third Lecture," in *Lectures on the Essence of Religion*, trans. Ralph Manheim (New York: Harper and Row, 1967), 207–8; and Feuerbach, "Twenty-fourth Lecture," in *Lectures on the Essence of Religion*, 219–23. And see Van A. Harvey, *Feuerbach and the Interpretation of Religion* (Cambridge: Cambridge University Press, 1995), 215–17.

110. Auguste Comte, *The Positive Philosophy of Auguste Comte*, vol. 1, 3d ed., trans. Harriet Martineau (London: Kegan Paul, Trench, Trübner, 1893), 1–2; and ibid., 2:160–65, 184.

111. Jastrow, *Study of Religion*, 63. See also Max Müller, *Introduction to the Science of Religion* (London: Longmans, Green, 1873); and Olender, *Languages of Paradise*, 91–92.

112. See Joseph M. Kitagawa, "History of Religions in America," in *The History of Religions: Understanding Human Experience* (Atlanta: Scholar's Press, 1987), 4–5, 16; and Jastrow, *Study of Religion*, 47–55, 351–79.

CHAPTER 2

1. Alfred C. Haddon, *History of Anthropology* (London: Watts and Co., [1910]), 137.

2. Paul Tillich, *Perspectives on Nineteenth and Twentieth Century Protestant Theol-*

ogy, ed. Carl E. Braaten (New York: Harper and Row, 1967), 46–47. See also in this regard Maureen Perkins, *The Reform of Time: Magic and Modernity* (London: Pluto Press, 2001).

3. E. Bolaji Idowi, *African Traditional Religion* (London: SCM Press, 1973), 191, quoted in Patrick F. Gesch, "Magic as a Process of Social Discernment," in *Powers, Plumes, and Piglets: Phenomena of Melanesian Religion*, ed. Norman C. Habel (Bedford Park, S. Aust.: Australian Association for the Study of Religions, 1979), 137.

4. Alexander Le Roy, *The Religion of the Primitives*, trans. Newton Thompson (New York: Macmillan, 1922), 218.

5. Ruth Benedict, "Religion," in *General Anthropology*, ed. Franz Boas (New York: Heath, 1938), 664 n. 1; and Wilhelm Wundt, *Elements of Folk Psychology: Outlines of a Psychological History of the Development of Mankind*, trans. Edward Leroy Schaub (London: George Allen and Unwin, 1916), 77. See also Tomoko Masuzawa, *In Search of Dreamtime: The Quest for the Origin of Religion* (Chicago: University of Chicago Press, 1993).

6. Felix M. Keesing, *Cultural Anthropology: The Science of Custom* (New York: Holt, Rinehart and Winston, 1958), 325; and E. E. Evans-Pritchard, *Theories of Primitive Religion* (Oxford: Clarendon, 1965), 20–77, particularly 25. See also Wilhelm Schmidt, *The Origin and Growth of Religion: Facts and Theories*, trans. H. J. Rose (London: Methuen, 1931); Eric J. Sharpe, *Comparative Religion: A History*, 2d ed. (La Salle, Ill.: Open Court, 1986), 27–96; and Stanley J. Tambiah, *Magic, Science, Religion, and the Scope of Rationality* (Cambridge: Cambridge University Press, 1990), 16–86.

7. Auguste Comte, *The Positive Philosophy of Auguste Comte*, vol. 2, 3d ed., trans. Harriet Martineau (London: Kegan Paul, Trench, Trübner, 1893), 151–252; and Max Müller, *Introduction to the Science of Religion* (London: Longmans, Green, 1873). See also Josiah Conder, *View of All Religions* (London: Jackson and Walford, 1838), 68–81; and William Burder, *A History of All Religions* (Philadelphia: W. A. Leary, 1848), 683–87.

8. See Herbert Spencer, *Principles of Sociology*, ed. Stanislav Andreski (Hamden, Conn.: Archon Books, 1969), 171–73, 446–49, 575–87; and Herbert Spencer, *On Social Evolution: Selected Writings*, ed. J. D. Y. Peel (Chicago: University of Chicago Press, 1972), particularly 207–8.

9. John Lubbock, Lord Avebury, *The Origin of Civilization and the Primitive Condition of Man: Mental and Social Condition of Savages*, 7th ed. (London: Longmans, Green, 1912), 163, 177–78, 181–208, 224. On the ancient roots of this distinction between magic and religion, see Fritz Graf, *Magic in the Ancient World*, trans. Franklin Philip (Cambridge, Mass.: Harvard University Press, 1997), 27.

10. On Tylor's significance in the development of anthropology, see Marvin Harris, *The Rise of Anthropological Theory: A History of Theories of Culture* (New York: Crowell, 1968), 140–216. For a valuable study of *Primitive Culture*, see Joan Leopold, *Culture in Comparative and Evolutionary Perspective: E. B. Tylor and the Making of Primitive Culture* (Berlin: Reimer, 1980).

11. Edward Burnett Tylor, *Primitive Culture: Researches into the Development of Mythology, Philosophy, Religion, Language, Art and Custom*, 3d American ed., vol. 1 (New York: Henry Holt, 1889), 420–29.

12. See ibid., 1:424; Tambiah, *Magic, Science, Religion*, 5, 19, 48; and Paul Bohannan, *Social Anthropology* (New York: Holt, Rinehart and Winston, 1963), 313.

13. See Wouter J. Hanegraaff, "The Emergence of the Academic Science of Magic: The Occult Philosophy in Tylor and Frazer," in *Religion in the Making: The Emergence of the Sciences of Religion*, ed. Arie L. Molendijk and Peter Pels (Leiden: Brill, 1998), 253–75, particularly 260; and Tylor, *Primitive Culture*, 1:16, 72, 112–13. For a classic overview of the concept of survivals, see Margaret T. Hodgen, *The Doctrine of Survivals: A Chapter in the History of Scientific Method in the Study of Man* (London: Allenson, 1936).

14. Tylor, *Primitive Culture*, 1:11, 116, 136–37.

15. Ibid., 1:138–39, 141–43.

16. Ibid., 1:156–59.

17. Tambiah, *Magic, Science, Religion*, 49–50; and Hanegraaff, "Academic Science of Magic," 261–71.

18. See Schmidt, *Origin and Growth of Religion*, 77–78, 91–117. Albert Réville, *Les religions des peuples non-civilisés*, 2 vols. (Paris: Librairie Fischbacher, 1883), particularly 2:221–56, and P. D. Chantepie de la Saussaye, *Manual of the Science of Religion*, trans. Beatrice S. Colyer-Fergusson (London: Longmans, Green, 1891), both sought to bridge between nature-myth theories and animism.

19. See James George Frazer, *The Golden Bough: A Study in Magic and Religion*, abridged ed. (New York: Macmillan, 1922), 11–13, 37–38. For a valuable account of the development of the text and the evolution of Frazer's typology, see Robert Fraser, *The Making of* The Golden Bough: *The Origins and Growth of an Argument* (New York: St. Martin's, 1990), particularly 120–23. Frazer attributes the label "homoeopathic magic" to Yrjö Hirn, *Origins of Art: A Psychological and Sociological Inquiry* (London: Macmillan, 1900), 282, and the label "imitative or mimetic magic" to Sidney Hartland, "Review of Frank Byron Jevons' *An Introduction to the History of Religion*," *Folk-lore* 8 (1897): 65. On the roots of the notion of "sympathetic magic," see Hanegraaff, "Academic Science of Magic," 266.

20. Frazer, *Golden Bough*, 48–60, 711.

21. Ibid., 50–52.

22. Ibid., 51–54; and Hanegraaff, "Academic Science of Magic," 265–73. See also Jonathan Z. Smith, *Drudgery Divine: On the Comparison of Early Christianities and the Religions of Late Antiquity* (Chicago: University of Chicago Press, 1990), 92 n. 14, 93, noting that most of Frazer's explicit references to Christianity involve Catholic ceremonial practices and take the form of polemics against "Pagano-papism."

23. Frazer, *Golden Bough*, 54–55.

24. Ibid., 56–59, 90–92, 711–12.

25. See Maurice Olender, *The Languages of Paradise: Race, Religion, and Philology in the Nineteenth Century*, trans. Arthur Goldhammer (Cambridge, Mass.: Harvard University Press, 1992), 82–105.

26. C. P. Tiele, *Elements of the Science of Religion*, vol. 2 (Edinburgh: William Blackwood, 1899), 135–42.

27. Andrew Lang, *Magic and Religion* (London: Longmans, Green, 1901), v, 9–12, 68–69; and see Lang, *The Making of Religion*, 2d ed. (London: Longmans, Green, 1900), 160–229.

28. Lang, *Magic and Religion*, 46–47.

29. Schmidt, *Origin and Growth of Religion*, 125, 137, 147–49, 160–65. See also Otto Pfleiderer, *Religion and Historic Faiths*, trans. Daniel A. Huebsch, authorized ed.

(New York: B. W. Huebsch, 1907), 79 (arguing that magic is a degeneration from "initial, naïve-religious ceremonies of worship"); and Le Roy, *Religion of the Primitives*, 60–61 (on the primitive intuition that the world has "an invisible, sovereign Master," an intuition that provides "the initial *substratum* of belief and religious worship").

30. Schmidt, *Origin and Growth of Religion*, 131, 151–58.

31. Ibid., 136–38, 147.

32. Ibid., 127, 155, 159.

33. See R. H. Codrington, *The Melanesians: Studies in Their Anthropology and Folklore* (Oxford: Clarendon, 1891); J. N. B. Hewitt, "Orenda and a Definition of Religion," *American Anthropologist*, n.s., 4 (1902): 33–46; and H. Philsooph, "Primitive Magic and Mana," *Man*, n.s., 6 (1971): 182–203.

34. John H. King, *The Supernatural: Its Origin, Nature, and Evolution*, vol. 1 (London: Williams and Norgate, 1892), 4–7, 89–102.

35. Ibid., 1:6–8, 36; 2:262; and see ibid., 1:28–44, 103–207.

36. R. R. Marett, "Preface to the First Edition," in *The Threshold of Religion*, 3d ed. (London: Methuen, 1914), viii–x; and Marett, "Introduction," in *Threshold of Religion*, xxix–xxx.

37. Marett, "Preface," xi–xiii; Marett, "Introduction," ix–x, xxi, xxxi; Marett, "Preanimistic Religion," in *Threshold of Religion*, 11–13; and Marett, "A Sociological View of Comparative Religion," in *Threshold of Religion*, 122–44.

38. Marett, "Preface," xiv; and Marett, "From Spell to Prayer," in *Threshold of Religion*, 32, 66–69.

39. Marett, "The Birth of Humility," in *Threshold of Religion*, 169, 176–79; Marett, "Is Taboo a Negative Magic?" in *Threshold of Religion*, 85; and Marett, "The Conception of Mana," in *Threshold of Religion*, 100.

40. R. R. Marett, *Faith, Hope and Charity in Primitive Religion* (Oxford: Clarendon, 1932), 38–39, 43–48, 134.

41. See Sigmund Freud, *Totem and Taboo: Some Points of Agreement between the Mental Lives of Savages and Neurotics*, trans. and ed. James Strachey (New York: Norton, 1989), 94–95, 114–15; Konrad Theodor Preuss, "Der Ursprung der Religion und Kunst," *Globus* 86 (1904): 321–92, and *Globus* 87 (1905): 333–419; and Preuss, "Das Irrationale in der Magie," in *Magie und Religion: Beiträge zu Einer Theorie der Magie*, ed. Leander Petzoldt (Darmstadt: Wissenschaftliche Buchgesellschaft, 1978), 223–47.

42. Marcel Mauss, *A General Theory of Magic*, trans. Robert Brain (London: Routledge and Kegan Paul, 1972), 12–14, 107, 116–19, 136–37. See also Henri Hubert and Marcel Mauss, "L'Origine des pouvoirs magiques dans les sociétés Australiennes," in *Mélanges d'histoire des religions*, 2d ed. (Paris: Librairie Félix Alcan, 1929), xvii–xxvi, 131–87; and Henri Hubert, *Essay on Time: A Brief Study of the Representation of Time in Religion and Magic*, ed. Robert Parkin, trans. Robert Parkin and Jacqueline Redding (Oxford: Durkheim, 1999).

43. Mauss, *General Theory of Magic*, 21–24, 89–90. And see Graf, *Magic in the Ancient World*, 25–26.

44. Mauss, *General Theory of Magic*, 9, 24 (emphasis deleted), 50, 86–88. For an early critique of Mauss and Hubert pointing out a range of internal inconsistencies in this text, see James H. Leuba, "How Magic Is to Be Differentiated from Religion," *Journal of Religious Psychology* 6 (1913): 422–26.

45. Robert H. Lowie, *Primitive Religion* (New York: Liveright, 1948), xiv–xvi. See also Lowie, *An Introduction to Cultural Anthropology*, rev. ed. (New York: Farrar and Rinehart, 1940), 304.

46. Lowie, *Primitive Religion*, 146–51.

47. See W. Robertson Smith, *Lectures on the Religion of the Semites: The Fundamental Institutions*, 3d ed., intro. Stanley A. Cook (New York: Macmillan, 1927), 54–55, 154.

48. Frank Byron Jevons, *An Introduction to the History of Religion*, 9th ed. (London: Methuen, 1927), 25.

49. Ibid., 25–27, 36–39.

50. Ibid., 42, 177–78; and Jevons, *An Introduction to the Study of Comparative Religion* (New York: Macmillan, 1920), 79–81, 86, 95–98. See also Irving King, *The Development of Religion: A Study in Anthropology and Social Psychology* (New York: Macmillan, 1910), 195.

51. Émile Durkheim, *The Elementary Forms of the Religious Life*, trans. Joseph Ward Swain (New York: Free Press, 1965), 52–59. See also Masuzawa, *In Search of Dreamtime*, 34–57.

52. Robertson Smith, *Religion of the Semites*, 264–65, cited at Durkheim, *Elementary Forms*, 61 n. 62.

53. Durkheim, *Elementary Forms*, 59–62, particularly n. 62 (emphasis deleted).

54. Ibid., 398–405.

55. For various influential critiques of Durkheim, see Edward Westermarck, *The Origin and Development of the Moral Ideas*, 2d ed., vol. 2 (1912; reprint, New York: Johnson Reprint Corporation, 1971), 753; Edwin Sidney Hartland, *Ritual and Belief: Studies in the History of Religion* (London: Williams and Norgate, 1914), 74–76, 89; Bronislaw Malinowski, "Magic, Science and Religion," in *Magic, Science and Religion and Other Essays*, ed. Robert Redfield (Glencoe, Ill.: Free Press, 1948), 57–59; and Jack Goody, "Religion and Ritual: The Definitional Problem," *British Journal of Sociology* 12 (1961): 146–47.

56. See Georg Wobbermin, *The Nature of Religion*, trans. Theophil Menzel and Daniel Sommer Robinson (New York: Crowell, 1933), 30; Joachim Wach, "The History of Religions: Theoretical Prolegomena to Its Foundation as a Scholarly Discipline (1924)," in *Introduction to the History of Religions*, ed. Joseph M. Kitagawa and Gregory D. Alles (New York: Macmillan, 1988), 44, 58–59; Edmund Leach, "Anthropology of Religion: British and French Schools," in *Nineteenth Century Religious Thought in the West*, vol. 3, ed. Ninian Smart, John Clayton, Steven Katz, and Patrick Sherry (Cambridge: Cambridge University Press, 1985), 215–62; and Walter H. Capps, *Religious Studies: The Making of a Discipline* (Minneapolis: Fortress, 1995), 94–96.

57. Hutton Webster, *Magic: A Sociological Study* (Stanford, Calif.: Stanford University Press, 1948), ix.

58. C. J. Bleeker, "The 'Entelecheia' of Religious Phenomena," in *Ways of Understanding Religion*, ed. Walter H. Capps (New York: Macmillan, 1972), 159.

59. See Robert N. Bellah, *Beyond Belief: Essays on Religion in a Post-traditional World* (New York: Harper and Row, 1970), 20–50. See also George Pepper, "Religion and Evolution," *Sociological Analysis* 31 (1970): 78–91; and James Fowler, *Stages of Faith: The Psychology of Human Development and the Quest for Meaning* (San Francisco: Harper and Row, 1981).

60. John Hick, *An Interpretation of Religion: Human Responses to the Transcendent* (New Haven, Conn.: Yale University Press, 1989), 12, 23–28, 252.

61. Ibid., 162–63.

62. Donate Pahnke, "Religion and Magic in the Modern Cults of the Great Goddess," in *Religion and Gender*, ed. Ursula King (Oxford: Blackwell, 1995), 166.

63. See Arnold Van Gennep, *The Rites of Passage*, trans. Monika B. Vizedom and Gabrielle L. Caffee, intro. Solon T. Kimball (Chicago: University of Chicago Press, 1960), 13; Huston Smith, *The Religions of Man* (New York: Harper and Brothers, 1958), 92; Melville J. Herskovits, *Cultural Anthropology* (New York: Knopf, 1955), 221, 225; and Alban G. Widgery, *The Comparative Study of Religions: A Systematic Survey* (Baroda: Luhana Mitra Steam Printing Press, 1922), 379.

64. William J. Goode, *Religion among the Primitives* (Glencoe, Ill.: Free Press, 1951), 50–54 (emphasis deleted); see also Goode, "Magic and Religion: A Continuum," *Ethnos* 14 (1949): 172–82.

65. Malinowski, "Magic, Science and Religion," 20–23, 35, 111; and Bronislaw Malinowski, "The Role of Magic and Religion," in *Reader in Comparative Religion: An Anthropological Approach*, 2d ed., ed. William A. Lessa and Evon Z. Vogt (New York: Harper and Row, 1965), 109–11. See also S. F. Nadel, "Malinowski on Magic and Religion," in *Man and Culture: An Evaluation of the Work of Bronislaw Malinowski*, ed. Raymond Firth (London: Routledge and Kegan Paul, 1957), 189–208.

66. Malinowski, "Magic, Science and Religion," 20–21, 67–69; and Malinowski, "Role of Magic and Religion," 104.

67. Malinowski, "Magic, Science and Religion," 69–70; and Malinowski, "Role of Magic and Religion," 109.

68. See, for example, A. R. Radcliffe-Brown, *Taboo* (Cambridge: Cambridge University Press, 1938), 39; Ruth Benedict, "Magic," in *Encyclopedia of the Social Sciences*, ed. Edwin R. A. Seligman, vol. 10 (New York: Macmillan, 1935), 42–45; Herskovits, *Cultural Anthropology*, 221; and Melford E. Spiro, "Religion: Problems of Definition and Explanation," in *Anthropological Approaches to the Study of Religion*, ed. Michael Banton (New York: Praeger, 1966), 85–126.

69. J. Milton Yinger, "The Sociology of Religion," in *Religion, Society and the Individual: An Introduction to the Sociology of Religion*, ed. J. Milton Yinger (New York: Macmillan, 1957), 42; Keith Thomas, *Religion and the Decline of Magic* (New York: Scribner, 1971), 636–38; and Jean Delumeau, *Catholicism between Luther and Voltaire: A New View of the Counter-Reformation*, intro. John Bossy, trans. J. Mosier (London: Burns and Oates, 1977), 172. For a variation of this theme seeking to distinguish between religion as the regular practices of a social group and magic as those performed in emergencies or crises, see Mischa Titiev, "A Fresh Approach to the Problem of Magic and Religion," *Southwestern Journal of Anthropology* 16 (1960): 292–98. See also Paul Tillich, "The Relation of Religion and Health: Religious, Magic, and Natural Healing Distinguished," *Pastoral Psychology* 5 (May 1954): 41–52.

70. Max Weber, *The Sociology of Religion*, trans. Ephraim Fischoff, intro. Talcott Parsons (Boston: Beacon Press, 1964), 20–31. See also Weber, *The Protestant Ethic and the Spirit of Capitalism*, trans. Talcott Parsons (New York: Scribner, 1958), 104–5, 117, 149; Weber, "The Social Psychology of the World Religions," in *From Max Weber: Essays in Sociology*, ed. and trans. Hans H. Gerth and C. Wright Mills (New York: Oxford University Press, 1946), 267–77; Mauss, *General Theory of Magic*, 141 (asserting

that religion is aimed "towards more metaphysical ends and is involved in the creation of idealistic images," while magic plays merely among the "fissures in the mystical world" and seeks out a practical role in everyday life); and Elizabeth K. Nottingham, *Religion: A Sociological View* (New York: Random House, 1971), 92 (religious systems develop to "encompass the whole of life" and offer "a total theory of both the supernatural and human society," while magic is largely "atomistic, something like an old-fashioned book of recipes or a home doctor manual").

71. William Sims Bainbridge and Rodney Stark, *The Future of Religion* (Berkeley: University of California Press, 1985), 6–7, 30, 110, 456.

72. Bryan Wilson, *Religion in Sociological Perspective* (Oxford: Oxford University Press, 1982), 171–74.

73. Mircea Eliade, *Patterns in Comparative Religion*, trans. Rosemary Sheed (London: Sheed and Ward, 1958), 108, 216–17; and Gregory Bateson, "Neither Supernatural nor Mechanical," in Gregory Bateson and Mary Catherine Bateson, *Angels Fear: Towards an Epistemology of the Sacred* (New York: Macmillan, 1987), 56.

74. See Tom F. Driver, *The Magic of Ritual: Our Need for Liberating Rites That Transform Our Lives and Our Communities* (San Francisco: HarperSanFrancisco, 1991), 168–71 (emphasis in original); and Van Gennep, *Rites of Passage*, 13.

75. Bruno Latour, *The Pasteurization of France*, trans. Alan Sheridan and John Law (Cambridge, Mass.: Harvard University Press, 1988), 213.

76. Timothy Fitzgerald, *The Ideology of Religious Studies* (New York: Oxford University Press, 2000), 15, 20. See also Michael J. Buckley, *At the Origins of Modern Atheism* (New Haven, Conn.: Yale University Press, 1987), 363.

77. Gerardus van der Leeuw, *Religion in Essence and Manifestation*, trans. J. E. Turner (Princeton, N.J.: Princeton University Press, 1986), 24–25, 545–46 (emphasis deleted). See also Richard J. Plantinga, "An Ambivalent Relationship to the Holy: Gerardus van der Leeuw on Religion," in *Religion in History: The Word, the Idea, the Reality*, ed. Michel Despland and Gérard Vallée (Waterloo, Ont.: Wilfrid Laurier University Press, 1992), 93–100; and George Alfred James, *Interpreting Religion: The Phenomenological Approaches of Pierre Daniël Chantepie de la Saussaye, W. Brede Kristensen, and Gerardus van der Leeuw* (Washington, D.C.: Catholic University of America Press, 1995), 201–63.

78. Van der Leeuw, *Religion in Essence and Manifestation*, 468–69, 547–60. Van der Leeuw's view of magic and science is echoed by C. S. Lewis, *Miracles: A Preliminary Study* (New York: Collier, 1978), 150: "The evil dream of Magic arises from finite spirit's longing to get that power [over nature without giving proper obedience to the divine]. The evil reality of lawless applied science (which is Magic's son and heir) is actually reducing large tracts of Nature to disorder and sterility at this very moment."

79. See Friedrich Schleiermacher, *The Christian Faith*, ed. H. R. Mackintosh and J. S. Stewart (Edinburgh: T. and T. Clark, 1989), 12–18; J. Edgar Wilson, *The Lord's Supper* (Nashville, Tenn.: Smith and Lamar, 1909) 27; and Paul H. Jones, *Christ's Eucharistic Presence: A History of the Doctrine* (New York: Peter Lang, 1994), 135.

80. C. P. Tiele, *Outlines of the History of Religion to the Spread of the Universal Religions*, trans. J. Estlin Carpenter, 7th ed. (London: Kegan Paul, Trench, Trübner, 1905), 10–11; Pfleiderer, *Religion and Historic Faiths*, 9, 79–80; and Jevons, *Introduction to the Study of Comparative Religion*, 152.

81. Rudolf Otto, *The Idea of the Holy*, trans. John W. Harvey (London: Oxford University Press, 1923), 33, 121–22; and Wobbermin, *Nature of Religion*, 244–51.

82. Nathan Söderblom, *The Living God: Basal Forms of Personal Religion* (London: Oxford University Press/Humphrey Milford, 1933), 18–19, 35–36; and Söderblom, "Holiness," in *Encyclopedia of Religion and Ethics*, ed. James Hastings, vol. 6 (Edinburgh: T. and T. Clark, 1913), 731–41. See also Joachim Wach, *Sociology of Religion* (Chicago: University of Chicago Press, 1944), 336, 353–63; Wach, *The Comparative Study of Religions*, ed. Joseph M. Kitagawa (New York: Columbia University Press, 1958), 52–53; W. Brede Kristensen, *The Meaning of Religion: Lectures in the Phenomenology of Religion*, trans. John B. Carman (The Hague: Martinus Nijhoff, 1960), 178; and Friedrich Heiler, *Erscheinungsformen un Wesen der Religion* (Stuttgart: Kohlhammer, 1961), 27.

83. Westermarck, *Origin and Development of the Moral Ideas*, 2:584, 649–52, 753; and W. H. R. Rivers, *Medicine, Magic, and Religion* (London: Kegan Paul, Trench, Trübner, 1924), 4, 119–20.

84. See Mauss, *General Theory of Magic*, 81–82; Edwin A. Burtt, *Man Seeks the Divine: A Study in the History and Comparison of Religions*, 2d ed. (New York: Harper and Row, 1964), 51; and Delumeau, *Catholicism between Luther and Voltaire*, 172. See also F. M. Cornford, *From Religion to Philosophy: A Study in the Origins of Western Speculation* (1912; reprint, Princeton, N.J.: Princeton University Press, 1991), 76–93; Hartland, *Ritual and Belief*, 74–76; Weber, *Sociology of Religion*, 26; Webster, *Magic*, 111; and Fritz Graf, "Prayer in Magic and Religious Ritual," in *Magika Hiera: Ancient Greek Magic and Religion*, ed. Christopher A. Faraone and Dirk Obbink (New York: Oxford University Press, 1991), 188–213.

85. See, for example, Marett, *Faith, Hope and Charity in Primitive Religion*, 133–35 (discussing the "commonplace" anthropological contrast between "the religious man who has learnt to say 'Thy will be done'" and "the magician who says 'My will be done'"); and E. Adamson Hoebel, *Man in the Primitive World: An Introduction to Anthropology* (New York: McGraw-Hill, 1949), 408–9 (stating that the Lord's Prayer epitomizes the religious attitude "with its 'Hallowed be thy name' [reverence]; 'Give us this day our daily bread' [petition]; 'Thine is the Kingdom, the Power and the Glory, forever' [subordination and awe]"). See also James H. Leuba, *A Psychological Study of Religion: Its Origin, Function, and Future* (New York: Macmillan, 1912), 151; Weber, *Sociology of Religion*, 25; Alexander A. Goldenweiser, *Anthropology: An Introduction to Primitive Culture* (New York: F. S. Crofts, 1937), 218; Lowie, *Primitive Religion*, 136–37; Nottingham, *Religion*, 91; Keith Roberts, *Religion in Sociological Perspective* (Homewood, Ill.: Dorsey Press, 1984), 68; and Stoddard Martin, *Orthodox Heresy: The Rise of "Magic" as Religion and Its Relation to Literature* (New York: St. Martin's, 1989), 8, 11–12, 225–30.

86. Hans-Joachim Schoeps, *The Religions of Mankind*, trans. Richard Winston and Clara Winston (Garden City, N.Y.: Doubleday, 1966), 23–24.

87. Thomas, *Religion and the Decline of Magic*, 41; and Hoebel, *Man in the Primitive World*, 409. See also Robert W. Scribner, "The Reformation, Popular Magic, and the 'Disenchantment of the World,'" *Journal of Interdisciplinary History* 23 (winter 1993): 476–77.

88. Edmund R. Leach, "Ritualization in Man in Relation to Conceptual and Social Development," *Philosophical Transactions of the Royal Society of London*, 29th ser.,

251 (1966): 524; E. E. Evans-Pritchard, *Nuer Religion* (Oxford: Oxford University Press, 1956), 104; and Ninian Smart, *Dimensions of the Sacred: An Anatomy of the World's Beliefs* (London: Fontana Press, 1997), 109. See also William Howells, *The Heathens: Primitive Man and His Religions* (Garden City, N.Y.: Doubleday, 1948), 49.

89.   Webster, *Magic*, 111–12; Graf, *Magic in the Ancient World*, 27; Leuba, "How Magic Is to Be Differentiated from Religion," 423; and Rafael Karsten, *The Origins of Religion* (London: Kegan Paul, Trench, Trübner, 1935), 205. See also E. O. James, *Comparative Religion* (London: Methuen, 1938), 57.

90.   T. Witton Davies, *Magic, Divination, and Demonology among the Hebrews and Their Neighbors* (London: James Clarke, [1897]), 1; and K. W. S. Kennedy, *Magic and Witchcraft* (London: Missionary Literature Supply, 1914), 13.

91.   Perkins, *Reform of Time*, 1–18.

92.   See Robert J. Baird, "How Religion Became Scientific," in *Religion in the Making*, 225–28.

93.   See Immanuel Kant, *Religion within the Limits of Reason Alone*, trans. Theodore M. Greene and Hoyt H. Hudson (New York: Harper Torchbooks, 1960), 79, 158–62; Mary Douglas, *Purity and Danger: An Analysis of Concepts of Pollution and Taboo* (London: Ark Paperbacks, 1984), 61–62; and FitzRoy Richard Somerset Raglan, *Jocasta's Crime: An Anthropological Study* (London: Methuen, 1933), vii.

94.   See Morris Jastrow Jr., *The Study of Religion* (London: Walter Scott, 1901), 108; and Roberts, *Religion in Sociological Perspective*, 71. See also Tiele, *Outlines of the History of Religion*, 10–11; Davies, *Magic, Divination, and Demonology*, 2, 24; and Roland Robertson, *The Sociological Interpretation of Religion* (Oxford: Basil Blackwell, 1970), 48–49, 106 n. 6.

95.   Le Roy, *Religion of the Primitives*, 223, 234–36, 306; at 234–35, Le Roy underscores the violence of European colonizers as well: "Without speaking of what takes place in the shoals of our European society, we have lately seen numerous representatives of the most civilized races who were living in the African world for the work of colonization, astonish the lowest savages by the extremity of their moral perversity, by their useless cruelty, and by their shameless degeneracy. So true is it that man is everywhere the same. . . . European civilization, in the forms it so often takes, disorganizes and dissolves the African family, introduces alcohol, spreads the gout, destroys the class distinctions of the Blacks, increases everywhere dreadful diseases. . . . But, everything considered, it has advantages, and we hope at least that we can contribute to make it better and render it a means of real progress for its African wards."

96.   Weber, *Sociology of Religion*, 28–30, 37–45, 74–75, 191.

97.   Hartland, *Ritual and Belief*, 88–89, 157; and Leuba, "How Magic Is to Be Differentiated from Religion," 426.

98.   Frederick Schleiter, *Religion and Culture: A Critical Survey of Methods of Approach to Religious Phenomena* (New York: Columbia University Press, 1919), 69; and Durkheim, *Elementary Forms*, 339.

99.   See Daniel Lawrence O'Keefe, *Stolen Lightning: The Social Theory of Magic* (New York: Continuum, 1982), 263–413; J. H. Driberg, *At Home with the Savage* (London: George Routledge, 1932), 189; Goode, *Religion among the Primitives*, 51; and Barbara Hargrove, *The Sociology of Religion: Classical and Contemporary Approaches*, 2d ed. (Arlington Heights, Ill.: Harlan Davidson, 1989), 90.

100.   Henry Presler, *Primitive Religions in India* (Madras: Christian Literature So-

ciety, 1971), 15–16, quoted in Earl E. Grant, "A Survey of Magic, Religion, and Science and the Development of an Analytical Framework of Magic" (M.T.M. thesis, Fuller Theological Seminary, 1982), 58–61.

101. Weber, *Sociology of Religion*, 23. See also Allan Menzies, *History of Religions* (London: John Murray, 1911), 74–75; George Peter Murdock, *Our Primitive Contemporaries* (New York: Macmillan, 1934), particularly 100–101, 386; and Herskovits, *Cultural Anthropology*, 226.

102. Malinowski, "Magic, Science and Religion," 56; Bronislaw Malinowski, *Coral Gardens and Their Magic: A Study of the Methods of Tilling the Soil and of Agricultural Rites in the Trobriand Islands* (London: George Allen and Unwin, 1935), 1:445, 2: 240–50; and Edmund Davison Soper, *The Religions of Mankind* (New York: Abingdon Press, 1921), 75–76. See also W. J. Perry, *The Origin of Magic and Religion* (London: Methuen, 1923), 7, 156–75; William Graham Sumner and Albert Galloway Keller, *The Science of Society* (New Haven, Conn.: Yale University Press, 1927), 1293–1301; Wach, *Sociology of Religion*, 355; Arturo Castiglioni, *Adventures of the Mind*, trans. V. Gianturco (New York: Knopf, 1946), 75–76; and Stephen Wilson, *The Magical Universe: Everyday Ritual and Magic in Pre-modern Europe* (London: Hambledon and London), 2000.

103. Benedict, "Magic," 40; Talcott Parsons, *The Structure of Social Action*, 2d ed. (New York: Free Press, 1949), 258, 259 n. 6; and Thomas F. O'Dea, *The Sociology of Religion* (Englewood Cliffs, N.J.: Prentice-Hall, 1966), 7. See also Stephen Fuchs, *The Origin of Man and His Culture* (Bombay: Asia Publishing House, 1963), 219; Judith Abel Willer, "A Theoretical Study of Magic, Science and Religion" (Ph.D. diss., University of Kansas, 1970), 17–19.

104. Werner Stark, *The Sociology of Religion: A Study of Christendom*, vol. 4 (New York: Fordham University Press, 1970), 240.

105. David Ray Griffin, "Of Minds and Molecules: Postmodern Medicine in a Psychosomatic Universe," in *The Reenchantment of Science*, ed. David Ray Griffin (Albany: State University of New York Press, 1988), 143–49; Perry, *Origin of Magic and Religion*, 8; and Morton Klass, *Ordered Universes: Approaches to the Anthropology of Religion* (Boulder, Colo.: Westview, 1995), 89.

106. See Frederick Schleiter, *Religion and Culture: A Critical Survey of Methods of Approach to Religious Phenomena* (New York: Columbia University Press, 1919), 115.

107. Buckley, *At the Origins of Modern Atheism*, 363.

108. See Philip J. Lee, *Against the Protestant Gnostics* (New York: Oxford University Press, 1987); and Horatio W. Dressler, *Outlines of the Psychology of Religion* (New York: Crowell, 1929), 322–24.

109. Dressler, *Outlines of the Psychology of Religion*, 392–93.

CHAPTER 3

1. David C. Lindberg, *The Beginnings of Western Science: The European Scientific Tradition in Philosophical, Religious, and Institutional Context, 600 B.C. to A.D. 1450* (Chicago: University of Chicago Press, 1992), 1–2. Portions of this chapter expand on my essay "The 'Magic' of 'Science': The Labeling of Ideas," in *Labeling: Pedagogy and Politics*, ed. Glenn M. Hudak and Paul Kihn (London: RoutledgeFalmer, 2001), 235–49.

2. See, for example, Sandra Harding, *Is Science Multicultural? Postcolonialisms, Feminisms, and Epistemologies* (Bloomington: Indiana University Press, 1998).

3. James George Frazer, *The Golden Bough: A Study in Magic and Religion*, abridged ed. (New York: Macmillan, 1922), 50; and Alexander Le Roy, *The Religion of the Primitives*, trans. Newton Thompson (New York: Macmillan, 1922), 35.

4. See, for example, the broad discussions of magical thought in Elman R. Service, *A Profile of Primitive Culture* (New York: Harper and Brothers, 1958); and Hans-Joachim Schoeps, *The Religions of Mankind*, trans. Richard Winston and Clara Winston (Garden City, N.Y.: Doubleday, 1966), 20–29.

5. Edward Burnett Tylor, *Primitive Culture: Researches into the Development of Mythology, Philosophy, Religion, Language, Art and Custom*, 3d American ed., vol. 1 (New York: Henry Holt, 1889), 112–23.

6. See John Locke, *An Essay concerning Human Understanding*, ed. Peter H. Nidditch (Oxford: Clarendon, 1975), bk. II, chap. 33, 395–98; David Hume, *A Treatise of Human Nature*, 2d ed., ed. P. H. Nidditch (Oxford: Clarendon, 1978), 10–12; Hume, *Enquiries concerning Human Understanding and concerning the Principles of Morals*, 3d ed., ed. P. H. Nidditch (Clarendon, 1975), 23–24, 50–53; and Tylor, *Primitive Culture*, 1:119, 127–28.

7. Tylor, *Primitive Culture*, 1:133–35; and Tylor, "Magic," in *Encyclopaedia Britannica*, 9th ed., vol. 15, 199–206, quoted in Wouter J. Hanegraaff, "The Emergence of the Academic Science of Magic: The Occult Philosophy in Tylor and Frazer," in *Religion in the Making: The Emergence of the Sciences of Religion*, ed. Arie L. Molendijk and Peter Pels (Leiden: Brill, 1998), 265.

8. Frazer, *Golden Bough*, 10–12.

9. Ibid., 11–13, 22, 37–38.

10. Ibid., 49–50. For related discussions of this view of magic as primitive science, see Alfred Lyall, *Asiatic Studies*, 1st ser. (London: John Murray, 1899); and Jan de Vries, "Magic and Religion," *History of Religion* 1 (1962): 214–20.

11. Frazer, *Golden Bough*, 19–20, 46–50, 712–13.

12. Ibid., 47–48, 92, 711–12.

13. Ibid., 48–49, 51–52, 711. On Frazer's ambivalent respect for the role of magic and superstition in social development, see Robert Fraser, *The Making of* The Golden Bough: *The Origins and Growth of an Argument* (New York: St. Martin's, 1990), 131–33.

14. Frank Byron Jevons, *An Introduction to the Study of Comparative Religion* (New York: Macmillan, 1920), 71–72, 77; and Jevons, *An Introduction to the History of Religion*, 9th ed. (London: Methuen, 1927), 27–35. See also Gustav Jahoda, *The Psychology of Superstition* (London: Allen Lane/Penguin, 1969), 35, discussing Mill's influence on late nineteenth-century theories of magic; and Fraser, *Making of* The Golden Bough, 120–21, on the links between Jevons and Frazer.

15. Jevons, *Introduction to the History of Religion*, 36–38; and Jevons, *Introduction to the Study of Comparative Religion*, 74–75, 100.

16. Morris Jastrow Jr., *The Study of Religion* (London: Walter Scott, 1901), 103; Salomon Reinach, *Cultes, mythes, et religions*, vol. 2 (Paris: Ernest Leroux, 1909), xv; and W. H. R. Rivers, *Medicine, Magic, and Religion* (London: Kegan Paul, Trench, Trübner, 1924), 120–21. See also F. M. Cornford, *From Religion to Philosophy: A Study in the Origins of Western Speculation* (1912; reprint, Princeton, N.J.: Princeton University Press, 1991), 139–42, affirming the general agreement that science originates in

"the practical impulse which drives man to extend his power over Nature, an impulse which found its first collective expression in magic."

17. Alfred C. Haddon, *Magic and Fetishism* (Chicago: Open Court, [1906?]), 53, 57; and Irving King, *The Development of Religion: A Study in Anthropology and Social Psychology* (New York: Macmillan, 1910), 169, 178–79, 202.

18. See Marcel Mauss, *A General Theory of Magic*, trans. Robert Brain (London: Routledge and Kegan Paul, 1972), 63, 75–76.

19. Ibid., 90–93, 97, 140–41.

20. Ibid., 141–44.

21. Ibid., 108, 124–25, 137.

22. Wilhelm Wundt, *Elements of Folk Psychology: Outlines of a Psychological History of the Development of Mankind*, trans. Edward Leroy Schaub (London: George Allen and Unwin, 1916), 91–94. And see Jahoda, *Psychology of Superstition*, 36; at ibid., 39, Jahoda quotes Wundt's student Alfred Lehmann, *Aberglaube und Zauberei* (Stuttgart: Enke, 1898), 725: "All the superstitious beliefs, whose natural context we tried to demonstrate here, were at the beginning only false interpretations of phenomena more or less inadequately observed."

23. See Lucien Lévy-Bruhl, *Primitive Mentality*, trans. Lilian A. Clare (New York: Macmillan, 1923), 36; Lévy-Bruhl, *How Natives Think*, trans. Lilian A. Clare (London: G. Allen and Unwin, 1926); and Lévy-Bruhl, *Primitives and the Supernatural*, trans. Lilian Clare (New York: Dutton, 1935). And see William I. Thomas, *Primitive Behavior: An Introduction to the Social Sciences* (New York: McGraw-Hill, 1937), 784, pointing out that in this thesis of a prelogical savage mind, Lévy-Bruhl "uses no other data than those from the field of magic."

24. E. E. Evans-Pritchard, "Lévy-Bruhl's Theory of Primitive Mentality," *Bulletin of the Faculty of Arts* (Cairo) 2, no. 2 (1934): 6–7.

25. Ibid., 8–13; Lucien Lévy-Bruhl, "Notebook III, June–August 1938," in *The Notebooks on Primitive Mentality*, trans. Peter Rivière (New York: Harper and Row, 1975), 47–49; and ibid., "Notebook X, January 1939," 173. For Franz Boas's critique of the notion of distinctive mental functioning among primitives, see Franz Boas, *The Mind of Primitive Man* (New York: Macmillan, 1927), particularly 114–15, 123; and Boas, *Anthropology and Modern Life*, intro. Ruth Bunzel (New York: Dover, 1986), 227–28. See also G. E. R. Lloyd, *Demystifying Mentalities* (Cambridge: Cambridge University Press, 1990), particularly 69, 144.

26. See Jean Piaget, *The Child's Conception of the World*, trans. Joan Tomlinson and Andrew Tomlinson (New York: Harcourt, Brace, 1929), 131–62, 389–94, particularly 131–32, 161–62.

27. Erwin H. Ackerknecht, "Problems of Primitive Medicine," in *Reader in Comparative Religion: An Anthropological Approach*, 2d ed., ed. William A. Lessa and Evon Z. Vogt (New York: Harper and Row, 1965), 395–96.

28. Ibid., 396–97.

29. Ibid., 399–400.

30. Ibid., 397, 399–402.

31. Claude Lévi-Strauss, *The Savage Mind* (Chicago: University of Chicago Press, 1966), 10–13, 219–20, 263.

32. Jack R. Goody, *The Domestication of the Savage Mind* (Cambridge: Cambridge University Press, 1977); and Christopher Robert Hallspike, *The Foundations of Primi-*

tive Thought (Oxford: Clarendon, 1979), 126. See also in this regard various essays in Robin Horton, *Patterns of Thought in Africa and the West: Essays on Magic, Religion and Science* (Cambridge: Cambridge University Press, 1993).

33. Raoul Allier, *The Mind of the Savage*, trans. Fred Rothwell (New York: Harcourt, Brace, [1929]), 21, 28.

34. Ibid., 29–30, 44–49, 61, 75, 92.

35. Ibid., 212–17, 270–72.

36. Wilhelm Schmidt, *The Origin and Growth of Religion: Facts and Theories*, trans. H. J. Rose (London: Methuen, 1931), 133–36. Versions of Schmidt's argument proved extremely popular among evangelical Christians. See, for example, Gordon Hedderly Smith, *The Missionary and Anthropology: An Introduction to the Study of Primitive Man for Missionaries* (Chicago: Moody Press, 1945), 43–44, asserting that Schmidt's view conforms with the scriptural view "of creation in holiness and subsequent apostasy."

37. R. R. Marett, *Faith, Hope and Charity in Primitive Religion* (Oxford: Clarendon, 1932), 135–36; and Marett, "From Spell to Prayer," in *The Threshold of Religion*, 3d ed. (London: Methuen, 1914), 36–37, 44–50, 60. See also Robert H. Lowie, *Primitive Religion* (New York: Liveright, 1948), 140–48; and Hutton Webster, *Magic: A Sociological Study* (Stanford, Calif.: Stanford, University Press, 1948), vii, 1, 38–39, 497–501.

38. Bronislaw Malinowski, "Magic, Science and Religion," in *Magic, Science and Religion and Other Essays*, ed. Robert Redfield (Glencoe, Ill.: Free Press, 1948), 1, 8–11, 17–18; and Malinowski, "The Role of Magic and Religion," in *Reader in Comparative Religion* 103.

39. Malinowski, "Magic, Science and Religion," 12–18, 58–60. For discussions of the role of magic and witchcraft in Melanesian sailing and trading, see Malinowski, *Argonauts of the Western Pacific* (London: George Routledge, 1922); in sexual relations, Malinowski, *The Sexual Life of Savages in North-Western Melanesia* (New York: Halcyon House, 1929); and in agriculture and other aspects of life among the Trobrianders, Malinowski, *Coral Gardens and Their Magic: A Study of the Methods of Tilling the Soil and of Agricultural Rites in the Trobriand Islands*, 2 vols. (London: George Allen and Unwin, 1935), particularly 1:62–68, 435–51.

40. Malinowski, "Magic, Science and Religion," 51, 66–67; and Malinowski, *Coral Gardens and Their Magic*, 2:62–64.

41. Malinowski, "Role of Magic and Religion," 105–6; and Malinowski, "Magic, Science and Religion," 51, 65.

42. See A. L. Kroeber, *Anthropology: Race, Language, Culture, Psychology, Prehistory*, rev. ed. (New York: Harcourt, Brace and World, 1948), 308–10, 603–4. See also Ruth Benedict, "Magic," in *Encyclopedia of the Social Sciences*, ed. Edwin R. A. Seligman, vol. 10 (New York: Macmillan, 1935), 42; Elizabeth K. Nottingham, *Religion: A Sociological View* (New York: Random House, 1971), 89–90; and Mary Douglas, *Purity and Danger: An Analysis of Concepts of Pollution and Taboo* (London: Ark Paperbacks, 1984), 58–59.

43. J. H. Driberg, *At Home with the Savage* (London: George Routledge, 1932), 42–43, 190–98. See also in this regard Kurt Seligman, *Magic, Supernaturalism and Religion* (New York: Pantheon, 1948), 322.

44. Evans-Pritchard, "Lévy-Bruhl's Theory of Primitive Mentality," 30–36; E. E. Evans-Pritchard, "The Intellectualist (English) Interpretation of Magic," *Bulletin of the*

Faculty of Arts (Cairo) 1, no. 2 (1933): 302–3; Evans-Pritchard, *Theories of Primitive Religion* (Oxford: Clarendon, 1965), 28–29; Benedict, "Magic," 39–41; and Ruth Benedict, "Religion," in *General Anthropology*, ed. Franz Boas (Boston: Heath, 1938), 634–38. See also Paul Blumberg, "Magic in the Modern World," *Sociology and Social Research* 47 (1963): 147–60, applying Malinowski's analysis to the modern world.

45. Alexander A. Goldenweiser, *Anthropology: An Introduction to Primitive Culture* (New York: F. S. Crofts, 1937), 208–15; see also Goldenweiser, *Early Civilization: An Introduction to Anthropology* (New York: Knopf, 1922), 193–97. See also on this theme Rachel O. Moore, *Savage Theory: Cinema as Modern Magic* (Durham, N.C.: Duke University Press, 2000).

46. Goldenweiser, *Anthropology*, 216–17, 420–21; and Goldenweiser, *Early Civilization*, 232–34.

47. Peter Winch, "Understanding a Primitive Society," *American Philosophical Quarterly* 1 (1964): 308–9; Kai Nielsen, *An Introduction to the Philosophy of Religion* (New York: St. Martin's, 1982), 80; and E. E. Evans-Pritchard, *Witchcraft, Oracles, and Magic among the Azande*, intro. Eva Gillies (Oxford: Clarendon, 1976). For a perspective similar to Winch's on this issue, see D. Z. Phillips, *Religion without Explanation* (Oxford: Basil Blackwell, 1976), 100–121.

48. Nielsen, *Introduction to the Philosophy of Religion*, 81–88, 129. For further critique of Winch's position, see I. C. Jarvie, in Michael Winkelman, "Magic: A Theoretical Reassessment," *Current Anthropology* 23 (1982): 48–49.

49. John Beattie, "Sorcery in Bunyoro," in *Witchcraft and Sorcery in East Africa*, ed. John Middleton and E. H. Winter (New York: Praeger, 1963), 29; Beattie, "On Understanding Ritual," in *Rationality*, ed. Bryan R. Wilson (Oxford: Basil Blackwell, 1970), 240–68; and Beattie, *Other Cultures: Aims, Methods and Achievements in Social Anthropology* (London: Routledge and Kegan Paul, 1966). See also Michal Buchowski, "The Controversy concerning the Rationality of Magic," trans. Stanislawa Buchowski *Ethnologia Polona* 12 (1986): 157–67.

50. See, for example, Raymond Firth, "Problem and Assumption in an Anthropological Study of Religion," *Journal of the Royal Anthropological Institute* 89 (1959): 129–48; Firth, "The Sociology of Magic (1954)," in *Tikopia Ritual and Belief* (London: George Allen and Unwin, 1967), 195–212; Mary MacDonald, "Magic, Medicine and Sorcery," *Point Series* 6 (1984): 195–211; MacDonald, "An Interpretation of Magic," *Religious Traditions: A Journal in the Study of Religion* 7–9 (1984–86): 83–104; and MacDonald, "Magic and the Study of Religion," *Religiologiques* 11 (1995): 137–53.

51. Edmund Leach, "Magical Hair," in *Myth and Cosmos: Readings in Mythology and Symbolism*, ed. John Middleton (Garden City, N.Y.: Natural History Press, 1967), 77–108, particularly 106–7. See also Leach, "Virgin Birth," in *Proceedings of the Royal Anthropological Institute for 1966* (London: Royal Anthropological Institute, 1967), 39–49; and Leach, "The Epistemological Background to Malinowski's Empiricism," in *Man and Culture: An Evaluation of the Work of Bronislaw Malinowski*, ed. Raymond Firth (London: Routledge and Kegan Paul, 1957), 129.

52. See I. C. Jarvie and Joseph Agassi, "The Problem of the Rationality of Magic," *British Journal of Sociology* 18 (1967): 55–74; and Joseph Agassi and I. C. Jarvie, "Magic and Rationality Again," *British Journal of Sociology* 24 (1973): 237–43. For further discussions of this debate, see Tom Settle, "The Rationality of Science *versus*

The Rationality of Magic," *Philosophy of Social Science* 1 (1971): 173–94; Antony Flew, "Anthropology and Rationality," *Question* 5 (January 1972): 90–99; and I. C. Jarvie, *Rationality and Relativism* (London: Routledge and Kegan Paul, 1984). For other prominent critiques of the symbolist approach, see Steven Lukes, "Some Problems about Rationality," in *Rationality*, 194–213; J. D. Y. Peel, "Understanding Alien Belief Systems," *British Journal of Sociology* 20 (1969): 69–84; and John Skorupski, *Symbol and Theory: A Philosophical Study of Theories of Religion in Social Anthropology* (Cambridge: Cambridge University Press, 1976), 60–64, 125–59.

53. See Robin Horton, "African Traditional Thought and Modern Science," in *Rationality*, 131–71; and Horton, "Tradition and Modernity Revisited," in *Rationality and Relativism*, ed. Martin Hollis and Steven Lukes (Cambridge, Mass.: MIT Press, 1982), 201–60, particularly 208–9. For John Beattie's critique of Horton, see John Beattie, "Ritual and Social Change," *Man*, n.s., 1 (1966): 60–74; Beattie, "On Understanding Ritual"; and Beattie, "Understanding African Traditional Religion: A Comment on Horton," *Second Order* 2, no. 2 (1973): 3–11. For a critique of the ethnocentric nature of Horton's comparison of European and African thought, see Stanley J. Tambiah, "Form and Meaning of Magical Acts: A Point of View," in *Modes of Thought: Essays on Thinking in Western and Non-Western Societies*, ed. Robin Horton and Ruth Finnegan (London: Faber and Faber, 1973), 224–29.

54. Agassi and Jarvie, "Magic and Rationality Again," 244.

55. Lindberg, *Beginnings of Western Science*, 355. For a valuable overview of the historiography of the scientific revolution, see H. Floris Cohen, *The Scientific Revolution: A Historiographic Inquiry* (Chicago: University of Chicago Press, 1994).

56. See Lindberg, *Beginnings of Western Science*, 355–57.

57. Cohen, *Scientific Revolution*, 116–18; and Lindberg, *Beginnings of Western Science*, 357.

58. Charles Singer, "Preface," in *From Magic to Science: Essays on the Scientific Twilight* (New York: Dover, 1958), xxiii; and Marie Boas, *The Scientific Renaissance, 1450–1630* (New York: Harper, 1962), 323.

59. Preserved Smith, *A History of Modern Culture*, 2 vols. (New York: Henry Holt, 1930), 1:451–55, 2:545.

60. Bertrand Russell, *A History of Western Philosophy* (New York: Simon and Schuster, 1945), 527, 536.

61. Karl R. Popper, *Realism and the Aim of Science*, ed. W. W. Bartley III (Totowa, N.J.: Rowman and Littlefield, 1983), 212; and Popper, *The Myth of the Framework: In Defense of Science and Rationality*, ed. M. A. Notturno (London: Routledge, 1994), 199.

62. See Pierre Duhem, *Medieval Cosmology: Theories of Infinity, Place, Time, Void, and the Plurality of Worlds*, ed. and trans. Roger Ariew (Chicago: University of Chicago Press, 1985); Alfred North Whitehead, *Science and the Modern World* (New York: Macmillan, 1925), 18–19; and M. B. Foster, "The Christian Doctrine of Creation and the Rise of Modern Science," *Mind* 43 (1934): 446–68, cited in Willem B. Drees, *Religion, Science and Naturalism* (Cambridge: Cambridge University Press, 1996), 78. See also Stanley Jaki, *Science and Creation: From Eternal Cycles to an Oscillating Universe* (Edinburgh: Scottish Academic Press, 1974); and Lindberg, *Beginnings of Western Science*, 357.

63. Robert K. Merton, "Puritanism, Pietism, and Science," *Sociological Review* 28 (1936): 1–30; Merton, *Science, Technology and Society in Seventeenth-Century England* (New York: Harper, 1970), 136; and Drees, *Religion, Science and Naturalism*, 81–86. For a discussion of Merton's thesis and its limitations, see Eugene M. Klaaren, *Religious Origins of Modern Science: Belief in Creation in Seventeenth-Century Thought* (Grand Rapids, Mich.: Eerdmans, 1977), particularly 7–11. See also I. B. Cohen, *Puritanism and the Rise of Modern Science: The Merton Thesis* (New Brunswick, N.J.: Rutgers University Press, 1990); and Peter Harrison, *The Bible, Protestantism, and the Rise of Natural Science* (Cambridge: Cambridge University Press, 1998).

64. See Lindberg, *Beginnings of Western Science*, 357–60; Cohen, *Scientific Revolution;* Lynn Thorndike, "The Place of Magic in the Intellectual History of Europe," in *Studies in History, Economics and Public Law*, ed. Faculty of Political Science of Columbia University, vol. 24 (New York: Columbia University Press, 1905), 1–110; and Thorndike, *A History of Magic and Experimental Science*, 8 vols. (New York: Columbia University Press, 1923–58). For other early versions of this thesis, see A. D. White, *A History of the Warfare of Science with Theology in Christendom* (New York: D. Appleton, 1896); and Seligman, *Magic, Supernaturalism and Religion*.

65. See Frances A. Yates, *Giordano Bruno and the Hermetic Tradition* (London: Routledge and Kegan Paul, 1964), 447–49; Yates, "The Hermetic Tradition in Renaissance Science," in *Art, Science, and History in the Renaissance*, ed. Charles S. Singleton (Baltimore: Johns Hopkins University Press, 1967), 272; and Cohen, *Scientific Revolution*, 110–11, 169–83, 285–96.

66. See P. M. Rattansi, "The Social Interpretation of Science in the Seventeenth Century," in *Science and Society 1600–1900*, ed. Peter Mathias (London: Cambridge University Press, 1972), 1–32; Bert Hansen, "Science and Magic," in *Science in the Middle Ages*, ed. David C. Lindberg (Chicago: University of Chicago Press, 1975), 483–500; Allen Debus, *Man and Nature in the Renaissance* (Cambridge: Cambridge University Press, 1978); Charles Webster, *From Paracelsus to Newton: Magic and the Making of Modern Science* (Cambridge: Cambridge University Press, 1982); Karin Johannisson, "Magic, Science, and Institutionalization in the Seventeenth and Eighteenth Centuries," in *Hermeticism and the Renaissance: Intellectual History and the Occult in Early Modern Europe*, ed. Ingrid Merkel and Allen G. Debus (Washington, D.C.: Folger Shakespeare Library, 1988), 251–61; and H. P. Nebelsick, *The Renaissance, the Reformation and the Rise of Science* (Edinburgh: T. and T. Clark, 1992).

67. Brian Easlea, *Witch Hunting, Magic and the New Philosophy: An Introduction to Debates of the Scientific Revolution, 1450–1750* (Brighton, England: Harvester Press, 1980), 89–93.

68. Ibid., 90–106, 124–26, 131, 151.

69. Ibid., 110–11, 134–37, 192; and René Descartes, "Discourse on the Method," pt. 6, in *The Philosophical Writings of Descartes*, vol. 1, trans. John Cottingham, Robert Stoothoff, and Dugald Murdoch (Cambridge: Cambridge University Press, 1995), 142–43.

70. Easlea, *Witch Hunting, Magic and the New Philosophy*, 220–21, 236–41.

71. For an overview of Yates's subsequent writings on this theme and the critical debate concerning Yates's thesis, see Brian P. Copenhaver, "Natural Magic, Hermeticism, and Occultism in Early Modern Science," in *Reappraisals of the Scientific Revolu-*

tion, ed. David C. Lindberg and Robert S. Westman (Cambridge: Cambridge University Press, 1990), 260–301.

72. Brian Vickers, "Introduction," in *Occult and Scientific Mentalities in the Renaissance* (Cambridge: Cambridge University Press, 1984), 5–6. For examples of essays in *Occult and Scientific Mentalities in the Renaissance* more hospitable to the notion that occult traditions played a role in the formulation and spread of new scientific knowledge, see Mordechai Feingold, "The Occult Tradition in the English Universities of the Renaissance: A Reassessment," 73–94; Richard S. Westfall, "Newton and Alchemy," 315–36; and Lotte Mulligan, " 'Reason,' 'Right Reason,' and 'Revelation' in Mid-Seventeenth-Century England," 375–401.

73. Vickers, "Introduction," 2, 8, 13–15, 31–44; see also Brian Vickers, "Analogy versus Identity: The Rejection of Occult Symbolism, 1580–1680," in *Occult and Scientific Mentalities in the Renaissance*, 95–163.

74. Vickers, "Introduction," 7, 34–36; and Horton, "African Traditional Thought and Modern Science," 153.

75. Vickers, "Introduction," 9–13, 35–36.

76. Vickers, "Introduction," 36–38; and Horton, "African Traditional Thought and Modern Science," 162.

77. Vickers, "Introduction," 38–39; and Horton, "African Traditional Thought and Modern Science," 169.

78. Vickers, "Introduction," 7, 41–42; Vickers quotes the latter characterizations of science from Ernest Gellner, "The Savage and the Modern Mind," in *Modes of Thought*, 171.

79. Vickers, "Introduction," 42–43.

80. Gellner, "The Savage and the Modern Mind," 176, quoted at Vickers, "Introduction," 43.

81. Gellner, "The Savage and the Modern Mind," 178, quoted at Vickers, "Introduction," 43–44.

82. See in this regard Patrick Curry, "Revisions of Science and Magic," *History of Science* 23 (1985): 303–6.

83. Vickers, "Introduction," 41–42.

84. Ibid., 39.

85. Lindberg, *Beginnings of Western Science*, 360.

86. Cohen, *Scientific Revolution*, 170.

87. Ibid., 176.

88. Ibid., 182.

89. Vickers, "Introduction," 39.

90. See John Hermann Randall Jr., *The Making of the Modern Mind: A Survey of the Intellectual Background of the Present Age*, rev. ed. (Cambridge, Mass.: Riverside Press, 1940), 224.

91. William Cecil Dampier, *A History of Science and Its Relations with Philosophy and Religion*, 3d ed. (Cambridge: Cambridge University Press, 1943), 57, 376. For a recent version of this claim concerning the humility of science, see Robert L. Park, "Voodoo Medicine in a Scientific World," in *After the Science Wars*, ed. Keith M. Ashman and Philip S. Baringer (London: Routledge, 2001), 140–50.

92. Carol Urquhart-Ross, "Styles of Knowledge: Mysticism, Magic and Science" (Ph.D. diss., University of Alberta, 1977), 270–71.

CHAPTER 4

1. David Hume, *Enquiries concerning Human Understanding and concerning the Principles of Morals*, 3d ed., ed. P. H. Nidditch (Oxford: Clarendon, 1975), 198.

2. Ibid., 198–99.

3. Ibid., 199.

4. Ibid., 200–201 n. 1.

5. See, for example, Mary Douglas, *Purity and Danger: An Analysis of Concepts of Pollution and Taboo* (London: Ark Paperbacks, 1984), 69.

6. Edward Said, *Culture and Imperialism* (New York: Vintage, 1994), 12, 14, 78, 170.

7. See C. G. Jung, *Memories, Dreams, Reflections*, ed. Aniela Jaffé, trans. Richard Winston and Clara Winston (New York: Vintage, 1965), 150; and Alex Owen, "Occultism and the 'Modern' Self in *Fin-de-Siècle* Britain," in *Meanings of Modernity: Britain from the Late-Victorian Era to World War II*, ed. Martin Daunton and Bernhard Rieger (Oxford: Berg, 2001), 85–86.

8. Sigmund Freud, *Totem and Taboo: Some Points of Agreement between the Mental Lives of Savages and Neurotics*, trans. and ed. James Strachey (New York: Norton, 1989), 97–98. For a discussion of Freud's analysis of superstition in his 1904 *Psychopathology of Everyday Life*, see Gustav Jahoda, *The Psychology of Superstition* (London: Allen Lane/Penguin, 1969), 55–57; Freud there argues that superstitions reflect unconscious thoughts unacceptable to the consciousness that are thus attributed to the external world through projection. For further discussion of Freud's theories of the origin of religion, see Tomoko Masuzawa, *In Search of Dreamtime: The Quest for the Origin of Religion* (Chicago: University of Chicago Press, 1993), particularly 76–161.

9. Freud, *Totem and Taboo*, 99, 104–7 (emphasis in original).

10. Ibid., 110–15; and Frederick Schleiter, *Religion and Culture: A Critical Survey of Methods of Approach to Religious Phenomena* (New York: Columbia University Press, 1919), 119–20.

11. Freud, *Totem and Taboo*, 107–9, 114; and Edward Benson, *Money and Magic in Montaigne: The Historicity of the Essais* (Geneva: Librairie Droz, 1995), 180.

12. Alfred Storch, *The Primitive Archaic Forms of Inner Experiences and Thought in Schizophrenia*, trans. Clara Willard (New York: Nervous and Mental Disease Publishing Company, 1924), 37–39, 55, 60; Charles Odier, *Anxiety and Magical Thinking*, trans. Marie-Louise Schoelly and Mary Jane Sherfey (New York: International Universities Press, 1956), 57, 63–64, 301; and Erich Fromm, *Escape from Freedom* (New York: Avon, 1965), 196–201.

13. Heinz Werner, *Comparative Psychology of Mental Development*, rev. ed. (New York: International Universities Press, 1957), 337–38, 352.

14. Ibid., 339–43, 361.

15. Ibid., 344–48, 370–76. For other theorists asserting that magic and superstition turn on an inadequate conceptualization of the nature of materiality and the laws of causality, see Renée A. Spitz, "The Genesis of Magical and Transcendent Cults (From Freud's IMAGO, X)," trans. Hella Freud Bernays, *American Imago: A Psychoanalytic Journal for Culture, Science and the Arts* 29 (spring 1972): 4–7; and B. F. Skinner, "Superstition in the Pigeon," *Journal of Experimental Psychology* 38 (1948): 168–72.

16. Leonard Zusne and Warren H. Jones, *Anomalistic Psychology: A Study of Magical Thinking* (Hillsdale, N.J.: Erlbaum, 1989), 17, 20, 27, 32.

17. See Alexander A. Goldenweiser, *Early Civilization: An Introduction to Anthropology* (New York: Knopf, 1922), 395; and Ruth Benedict, "Magic," in *Encyclopedia of the Social Sciences*, ed. Edwin R. A. Seligman, vol. 10 (New York: Macmillan, 1935), 43.

18. Paul Radin, *Primitive Religion: Its Nature and Origin* (New York: Viking, 1937), 7–8, 25–30, 59–65, 150. See also Alexander Le Roy, *The Religion of the Primitives*, trans. Newton Thompson (New York: Macmillan, 1922), 218, stating that magic arises from "the primitive's . . . irresistible desire to satisfy his passions (which he shares with all humanity)."

19. Pamela Thurschwell, *Literature, Technology and Magical Thinking, 1880–1920* (Cambridge: Cambridge University Press, 2001), 6–7.

20. Géza Róheim, "The Origin and Function of Magic," in *Magic and Schizophrenia*, ed. Warner Muensterberger and S. H. Posinsky (New York: International Universities Press, 1955), 3, 10–11; and Róheim, *Psychoanalysis and Anthropology: Culture, Personality and the Unconscious* (New York: International Universities Press, 1950), 478. For Róheim's earlier compendium of magical practices, see Róheim, *Animism, Magic, and the Divine King* (London: Kegan Paul, Trench, Trübner, 1930), exploring particularly the role of castration anxiety in the development of magical practices.

21. Róheim, "Origin and Function of Magic," 44–47.

22. Ibid., 63, 81–82.

23. Ibid., 82–83 (emphasis deleted).

24. Jahoda, *Psychology of Superstition*, 9–10, 62, 134–35, 143–47; see also Zusne and Jones, *Anomalistic Psychology*, 242, rejecting what they see as Jahoda's relativism.

25. Ioan P. Couliano, *Eros and Magic in the Renaissance*, trans. Margaret Cook (Chicago: University of Chicago Press, 1987), xviii, 104, 124.

26. Ibid., 89–90, 104.

27. Jean-Paul Sartre, *The Emotions: Outline of a Theory*, trans. Bernard Frechtman (New York: Philosophical Library, 1948), 58–60, 75–76, 83–85.

28. Raoul Allier, *The Mind of the Savage*, trans. Fred Rothwell (New York: Harcourt, Brace, [1929]), x.

29. Edward Burnett Tylor, *Primitive Culture: Researches into the Development of Mythology, Philosophy, Religion, Language, Art and Custom*, vol. 1, 3d American ed. (New York: Henry Holt, 1889), 134.

30. Marcel Mauss, *A General Theory of Magic*, trans. Robert Brain (London: Routledge and Kegan Paul, 1972), 96–97; Bronislaw Malinowski, "Magic, Science and Religion," in *Magic, Science and Religion and Other Essays*, ed. Robert Redfield (Glencoe, Ill.: Free Press, 1948), 63, 68; and E. O. James, *Comparative Religion* (London: Methuen, 1938), 69.

31. Tylor, *Primitive Culture*, 1:133–34; and Frank Byron Jevons, *An Introduction to the Study of Comparative Religion* (New York: Macmillan, 1920), 75, 101–2.

32. Lindsay Dewar, *Magic and Grace* (London: Society for Promoting Christian Knowledge, 1929), 21, 24–26 n. 1, 29.

33. R. R. Marett, *Faith, Hope and Charity in Primitive Religion* (Oxford: Clarendon, 1932), 146–47.

34. Hutton Webster, *Magic: A Sociological Study* (Stanford, Calif.: Stanford University Press, 1948), 477–89, 499–501.

35. See E. William Monter, "La sodomie à l'époque moderne en Suisse romande," *Annales: Économies-sociétés-civilisations* 29 (1974): 1023–33; Norman Cohn, *Europe's Inner Demons: An Inquiry Inspired by the Great Witch Hunt* (New York: Basic Books, 1975), 16–125; E. William Monter, *Witchcraft in France and Switzerland: The Borderlands during the Reformation* (Ithaca, N.Y.: Cornell University Press, 1976), 118–41, 197; Christina Larner, *Enemies of God: The Witch-Hunt in Scotland* (London: Chatto and Windus, 1981), 51, 92–93, 102; and Retha M. Warnicke, "Sexual Heresy at the Court of Henry VIII," *Historical Journal* 30 (1987): 247–68.

36. Rudi C. Bleys, *The Geography of Perversion: Male-to-Male Sexual Behaviour outside the West and the Ethnographic Imagination, 1750–1918* (New York: New York University Press, 1995), 117–21, 169, 173, 190, 236.

37. Waldemar Bogoras, *The Chukchee*, ed. Franz Boas (Leiden: Brill, 1909), 415–16, 421, 426.

38. Ibid., 449–51.

39. Ibid., 451–52.

40. Ibid., 451, 453–55.

41. Ibid., 455.

42. Edward Westermarck, *The Origin and Development of the Moral Ideas*, 2d ed., (1912; reprint, New York: Johnson Reprint Corporation, 1971), 1:593 n. 1, 2:405–21, 2:564–65, 2:851.

43. Ibid., 2:458, 465, 484; see also ibid., 2:459 (concerning the *basir* of the Dyaks, "men who make their living by witchcraft and debauchery"); 2:472 (among the Kadiak, effeminate men were "held in repute by the people, most of them being wizards"); 2:477 (concerning the link between pederasty and sorcery among ancient Scandinavians); and 1:484 n. 1 (among the Patagonians, male wizards are chosen from among effeminate children who are "obliged, as it were, to leave their sex, and to dress themselves in female apparel").

44. Arnold Van Gennep, *The Rites of Passage*, trans. Monika B. Vizedom and Gabrielle L. Caffee, intro. Solon T. Kimball (Chicago: University of Chicago Press, 1960), 171–72.

45. Edward Carpenter, *Intermediate Types among Primitive Folk: A Study in Social Evolution* (London: George Allen, 1914), 16–54, particularly 12, 39–41. At ibid., 17–18, Carpenter quotes Reclus's description of the transformation of Inoit Choupans who often become magicians and priests: "Has a boy with a pretty face also a graceful demeanour? The mother no longer permits him to associate with companions of his own age, but clothes him and brings him up as a girl. Any stranger would be deceived as to his sex."

46. Ibid., 47–48, 59–60, 171–72.

47. Ruth Benedict, "Religion," in *General Anthropology*, ed. Franz Boas (New York: Heath, 1938), 649–50.

48. Alexander A. Goldenweiser, *Anthropology: An Introduction to Primitive Culture* (New York: F. S. Crofts, 1937), 249, 251, 259; and Webster, *Magic*, 191–93, 381.

49. Mircea Eliade, *Shamanism: Archaic Techniques of Ecstasy*, trans. Willard R. Trask (New York: Pantheon, 1964), 257–58.

50. See, for example, Herman Nunberg, *Practice and Theory of Psychoanalysis*

(New York: International Universities Press, 1948), 150–65; Erwin H. Ackerknecht, "Problems of Primitive Medicine," in *Reader in Comparative Religion: An Anthropological Approach*, 2d ed., ed. William A. Lessa and Evon Z. Vogt (New York: Harper and Row, 1965), 397; H. G. Quaritch Wales, *Prehistory and Religion in South-East Asia* (London: Bernard Quaritch, 1957), 72; Louis C. Faron, "Symbolic Values and the Integration of Society among the Mapuche of Chile," in *Myth and Cosmos: Readings in Mythology and Symbolism*, ed. John Middleton (Garden City, N.Y.: Natural History Press, 1967), 177–78; Roger Walsh, "The Psychological Health of Shamans: A Reevaluation," *Journal of the American Academy of Religion* 65 (1997): 101–24; Marjorie Mandelstam Balzer, "Sacred Genders in Siberia: Shamans, Bear Festivals, and Androgyny," in *Gender Reversals and Gender Cultures: Anthropological and Historical Perspectives*, ed. Sabrina Petra Ramet (London: Routledge, 1999); and Claudia Schiffer quoted in *The Advocate* (May 25, 1999): 10, concerning the popular connotations of magic: "People immediately think of Siegfrid and Roy. They just assume if someone is involved in magic that maybe they're gay."

51. Mauss, *General Theory of Magic*, 27–28. For an elaboration of this theme, see Claude Lévi-Strauss, "The Sorcerer and His Magic," in *Structural Anthropology*, trans. Claire Jacobson and Brooke Grundfest Schoepf (New York: Basic Books, 1963), 167–85.

52. Robert H. Lowie, *Primitive Religion* (New York: Liveright, 1948), 311; Radin, *Primitive Religion*, 106–7 (emphasis deleted), 154; E. Adamson Hoebel, *Man in the Primitive World: An Introduction to Anthropology* (New York: McGraw-Hill, 1949), 415; Carleton S. Coon, *The Story of Man: From the First Human to Primitive Culture and Beyond*, 2d ed. (New York: Knopf, 1962), 105–6; and Joachim Wach, *Sociology of Religion* (Chicago: University of Chicago Press, 1944), 354–55. See also in this regard E. O. James, *The Beginnings of Religion: An Introductory and Scientific Study* (London: Hutchinson's University Library, [1949]), 47.

53. Spitz, "Genesis of Magical and Transcendent Cults," 4–7; William Graham Sumner and Albert Galloway Keller, *The Science of Society* (New Haven, Conn.: Yale University Press, 1927), 1291; Arturo Castiglioni, *Adventures of the Mind*, trans. V. Gianturco (New York: Knopf, 1946), 62–74; Webster, *Magic*, 243; and T. P. Vukanovic, "Obscene Objects in Balkan Religion and Magic," *Folklore* 92 (1981): 43–53.

54. For a discussion of the broader modern dialectic of knowledge and concealment shaping such forms of rhetorical slippage, see Eve Kosofsky Sedgwick, *Epistemology of the Closet* (Berkeley: University of California Press, 1990).

55. See also Ruth Benedict, "Anthropology and the Abnormal," in *An Anthropologist at Work: Writings of Ruth Benedict*, ed. Margaret Mead (Boston: Houghton Mifflin, 1959), 262–83, particularly 267–68.

56. Herbert Spencer, *Principles of Sociology*, abridged ed., ed. Stanislav Andreski (Hamden, Conn.: Archon Books, 1969), 270–73; and Spencer, *On Social Evolution: Selected Writings*, ed. J. D. Y. Peel (Chicago: University of Chicago Press, 1972), 222–23.

57. James George Frazer, *The Golden Bough: A Study in Magic and Religion*, abridged ed. (New York: Macmillan, 1922), 45–47; and Frazer, *The Devil's Advocate: A Plea for Superstition* (London: Macmillan, 1927), 4.

58. Frazer, *Golden Bough*, 47–48, 59–60; and Frazer, *Devil's Advocate*, 4, 20–43.

59. Wilhelm Wundt, *Elements of Folk Psychology: Outlines of a Psychological His-*

tory of the Development of Mankind, trans. Edward Leroy Schaub (London: George Allen and Unwin, 1916), 84–85, 94–109. See also Yrjö Hirn, *The Origins of Art: A Psychological and Sociological Inquiry* (London: Macmillan, 1900); Webster, *Magic*, 501–2; Harry Holbert Turney-High, *General Anthropology* (New York: Crowell, 1949), 118–19; and Pascual Gisbert, *Preliterate Man: A Synthetic View of "Primitive" Man* (Bombay: Manaktalas, 1967), 132.

60. Webster, *Magic*, 262–66, 279, 290–93.

61. Charles Singer, "Preface," in *From Magic to Science: Essays on the Scientific Twilight* (New York: Dover, 1958), xxi.

62. Tylor, *Primitive Culture*, 1:156–57.

63. Bronislaw Malinowski, "The Role of Magic and Religion," in *Reader in Comparative Religion: An Anthropological Approach*, 2d ed., ed. William A. Lessa and Evon Z. Vogt (New York: Harper and Row, 1965), 110; and Goldenweiser, *Anthropology*, 218, 420 n. 11. See also Keith Thomas, *Religion and the Decline of Magic* (New York: Scribner, 1971), 566; Elizabeth K. Nottingham, *Religion: A Sociological View* (New York: Random House, 1971), 162; Johnnetta B. Cole, ed., *Anthropology for the Eighties: Introductory Readings* (New York: Free Press, 1982), 369 (citing 1950s McCarthyism as an example of a witch-hunt aimed at preserving the social status quo); and Ronald L. Grimes, *Beginnings in Ritual Studies* (Lanham, Md.: University Press of America, 1982), 47.

64. W. Robertson Smith, *Lectures on the Religion of the Semites: The Fundamental Institutions*, 3d. ed., intro. Stanley A. Cook (New York: Macmillan, 1927), 154; and Edwin Sidney Hartland, *Ritual and Belief: Studies in the History of Religion* (London: Williams and Norgate, 1914), 15, 159 (quoting John H. Weeks, *Among Congo Cannibals: Experiences, Impressions and Adventures during a Thirty Years' Sojourn amongst the Boloki and Other Congo Tribes* [London: Seeley, Service and Co., 1913], 177). See also in this regard Nottingham, *Religion*, 90–91; and Thomas, *Religion and the Decline of Magic*, 539–40.

65. Webster, *Magic*, 455–59 (also citing Weeks's *Among Congo Cannibals*), 506–7.

66. Sumner and Keller, *Science of Society*, 1324; and John J. Honigmann, *The World of Man* (New York: Harper and Row, 1959), 152–53, 189, 685–88.

67. See John Hick, *An Interpretation of Religion: Human Responses to the Transcendent* (New Haven, Conn.: Yale University Press, 1989), 23; and Maureen Perkins, *The Reform of Time: Magic and Modernity* (London: Pluto Press, 2001).

68. Nathan Söderblom, *The Living God: Basal Forms of Personal Religion* (London: Oxford University Press/Humphrey Milford, 1933), 33. See also in this regard William Butler Yeats, "Magic," in *Ideas of Good and Evil* (London: Bullen, 1903), 49, 66, where Yeats describes magic as the province of "those lean and fierce minds who are at war with their time, who cannot accept the days as they pass, simply and gladly."

69. Webster, *Magic*, 373; and Irving King, *The Development of Religion: A Study in Anthropology and Social Psychology* (New York: Macmillan, 1910), 195. See also Victor Turner, "Witchcraft and Sorcery: Taxonomy versus Dynamics," *Africa* 34 (1964): 324.

70. Godfrey Lienhardt, "Some Notions of Witchcraft among the Dinka," *Africa* 21 (1951): 317.

71. Max Weber, *General Economic History*, trans. Frank H. Knight (Glencoe, Ill.: Free Press, 1950), 322–23, 354–56, 360–69. See also Roger O'Toole, *Religion: Classic Sociological Approaches* (Toronto: McGraw-Hill Ryerson, 1984), 141–42; Derek Sayer,

Capitalism and Modernity: An Excursus on Marx and Weber (London: Routledge, 1991), 112–13; and Talcott Parsons, *The Structure of Social Action*, 2d ed. (New York: Free Press, 1949), 565–66, 673–74.

72. Tylor, *Primitive Culture*, 1:112.

73. Frazer, *Golden Bough*, 11, 41–43, 62–63; and James George Frazer, *The Magical Origin of Kings* (London: Macmillan, 1920), 78. For further examples of magical practices within contemporary Europe, see Frazer, *Golden Bough*, 16–19, 28–45, 239–40.

74. Frazer, *Golden Bough*, 55–56; and James George Frazer, *Man, God and Immortality: Thoughts on Human Progress* (London: Macmillan, 1927), 218–19.

75. See Malinowski, "Magic, Science and Religion," 50; and Malinowski, "Role of Magic and Religion," 105.

76. Benedict, "Magic," 41. See also William Howells, *The Heathens: Primitive Man and His Religions* (Garden City, N.Y.: Doubleday, 1948), 51, stating with regard to contemporary magic: "This business goes on today in our own country and in Europe (I understand that the Balkans take most of the ribbons)."

77. Mauss, *General Theory of Magic*, 138–39. See also Nottingham, *Religion*, 103–4, concerning the persistence of magic in modern technological society particularly in areas relating to "the hazards of economic arrangements, status striving, and job security." For exploration of magic as an index of social pressures on individuals, see Daniel Lawrence O'Keefe, *Stolen Lightning: The Social Theory of Magic* (New York: Continuum, 1982), 414–57.

78. Franz Neumann, *Behemoth: The Structure and Practice of National Socialism 1933–44* (Toronto: Oxford University Press, 1944), 95–97, 439; Castiglioni, *Adventures of the Mind*, 63–68, 112–17, 405–16; Louis Pauwels and Jacques Bergier, *The Morning of the Magicians*, trans. Rollo Myers (New York: Stein and Day, 1963), 173–82 (particularly 196, asserting that the swastika has always been considered a magic sign); and Nicholas Goodrick-Clarke, *The Occult Roots of Nazism* (New York: New York University Press, 1985), 217–25. See also Nottingham, *Religion*, 103–4; and V. R. Padgett and D. O. Jorgenson, "Superstition and Economic Threat: Germany, 1918–1940," *Personality and Social Psychology Bulletin* 8 (1982): 736–41.

79. See Theodor W. Adorno, "The Stars Down to Earth: The *Los Angeles Times* Astrology Column," in *The Stars Down to Earth and Other Essays on the Irrational in Culture*, ed. Stephen Crook (New York: Routledge, 1994), 34–35; and Stephen Crook, "Introduction: Adorno and Authoritarian Irrationalism," in Adorno, *Stars Down to Earth*, 1–33. See also Theodor W. Adorno, Else Frenkel-Brunswik, Daniel J. Levinson, and R. Nevitt Sanford, *The Authoritarian Personality* (New York: Harper and Row, 1950); and Max Horkheimer and Theodor W. Adorno, *Dialectic of Enlightenment* (New York: Continuum, 1993), 3–42, 120–67.

80. Adorno, "Stars Down to Earth," 38, 41, 51–59, 111–14 (emphasis in original); and Theodor Adorno, "Theses against Occultism," in *Minima Moralia: Reflections from Damaged Life*, trans. E. F. N. Jephcott (London: NLB, 1974), 240.

81. Raymond Williams, "Advertising: The Magic System," in *Problems in Materialism and Culture* (London: Verso, 1980), 185–89. For other commentaries on the perverse magic of advertising, see Nottingham, *Religion*, 104; and Grimes, *Beginnings in Ritual Studies*, 47. See also Pierre Bourdieu, "The Production of Belief: Contribution to an Economy of Symbolic Goods," in *The Field of Cultural Production: Essays on Art*

and Literature, ed. and intro. Randal Johnson (New York: Columbia University Press, 1993), 81, concerning the magic of contemporary art markets.

82. Stephen R. L. Clark, *The Mysteries of Religion: An Introduction to Philosophy through Religion* (Oxford: Basil Blackwell, 1986), 53–56. For a related recent argument see Richard Stivers, *Technology as Magic: The Triumph of the Irrational* (New York: Continuum, 1999).

83. Tylor, *Primitive Culture*, 1:113.

84. Ibid., 1:113–15.

85. Mauss, *General Theory of Magic*, 28–32, 40, 120–21.

86. P. D. Chantepie de la Saussaye, *Manual of the Science of Religion*, trans. Beatrice S. Colyer-Fergusson (London: Longmans, Green, 1891), 132; and Westermarck, *Origin and Development of the Moral Ideas*, 1:584, 619–20, 666–69, 715–16. See also King, *Development of Religion*, 197; and A. L. Kroeber, *Anthropology: Race, Language, Culture, Psychology, Prehistory*, rev. ed. (New York: Harcourt, Brace and World, 1948), 298, 380; and G. E. R. Lloyd, *Demystifying Mentalities* (Cambridge: Cambridge University Press, 1990), 40–44.

87. Max Weber, *The Sociology of Religion*, trans. Ephraim Fischoff (Boston: Beacon Press, 1964), 80–117 (particularly 89, 98–102, 108), 124–25. See also Talcott Parsons, "Introduction," in Weber, *Sociology of Religion*, xl; and Max Weber, "The Social Psychology of the World Religions," in *From Max Weber: Essays in Sociology*, ed. and trans. Hans H. Gerth and C. Wright Mills (New York: Oxford University Press, 1946), 267–301. Weber's theme of religion as a compensatory response for deprived peoples has been amplified by Weber's successors in the sociology of religion. See, for example, Charles Y. Glock, "The Role of Deprivation in the Origin and Evolution of Religious Groups," in *Religion and Social Conflict*, ed. Robert Lee and Martin E. Marty (New York: Oxford University Press, 1964), 24–26; and Charles Y. Glock, B. B. Ringer, and E. R. Babbie, *To Comfort and to Challenge* (Berkeley: University of California Press, 1967).

88. Thomas, *Religion and the Decline of Magic*, 520–22, 533, 561.

89. David Hume, "The Natural History of Religion," in *Writings on Religion*, ed. Antony Flew (La Salle, Ill.: Open Court, 1992), 119.

90. Voltaire, "Questions sur l'Encyclopédie," quoted by Gábor Klaniczay, "The Decline of Witches and the Rise of Vampires under the Eighteenth-Century Habsburg Monarchy," in *The Uses of Supernatural Power: The Transformation of Popular Religion in Medieval and Early-Modern Europe*, ed. Gábor Klaniczay (Oxford: Polity Press, 1990), 187. And see Voltaire, "Vampires," in *A Philosophical Dictionary*, vol. 10, in *The Works of Voltaire: A Contemporary Version*, vol. 14, trans. William F. Fleming (Paris: E. R. DuMont, 1901), 144.

91. J. H. Driberg, *At Home with the Savage* (London: George Routledge, 1932), 199.

92. Ibid., 200–201.

93. Webster, *Magic*, 504–6.

94. See as examples Allier, *Mind of the Savage*; and Gordon Hedderly Smith, *The Missionary and Anthropology: An Introduction to the Study of Primitive Man for Missionaries* (Chicago: Moody Press, 1945).

95. Bleys, *Geography of Perversion*, 267–68.

96. See Perkins, *Reform of Time*.

97. Said, *Culture and Imperialism*, 7. See also Ira J. Cohen, *Structuration Theory* (New York: St. Martin's, 1989); Anthony Giddens, *Consequences of Modernity* (Stanford, Calif.: Stanford University Press, 1990); Timothy Mitchell, *Colonising Egypt* (Berkeley: University of California Press, 1991), 34–94; and Roger Friedland and Deirdre Boden, "NowHere: An Introduction to Space, Time and Modernity," in *NowHere: Space, Time and Modernity*, ed. Roger Friedland and Deirdre Boden (Berkeley: University of California Press, 1994), 29–32.

98. See Tylor, *Primitive Culture*, 1:118–19, 156.

99. G. W. F. Hegel, *Lectures on the Philosophy of Religion: The Lectures of 1827*, ed. Peter C. Hodgson, trans. R. F. Brown, P. C. Hodgson, and J. M. Stewart (Berkeley: University of California Press, 1988), 201–3 (emphasis in original).

100. See Marshall Berman, *All That Is Solid Melts into Air: The Experience of Modernity* (New York: Simon and Schuster, 1982), 15.

101. See Gilles Deleuze and Félix Guattari, *A Thousand Plateaus: Capitalism and Schizophrenia*, trans. Brian Massumi (Minneapolis: University of Minnesota Press, 1987), 490–92.

102. Friedland and Boden, "NowHere," 37.

103. E. P. Thompson, "Anthropology and the Discipline of Historical Context," *Midland History* 1, no. 3 (spring 1972): 51–54.

104. Donate Pahnke, "Religion and Magic in the Modern Cults of the Great Goddess," in *Religion and Gender*, ed. Ursula King (Oxford: Blackwell, 1995), 173–74.

105. See David Farren, *The Return of Magic* (New York: Harper and Row, 1972), 101, 103; and Ariel Glucklich, *The End of Magic* (New York: Oxford University Press, 1997), 12, 22, 97–117. For related arguments, see Catharine Cook Smith, *In Defense of Magic: The Meaning and Use of Symbol and Rite* (New York: Dial Press, 1930); Tanya Luhrmann, *The Persuasions of the Witch's Craft* (Oxford: Oxford University Press, 1989); Theophus H. Smith, *Conjuring Culture: Biblical Formations of Black America* (New York: Oxford University Press, 1994); Paul Heelas, *The New Age Movement* (Oxford: Blackwell, 1996), particularly 25–26; and B. J. Gibbons, *Spirituality and the Occult: From the Renaissance to the Modern Age* (London: Routledge, 2001).

106. See Wouter J. Hanegraaff, *New Age Religion and Western Culture: Esotericism in the Mirror of Secular Thought* (Leiden: Brill, 1996), 84. See also Stanley Diamond, *In Search of the Primitive: A Critique of Civilization*, forward by Eric R. Wolf (New Brunswick, N.J.: Transaction, 1974), 139; and Jean Comaroff and John L. Comaroff, "Introduction," in *Modernity and Its Malcontents: Ritual and Power in Postcolonial Africa*, ed. Jean Comaroff and John L. Comaroff (Chicago: University of Chicago Press, 1993), xi–xxxvii.

107. Michael Taussig, *Shamanism, Colonialism, and the Wild Man: A Study in Terror and Healing* (Chicago: University of Chicago Press, 1987), xiii, 211.

108. Ibid., xiv, 37, 99–200. See also Michael Taussig, "Reification and the Consciousness of the Patient," in *The Nervous System* (New York: Routledge, 1992), 83–88; Taussig, "The Rise and Fall of Marxist Anthropology," *Social Analysis* 21 (August 1987): 110–11; and Georg Lukács, "Reification and the Consciousness of the Proletariat," in *History and Class Consciousness: Studies in Marxist Dialectics*, trans. Rodney Livingstone (Cambridge, Mass.: MIT Press, 1971), 93–99, 114–21.

109. Taussig, *Shamanism*, 10 (paraphrasing Frederick R. Karl, *Joseph Conrad: The Three Lives* [New York: Farrar, Straus and Giroux, 1979], 286 [emphasis in *Shamanism*]), 473.

110. Lawrence Grossberg, "The Space of Culture, the Power of Space," in *The Post-colonial Question: Common Skies, Divided Horizons*, ed. Iain Chambers and Lidia Curti (London: Routledge, 1996), 184–86.

CONCLUSION

1. Ernst Cassirer, *The Philosophy of Symbolic Forms*, vol. 2, *Mythical Thought*, trans. Ralph Manheim (New Haven, Conn.: Yale University Press, 1955), 24, 68, 221–24. For a critique of Cassirer's view of magical language, see Stanley J. Tambiah, "The Magical Power of Words," *Man*, n.s., 3 (1968): 175–208, particularly 187–88, 202, where Tambiah rejects Cassirer's claim that primitive magic is based on "the belief in a real identity between word and thing," and argues instead that such magic represents "true, relational metaphorical thinking." In magic, Tambiah states, the "savage mind . . . ingeniously conjoins the expressive and metaphorical qualities of language with the operational and empirical properties of technical activity."

2. Leonard Zusne and Warren H. Jones, *Anomalistic Psychology: A Study of Magical Thinking* (Hillsdale, N.J.: Erlbaum, 1989), 17–27. For a rich elaboration of magic as based on the power of words, see Raymond Firth, "The Sociology of Magic (1954)," in *Tikopia Ritual and Belief* (London: George Allen and Unwin, 1967), 195–212.

3. See Thomas M. Greene, "Language, Signs and Magic," in *Envisioning Magic: A Princeton Seminar and Symposium*, ed. Peter Schäfer and Hans G. Kippenberg (Leiden: Brill, 1997), 255–72, quoting Reginald Scot, *The Discoverie of Witchcraft*, ed. Montague Summers (1930; reprint, New York: Dover, 1972), 189, and William Perkins, *A Discourse of the Damned Art of Witchcraft* in *Works* (London: James Boler, 1631), 3: 631.

4. W. J. Perry, *The Origin of Magic and Religion* (London: Methuen, 1923), 8; William Graham Sumner and Albert Galloway Keller, *The Science of Society* (New Haven, Conn.: Yale University Press, 1927), 1317; William Howells, *The Heathens: Primitive Man and His Religions* (Garden City, N.Y.: Doubleday, 1948), 47–48; Werner Stark, *The Sociology of Religion: A Study of Christendom*, vol. 4 (New York: Fordham University Press, 1970), 240; and Morton Klass, *Ordered Universes: Approaches to the Anthropology of Religion* (Boulder, Colo.: Westview, 1995), 89.

5. Timothy Mitchell, *Colonising Egypt* (Berkeley: University of California Press, 1988), 79.

6. Bruno Latour, *The Pasteurization of France*, trans. Alan Sheridan and John Law (Cambridge, Mass.: Harvard University Press, 1988), 180.

7. Alexander Le Roy, *The Religion of the Primitives*, trans. Newton Thompson (New York: Macmillan, 1922), 298; and Howells, *Heathens*, 48.

8. Frank Byron Jevons, An *Introduction to the Study of Comparative Religion* (New York: Marmillan, 1920), 70; and Howells, *Heathens*, 47.

9. Ruth Benedict, "Magic," in *Encyclopedia of the Social Sciences*, ed. Edwin R. A. Seligman, vol. 10 (New York: Macmillan, 1935), 42; and Tom F. Driver, *The Magic of Ritual: Our Need for Liberating Rites That Transform Our Lives and Our Communities*

(San Francisco: HarperSanFrancisco, 1991), 168–76. See also in this regard Catharine Cook Smith, *In Defense of Magic: The Meaning and Use of Symbol and Rite* (New York: Dial Press, 1930); and Síân Reid, "As I Do Will, So Mote It Be: Magic as Metaphor in Neo-Pagan Witchcraft," in *Magical Religion and Modern Witchcraft*, ed. James R. Lewis (Albany: State University of New York Press, 1996), 141–67.

10. Latour, *Pasteurization of France*, 209.

Selected Bibliography

Ackerknecht, Erwin H. "Problems of Primitive Medicine." In *Reader in Comparative Religion: An Anthropological Approach*, 2d ed., ed. William A. Lessa and Evon Z. Vogt, 395–402. New York: Harper and Row, 1965.

Adorno, Theodor. *Minima Moralia: Reflections from Damaged Life*. Translated by E. F. N. Jephcott. London: NLB, 1974.

———. *The Stars Down to Earth and Other Essays on the Irrational in Culture.* Edited by Stephen Crook. London: Routledge, 1994.

Agassi, Joseph, and I. C. Jarvie. "Magic and Rationality Again." *British Journal of Sociology* 24 (1973): 236–45.

———, eds. *Rationality: The Critical View*. Dordrecht: Martinus Nijhoff, 1987.

Allier, Raoul. *The Mind of the Savage*. Translated by Fred Rothwell. New York: Harcourt, Brace, [1929].

Anglo, Sidney, ed. *The Damned Art: Essays in the Literature of Witchcraft*. London: Routledge and Kegan Paul, 1977.

Ankarloo, Bengt, and Stuart Clark, eds. *Witchcraft and Magic in Europe: The Twentieth Century*. Philadelphia: University of Pennsylvania Press, 1999.

Ankarloo, Bengt, and Gustav Henningsen, eds. *Early Modern European Witchcraft: Centres and Peripheries*. Oxford: Clarendon, 1990.

Apter, Emily, and William Pietz, eds. *Fetishism as Cultural Discourse*. Ithaca, N.Y.: Cornell University Press, 1993.

Bacon, Francis. *The Works of Francis Bacon*. Edited by James Spedding, Robert Leslie Ellis, and Douglas Denon Heath. 15 vols. London: Longman, 1857–74.

Baird, Robert J. "How Religion Became Scientific." In *Religion in the Making: The Emergence of the Sciences of Religion*, ed. Arie L. Molendijk and Peter Pels, 205–29. Leiden: Brill, 1998.

Barstow, Anne Llewellyn. *Witchcraze: A New History of the European Witch Hunts.* San Francisco: Pandora/HarperCollins, 1994.

Beattie, John H. M. "Sorcery in Bunyoro." In *Witchcraft and Sorcery in East Africa,* ed. John Middleton and E. H. Winter, 27–55. New York: Praeger, 1963.

———. "Ritual and Social Change." *Man,* n.s., 1 (1966): 60–74.

———. "On Understanding Ritual." In *Rationality,* ed. Bryan R. Wilson, 240–68. Oxford: Basil Blackwell, 1970.

———. "Understanding Traditional African Religion: A Comment on Horton." *Second Order* 2, no. 2 (1973): 3–11.

Bellah, Robert N. *Beyond Belief: Essays on Religion in a Post-traditional World.* New York: Harper and Row, 1970.

Benavides, Gustavo. "Magic, Religion, Materiality." *Historical Reflections/Réflexions Historiques* 23 (1997): 301–30.

———. "Modernity." In *Critical Terms for Religious Studies,* ed. Mark C. Taylor, 186–204. Chicago: University of Chicago Press, 1998.

Benedict, Ruth. "Magic." In *Encyclopedia of the Social Sciences,* ed. Edwin R. A. Seligman, 10:39–44. New York: Macmillan, 1935.

———. "Religion." In *General Anthropology,* ed. Franz Boas, 627–65. New York: Heath, 1938.

———. *An Anthropologist at Work: Writings of Ruth Benedict.* Edited by Margaret Mead. Boston: Houghton Mifflin, 1959.

Bernal, Martin. *Black Athena: The Afroasiatic Roots of Classical Civilization.* Vol. 1, *The Fabrication of Ancient Greece 1785–1985.* New Brunswick, N.J.: Rutgers University Press, 1987.

Betts, Raymond R. *Europe Overseas: Phases of Imperialism.* New York: Basic Books, 1968.

Bleys, Rudi C. *The Geography of Perversion: Male-to-Male Sexual Behaviour outside the West and the Ethnographic Imagination, 1750–1918.* New York: New York University Press, 1995.

Boas, Marie. *The Scientific Renaissance 1450–1630: The Rise of Modern Science.* New York: Harper; 1962.

Bogoras, Waldemar. *The Chuckchee.* Edited by Franz Boas. Leiden: Brill, 1909.

Bovenschen, Silvia. "The Contemporary Witch, the Historical Witch and the Witch Myth: The Witch Subject of the Appropriation of Nature and Object of the Domination of Nature." *New German Critique* 15 (fall 1978): 83–119.

Brann, Noel L. "The Proto-Protestant Assault upon Church Magic: The 'Errores Bohemanorum' according to the Abbott Trithemius (1462–1516)." *Journal of Religious History* 12 (June 1982): 9–22.

Briggs, Robin. *Witches and Neighbors: The Social and Cultural Context of European Witchcraft.* New York: Penguin, 1996.

Brink, Jean R., Allison P. Coudert, and Maryanne C. Horowitz, eds. *The Politics of Gender in Early Modern Europe.* Kirksville, Mo.: Sixteenth Century Journal Publishers, 1989.

Brinton, Daniel Garrison. *Religions of Primitive Peoples.* 1897. Reprint, New York: Negro Universities Press, 1969.

Buchowski, Michal. "The Controversy concerning the Rationality of Magic." Translated by Stanislawa Buchowski. *Ethnologia Polona* 12 (1986): 157–67.

Buckley, Michael J. *At the Origins of Modern Atheism*. New Haven, Conn.: Yale University Press, 1987.

Carpenter, Edward. *Intermediate Types among Primitive Folk: A Study in Social Evolution*. London: George Allen, 1914.

Cassirer, Ernst. *The Philosophy of Symbolic Forms*. Vol. 2, *Mythical Thought*. Translated by Ralph Manheim. New Haven, Conn.: Yale University Press, 1955.

Chantepie de la Saussaye, P. D. *Manual of the Science of Religion*. Translated by Beatrice S. Colyer-Fergusson. London: Longmans, Green, 1891.

Child, Alice B., and Irvin L. Child. *Religion and Magic in the Life of Traditional Peoples*. Englewood Cliffs, N.J.: Prentice-Hall, 1993.

Clark, Stephen R. L. *The Mysteries of Religion: An Introduction to Philosophy through Religion*. Oxford: Basil Blackwell, 1986.

Clark, Stuart. *Thinking with Demons: The Idea of Witchcraft in Early Modern Europe*. Oxford: Clarendon, 1997.

Cohen, H. Floris. *The Scientific Revolution: A Historiographic Inquiry*. Chicago: University of Chicago Press, 1994.

Cohen, I. B. *Puritanism and the Rise of Modern Science: The Merton Thesis*. New Brunswick, N.J.: Rutgers University Press, 1990.

Cohn, Norman. *Europe's Inner Demons: An Inquiry Inspired by the Great Witch Hunt*. New York: Basic Books, 1975.

Comte, Auguste. *The Positive Philosophy of Auguste Comte*. 2 vols. 3d ed. Translated by Harriet Martineau. London: Kegan Paul, Trench, Trübner, 1893.

Condorcet, Marquis de. *Esquisse d'un tableau historique des progrès de l'esprit humain*. Introduction by Alain Pons. Paris: GF Flammarion, 1988.

Cook, Stanley A. *The Study of Religions*. London: Adam and Charles Black, 1914.

Copenhaver, Brian P. "Natural Magic, Hermeticism, and Occultism in Early Modern Science." In *Reappraisals of the Scientific Revolution*, ed. David C. Lindberg and Robert S. Westman, 261–301. Cambridge: Cambridge University Press, 1990.

Couliano, Ioan P. *Eros and Magic in the Renaissance*. Translated by Margaret Cook. Chicago: University of Chicago Press, 1987.

Cunningham, Graham. *Religion and Magic: Approaches and Theories*. New York: New York University Press, 1999.

Curtin, Philip D., ed. *Imperialism*. New York: Harper and Row, 1971.

Dampier, William Cecil. *A History of Science and Its Relations with Philosophy and Religion*. 3d ed. Cambridge: Cambridge University Press, 1943.

Debus, Allen. *Man and Nature in the Renaissance*. Cambridge: Cambridge University Press, 1978.

Delumeau, Jean. "Les réformateurs et la superstition." In *Actes du Colloque L'Amiral de Coligny et son temps*, 451–87. Paris: Société de L'Histoire du Protestantisme Français, 1974.

———. *Catholicism between Luther and Voltaire: A New View of the Counter-Reformation*. Introduction by John Bossy. Translated by J. Moiser. London: Burns and Oates, 1977.

Descartes, René. *The Philosophical Writings of Descartes*. 2 vols. Translated by John Cottingham, Robert Stoothoff, and Dugald Murdoch. Cambridge: Cambridge University Press, 1995.

De Vries, Jan. "Magic and Religion." *History of Religions* 1 (1962): 214–21.

Douglas, Mary. *Purity and Danger: An Analysis of Concepts of Pollution and Taboo.* London: Ark Paperbacks, 1984.

Dressler, Horatio W. *Outlines of the Psychology of Religion.* New York: Crowell, 1929.

Driberg, J. H. *At Home with the Savage.* London: George Routledge, 1932.

Driver, Tom F. *The Magic of Ritual: Our Need for Liberating Rites That Transform Our Lives and Our Communities.* San Francisco: HarperSanFrancisco, 1991.

During, Simon. *Modern Enchantments: The Cultural Power of Secular Magic.* Cambridge, Mass.: Harvard University Press, 2002.

Durkheim, Émile. *The Elementary Forms of Religious Life.* Translated by Joseph Ward Swain. New York: Free Press, 1965.

Easlea, Brian. *Witch Hunting, Magic and the New Philosophy: An Introduction to Debates of the Scientific Revolution, 1450–1750.* Brighton, England: Harvester Press, 1980.

Ehnmark, Erland. "Religion and Magic—Frazer, Söderblom, and Hägerström." *Ethos* 21, nos. 1–2 (1956): 1–10.

Eilberg-Schwartz, Howard. "Witches of the West: Neopaganism and Goddess Worship as Enlightenment Religions." *Journal of Feminist Studies in Religion* 5 (1989): 77–95.

Eliade, Mircea. *Patterns in Comparative Religion.* Translated by Rosemary Sheed. London: Sheed and Ward, 1958.

———. *Shamanism: Archaic Techniques of Ecstasy.* Translated by Willard R. Trask. New York: Pantheon, 1964.

———. *Occultism, Witchcraft, and Cultural Fashions: Essays in Comparative Religions.* Chicago: University of Chicago Press, 1976.

Evans-Pritchard, E. E. "The Intellectualist (English) Interpretation of Magic." *Bulletin of the Faculty of Arts* (Cairo) 1, no. 2 (1933): 282–311.

———. "Lévy-Bruhl's Theory of Primitive Mentality." *Bulletin of the Faculty of Arts* (Cairo) 2, no. 2 (1934): 1–36.

———. *Theories of Primitive Religion.* Oxford: Clarendon, 1965.

———. *Witchcraft, Oracles, and Magic among the Azande.* Introduction by Eve Gillies. Oxford: Clarendon, 1976.

Evens, T. M. S. "On the Social Anthropology of Religion." *Journal of Religions* 62 (October 1982): 376–91.

Farren, David. *The Return of Magic.* New York: Harper and Row, 1972.

Favret-Saada, Jeanne. *Deadly Words: Witchcraft in the Bocage.* Translated by Catherine Cullen. Cambridge: Cambridge University Press, 1980.

Feuerbach, Ludwig. *Lectures on the Essence of Religion.* Translated by Ralph Manheim. New York: Harper and Row, 1967.

Firth, Raymond. "Problem and Assumption in the Anthropological Study of Religion." *Journal of the Royal Anthropological Institute* 89 (1959): 129–48.

———. "The Sociology of Magic (1954)." In *Tikopia Ritual and Belief,* 195–212. London: George Allen and Unwin, 1967.

Fitzgerald, Timothy. *The Ideology of Religious Studies.* New York: Oxford University Press, 2000.

Fraser, Robert. *The Making of* The Golden Bough: *The Origins and Growth of an Argument.* New York: St. Martin's, 1990.

Frazer, James George. *The Magical Origin of Kings.* London: Macmillan, 1920.

————. *The Golden Bough: A Study in Magic and Religion*. Abridged ed. New York: Macmillan, 1922.

————. *Man, God and Immortality: Thoughts on Human Progress*. London: Macmillan, 1927.

Freud, Sigmund. *The Future of an Illusion*. Translated and edited by James Strachey. New York: Norton, 1989.

————. "Obsessive Action and Religious Practice." In *The Freud Reader*, ed. Peter Gay, 429–36. New York: Norton, 1989.

————. *Totem and Taboo: Some Points of Agreement between the Mental Lives of Savages and Neurotics*. Translated and edited by James Strachey. New York: Norton, 1989.

Friedland, Roger, and Deirdre Boden, eds. *NowHere: Space, Time and Modernity*. Berkeley: University of California Press, 1994.

Fromm, Erich. *Escape from Freedom*. New York: Avon, 1965.

Geertz, Hildred. "An Anthropology of Religion and Magic, I." *Journal of Interdisciplinary History* 6 (summer 1975): 71–89.

Gellner, Ernest. "The Savage and the Modern Mind." In *Modes of Thought: Essays on Thinking in Western and Non-Western Societies*, ed. Robin Horton and Ruth Finnegan, 162–81. London: Faber and Faber, 1973.

Gesch, Patrick F. "Magic as a Process of Social Discernment." In *Powers, Plumes, and Piglets: Phenomena of Melanesian Religion*, ed. Norman C. Habel, 137–47. Bedford Parks, S. Aust.: Australian Association for the Study of Religions, 1979.

Glucklich, Ariel. *The End of Magic*. New York: Oxford University Press, 1997.

Goldenweiser, Alexander A. *Early Civilization: An Introduction to Anthropology*. New York: Knopf, 1922.

————. *Anthropology: An Introduction to Primitive Culture*. New York: F. S. Crofts, 1937.

Goode, William J. "Magic and Religion: A Continuum." *Ethnos* 14 (1949): 172–82.

————. *Religion among the Primitives*. Glencoe, Ill.: Free Press, 1951.

Goody, Jack. "Religion and Ritual: The Definitional Problem." *British Journal of Sociology* 12 (1961): 142–64.

Grossberg, Lawrence. "The Space of Culture, the Power of Space." In *The Post-colonial Question: Common Skies, Divided Horizons*, ed. Iain Chambers and Lidia Curti, 169–88. London: Routledge, 1996.

Haddon, Alfred C. *Magic and Fetishism*. Chicago: Open Court, [1906?].

————. *History of Anthropology*. London: Watts and Co., [1910].

Hammond, Dorothy. "Magic: A Problem in Semantics." *American Anthropologist* 72 (1970): 1349–56.

Hanegraaff, Wouter J. *New Age Religion and Western Culture: Esotericism in the Mirror of Secular Thought*. Leiden: Brill, 1996.

————. "The Emergence of the Academic Science of Magic: The Occult Philosophy in Tylor and Frazer." In *Religion in the Making: The Emergence of the Sciences of Religion*, ed. Arie L. Molendijk and Peter Pels, 253–75. Leiden: Brill, 1998.

Hansen, Bert. "Science and Magic." In *Science in the Middle Ages*, ed. David C. Lindberg, 483–506. Chicago: University of Chicago Press, 1978.

————. "The Complementarity of Science and Magic before the Scientific Revolution." *American Scientist* 74 (March–April 1986): 128–36.

Hargrove, Barbara. *The Sociology of Religion: Classical and Contemporary Approaches.* 2d ed. Arlington Heights, Ill.: Harlan Davidson, 1989.

Hartland, Edwin Sidney. *Ritual and Belief: Studies in the History of Religion.* London: Williams and Norgate, 1914.

Hegel, G. W. F. *Lectures on the Philosophy of Religion: The Lectures of 1827.* Edited by Peter C. Hodgson. Translated by R. F. Brown, P. C. Hodgson, and J. M. Stewart. Berkeley: University of California Press, 1988.

Herbert, Edward, Lord of Cherbury. *De Veritate.* Translated by Meyrick H. Carré. 1937. Reprint, London: Routledge/Thoemmes Press, 1992.

Herskovits, Melville J. *Cultural Anthropology.* New York: Knopf, 1955.

Hewitt, J. N. B. "Orenda and a Definition of Religion." *American Anthropologist,* n.s., 4 (1902): 33–46.

Hick, John. *An Interpretation of Religion: Human Responses to the Transcendent.* New Haven, Conn.: Yale University Press, 1989.

Hobbes, Thomas. *Leviathan.* Edited by Richard Tuck. Cambridge: Cambridge University Press, 1991.

Hodgson, Margaret T. *The Doctrine of Survivals: A Chapter in the History of Scientific Method in the Study of Man.* London: Allenson, 1936.

Hoebel, E. Adamson. *Man in the Primitive World: An Introduction to Anthropology.* New York: McGraw-Hill, 1949.

Hollis, Martin, and Steven Lukes, eds. *Rationality and Relativism.* Cambridge, Mass.: MIT Press, 1982.

Horton, Robin. "African Traditional Thought and Western Science." *Africa* 37 (1967): 50–71.

———. "Tradition and Modernity Revisited." In *Rationality and Relativism,* ed. Martin Hollis and Steven Lukes, 201–60. Cambridge, Mass.: MIT Press, 1982.

———. *Patterns of Thought in Africa and the West: Essays in Magic, Religion and Science.* Cambridge: Cambridge University Press, 1993.

Horton, Robin, and Ruth Finnegan, eds. *Modes of Thought.* London: Faber and Faber, 1973.

Howells, William. *The Heathens: Primitive Man and His Religions.* Garden City, N.Y.: Doubleday, 1948.

Hubert, Henri, and Marcel Mauss. "L'Origine des pouvoirs magiques dans les sociétés Australiennes." In *Mélanges d'histoire des religions,* 131–87. 2d ed. Paris: Librairie Félix Alcan, 1929.

Hume, David. *Enquiries concerning Human Understanding and concerning the Principles of Morals.* 3d ed. Edited by P. H. Nidditch. Oxford: Clarendon Press, 1975.

———. *Writings on Religion.* Edited by Antony Flew. La Salle, Ill.: Open Court, 1992.

Jahoda, Gustav. *The Psychology of Superstition.* London: Allen Lane/Penguin, 1969.

James, E. O. *Comparative Religion.* London: Methuen, 1938.

———. *The Beginnings of Religion: An Introductory and Scientific Study.* London: Hutchinson's University Library, [1949].

Jarvie, I. C., and Joseph Agassi. "The Problem of the Rationality of Magic." *British Journal of Sociology* 18 (1967): 55–74.

Jastrow, Morris, Jr. *The Study of Religion.* London: Walter Scott, 1901.

Jevons, Frank Byron. "The Definition of Magic." *Sociological Review* 1 (April 1908): 105–17.

———. "Magic and Religion." *Folklore* 18 (1917): 259–78.

———. *An Introduction to the Study of Comparative Religion.* New York: Macmillan, 1920.

———. *An Introduction to the History of Religion.* 9th ed. London: Methuen, 1927.

Jones, Paul H. *Christ's Eucharistic Presence: A History of the Doctrine.* New York: Peter Lang, 1994.

Kant, Immanuel. *Critique of Judgment.* Translated by J. H. Bernard. New York: Hafner Press, 1951.

———. *Religion within the Limits of Reason Alone.* Translated by Theodore M. Greene and Hoyt H. Hudson. New York: Harper Torchbooks, 1960.

———. *Critique of Pure Reason.* Unabridged ed. Translated by Norman Kemp Smith. New York: St. Martin's, 1965.

Karsten, Rafael. *The Origins of Religion.* London: Kegan Paul, Trench, Trübner, 1935.

Keesing, Felix M. *Cultural Anthropology: The Science of Custom.* New York: Holt, Rinehart and Winston, 1958.

King, Irving. *The Development of Religion: A Study in Anthropology and Social Psychology.* New York: Macmillan, 1910.

King, John H. *The Supernatural: Its Origin, Nature, and Evolution.* 2 vols. London: Williams and Norgate, 1892.

King, Richard. *Orientalism and Religion: Postcolonial Theory, India and "The Mystic East."* London: Routledge, 1999.

Klass, Morton. *Ordered Universes: Approaches to the Anthropology of Religion.* Boulder, Colo.: Westview, 1995.

Kors, Alan C., and Edward Peters, eds. *Witchcraft in Europe 1100–1700: A Documentary History.* Philadelphia: University of Pennsylvania Press, 1972.

Kristensen, W. Brede. *The Meaning of Religion: Lectures in the Phenomenology of Religion.* Translated by John B. Carman. The Hague: Martinus Nijhoff, 1960.

Kroeber, A. L. *Anthropology: Race, Language, Culture, Psychology, Prehistory.* Rev. ed. New York: Harcourt, Brace and World, 1948.

Lang, Andrew. *The Making of Religion.* 2d ed. London: Longmans, Green, 1900.

———. *Magic and Religion.* London: Longmans, Green, 1901.

Larner, Christina. *Enemies of God: The Witch-Hunt in Scotland.* London: Chatto and Windus, 1981.

———. *Witchcraft and Religion: The Politics of Popular Belief.* Edited by Alan Macfarlane. Oxford: Basil Blackwell, 1984.

Latour, Bruno. *The Pasteurization of France.* Translated by Alan Sheridan and John Law. Cambridge, Mass.: Harvard University Press, 1988.

———. *We Have Never Been Modern.* Translated by Catherine Porter. Cambridge, Mass.: Harvard University Press, 1993.

Le Roy, Alexander. *The Religion of the Primitives.* Translated by Newton Thompson. New York: Macmillan, 1922.

Leach, Edmund R. "Magic." In *A Dictionary of the Social Sciences.* Edited by Julius Gould and William L. Kolb, 398–99. New York: Free Press, 1964.

———. "Magical Hair." In *Myth and Cosmos: Readings in Mythology and Symbolism,* ed. John Middleton, 77–108. Garden City, N.Y.: Natural History Press, 1967.

Lee, Philip J. *Against the Protestant Gnostics*. New York: Oxford University Press, 1987.

Leeuw, Gerardus van der. *Religion in Essence and Manifestation*. Translated by J. E. Turner. Princeton, N.J.: Princeton University Press, 1986.

Lehmann, Arthur C., and James E. Myers, eds. *Magic, Witchcraft, and Religion: An Anthropological Study of the Supernatural*. Palo Alto, Calif.: Mayfield, 1985.

Leibniz, Gottfried Wilhelm. *Philosophical Writings*. Edited by G. H. R. Parkinson. Translated by Mary Morris and G. H. R. Parkinson. London: J. M. Dent, 1973.

Leopold, Joan. *Culture in Comparative and Evolutionary Perspective: E. B. Tylor and the Making of Primitive Culture*. Berlin: Reimer, 1980.

Leuba, James H. *A Psychological Study of Religion: Its Origin, Function, and Future*. New York: Macmillan, 1912.

Levack, Brian P. *The Witch-Hunt in Early Modern Europe*. London: Longman, 1987.

Lévi-Strauss, Claude. *Structural Anthropology*. Translated by Claire Jacobson and Brooke Grundfest Schoepf. New York: Basic Books, 1963.

———. *The Savage Mind*. Chicago: University of Chicago Press, 1966.

———. *Structural Anthropology*. Vol. 2. Translated by Monique Layton. New York: Basic Books, 1976.

———. *Introduction to the Work of Marcel Mauss*. Translated by Felicity Baker. London: Routledge and Kegan Paul, 1987.

Lévy-Bruhl, Lucien. *Primitive Mentality*. Translated by Lilian Clare. New York: Macmillan, 1923.

———. *How Natives Think*. Translated by Lilian Clare. New York: Washington Square Press, 1966.

———. *The Notebooks on Primitive Mentality*. Translated by Peter Rivière. New York: Harper and Row, 1975.

Lewis, James R., ed. *Magical Religion and Modern Witchcraft*. Albany: State University of New York Press, 1996.

Lindberg, David C. *The Beginnings of Western Science: The European Scientific Tradition in Philosophical, Religious, and Institutional Context, 600 B.C. to A.D. 1450*. Chicago: University of Chicago Press, 1992.

Lloyd, G. E. R. *Demystifying Mentalities*. Cambridge: Cambridge University Press, 1990.

Locke, John. *The Reasonableness of Christianity*. Edited by I. T. Ramsey. Stanford, Calif.: Stanford University Press, 1958.

———. *An Essay Concerning Human Understanding*. Edited by Peter H. Nidditch. Oxford: Clarendon, 1975.

Lowie, Robert H. *An Introduction to Cultural Anthropology*. Rev. ed. New York: Farrar and Rinehart, 1940.

———. *Primitive Religion*. New York: Liveright, 1948.

Lubbock, John, Lord Avebury. *The Origin of Civilization and the Primitive Condition of Man: Mental and Social Condition of Savages*. 7th ed. London: Longmans, Green, 1912.

Lukes, Steven. "Some Problems about Rationality." In *Rationality*, ed. Bryan R. Wilson, 194–213. Oxford: Basil Blackwell, 1970.

MacDonald, Mary N. "Magic, Medicine and Sorcery." *Point Series* 6 (1984): 195–211.

———. "An Interpretation of Magic." *Religious Traditions: A Journal in the Study of Religion* 7–9 (1984–86): 83–104.

————. "Magic and the Study of Religion." *Religiologiques* 11 (1995): 137–53.

MacKenzie, John M. *Orientalism: History, Theory and the Arts.* Manchester: Manchester University Press, 1995.

Malinowski, Bronislaw. *Coral Gardens and Their Magic: A Study of the Methods of Tilling the Soil and of Agricultural Rites in the Trobriand Islands.* 2 vols. London: George Allen and Unwin, 1935.

————. "Magic, Science, and Religion." In *Magic, Science and Religion and Other Essays,* ed. Robert Redfield, 17–92. Glencoe, Ill.: Free Press, 1948.

————. "The Role of Magic and Religion." In *Reader in Comparative Religion: An Anthropological Approach,* ed. William A. Lessa and Evon Z. Vogt, 102–12. 2d ed. New York: Harper and Row, 1965.

Marett, R. R. *The Threshold of Religion.* 3d ed. London: Methuen, 1914.

————. "Magic." In *Encyclopedia of Religion and Ethics,* ed. James Hastings, 245–52. Edinburgh: T. and T. Clark, 1930.

————. *Faith, Hope and Charity in Primitive Religion.* Oxford: Clarendon, 1932.

Masuzawa, Tomoko. *In Search of Dreamtime: The Quest for the Origin of Religion.* Chicago: University of Chicago Press, 1993.

Mauss, Marcel. *A General Theory of Magic.* Translated by Robert Brain. London: Routledge and Kegan Paul, 1972.

McCutcheon, Russell. *Manufacturing Religion: The Discourse on Sui Generis Religion and the Politics of Nostalgia.* New York: Oxford University Press, 1997.

Mencken, H. L. *Treatise on the Gods.* New York: Knopf, 1930.

Merkel, Ingrid, and Allen G. Debus, eds. *Hermeticism and the Renaissance: Intellectual History and the Occult in Early Modern Europe.* Washington, D.C.: Folger Shakespeare Library, 1988.

Midelfort, H. C. Erik. "Recent Witch Hunting Research, or Where Do We Go from Here?" *Papers of the Bibliographical Society of America* 62 (1968): 373–420.

————. *Witch Hunting in Southwestern Germany 1562–1684: The Social and Intellectual Foundations.* Stanford, Calif.: Stanford University Press, 1972.

————. "Were There Really Witches?" In *Transition and Revolution: Problems and Issues of European Renaissance and Reformation History,* ed. Robert M. Kingdon, 189–205. Minneapolis: Burgess, 1974.

Millen, Ron. "The Manifestation of Occult Qualities in the Scientific Revolution." In *Religion, Science, and Worldview: Essays in Honor of Richard S. Westfall,* ed. Margaret J. Osler and Paul L. Farber, 185–216. Cambridge: Cambridge University Press, 1985.

Molnár, Attila K. "The Construction of the Notion of Religion in Early Modern Europe." *Method and Theory in the Study of Religion* 14 (2002): 47–60.

Monter, E. William. *Witchcraft in France and Switzerland: The Borderlands during the Reformation.* Ithaca, N.Y.: Cornell University Press, 1976.

————. *Ritual, Myth and Magic in Early Modern Europe.* Athens: Ohio University Press, 1983.

Morgan, Lewis Henry. *Ancient Society or Research in the Lines of Human Progress from Savagery through Barbarism to Civilization.* New York: Henry Holt, 1907.

Morris, Brian. *Anthropological Studies of Religion: An Introductory Text.* Cambridge: Cambridge University Press, 1987.

Müller, Max. *Introduction to the Science of Religion.* London: Longmans, Green, 1873.

Neusner, Jacob, Ernest S. Frerichs, and Paul Virgil McCracken Flesher, eds. *Religion, Science, and Magic: In Concert and in Conflict.* New York: Oxford University Press, 1989.

O'Dea, Thomas F. *The Sociology of Religion.* Englewood Cliffs, N.J.: Prentice-Hall, 1966.

Odier, Charles. *Anxiety and Magical Thinking.* Translated by Marie-Louise Schoelly and Mary Jane Sherfey. New York: International Universities Press, 1956.

O'Keefe, Daniel Lawrence. *Stolen Lightning: The Social Theory of Magic.* New York: Continuum, 1982.

Olender, Maurice. *The Languages of Paradise: Race, Religion, and Philology in the Nineteenth Century.* Translated by Arthur Goldhammer. Cambridge, Mass.: Harvard University Press, 1992.

Osler, Margaret J. *Divine Will and the Mechanical Philosophy: Gassendi and Descartes on Contingency and Necessity in the Created World.* Cambridge: Cambridge University Press, 1994.

O'Toole, Roger. *Religion: Classic Sociological Approaches.* Toronto: McGraw-Hill Ryerson, 1984.

Owen, Alex. "Occultism and the 'Modern' Self in *Fin-de-Siècle* Britain." In *Meanings of Modernity: Britain from the Late-Victorian Era to World War II,* ed. Martin Daunton and Bernhard Rieger, 71–96. Oxford: Berg, 2001.

Parsons, Talcott. *Structure of Social Action.* 2nd ed. New York: Free Press, 1949.

Perkins, Maureen. *The Reform of Time: Magic and Modernity.* London: Pluto Press, 2001.

Perry, W. J. *The Origin of Magic and Religion.* London: Methuen, 1923.

Pettersson, Olof. "Magic—Religion: Some Marginal Notes to an Old Problem." *Ethnos* 22, nos. 3–4 (1957): 109–19.

Pfleiderer, Otto. *Religion and Historic Faiths.* Translated by Daniel A. Huebsch. Authorized ed. New York: B. W. Huebsch, 1907.

Philsooph, H. "Primitive Magic and Mana." *Man,* n.s., 6 (1971): 182–203.

Piaget, Jean. *The Child's Conception of the World.* Translated by Joan Tomlinson and Andrew Tomlinson. New York: Harcourt, Brace, 1929.

Popkin, Richard H. *The History of Scepticism from Erasmus to Spinoza.* Berkeley: University of California Press, 1979.

Popper, Karl. *Realism and the Aim of Science.* Edited by W. W. Bartley III. Totowa, N.J.: Rowman and Littlefield, 1983.

———. *The Myth of the Framework: In Defense of Science and Rationality.* Edited by M. A. Notturno. London: Routledge, 1994.

Preuss, Konrad Theodor. "Das Irrationale in der Magie." In *Magie und Religion: Beiträge zu einer Theorie der Magie,* ed. Leander Petzoldt, 223–47. Darmstadt: Wissenschaftliche Buchgesellschaft, 1978.

Quaife, G. R. *Godly Zeal and Furious Rage: The Witch in Early Modern Europe.* London: Croom Helm, 1987.

Radcliffe-Brown, A. R. *Taboo.* Cambridge: Cambridge University Press, 1938.

Radin, Paul. *Primitive Religion: Its Nature and Origin.* New York: Viking, 1937.

Randall, John Hermann, Jr. *The Making of the Modern Mind: A Survey of the Intellectual Background of the Present Age.* Rev. ed. Cambridge, Mass.: Riverside Press, 1940.

Richards, Jeffrey. *Sex, Dissidence and Damnation: Minority Groups in the Middle Ages.* London: Routledge, 1991.

Rivers, W. H. R. *Medicine, Magic, and Religion.* London: Kegan Paul, Trench, Trübner, 1924.

Róheim, Géza. *Animism, Magic, and the Divine King.* London: Kegan Paul, Trench, Trübner, 1930.

————. *Psychoanalysis and Anthropology: Culture, Personality and the Unconscious.* New York: International Universities Press, 1950.

————. *Magic and Schizophrenia.* Edited by Warner Muensterberger and S. H. Posinsky. New York: International Universities Press, 1955.

Roper, Lyndal. *Oedipus and the Devil: Witchcraft, Sexuality, and Religion in Early Modern Europe.* London: Routledge, 1994.

Russell, Jeffrey B. *Witchcraft in the Middle Ages.* Ithaca, N.Y.: Cornell University Press, 1972.

Sartre, Jean-Paul. *The Emotions: Outline of a Theory.* Translated by Bernard Frechtman. New York: Philosophical Library, 1948.

Scarre, Geoffrey. *Witchcraft and Magic in Sixteenth- and Seventeenth-Century Europe.* Atlantic Highlands, N.J.: Humanities Press International, 1987.

Schleiermacher, Friedrich. *The Christian Faith.* Edited by H. R. Mackintosh and J. S. Stewart. Edinburgh: T. and T. Clark, 1989.

Schmidt, Wilhelm. *The Origin and Growth of Religion: Facts and Theories.* Translated by H. J. Rose. London: Methuen, 1931.

Schneider, Jane. "Spirits and the Spirit of Capitalism." In *Religious Orthodoxy and Popular Faith in European Society,* ed. Ellen Badone, 24–54. Princeton, N.J.: Princeton University Press, 1990.

Schoeneman, Thomas J. "The Witch Hunt as a Culture Change Phenomenon." *Ethos* 3 (1975): 529–54.

Schoeps, Hans-Joachim. *The Religions of Mankind.* Translated by Richard Winston and Clara Winston. Garden City, N.Y.: Doubleday, 1966.

Scot, Reginald. *The Discoverie of Witchcraft.* Edited by Montague Summers. 1930. Reprint, New York: Dover, 1972.

Scribner, Robert W. "The Reformation, Popular Magic, and the 'Disenchantment of the World.' " *Journal of Interdisciplinary History* 23 (winter 1993): 475–94.

Seligman, Kurt. *Magic, Supernaturalism and Religion.* New York: Pantheon, 1948.

Sharpe, Eric J. *Comparative Religion: A History.* 2d ed. La Salle, Ill.: Open Court, 1986.

Shumaker, Wayne. *Natural Magic and Modern Science.* Binghamton, N.Y.: Medieval and Renaissance Texts and Studies, 1989.

Singer, Charles, ed. *From Magic to Science: Essays on the Scientific Twilight.* New York: Dover, 1958.

Skorupski, John. *Symbol and Theory: A Philosophical Study of Theories of Religion in Social Anthropology.* Cambridge: Cambridge University Press, 1976.

Smith, Catharine Cook. *In Defense of Magic: The Meaning and Use of Symbol and Rite.* New York: Dial Press, 1930.

Smith, Gordon Hedderly. *The Missionary and Anthropology: An Introduction to the Study of Primitive Man for Missionaries.* Chicago: Moody Press, 1945.

Smith, Jonathan Z. *To Take Place.* Chicago: University of Chicago Press, 1987.

———. *Drudgery Divine: On the Comparison of Early Christianities and the Religions of Late Antiquity*. Chicago: University of Chicago Press, 1990.

———. "Religion, Religions, Religious." In *Critical Terms for Religious Studies*, ed. Mark C. Taylor, 269–94. Chicago: University of Chicago Press, 1998.

Smith, Preserved. *A History of Modern Culture*. 2 vols. New York: Henry Holt, 1930.

Smith, Theophus H. *Conjuring Culture: Biblical Formations of Black America*. New York: Oxford University Press, 1994.

Smith, W. Robertson. *Lectures on the Religion of the Semites: The Fundamental Institutions*. 3d ed. Introduction and additional notes by Stanley A. Cook. New York: Macmillan, 1927.

Smith, Wilfred Cantwell. *The Meaning and End of Religion*. Minneapolis: Fortress, 1991.

Söderblom, Nathan. "Holiness." In *Encyclopedia of Religion and Ethics*, ed. James Hastings, 6: 731–41. Edinburgh: T. and T. Clark, 1913.

———. *The Living God: Basal Forms of Personal Religion*. London: Oxford University Press/Humphrey Milford, 1933.

Spencer, Herbert. *Principles of Sociology*. Edited by Stanislav Andreski. Hamden, Conn.: Archon Books, 1969.

———. *On Social Evolution: Selected Writings*. Edited by J. D. Y. Peel. Chicago: University of Chicago Press, 1972.

Spinoza, Benedict de. *A Theologico-Political Treatise and A Political Treatise*. Translated by R. H. M. Elwes. New York: Dover, 1951.

Spitz, Renée A. "The Genesis of Magical and Transcendent Cults (From Freud's IMAGO X)." Translated by Hella Freud Bernays. *American Imago: A Psychoanalytic Journal for Culture, Science and the Arts* 29 (spring 1972): 2–10.

Stark, Werner. *The Sociology of Religion: A Study of Christendom*. 4 vols. New York: Fordham University Press, 1970.

Storch, Alfred. *The Primitive Archaic Forms of Inner Experiences and Thought in Schizophrenia*. Translated by Clara Willard. New York: Nervous and Mental Disease Publishing Company, 1924.

Sumner, William Graham, and Albert Galloway Keller. *The Science of Society*. New Haven, Conn.: Yale University Press, 1927.

Tambiah, Stanley J. "The Magical Power of Words." *Man*, n.s., 3 (1968): 175–208.

———. "Form and Meaning of Magical Acts: A Point of View." In *Modes of Thought: Essays on Thinking in Western and Non-Western Societies*, ed. Robin Horton and Ruth Finnegan, 199–229. London: Faber and Faber, 1973.

———. *Magic, Science, Religion, and the Scope of Rationality*. Cambridge: Cambridge University Press, 1990.

Taussig, Michael. *The Devil and Commodity Fetishism*. Chapel Hill: University of North Carolina Press, 1980.

———. *Shamanism, Colonialism, and the Wild Man: A Study in Terror and Healing*. Chicago: University of Chicago Press, 1987.

———. *The Nervous System*. New York: Routledge, 1992.

———. *The Magic of the State*. New York: Routledge, 1997.

Thomas, Keith. "The Relevance of Social Anthropology to the Historical Study of English Witchcraft." In *Witchcraft Confessions and Accusations*, ed. Mary Douglas, 47–79. London: Tavistock, 1970.

————. *Religion and the Decline of Magic*. New York: Scribner, 1971.

————. "An Anthropology of Religion and Magic, II." *Journal of Interdisciplinary History* 6 (summer 1975): 91–109.

Thompson, E. P. "Anthropology and the Discipline of Historical Context." *Midland History* 1, no. 3 (spring 1972): 41–55.

Thorndike, Lynn. "The Place of Magic in the Intellectual History of Europe." In *Studies in History, Economics and Public Law*, ed. Faculty of Political Science of Columbia University, 24: 1–110. New York: Columbia University Press, 1905.

————. *A History of Magic and Experimental Science*. 8 vols. New York: Columbia University Press, 1934–58.

Thurschwell, Pamela. *Literature, Technology and Magical Thinking, 1880–1920*. Cambridge: Cambridge University Press, 2001.

Tiele, C. P. *Elements of the Science of Religion*. 2 vols. Edinburgh: William Blackwood and Sons, 1897–99.

————. *Outlines of the History of Religion to the Spread of the Universal Religions*. Translated by J. Estlin Carpenter. 7th ed. London: Kegan Paul, Trench, Trübner, 1905.

Tillich, Paul. "The Relation of Religion and Health: Religious, Magic, and Natural Healing Distinguished." *Pastoral Psychology* 5 (May 1954): 41–52.

————. *Perspectives on Nineteenth and Twentieth Century Protestant Theology*. Edited by Carl E. Braaten. New York: Harper and Row, 1967.

Trevor-Roper, H. R. *The European Witch-Craze of the Sixteenth and Seventeenth Centuries*. Harmondsworth, England: Penguin, 1969.

Turner, Victor. "Witchcraft and Sorcery: Taxonomy versus Dynamics." *Africa* 34 (1964): 314–24.

Tylor, Edward Burnett. *Primitive Culture: Researches into the Development of Mythology, Philosophy, Religion, Language, Art and Custom*. 3d American ed. 2 vols. New York: Henry Holt, 1889.

Van Gennep, Arnold. *The Rites of Passage*. Translated by Monika B. Vizedom and Gabrielle L. Caffee. Introduction by Solon T. Kimball. Chicago: University of Chicago Press, 1960.

Vickers, Brian, ed. *Occult and Scientific Mentalities in the Renaissance*. Cambridge: Cambridge University Press, 1984.

Voltaire. "A Philosophical Dictionary." In *The Works of Voltaire: A Contemporary Version*. Vols. 5–14. Translated by William F. Fleming. Introduction by Oliver H. G. Leigh. Critique and biography by John Morley. Paris: E. R. DuMont, 1901.

Wach, Joachim. *Sociology of Religion*. Chicago: University of Chicago Press, 1944.

Wax, Murray, and Rosalie Wax. "The Notion of Magic." *Current Anthropology* 4 (1963): 495–518.

Wax, Rosalie, and Murray Wax. "The Magical World View." *Journal for the Scientific Study of Religion* 1 (1962): 179–88.

Weber, Max. "The Social Psychology of the World Religions." In *From Max Weber: Essays in Sociology*, ed. and trans. Hans H. Gerth and C. Wright Mills, 267–301. New York: Oxford University Press, 1946.

————. *The Protestant Ethic and the Spirit of Capitalism*. Translated by Talcott Parsons. New York: Scribner, 1958.

————. *The Sociology of Religion*. Translated by Ephraim Fischoff. Introduction by Talcott Parsons. Boston: Beacon Press, 1964.

Webster, Charles. *From Paracelsus to Newton: Magic and the Making of Modern Science.* Cambridge: Cambridge University Press, 1982.

Webster, Hutton. *Magic: A Sociological Study.* Stanford, Calif.: Stanford University Press, 1948.

Werner, Heinz. *Comparative Psychology of Mental Development.* Rev. ed. New York: International Universities Press, 1957.

Westermarck, Edward. *The Origin and Development of the Moral Ideas.* 2d ed. 2 vols. 1912. Reprint, New York: Johnson Reprint Corporation, 1971.

Whitehead, Alfred North. *Science and the Modern World.* New York: Macmillan, 1925.

Wiesner, Merry E. *Women and Gender in Early Modern Europe.* Cambridge: Cambridge University Press, 1993.

Wilson, Bryan, ed. *Rationality.* Oxford: Basil Blackwell, 1979.

Winch, Peter. "Understanding a Primitive Society." *American Philosophical Quarterly* 1 (1964): 307–24.

Winkelman, Michael. "Magic: A Theoretical Assessment." *Current Anthropology* 23 (1982): 37–66.

Wobbermin, Georg. *The Nature of Religion.* Translated by Theophil Menzel and Daniel Sommer Robinson. New York: Crowell, 1933.

Worgul, George S. *From Magic to Metaphor: A Validation of Christian Sacraments.* New York: Paulist Press, 1980.

Wundt, Wilhelm. *Elements of Folk Psychology: Outlines of a Psychological History of the Development of Mankind.* Translated by Edward Leroy Schaub. London: George Allen and Unwin, 1916.

Yates, Frances A. *Giordano Bruno and the Hermetic Tradition.* London: Routledge and Kegan Paul, 1964.

———. "The Hermetic Tradition in Renaissance Science." In *Art, Science, and History in the Renaissance,* ed. Charles S. Singleton, 255–74. Baltimore: Johns Hopkins University Press, 1967.

Yinger, J. Milton. *The Scientific Study of Religion.* New York: Macmillan, 1970.

———, ed. *Religion, Society and the Individual: An Introduction to the Sociology of Religion.* New York: Macmillan, 1957.

Zetterberg, J. Peter. "The Mistaking of 'the Mathematicks' for Magic in Tudor and Stuart England." *Sixteenth Century Journal* 11 (spring 1980): 83–97.

Zusne, Leonard, and Warren H. Jones. *Anomalistic Psychology: A Study of Magical Thinking.* Hillsdale, N.J.: Erlbaum, 1989.

Index

Racism, sexism shaped have profoundly shaped the discourse on magic, as it has shaped the definition of the modern world.

- ironic that an era characterized by progress toward "the good society" be defined by racism, sexism, among others.

How has discourse on magic shaped post-modern world?

Modernity - sought to define

Codification of magic as deviant still with us.
- neurosis
- gay, etc.
- defies norms 191

Magic threat to the ~~death~~ Binaries set up in modernity.
- Male, female
- fantasy, reality
- deviance, morality

Magic as threat to social change (196)
- individualistic 198